THE EXCESSIVE SUBJECT

THE EXCESSIVE SUBJECT

A New Theory of Social Change

Molly Anne Rothenberg

polity

First published in 2010 by Polity Press

Polity Press
65 Bridge Street
Cambridge CB2 1UR, UK

Polity Press
350 Main Street
Malden, MA 02148, USA

ISBN-13: 978-0-7456-4823-1
ISBN-13: 978-0-7456-4824-8 (paperback)

A catalogue record for this book is available from the British Library.

Typeset in 10 on 12 pt Sabon
by Servis Filmsetting Ltd, Stockport, Cheshire

For further information on Polity, visit our website: www.polity.co.uk

Contents

Acknowledgments

My debts to colleagues and other scholars are too many to be encompassed in a prefatory acknowledgment. Many will recognize themselves in the notes and bibliography, but I wish to mention here a few people to whom I feel especially indebted. I owe profound thanks to Slavoj Žižek for encouraging my efforts to make sense of the fundamental questions of social change. Dennis Foster and Nina Schwartz gave me the incomparable gifts of taking pleasure in my work, offering shelter during storms, and commenting incisively on drafts. Geoffrey Galt Harpham's support during the project's long gestation has touched me deeply. Teresa Toulouse pushed me to think harder and write better: many of the improvements to this manuscript were due to her efforts. I am grateful to Molly Abel Travis for her guidance in addressing complex problems at an early stage. Words fail me in expressing my gratitude for Idelber Avelar's generosity. My collaboration with Joseph Valente gave me an initial introduction to some of these topics. Robert Kaufman and Bruno Bosteels have both given generously of their time and expertise. My early work on this project was enhanced by Mellon seminars at Tulane University with Fredric Jameson on Adorno and with Slavoj Žižek. Thanks to the University of California at Irvine Humanities Research Institute for inviting me to participate in the Seminar in Experimental Critical Theory, organized by Julia Lupton and Ken Reinhardt, where the lineaments of this theory first became clear to me. I especially wish to thank Joan Copjec, Eric Santner, Alenka Zupančič, Peter Hallward, and Mladen Dolar for clarifying conversations.

A small portion of the discussion from Chapter 3 appeared in a different form in "Articulating Social Agency in *Our Mutual Friend*: Problems with Performances, Practices, and Political Efficacy," in *English Literary History* 71 (2004): 719–49. A version of Chapter 4 first appeared as "Embodied Political Performativity in *Excitable Speech*: Butler's Psychoanalytic Revision of Historicism," *Theory, Culture and Society* 23 (July 2006): 71–93. Tulane University has assisted me with a Georges Lurcy grant and a sabbatical leave. I wish to thank my departmental colleagues at Tulane for their patience and good humor as I labored to shape this project. I am especially grateful to my anonymous readers for Polity Press. Many thanks to the wonderful people at Polity, in particular Emma Hutchinson (whose encouragement and expertise brought the project to fruition), Rachel Donnelly, David Drummond, Sarah Dodgson, Clare Ansell, and Tim Clark. Becky Parmenter has been a constant support. To Doris, Herbert, Norrie, Michael, Carol, Nathaniel, and Benjamin, thank you for your love and for your wise-cracks: I have needed both. This book is dedicated to my husband, Jonathan Riley, who knows why.

Molly Anne Rothenberg
Tulane University
June 2009

List of Abbreviations

BTM   Judith Butler, *Bodies That Matter*
E   Ernesto Laclau, *Emancipations*
ES   Judith Butler, *Excitable Speech*
IBK   Slavoj Žižek, *Iraq: The Broken Kettle*
ID   Simon Critchley, *Infinitely Demanding*
LP   Pierre Bourdieu, *Logic of Practice*
MR   Félix Guattari, *Molecular Revolution*
MWE   Giorgio Agamben, *Means Without End*
OC   Alain Badiou, "On the Connection between Adorno's *Negative Dialectics* and a Particular Assessment of Wagner*"
OSP   Jacques Rancière, *On the Shores of Politics*
OWB   Slavoj Žižek, *Organs Without Bodies*
PEL   Michel de Certeau, *The Practice of Everyday Life*
PV   Slavoj Žižek, *The Parallax View*
RG   Slavoj Žižek, *Revolution at the Gates*
WDR   Slavoj Žižek, *Welcome to the Desert of the Real*

Foreword

With the Keen Edge of a Knife

Slavoj Žižek

Molly Rothenberg's book opens with a reference to Italo Calvino's "A Beautiful March Day," a story about the death of Julius Caesar. In his idiosyncratic description of the conspiracy, Calvino focuses on the unintended consequences of the act of killing Caesar: while the conspirators wanted to kill a tyrant and thereby restore Rome to its republican glory, their act effectively abolishes the very conditions which sustained its intended meaning. As Rothenberg explains:

> The very world in which it made sense to get rid of Caesar also vanishes with those dagger strokes – not because Caesar held that world together, but because the assassins could not foresee that their act would also transform the way the act itself would later be judged, even by themselves. They could not factor in the historicity of their action; neither they nor anyone else could predict or govern how the future would interpret the assassination. Put another way, we could say that there was simply no way for them to take into account the *retroversive* effect of future interpretations.

What we encounter here is the key feature of the Symbolic: this passage renders the fundamental "openness" the Symbolic introduces into a closed order of reality. Once we enter the Symbolic, things never simply are, they all "will have been"; they as it were borrow (part of) their being from the future. Rothenberg evokes a wonderfully cruel example of a tender statement – "Carl smiled as he gently stroked the velvety skin of his lover..." – completed by a supplement which brutally changes the meaning of the first part: "...with the keen edge of a knife." And, as Rothenberg points out, the cause of this irreducible "openness" of the Symbolic is not its excessive complexity (we never know in what decentered context our statement will be inscribed), but the much more refined, properly dialectical impossibility of taking into account the way our own intervention will transform the field. The speaking subject cannot take into account the way it is itself "counted" in the signifying series; with regard to its own inclusion, it is irreducibly split, redoubled; or, to quote a joke often mentioned by Lacan: "I have three brothers, Paul, Robert and myself."

This "retroversive effect" concerns the very core of the relationship between Hegel and Marx: it provides the main reason why, today, one should return from Marx to Hegel and enact a "materialist reversal" of Marx himself. To approach this complex issue, let me begin with Gilles Deleuze's notion of a *pure past*: not the past into which present things pass, but an absolute past "where all events, including those that have sunk without trace, are stored and remembered as their passing away,"[1] a virtual past which already contains also things which are still present. A present can become past because in a way it is so already, it can perceive itself as part of the past ("what we are doing now is [will have been] history"); as Deleuze puts it: "It is with respect to the pure element of the past, understood as the past in general, as an a priori past, that a given former present is reproducible and the present present is able to reflect itself."[2] Does this mean that the pure past involves a thoroughly deterministic notion of the universe in which everything still to happen (to come) – all actual spatio-temporal deployment – is already part of an immemorial/atemporal virtual network? No, and for a very precise reason: because "the pure past must be all the past but must also be amenable to change through the occurrence of any new present."[3] It was none other than T. S. Eliot, the great conservative, who first clearly formulated this link between our dependence on tradition and our power to change the past:

> [tradition] cannot be inherited, and if you want it you must obtain it by great labour. It involves, in the first place, the historical sense, which we may call nearly indispensable to anyone who would continue to be a poet beyond his twenty-fifth year; and the historical sense involves a perception, not only of the pastness of the past, but of its presence; the historical sense compels a man to write not merely with his own generation in his bones, but with a feeling that the whole of the literature of Europe from Homer and within it the whole of the literature of his own country has a simultaneous existence and composes a simultaneous order. This historical sense, which is a sense of the timeless as well as of the temporal and of the timeless and of the temporal together, is what makes a writer traditional. And it is at the same time what makes a writer most acutely conscious of his place in time, of his contemporaneity.

No poet, no artist of any art, has his complete meaning alone. His significance, his appreciation is the appreciation of his relation to the dead poets
and artists. You cannot value him alone; you must set him, for contrast
and comparison, among the dead. I mean this as a principle of æsthetic,
not merely historical, criticism. The necessity that he shall conform, that
he shall cohere, is not one-sided; what happens when a new work of art is
created is something that happens simultaneously to all the works of art
which preceded it. The existing monuments form an ideal order among
themselves, which is modified by the introduction of the new (the really
new) work of art among them. The existing order is complete before the
new work arrives; for order to persist after the supervention of novelty,
the *whole* existing order must be, if ever so slightly, altered; and so the
relations, proportions, values of each work of art toward the whole are
readjusted; and this is conformity between the old and the new. Whoever
has approved this idea of order, of the form of European, of English literature, will not find it preposterous that the past should be altered by the
present as much as the present is directed by the past. And the poet who is
aware of this will be aware of great difficulties and responsibilities. ...
    What happens is a continual surrender of himself as he is at the moment
to something which is more valuable. The progress of an artist is a continual self-sacrifice, a continual extinction of personality. There remains
to define this process of depersonalization and its relation to the sense of
tradition. It is in this depersonalization that art may be said to approach
the condition of science.[4]

When Eliot writes that, in judging a living poet, "*you must set him
among the dead,*" he formulates precisely an example of Deleuze's pure
past. And when he writes that "the existing order is complete before the
new work arrives; for order to persist after the supervention of novelty,
the *whole* existing order must be, if ever so slightly, altered; and so the
relations, proportions, values of each work of art toward the whole are
readjusted," he no less clearly formulates the paradoxical link between
the completeness of the past and our capacity to change it retroactively:
precisely because the pure past is complete, each new work re-arranges
its entire balance. Recall Borges' precise formulation of the relationship between Kafka and his multitude of precursors, from old Chinese
authors to Robert Browning: "Kafka's idiosyncrasy, in greater or lesser
degree, is present in each of these writings, but if Kafka had not written
we would not perceive it; that is to say, it would not exist. ... each writer
creates his precursors. His work modifies our conception of the past, as
it will modify the future."[5] Hence the properly dialectical solution of the
dilemma, "is it really there, in the source, or did we just read it into the
source?," is thus: it is there, but we can only perceive and state this retroactively, from today's perspective.
    Here, Peter Hallward falls short in his otherwise excellent *Out of*

This World,[6] where he stresses only that aspect of the pure past as the virtual field in which the fate of all actual events is sealed in advance, since "everything is already written" in it. At this point, where we view reality *sub specie aeternitatis*, absolute freedom coincides with absolute necessity and its pure automatism: to be free means to let oneself freely flow in/with the substantial necessity. This topic reverberates even in recent cognitivist debates on the problem of free will. Compatibilists like Daniel Dennett have an elegant solution to the incompatibilists' complaints about determinism:[7] when incompatibilists complain that our freedom cannot be combined with the fact that all our acts are part of a great chain of natural determinism, they secretly make an unwarranted ontological assumption: they first assume that we (as the Self, or the free agent) somehow stand *outside* reality, and then go on to complain how they feel oppressed by the notion that reality with its determinism controls them totally. This is what is wrong with the notion of our being "imprisoned" by chains of the natural determinism: we thereby obfuscate the fact that we are *part of* reality, that the (possible, local) conflict between our "free" striving and an external reality resisting to it is a conflict inherent in reality itself. That is to say, there is nothing "oppressive" or "constraining" about the fact that our innermost strivings are (pre) determined: when we feel thwarted in our freedom by the constraining pressure of external reality, there must be something in us, some desire or striving, which is thus thwarted, but where should this striving come if not from this same reality? Our "free will" does not then in some mysterious way "disturb the natural course of things," it is part and parcel of this course. For us to be "truly" and "radically" free, this would entail there being no positive content imposed on our free act – if we want nothing "external" and particular or given to determine our behavior, then "this would involve being free of every part of ourselves."[8] When a determinist claims that our free choice is "determined," this does not mean that our free will is somehow constrained, that we are forced to act *against* our free will. What is "determined" is rather the very thing that we want to do "freely," i.e., without being thwarted by external obstacles.

So, back to Hallward: while he is right to emphasize that, for Deleuze, freedom "isn't a matter of human liberty but of liberation *from* humanity,"[9] of fully submerging oneself in the creative flux of absolute Life, the political conclusion he draws from this seems too hasty: "The immediate political implication of such a position ... is clear enough: since a free mode or monad is simply one that has eliminated its resistance to the sovereign will that works through it, so then it follows that the more absolute the sovereign's power, the more 'free' are those subject to it."[10] But does Hallward not ignore the retroactive movement on which Deleuze also insists, namely, how this eternal pure past which fully determines us is itself subjected to retroactive change? We are thus simultaneously both less free and more free than we think: we are thoroughly passive, determined by and dependent on the past, but we have the freedom to define the scope of this determination, that is, to (over)determine the past which will determine us. Deleuze is here unexpectedly close to Kant, for whom, though I am determined by causes, I (can) retroactively determine which causes will determine me – we, subjects, are passively affected by pathological objects and motivations; but, in a reflexive way, we ourselves have the minimal power to accept (or reject) being affected in this way. In other words, we may retroactively determine the causes allowed to determine us, or, at least, the *mode* of this linear determination.

"Freedom" is thus inherently retroactive: at its most elementary, it is not simply a free act which, out of nowhere, initiates a new causal link, but is a retroactive act of endorsing which link or sequence of necessities will determine me. Here, one should add a Hegelian twist to Spinoza: freedom is not simply "recognized/known necessity," but recognized/assumed necessity, the necessity constituted/actualized through this recognition. So when Deleuze refers to Proust's description of Vinteuil's music that haunts Swann – "as if the performers not so much played the little phrase as executed the rites necessary for it to appear" – he is evoking the necessary illusion: generating the sense-event is experienced as ritualistic evocation of a pre-existing event, as if the event was already there, waiting for our call in its virtual presence.

What directly resonates in this topic is, of course, the Protestant motif of predestination. Far from being a reactionary theological motif, predestination is a key element of the materialist theory of sense, on condition that we read it along the lines of the Deleuzian opposition between the virtual and the actual. That is to say, predestination does not mean that our fate is sealed in an actual text existing from eternity in the divine mind; the texture which predestines us belongs to the purely virtual eternal past which, as such, can be retroactively rewritten by our act. This, perhaps, would have been the ultimate meaning of the singularity of Christ's incarnation: it is an *act* which radically changes our destiny. Prior to Christ, we were determined by Fate, caught in the cycle of sin and its payment; but Christ's erasing of our past sins means precisely that his sacrifice changes our virtual past and thus sets us free. When Deleuze writes that "my wound existed before me; I was born to embody it," does this variation on the theme of the Cheshire cat and its smile from *Alice in Wonderland* (the cat was born to embody its smile) not provide a perfect formula of Christ's sacrifice: Christ was born to embody his wound, to be crucified? The problem is the literal teleological reading of this proposition: as if the actual deeds of a person merely actualize their atemporal-eternal fate inscribed in their virtual idea:

Caesar's only real task is to become worthy of the events he has been created to embody. *Amor fati.* What Caesar actually does adds nothing to what he virtually is. When Caesar actually crosses the Rubicon this involves no deliberation or choice since it is simply part of the entire, immediate expression of Caesarness, it simply unrolls or "unfolds something that was encompassed for all times in the notion of Caesar."[11]

However, what about the retroactivity of a gesture which (re)constitutes this past itself? This, perhaps, is the most succinct definition of what an authentic *act* is: in our ordinary activity, we effectively just follow the (virtual-fantasmatic) coordinates of our identity, while an act proper is the paradox of an actual move which (retroactively) changes the very virtual "transcendental" coordinates of its agent's being – or, in Freudian terms, which not only changes the actuality of our world but also "moves its underground." We have thus a kind of reflexive "folding back of the condition onto the given it was the condition for":[12] while the pure past is the transcendental condition for our acts, our acts not only create new actual reality, they also retroactively change this very condition. This brings us to the central problem of Deleuze's ontology: how are the virtual and the actual related? "Actual things express Ideas but are not caused by them."[13] The notion of causality is limited to the interaction of actual things and processes; on the other hand, this interaction also causes virtual entities (Sense, Ideas). Deleuze is not an idealist; Sense is for him always an ineffective sterile shadow accompanying actual things. What this means is that, for Deleuze, (transcendental) *genesis and causality are totally opposed*, they move at different levels: "Actual things have an identity, but virtual ones do not, they are pure variations. An actual thing must change – become something different – in order to express something. Whereas, the expressed virtual thing does not change – only its relation to other virtual things, other intensities and Ideas changes."[14]

How does this relation change? *Only through the changes in actual things which express Ideas, since the entire generative power lies in actual things*: Ideas belong to the domain of Sense which is "only a vapor which plays at the limit of things and words"; as such, Sense is "the Ineffectual, a sterile incorporeal deprived of its generative powers."[15] Think about a group of dedicated individuals fighting for the Idea of Communism: in order to grasp their activity, we have to take into account the virtual Idea. But this Idea is in itself sterile, has no proper causality: all causality lies in the individuals who "express" it.

The lesson to be drawn from the basic paradox of Protestantism (how is it possible that a religion which taught predestination sustained capitalism, the greatest explosion of human activity and freedom in history) is that freedom is neither grasped necessity (the vulgata from Spinoza to Hegel and traditional Marxists) nor overlooked (ignored) necessity (the cognitivist and brain science thesis: freedom is the "user's illusion" of our consciousness, unaware of the bio-neuronal processes that determine it), but *a necessity which is presupposed and/as unknown/unknowable.* We know that everything is predetermined, but we do not know *which* is our predetermined destiny, and it is this uncertainty which impels us into incessant activity.

This is how one should differentiate historicity proper from organic evolution. In the latter, a universal Principle is slowly and gradually differentiating itself; as such, it remains the calm underlying all-encompassing ground that unifies the bustling activity of struggling individuals, the endless process of generation and corruption that is the "cycle of life." In history proper, on the contrary, the universal Principle is caught in an "infinite" struggle with itself; that is, the struggle is each time a struggle for the fate of the universal itself. This is why the eminently "historical" moments are those of great collisions when a whole form of life is threatened, when reference to established social and cultural norms no longer guarantees a minimum of stability and cohesion. In such open situations, a new form of life has to be invented. It is at this point that Hegel locates the role of great heroes, operating in a pre-legal, stateless zone: their violence is not bound by the usual moral rules, they enforce a new order with a subterranean vitality that shatters all established forms. According to the usual *doxa* on Hegel, these heroes follow their instinctual passions, their true motifs and goals remain unclear to themselves, since they are unconscious instruments of the deeper historical necessity of giving birth to a new spiritual life form. However, as Gerard Lebrun points out, one should not here impute to Hegel the standard teleological notion of a hidden Reason pulling the strings of the historical process, following a plan established in advance and using the passions of individuals as the instruments of its implementation. First, since the meaning of their acts is a priori inaccessible to the individuals who accomplish them, heroes included, there is no "science of politics" able to predict the course of events: "nobody ever has the right to declare himself depositary of the Spirit's self-knowledge,"[16] and this impossibility "spares Hegel the fanaticism of 'objective responsibility'."[17] In other words, there is no place in Hegel for the Marxist-Stalinist figure of the communist revolutionary who understands historical necessity and posits himself as the instrument of its implementation. However, it is crucial to add a further twist here: if all we do is assert this impossibility, then we are still "conceiving the Absolute as Substance, not as Subject" – i.e., we still assume some pre-existing Spirit imposing its substantial Necessity on history, we just accept that insight into this Necessity is inaccessible for us. From a consequent Hegelian standpoint, one should go a crucial step further and insist that historical Necessity does not pre-exist the contingent process of its actualization, i.e., that the historical process is also in itself "open," undecided – this confused mixture "generates sense *insofar as it unravels itself*":

> It is people, and they only, who make history, while Spirit explicates itself through this making. ... The point is not, as in a naïve theodicy, to find a justification for every event. In actual time, no heavenly harmony resonates in the sound and fury. It is only once this tumult recollects itself in the past, once what took place is conceived, that we can say, to put it briefly, that the "course of History" is a little bit better outlined. History runs forward only for those who look at it backwards; it is linear progression only in retrospect. ... The Hegelian 'providential necessity' has so little authority that it seems as if it learns from the run of things in the world which were its goals.[18]

This is how one should read Hegel's thesis that, in the course of the dialectical development, things "become what they are": it is not that a temporal deployment merely actualizes some pre-existing atemporal conceptual structure – this atemporal conceptual structure itself is the result of contingent temporal decisions. Let us take the exemplary case of a contingent decision whose outcome defines the agent's entire life: Caesar's crossing of the Rubicon:

> It is not enough to say that crossing the Rubicon is part of the complete notion of Caesar. One should rather say that Caesar is defined by the fact that he crossed the Rubicon. His life didn't follow a scenario written in the book of some goddess: there is no book which would already have contained the relations of Caesar's life, for the simple reason that his life itself is this book, and that, at every moment, an event is in itself its own narrative.[19]

But why shouldn't we then say that there is simply no atemporal conceptual structure, that all there is is the gradual temporal deployment? Here we encounter the properly dialectical paradox which defines true historicity as opposed to evolutionist historicism, and which was formulated much later, in French structuralism, as the "primacy of synchrony over diachrony." Usually, this primacy was taken to indicate structuralism's ultimate denial of historicity: an historical development can be reduced to the (imperfect) temporal deployment of a pre-existing atemporal matrix of all possible variations/combinations. This simplistic notion of the "primacy of synchrony over diachrony" overlooks the (properly dialectical) point, made long ago by (among others) T. S. Eliot (as quoted above) on how each truly new artistic phenomenon not only designates a break from the entire past, but retroactively changes this past itself. At every historical conjuncture, the present is not only present, it also encompasses a perspective on the past immanent to it – after the disintegration of the Soviet Union in 1991, say, the October Revolution is no longer the same historical event; no longer the beginning of a new progressive epoch in the history of humanity, but (from the triumphant liberal-capitalist perspective) the beginning of a catastrophic mis-direction of history which reached its end in 1991. Or, to return to Caesar, once he crossed Rubicon his previous life appeared in a new way, as a preparation for his later world-historical role, that is, it was transformed into part of a totally different life story. This is what Hegel calls "totality" and what structuralism calls "synchronic structure": a historical moment which is not limited to the present but includes its own past and future, i.e., the way the past and the future appeared to and from this moment.

The main implication of treating the Symbolic order as such a totality is that, far from reducing it to a kind of transcendental *a priori* (a formal network, given in advance, which limits the scope of human practice), one should follow Lacan and focus on how gestures of symbolization are entwined with and embedded in the process of collective practice. What Lacan elaborates as the "twofold moment" of the symbolic function reaches far beyond the standard theory of the performative dimension of speech as developed in the tradition from J.L. Austin to John Searle: "The symbolic function presents itself as a twofold movement in the subject: man makes his own action into an object, but only to return its foundational place to it in due time. In this equivocation, operating at every instant, lies the whole progress of a function in which action and knowledge alternate."[20] The historical example evoked by Lacan to clarify this "twofold movement" is indicative in its hidden references: "in phase one, a man who works at the level of production in our society considers himself to belong to the ranks of the proletariat; in phase two, in the name of belonging to it, he joins in a general strike."[21]

Lacan's (implicit) reference here is to Lukács's *History and Class Consciousness*, a classic Marxist work from 1923 whose widely acclaimed French translation was published in the mid 1950s. For Lukács, consciousness is opposed to mere knowledge of an object: knowledge is external to the known object, while consciousness is in itself "practical," an act which changes its very object. (Once a worker "considers himself to belong to the ranks of the proletariat," this changes his very reality: he acts differently.) One does something, one counts oneself as (declares oneself) the one who did it, and, on the base of this declaration, one does something new – the proper moment of subjective transformation occurs at the moment of declaration, not at the moment of action. This reflexive moment of declaration means that every utterance not only transmits some content, but simultaneously *renders how the subject relates to this content*. Even the most down-to-earth objects and activities always contain such a declarative dimension, which constitutes the ideology of everyday life.

However, Lukács remains all too idealist when he proposes simply to replace the Hegelian Spirit with the proletariat as the Subject-Object of History: Lukács is here not really Hegelian, but a pre-Hegelian idealist.[22] One is even tempted to talk here about Marx's "idealist reversal of Hegel": in contrast to Hegel, who was well aware that the owl of Minerva takes flight only at dusk, after the fact (i.e., that Thought follows Being – which is why, for Hegel, there can be no scientific insight into the future of society), Marx reasserts the primacy of Thought: the owl of Minerva (German contemplative philosophy) should be replaced by the singing of the Gallic rooster (French revolutionary thought) announcing the proletarian revolution. In the proletarian revolutionary act, Thought will precede Being. Marx thus sees in Hegel's motif of the owl of Minerva an indication of the secret positivism of Hegel's idealist speculation: Hegel leaves reality the way it is. Hegel's reply is that the delay of consciousness does not imply any naive objectivism, so that consciousness is caught in a transcendent objective process. What is inaccessible is the impact of the subject's act itself, its own inscription into objectivity. Of course thought is immanent to reality and changes it, but not as fully self-transparent self-consciousness, not as an Act aware of its own impact. A Hegelian thus accepts Lukács's notion of consciousness as opposed to mere knowledge: the latter is external to its object, while the former is an act which changes its object. What one should add is that self-consciousness itself is unconscious: we are not aware of the point of our self-consciousness.

If there was ever a critic of the fetishizing effect of fascinatingly dazzling "leitmotifs" it was Adorno. In his devastating analysis of Wagner, he tries to demonstrate how the Wagnerian leitmotifs serve as the fetishized elements of easy recognition and thus constitute a kind of inner-structural commodification of his music.[23] How, then, can one not but admire the supreme irony of locating traces of this same fetishizing procedure in Adorno's own writings? Many of his provocative one-liners do effectively express a profound insight or at least touch on a crucial point (recall his "Nothing is more true in psychoanalysis than its exaggerations."); however, more often than his partisans care to admit, Adorno gets caught up in his own game, enamored of his own ability to produce dazzlingly "effective" paradoxical statements at the expense of theoretical substance (recall the famous line from *Dialectic of Enlightenment* on how Hollywood's ideological manipulation of social reality realizes Kant's idea of the transcendental constitution of reality). In such cases, where the dazzling "effect" of the unexpected short-circuit (here between Hollywood cinema and Kantian ontology) effectively overshadows the immanent line of argumentation, the brilliant paradox works precisely as does the Wagnerian leitmotif (according to Adorno): instead of serving as a nodal point of the complex network of structural mediations, it generates idiotic pleasure by focusing attention on itself. Adorno was undoubtedly unaware of this unintended self-reflexivity: that his critique of Wagnerian leitmotifs amounted to a critique of his own writing. Is this not an exemplary case of the unconscious reflexivity of thinking? When criticizing his opponent Wagner, Adorno was effectively deploying a critical allegory about his own style of writing – in Hegelese, the truth of his relating to the Other was a self-relating.

Let us then conclude with a reference to another story by Calvino, "A King Listens,"[24] where one should apply "the keen edge of a knife" to generate a strong retroversive effect that makes Calvino's own weakness palpable. "A King Listens" focuses on the sense of hearing: in an anonymous kingdom, the royal palace becomes a giant ear and the king, obsessed and paralyzed by fears of rebellion, tries to hear every fragile sound that reverberates through the palace – the footsteps of servants, whispers and conversations, fanfare trumpets at the raising of the flag, ceremonies and riots, the sounds of the city outside, etc. He cannot see their source, but is obsessed by interpreting the meaning of the sounds and the destiny they are predicting. This state of interpretive paranoia only seems to halt when he hears something that completely enchants him: through the window the wind brings the voice of a woman singing, a voice of pure beauty, unique and irreplaceable. For the king it is the sound of freedom; he steps out of the palace into the open space and mingles with the crowd... The first thing to bear in mind here is that this king is not the traditional monarch, but a modern totalitarian tyrant: the traditional king doesn't care about his environment, he arrogantly ignores it and leaves the job of preventing plots to his ministers. It is the modern Leader who is obsessed by plots – "to rule is to interpret" is the perfect formula of Stalinism, *the* system of an endless paranoiac hermeneutics. So when the king is seduced by the pure feminine voice of immediate life-pleasure, this is obviously (although unfortunately not for Calvino himself) a fantasy: precisely the fantasy of breaking out of the closed circle of representations and re-joining the pure outside of the innocent presence of the voice – a voice which is in excess of the self-mirroring prison-house of representations, that is, which needs no interpretation but merely enjoys its own exercise. What is missing here is the way this innocent externality of the voice is itself already reflexively marked by the mirror of interpretive representations. This is why one can imagine an alternative ending for the story, missing in Calvino's narrative: when the king exits the palace, following the voice, he is immediately arrested; the beautiful voice was simply an instrument of the plotters to lure the king out of the safety of the palace. One can be sure that, after a thorough police interrogation, the woman would have sung a different song . . .

Is the ultimate consequence of Rothenberg's outstanding book then a negative one? Should we refrain from large social actions since, for structural reasons, they always lead to unintended (and as such potentially catastrophic) results? A further distinction has to be drawn here: between the "openness" of the ongoing symbolic activity caught in the "retroversive effect" (whereby the meaning of each of its elements is decided retroactively) and the act in a much stronger sense of the term. In the first case, the unintended consequences of our acts are due simply to the big Other, to the complex symbolic network which overdetermines (and thus displaces) their meaning. In the second case, the unintended consequences emerge from the very failure of the big Other, that is, from the way our act not only relies on the big Other, but also radically challenges and transforms it. The awareness that the power of a proper act is to retroactively create its own conditions of possibility should not make us afraid to embrace what, prior to the act, appears as impossible. Only in this way will our act touch the real. It is around this traumatic point that Rothenberg's book circulates, and this is what makes reading it not only worthwhile, but a necessity.

Notes

1 James Williams, *Gilles Deleuze's* Difference and Repetition: *A Critical Introduction and Guide*, Edinburgh: Edinburgh University Press 2003, p. 94.

2 Gilles Deleuze, *Difference and Repetition*, London: Continuum Books 2001, p. 81.

3 Williams, *Gilles Deleuze's* Difference and Repetition, p. 96.

4 T. S. Eliot, "Tradition and the Individual Talent," originally published in *The Sacred Wood: Essays on Poetry and Criticism*, London: Methuen 1920.

5 Jorge Luis Borges, *Other Inquisitions: 1937–52*, New York: Washington Square Press 1966, p. 113.

6 See Peter Hallward, *Out of This World: Deleuze and the Philosophy of Creation*, London: Verso 2006.

7 See Daniel Dennett, *Freedom Evolves*, Harmondsworth: Penguin Books 2003.

8 Nicholas Fearn, *Philosophy. The Latest Answers to the Oldest Questions*, London: Atlantic Books 2005, p. 24.

9 Hallward, *Out of This World*, p. 139.

10 Ibid.

11 Ibid., p. 54.

12 Williams, *Gilles Deleuze's* Difference and Repetition, p. 109.

13 Ibid., p. 200.

14 Ibid.
15 Deleuze, *Difference and Repetition*, p. 156.
16 Gerard Lebrun, *L'envers de la dialectique. Hegel a la lumiere de Nietzsche*, Paris: Editions du Seuil 2004, p. 40.
17 Ibid., p. 41.
18 Ibid., pp. 41–4.
19 Ibid., p. 87.
20 Jacques Lacan, *Écrits*, New York: Norton 2002, pp. 72–3.
21 Ibid., p. 73.
22 See Georg Lukács, *History and Class Consciousness*, Cambridge, MA: MIT Press 1972.
23 See Theodor W. Adorno, *In Search of Wagner*, London: Verso 2005.
24 Italo Calvino, "A King Listens," in *Under the Jaguar Sun*, London: Vintage 1993.

Introduction: The Excess of Everyday Life

... withdrawing my dagger I'm overcome by a sort of vertigo, a feeling of emptiness, of being alone, not here in Rome, today, but forever after, in the centuries to come, the fear that people won't understand what we did here today, that they won't be able to do it again, that they will remain distant and indifferent as this beautiful calm morning in March.
Italo Calvino, "A Beautiful March Day"[1]

The senators who damned Julius Caesar as a tyrant argued that killing him was the only way to liberate Rome. In their logic, we find the most common gesture of every political program and every call for social change: identify a problem, locate its cause, and then eliminate that cause to solve the problem. This logic seems so self-evident as to be virtually tautological. But Calvino exposes its flaw. Killing Caesar not only eliminates the tyrant, it changes the conditions by which that action acquires its meaning. The very world in which it made sense to get rid of Caesar also vanishes with those dagger strokes – not because Caesar held that world together, but because the assassins could not foresee that their act would also transform the way the act itself would later be judged, even by themselves. They could not factor in the historicity of their action; neither they nor anyone else could predict or govern how the future would interpret the assassination. Put another way, we could say that there was simply no way for them to take into account the *retroversive* effect of future interpretations.

"Retroversion" is one of the most common but least acknowledged forces in human social relations. We encounter it in every use of language. When you read that "Carl smiled as he gently stroked the velvety skin of his lover," you may find your initial picture of this apparent love scene altered irrevocably by the next phrase: "with the keen edge of a knife." Using language means making constant adjustments as the field of meaning widens, narrows, and then circles back on itself. The opportunity and the need for such adjustment is ever-present but has unpredictable effects. One person may be jolted out of a chain of associations, forced to re-evaluate the beginning of that chain by a word that has no particular effect on another person. It is easy enough to imagine a reader who would not read the first phrase as a love scene but rather as the opening of a horror story: such a person may not be vulnerable to the kind of blunt retroversion that would otherwise strike at the mention of the knife. At the same time, we could imagine another reader for whom every word in the first clause works backward to warp or inflect the words that precede it, even before the knife makes its appearance. For example, the reader might at first imagine "velvety skin" to be referring to Carl's own body, and would then re-work the whole scene – from auto-stimulation to interpersonal sexual relations – at the moment of encountering the word "lover." But once the jolt occurs, the opening of the sentence, the opening that sets us up for the jolt down the line, will be transformed permanently in this retroversive movement. In a kind of *Back to the Future* scenario, the original causes – words such as "smile" and "stroked" – are altered in their significance by the effects they produce. Time seems to loop back on itself.

Were we to consider the difference between the way a heterosexual and a homosexual reader might imagine this scene, we could explore another set of possible retroversive effects. In other words, the very conditions by which these sentences acquire their meaning shift not only as we add words and phrases but also as the particularities of the people involved are taken into account. When we read or talk with each other, we make just such (often minute or unconscious) adjustments to the fantasmatic dimension of our associative chains and to those we postulate as operating in our interlocutors. One of the great pleasures of learning to read attentively, of course, is to register such micro-adjustments, even to imagine ourselves as having different concerns, interests, and personal histories. But if we are in the business of trying to promote social change, things become more difficult once we acknowledge that retroversion is constantly in play as a function not only of individual signifying acts but also of interactions among individuals.

So, Calvino's story points to a double problem facing contemporary theories of social change. In the first place, we are used to conceiving of change in a linear way: I strike a stationary billiard ball with a cue and it rolls into the corner pocket. First comes the cause, then the effect. But retroversive causality challenges that linearity, as if the act of striking the ball into the pocket could loop backward in time to change the initial position of the ball on the table. Of course, physical forces at human scale rarely exhibit retroversive causality, although physicists describe the quantum world as a phantasmagoria of such phenomena. On the other hand, social forces seem always to exhibit retroversive causality, precisely because they necessarily involve signification, meaning, or interpretation. As soon as we have a social situation, we are in the world of signifiers: the signifier is always subject to the law of retroversion. Clearly then, once we notice the phenomenon of retroversion and try to take it into account, we face the difficulty of defining the concept of "change." For if our social interactions necessarily operate with retroversion, then our everyday ideas about generating change come into question. If we identify a problem, as Rome's senators did, and then act to change it, how should we model the operation of retroversive causality? Indeed, can it be modeled at all?

In the second place, by describing sociality as saturated with the unpredictability of retroversive signification, we call into question some familiar ideas about what we mean by social interaction. As we shall see, the usual sorts of interpersonal activities – joining a club, going to church, bringing a lawsuit, attending university – that we typically conceive in terms of individual units engaging in delimited actions for specifiable ends start to look incredibly complicated. The very idea of the "social" has to be revisited once retroversion enters the picture. How is it possible to address the concept of social change when we seem to be talking about a fluctuating social field formed from the mutually constitutive interactions of retroversive effects?

To a person dedicated to trying to make the world a better place, such reflections might seem beside the point. After all, can't we identify real problems that exist at a material level rather than at the level of language or interpretations? What difference does retroversion make when we're trying to abolish hunger? Why consider the social field as a congeries of forces in flux when people around the world are subjected to oppression, violence, and death? Let's attempt to solve the practical problems, and leave the theoreticians to their ivory tower cogitations. Without a doubt this approach has its appeal. Yet the history of efforts to change the world for the better indicate forcefully how poorly it has worked. Violence, poverty, oppression – this familiar litany of woe begs the question as to why we have failed to cross a single item off the list. For despite our best efforts to identify and address their causes, such serious problems seem to be permanent fixtures of every modern society.

We have laid the blame at many doors, including lack of sympathy and common values, human propensities for greed and power, the rhizomatic properties of global capitalist institutions, the weakness of political systems, the strength of hegemonic ideologies, the micro-fluctuations of power, and the madness of individual rulers. No one would argue that identifying the causes of these problems is easy. Think for a moment of the difficulties facing anyone who wants to address poverty. What causes poverty? It seems unlikely that every poverty-stricken person is poor for the same reason, given the myriad different circumstances of poor people on the planet. Some have their land taken away, some fall ill; some manage their money poorly, some lose their jobs; some are victims of disaster, some are victims of hoaxes. How should we group these people in order to best address poverty? By psychological type? By urban or rural setting? By skill set? By country? By degree of agency? By economic system? For example, if we think that poverty has its roots in a worldwide economic system, then we have to figure out how that system works (and works differentially) on individuals, groups, industries, and governmental processes, and then design a new system that would not only enrich the present poor but also would not impoverish hosts of other people in the process. How do we decide what is the proper scale for our focus? How do we handle the mass of variables at every scale as well as the complexity of their interactions?

Attempts to handle these factors (among many others) have generated a demand for new disciplinary methods to bring analytic clarity to such chaos. Yet, because every analysis takes its orientation from some model of the structure and operations of social interactions, and because every model inevitably reduces social complexity in order to manage it, these analyses necessarily produce a distorted picture of the complexities of the social field. In modern times, discourses of social change have struggled with these twin difficulties of empirical multiplicity and theoretical reduction. These discourses tend either to emphasize the importance of studying interactions among particulars to arrive inductively at a sense of relevant causes, or they begin with a framework that distinguishes cause from effect in an *a priori* way (e.g., economic base, ideological superstructure). A good example of the first type is statistical analysis; a good example of the second is Marxist theory.

As a consequence of this shared inheritance of fundamental approaches, when it comes to theorizing social change, no matter which approach is being used, we repeatedly encounter familiar but apparently insoluble questions about the forces generating social forms and the counter-forces that might be marshaled to check or change them. The literature is littered with such puzzles. How is the social field structured? Is it generated by dominant forces or by aggregates of chance activities? Do we produce society or does it produce us? If they are mutually constitutive, how do we distinguish the contribution of each? If social forces perpetuate themselves by producing social subjects pre-programmed to follow their dictates, how do we achieve agency? How can power be created, husbanded, distributed, channeled, or governed? Should we form political groups based on universal characteristics or particular identities – or on something else? What group forms and activities will create the greatest political traction? If we desire change, should we place our bet on pragmatic political action, which might involve violence and inequities, or on ethical principle, which might hamstring us and leave the status quo intact? These questions – well known to anyone who has tried to model the causes of social effects with a view to promoting change – seem constantly to shift focus from the trees to the forest and back again, without offering much in the way of new prospects, new models, or new approaches.

Now, however, something new has made an appearance. This book tells the story of a new theory of social change that challenges standard concepts of causality and traditional definitions of the "social" in large part by taking account of the retroversion that permeates social interactions. This new theory of social change has been developing in the work of cultural theorists, sociologists, philosophers of science, and psychoanalytic thinkers. No single author articulates the theory as a whole. However, by putting eminent theorists, such as Pierre Bourdieu, Michel de Certeau, Judith Butler, Theodor Adorno, Slavoj Žižek, Emmanuel Levinas, Giorgio Agamben, Bruno Latour and Alain Badiou into conversation with one another, in this book I have presented the fundamental features of this theory and demonstrated its innovations and limitations for thinking through social change in a political as well as ethical register. In order to help the reader appreciate the innovations on offer, I want here to outline its starting point and define some key terms.

Articulating the Cause of the Social Field

Any theory of social change with political aspirations faces an apparently insurmountable task. On the one hand, it must provide a credible causal analysis that targets the source of social problems. On the other hand, achieving such credibility seems impossible in the face of the complexity of the interactions among social actors and contingent conditions. Only from God's perspective can the sheer number of interrelated variables within the complex social space resolve themselves into neat bundles making it possible to differentiate cause from effect. And we can add further difficulties. To construct a plausible scenario of social change, we would have to have some means of following effects through time, in all their manifold concatenations, to discover their origin in a significant cause. We would also have to have some means of judging which effects are most significant and for which period of time. How, for example, are we to analyze the determinants of any given social fact – say, the poverty of children in America – in the face of a plethora of possible historical, economic, ideological, biological, familial, personal, and environmental factors if we cannot isolate, at least provisionally and theoretically, a domain of causes prior to and independent of the effects they produce? Distinguishing cause from effect scientifically seems to be the *sine qua non* of a politically relevant theory of social change.

Marx's signal achievement in this respect was his description of a social field split into two tiers, base and superstructure, allowing for the "scientific" disentanglement of cause from effect, and thus addressing the problem of causes being indistinguishable from effects. But in the absence of some transcendental position from which to make that distinction, the sequestration of causes from the effects they produce creates a fatal separation, such that nothing remains to guarantee the very connection one has set out to explain – namely, the link between the cause and the field of effects. For if the cause is radically other than its effects, if it is not *in some way* part of the field it produces, then it cannot be seen in relation to that field *as its cause*. In fact, the field itself threatens to fall apart, since nothing holds its elements together in relation to each other.

In response to this problem, later Marxist theorizing takes on the task of articulating plausible mechanisms by which a cause might be brought back into touch with its effects. In Marxian theories, such mechanisms include the intellectual's role in transforming class consciousness, Althusser's emphasis on overdetermination, Gramsci's invention of hegemony, and Williams' attempts to rethink the base. As we shall see in chapter 3, Pierre Bourdieu invents the concept of the *habitus* – an embodied set of durable predispositions installed by external conditions – explicitly to serve this purpose. But perhaps the effort best known to North American readers is Michel Foucault's theory of immanent power relations:

> It seems to me that power must be understood in the first instance as the multiplicity of force relations immanent in the sphere in which they operate and which constitute their own organization; as the process which, through ceaseless struggles and confrontations, transforms, strengthens, or reverses them; as the support which these force relations find in one another, thus forming a chain or a system, or on the contrary, the disjunctions and contradictions which isolate them from one another; and lastly, as the strategies in which they take effect, whose general design or institutional crystallization is embodied in the state apparatus, in the formulation of the law, in the various social hegemonies.[2]

By this means, Foucault links causes directly with their effects. Unfortunately, in this model, cause and effect are brought so closely together that the two tiers collapse into one: anything can be a cause of anything (or everything) else in this "moving substrate of force relations."[3] In so doing, cause once again becomes indistinguishable from effect, dissolved within the very positivity of the relation it supposedly produces. It would seem that we must accept either the flaw of *non sequitur* in the Marxian transcendentalist model or the flaw of *nondifferentiation* in the Foucaultian immanentist model.

In order to address this set of problems, Joan Copjec has taken up the challenge of articulating a psychoanalytic position against Foucault and his followers. She locates the crux of their disagreement by showing that the model of social relationality which underwrites Foucault's analyses of the implication of power and knowledge – and serves as the standard for cultural studies – *reduces* society to its immanent power relations, which are identified in terms of positive categories or properties. In this way, Foucault avoids the Marxian error of locating the principle of social regulation outside the realm of the social but commits the reciprocal error of failing to provide any place from which resistance could be mounted. As Copjec puts it:

> While the Foucauldian focus on *relations* of power and knowledge is widely hailed as a necessary corrective to more naïve political theories, we will contend that his reduction of society to these relations is problematic . . . [P]ower was no longer conceived by Foucault as an external force that exerted itself on society, but as immanent within society, the "fine, differentiated, continuous" network of uneven relations that constituted the very matter of the social. . . . Now, it is with this notion of immanence, this conception of a cause that is immanent within the field of its effects, with which this book quarrels and repeatedly condemns as historicist. . . . We are calling historicist the reduction of society to its indwelling network of relations of power and knowledge.[4]

Copjec agrees with Foucault's criticism of the Marxian solution, explaining that there cannot be some exception to the field of relations that causes all the others while being itself immune to causation. A great advantage of the Foucaultian solution is that causes (powers) subsist within the field in question. All the same, Foucault's attempts to avoid importing some transcendent externality lead him to adopt a model that not only cannot satisfactorily distinguish cause from effect but also, and on that account, cannot provide for any resistance to the system itself that does not translate back into the power that is the target of that resistance. Subjects determined by the immanent relations of the system can never stand in a position *counter* to that system, determined as they are *by* it. In this scenario, no element remains undetermined – that is, *contingent* – and thus potentially subversive of the system.

Academic historicists allied under the banner of cultural studies have responded to this criticism by pointing out that the contingency minimally required for resistance to the determining system could arise from the multiplicity of discourses circulating within it: no subject is determined unilaterally by one discourse, so the inevitable discordances among the various discourses determining the subject can provide for a "new" entity, one not predictable from the component discourses. Unfortunately, however, in the Foucaultian model, the very conflict that is taken to signal the subject's nondetermination, its potential positioning against its determinations, proves to be the means by which knowledge and power are produced and consolidated – the very means, in other words, which situate the subject in its determinations. The lines of power that run through the social field are productive of subjects, not just of prohibitions on them. What is more, this productive power works in more than one direction simultaneously, so that what looks like a prohibition actually conceals a formative force. Copjec makes the point this way:

> the simple atomization and multiplication of subject positions and this *partes extra partes* description of conflict does not lead to a radical undermining of knowledge or power. Not only is it the case that at each stage what is produced is conceived in Foucauldian theory to be a determinate thing or position, but, in addition, knowledge and power are conceived as the overall effect of the relations among the various conflicting positions and discourses. Differences do not threaten panoptic power; they feed it.[5]

In sum, the Foucaultian solution is "ultimately *resistant to resistance*, unable to conceive of a discourse that would refuse rather than refuel power."[6] Foucault's model of power cannot deliver a plausible account of social change.

So, until recently, social theorists have articulated their positions vis-à-vis two opposed causal models, one describing the cause as exceptional to the field of its effects (a two-tier model) and one describing the cause as entangled within a field of causes indistinguishable from their effects (a one-tier model). For convenience, I refer to these as the model of external causation and the model of immanent causation. They are strictly complementary: each attempts to correct the deficits of the other. Marxism is a good example of external causation: the field of effects (superstructure) is analytically distinct from its underlying cause (economic base), which appears as an exception to the field. But the separation of cause and effect for the purposes of analysis brings its own problems: for one, in the lived social world such distinctions are very difficult to make, and, for another, once cause is separated from effect, it is difficult to account for the links between them – that is, as Hume noted, it is difficult to find the very causation of causality. Another way to put this is to say that external causation reifies the cause as being so entrenched and having such dominance that the prospect of altering it seems impossible.

Immanent causation, exemplified in the work of Foucault and Deleuze (and sometimes going under the name of "neo-Spinozism"), treats causes and effects as mutually conditioning one another within the same field. In this way, immanent causation rectifies the problems that bedevil external causation by more adequately reflecting the state of affairs in the social world and by accepting the possibility of reciprocal causes. But immanent causation has its own drawbacks because the model provides no means for distinguishing causes from their consequences in a way that would enable an analysis. Put another way, the sheer volume and volatility of particulars makes it unlikely that one can find the lever for change.

While partisans of one approach may argue for the superiority of their chosen model, including all the ways that a given advance on their side vitiates any criticism from the other, their counter-partisans are quick to demonstrate how these so-called advances are simply the old model tricked out in new clothes. So, for example, when Althusser proposes to avoid the causal traps of classical Marxist thought via the mechanism of overdetermination of superstructural elements, his immanentist critics have no problem discerning his continued reliance on just those aspects of Marxist causality that he claims to have left behind. They are right, but so too are the critics of the "new" immanentism propounded by theorists such as Deleuze or Hardt and Negri. It has seemed impossible to overcome this divide. The disciplinary boundaries between history and sociology, to take one salient example, exemplify this dichotomy, which then gets played out within each discipline, as in the question of the priority of agency versus structure (see, for example, Giddens' *The Constitution of Society*).

Once we see the complementary nature of these two models, however, an opening appears. The challenge is to theorize a cause that is both exceptional to the social field, *à la* the Marxist meta-cause, and internal to the field, *à la* the Foucaultian immanent cause. Such an external/internal ("extimate") cause not only has to supply a means of keeping cause and effect distinct, unlike the causal field in the Foucaultian model, it must also forge a link between cause and effect within the social field of effects, unlike the Marxist model. Thanks to the work of a number of talented theorists, this third option is available. Departing from longstanding dissatisfactions with the dominant paradigms of the structure and function of social power represented by Marx and Foucault, and aligning themselves against sheer empirical studies, these theorists establish the need for an alternative model of social space, power, and causality. They tackle head on the problem of theorizing what is apparently an incomprehensible complexity by identifying a type of external/internal causality – I refer to it as "extimate causality" for reasons that will become clear in a moment. It will be the burden of this book to show that extimate causality has the special property of producing and disseminating a certain type of *excess* that is central to the establishment and maintenance of the social field itself.

Speaking in terms of the social arena, we could describe the significance of extimate causality in the following way. We have seen that social relations depend upon retroversive signification, which is one way of saying that the social dimension of subjectivity is irremediably *excessive*. Extimate causality names the operation that generates subjects in their social dimension – that is, the operation that gives us social identities, properties, and relationships. In producing the social subject, extimate causality also leaves a remainder or indeterminacy, so that every subject bears some unspecifiable excess within the social field. Every subject is an "excessive" subject. For convenience, I refer to this excessive subject – the subject born of and bearing excess – as the "Möbius subject" because the topology of the Möbius band (with its apparently impossible configuration of two sides that turn out to be the same) provides a convenient model for understanding how, at every point in the social field, an irreducible excess attends social relations, as we will see in chapter 2.

In fact, although it seems paradoxical, this excess is what makes the systematicity of the social field itself possible (and hence susceptible to analysis). For example, we can never know for certain what others think of us, but this inability is precisely what makes it necessary for us to continue to participate in the social field itself, for the social field is the only place in which we can even try to find out what we mean to others. We could say that the excess produced by the extimate cause of subjectivity is both the obstacle to our knowing our meaning as social beings and the necessary ingredient of the social field within which we obtain the only meaning that we will ever have, however uncertain.

The key contribution made by these theorists involves their unique handling of this excess. Other theories of social change, subject formation, and political alliance may acknowledge it (without however understanding the production of the excess by the operation of extimate causality), but they invariably conceive of its *elimination* as necessary to their projects because it seems to them that the excess of each subject stands only as an obstacle to secure self-knowledge, solidarity, or stable political regimes. However, as theorists of extimate causality make clear, the excess is ineradicable. Hence any theory of social change must either find a way to include it or doom itself to rehearsing the same problems again and again.

Structure of the Book

Until now, the writers developing this theory – for example, Žižek, Copjec, Badiou, and Alenka Zupančič – have all been to some degree associated with Lacanian psychoanalysis. One gets an impression of the importance of extimate causality from reading neo-Lacanian discussions of St. Paul, Spinoza, Kant, Schelling, Hegel, Marx, Freud, and Nietzsche, in which it appears that the history of Western philosophy has been a history of the search for this third form of causality. However, I must stress that the extimate cause is not a psychoanalytic concept per se, having emerged first in set theory, then topology, and finally in what is known as paraconsistent logic, a branch of symbolic logic. (Readers will need no particular familiarity with these fields; the significance of these concepts will be explained here in terms accessible to the general academic reader.) Lacan coined the term "extimacy" to describe the form of causality peculiar to the subject of the unconscious. He was the first to see how extimate causality, the concept necessary to explain the advent of the subject, also recalibrates the investigation of social relations, a topic he takes up most rigorously in Seminar 17, *L'envers de la psychanalyse* (*The Other Side of Psychoanalysis*).[7] It will become obvious to my readers that this "other side" must be understood in terms of the Möbius band (or other topologically similar objects defined as "non-orientable").

It is then an accident of the history of intellectual inquiry that, despite some valiant efforts to create a wider audience for it, the most interesting discourse available to the humanities for thinking causality, solidarity, and social change became sequestered in a relatively small corner of the academy, thanks to the repudiation of psychoanalysis on other grounds by Deleuze, Foucault, and Butler, among others, over the past thirty years. Now that Žižek, for instance, is becoming more explicit about current political policies and the effects of globalization, it is more important than ever to understand the central role that the extimate cause plays in his thinking – but because he switches so rapidly from one philosophical framework (or illustrative anecdote) to another, it can be difficult to catch precisely how he uses the concept of the extimate cause to theorize social change.

In an attempt to overcome this unfortunate sequestration of extimate causality and the precise kind of subject it produces, I offer here case studies of seminal theorists of social change: Bourdieu (*The Logic of Practice*), de Certeau (*The Practice of Everyday Life*), Butler (*Excitable Speech*), Laclau (*Emancipations*), and Žižek (*Organs Without Bodies*; *Revolution at the Gates*; *The Parallax View*). I chose these authors because they are leading lights in their respective fields as well as widely recognized contributors to social theory and cultural studies, whatever their home discipline (social science research in the case of Bourdieu, gender/sexuality studies in Butler's case, political theory in the case of Laclau, etc.). Each author provides an entry point to a key question in social change theory, and critique of their work establishes the need for and value of the extimate cause and the Möbius subject with respect to each question. I take up the work of Bourdieu and de Certeau to address the preeminent theories for linking subjects to the social field. My discussion of Butler focuses on theories of subject formation and social agency. I address Laclau's political thought as it centers on the problem of creating and stabilizing politically active groups in democratic interaction. In Žižek's work, I engage with issues of the nature and temporality of the political act and the connection between the political and the ethical subject. In each chapter, I discuss the featured thinker with reference to other theorists whose work illuminates some facet of extimate causality. Aristotle, Bruno Latour, Jacques Rancière, Jean-Luc Nancy, Simon Critchley, Emmanuel Levinas, Giorgio Agamben, Theodor Adorno, Félix Guattari, and Alain Badiou, among others, provide crucial perspectives.

I have another reason for choosing the authors featured in each chapter: each turns to psychoanalysis (often surprisingly) to break the deadlock between external and immanent causation. What makes their work so exciting is their creativity in attempting to break that deadlock as they come to recognize the need for some alternative – as they grope towards the significance of what I am calling the extimate cause. From my point of view, these discussions become particularly fruitful at the point when, having acknowledged the need for extimate causality, the author misrecognizes its nature and function in a way characteristic of that author. My own commentary on these theories focuses on the degree to which each author meets his or her own acknowledged need for the function of extimate causality and an excessive subject only to disavow those concepts precisely at the point when they threaten to undermine cherished assumptions about the source and reach of the individual's power to effect social change. I take advantage of these different misrecognitions (and the missed opportunities the authors themselves are trying to seize) to relate the implications of extimate causality and Möbius subjectivity for social change theory. Countering the current refrain that psychoanalysis is ahistorical and illegitimately universalizing, my discussion shows the advantages of this theory for the historicist project of cultural studies and its concomitant emancipatory aims. The book is designed for the reader who, having glimpsed the significance of extimate causality in the stimulating work of thinkers like those showcased here, wishes to investigate its advantages and limitations.

The range of topics taken up here presented me with a quandary: how could I do justice to the network of philosophical issues and scholarly debates weaving through the book without risking obscuring the lines of the story I wanted to tell? If I devoted myself to attempting to demonstrate my theoretical proficiency in these debates, I would either have to write a series of learned treatises or employ a theoretical shorthand that might be useful for the adept but risk confusing others. At the same time, I knew that I would have to try to provide some access to the complexities of neo-Lacanian psychoanalytic theory for uninitiated readers. I decided that a linked series of case studies, each of which would include a targeted summary, exposition, analysis, and critique, would best serve readers who have fundamental questions about social change and who need a road map for further inquiry.

The first chapter describes the need to define the "social" as a site of excess and investigates the role of the extimate cause in generating the social field. The second chapter contains the heart of the theoretical explanation of extimate causality and the nature of the Möbius subject. It provides the reader with the terms and theoretical tools that should enable her to recognize the function and advantage of the Möbius subject for conceptualizing the nature of the social arena as a "non-orientable object," the possibilities for group formation and stability, the temporality of political acts, and their ethical dimension. To help the reader see these advantages, the concluding section of the chapter puts the extimate cause and Möbius subjectivity to work in readings of the theories of two political philosophers: Rancière's analysis of the political nature of subjects in classical Greek thought, and Agamben's proposal for a new topology for thinking the political. With the caveat that I highlight only those features of these accounts which best elucidate the Möbius subject rather than providing a full discussion of all the issues, I argue that these philosophers demonstrate the potential of that subject for the politics of social change. With these tools and examples in hand, the reader should be able to judge the importance of the forms of disavowal of extimate causality (and the functions of excess it generates in the social field) specific to each of the authors discussed in the remaining chapters.

Chapter 3 assesses the implications of the extimate cause and the role of retroversive temporality in the production of the subject of social change in two theorists – Bourdieu and de Certeau – who have devoted their careers to trying to square the circle of immanent and external causation using psychoanalytic tools. Their work helps us to see the need for new causal models to theorize the reciprocal effects of subjects and social structures. Chapter 4 undertakes an investigation of Butler's extraordinary attempts to bring Lacan together with Derrida and Bourdieu in order to grapple with the problem of the determinants of the subject and the limitations of agency: the problems she encounters point up the need for a different account of subject formation based on extimacy. In chapter 5, I analyze Laclau's sophisticated deployment of Lacanian thought to articulate the production of collective political groups and the possibility of radical democratic interaction. I use the problems he encounters in his analysis to explore the kinds of social relations available to Möbius subjects and the types of collective political agency that can result from them. In chapter 6, I examine Žižek's reflections on the nature of the political act, drawn from Benjamin, Badiou, and Lacan, in particular the retroversive temporality particular to the Möbius subject as political and ethical subject. The limitations of Žižek's theory help to highlight the virtues of tracing "excess" as a means of conducting complex social analysis. The concluding sections of this chapter explore the relationship between the subjective destitution for which Žižek claims political efficacy, the Adornian concept of the constellation, and the Lacanian theory of the *sinthome*. Chapter 7, the final chapter, assesses the value of extimate causality and Möbius subjectivity for the political valence of ethics by comparing the implications of Žižek's thought with the work of Critchley and Levinas. Here I address the possibility that the intrasubjective relation of de-personalization or symbolic divestiture, which appears in the theory of the constellation as well as the *sinthome*, provides another entry point into the question of how individual efforts can generate social effects. The conclusion to this final chapter takes up Guattari's early works to link individual symbolic divestiture with the problematic of group transformation in a revolutionary political key.

All of the major themes of this study come into play in the final chapter, which traces in a different register the arc of the book through issues of subjectification and political agency, to emancipatory politics and the nature of revolutionary acts, and finally to the ethical and transformative potential of a praxis based on the recognition of Möbius subjectivity in order to provide a more solid footing for historicist work that promotes social change. The fundamental tools of the formal negation, the extimate cause, the Möbius subject, retroversive temporality, and the non-orientable social field are explained and applied throughout. I hope my readers will find these tools, first developed in psychoanalytic discourse, useful guides as they develop their own approaches to the problems of social change.

I

What Does the "Social" in Social Change Mean?

ᘒᘒ

The Social Field in Flux

Calvino's story, "A Beautiful March Day," raises important issues about the stability of social ties, the nature of political acts, and the historicity of interpretation. The view of social life in this story suggests a provisionality and a fragility of the social realm that is not usually in evidence in the standard discourse of social theory, where it seems that social forces have the power to shape just about everything. In these classic accounts, "social" refers to a special arena, force, or medium that guarantees the coordination and meaning of all activity. According to this paradigm, the "social" functions both as the glue and the governor of activity. It is assumed to have an independent existence, with its own properties and powers, while at the same time being the most general feature of all human activity. Although typically distinguished from politics, economics, and culture, which are conceived as subsets of its more general category, "society" and "the social" nonetheless in fact have no readily identifiable defining quality.[1]

Sometimes this fundament or force is conceived, à la vulgar Marxism, as thoroughly saturating everything, so that nothing escapes its shaping power. Sometimes it appears to be less potent, as in Michel de Certeau's work on everyday practices, where it permits some individual creativity but only within set limits. In any case, its theorists assume that this force pre-exists the activities it conditions, arguing that it serves as the very ontological ground of all human activity and relationality. They take it as axiomatic that these various activities acquire their meaning and function by means of this "social" force.

Bruno Latour has identified this view of the social as the default position of contemporary sociology which assumes "the existence of a specific sort of phenomenon variously called 'society', 'social order', 'social practice', 'social dimension', or 'social structure'."[2] He elaborates the familiar tenets of this sociology, which have come to seem incontrovertible:

> there exists a social "context" in which non-social activities take place; it is a specific domain of reality; it can be used as a specific type of causality to account for the residual aspects that other domains (psychology, law, economics, etc.) cannot completely deal with; it is studied by specialized scholars called sociologists or socio-(x) – "x" being the placeholder for the various disciplines; since ordinary agents are always "inside" a social world that encompasses them, they can at best be "informants" about this world and, at worst, blinded to its existence, whose full effect is only visible to the social scientist's more disciplined eyes; no matter how difficult it is to carry on those studies, it is possible for them to roughly imitate the successes of the natural sciences by being as objective as other scientists thanks to the use of quantitative tools. . .[3]

For sociologists, the social "force" governs all sorts of activities from behind the curtain, or it is what guarantees that these activities all have the same context, conditions, and causes.

But what if the social is not a specific domain or force standing behind these activities? What if, instead, we understand the "social" to be merely the provisional product of "re-association and re-assembling," as Latour puts it?[4] Latour likens the assumption of an *a priori* social domain to the theory of ether in physics, an entity brought in to explain what classical physics could not. Just as the ether theory's explanatory value dropped to zero once physics adopted the framework of relativity, so "social forces" become superfluous once we recognize that individual activity is always working – sometimes successfully, sometimes not – to regenerate the space in which the individual can be meaningful. The social isn't always already there, holding individuals together. Rather, individuals act in order to "re-assemble" the social.

Even the most "objective" and "fact-based" parts of our world are functions of this activity, as Latour details in his work on the production of science. He starts his inquiry into the assemblage of the social with what he calls the "simplest of all possible situations: when someone utters a statement, what happens when the others believe it or don't believe it."[5] He summarizes the various responses and rhetorical strategies which can result (such as misquotation, enlistment, neglect, embedding) – and the many venues in which these responses may appear (such as scientific journals, classrooms, laboratories, dinner tables) – to demonstrate the production of facts in science:

By itself a given sentence is neither a fact nor a fiction; it is made so by others, later on. You make it more of a fact if you insert it as a closed, obvious, firm and packaged premise leading to some other less closed, less obvious, less firm and less united consequence. . . . listeners make sentences less of a fact if they take them back where they came from, to the mouths and hands of whoever made them. . . . with every new retort added to the debate, the status of the original discovery . . . *will be modified . . . the status of a statement depends on later statements.*[6]

Remember, Latour is describing the process by which *scientific* discoveries are made and validated. As he sums it up: *"the fate of what we say and make is in later users' hands* . . . [and] the construction of facts and machines is a *collective* process."[7] The commonplace and obvious elements of our world emerge only on account of the possibility of their being (mis)construed, taken up, or appropriated by others. His point is not that facts are fictions but rather that the most provable, useful, *true* fact only comes to be accepted as such through negotiations, appropriations, debates, and so forth. All facts are liable to appropriation, contextual embedding, and deployment in the service of some agenda.

This is not to say, however, that the social is reducible to culture or discourse. Making the move to replace "social" with "cultural" or "discursive" does nothing to establish more specificity or to create greater theoretical reach. In this book, I will be following the suggestion of Keith Baker and William Sewell that we use "social" to refer to "the totality of the 'interdependence of human relations.'"[8] These relations are always both fluctuating and creating flux, stabilized and stabilizing. But what is most important about them, what makes them susceptible to analysis, is that they are mediated. As Sewell puts it, "the various *mediations* that place people into 'social' relations with one another . . . may not make them companions but . . . [do] make them interdependent members of each other's worlds."[9] So, rather than taking as given the various units of society and then studying them as autonomous, already constituted entities (individuals, institutions, nations, etc.) which can have some impact on one another or come into conflict with one another, we must consider the ways in which specific modes of relationality make different properties of the entities in question *signify* differently. What is more, we must consider how, at a given time or over time, these various signifying modes articulate differentially with one another.

As we shall see, the impossibility of immediate (immanent) communication will be decisive for the generation and sustenance of social subjects in a social field. It is particularly important to keep in mind that signification – the process of bestowing meaning – does not function by way of the intentions of speakers or authors but rather by way of the appropriation of the signifier by the auditor or reader. That is, in the hypothesis we are pursuing about the nature of the social field, any act of signification not only articulates differentially to other acts embedded in different modes of relationality and signification but also involves aleatory processes, such as unpredictably linked affects, unconscious motives, or unintended consequences, which may or may not be knowable by individuals or even cognizable at the level of the individual.[10]

Let's return to Calvino for a moment to see how these reflections have a bearing. Calvino describes a social world in danger of disintegrating: this is where he parts company with the larger traditions of social thought. When the narrator realizes he cannot control the interpretation of his act, he imagines that he risks becoming completely meaningless. He feels alone in an empty world, infinitely distanced from others. To him, the inability to guarantee how others will interpret him spells the dissolution of the social itself. The story registers this fragility. Yet the narrator's fear that his vulnerability to interpretation renders him meaningless and destroys his social ties is based on a mistake about the effects of interpretative unpredictability. The fact that he cannot know his meaning for others does not doom him to meaninglessness, nor does it radically disconnect him from others. It simply speaks to the reality of social life. We are always in the process of trying to re-assemble what is threatening to disperse.

Calvino's story allows us to glimpse a social world that has to be put together from "connections" that are neither secure nor produced by some special, *a priori* force. This world has to be generated anew continually by countless acts of interpretation, innumerable efforts to make oneself signify in a particular way, even though one can never know for sure if one has succeeded, within constraints or modalities of relationality that operate at a level beyond the cognizance of individuals. The "social" itself refers to hard-won yet ever-precarious outcomes of activities undertaken precisely because signification is not a function of intentionality but of appropriability. Put another way: if the possibility of appropriation did not exist, there would be no social realm.[11]

Jean-Luc Nancy has commented extensively on the mistake that theorists of social change make when they distinguish the "social" world of such interpretations and assemblages from a world of human interaction assumed to be comprised of ever-present, perduring, and predictable links between people ("community"). Communality, in their view, is prior to all signification, impervious to destabilizing interpretations, and grounded in ontological realities that lie beneath, behind, or beyond the activities of humankind. Communality, it is imagined, guarantees communication as communion. Such critics lament the substitution of the observed fluctuation of "social" ties for the (fantasized) more stable, authentic, organic, or immanent ties of a "lost" community:

What this community has "lost" – the immanence and the intimacy of a communion – is lost only in the sense that such a "loss" is constitutive of "community" itself. It is not a loss: on the contrary, immanence, if it were to come about, would instantly suppress community, or communication, as such . . . Community therefore occupies a singular place: it assumes the impossibility of its own immanence, the impossibility of a communitarian being in the form of a subject. In a certain sense community acknowledges and inscribes – this is its peculiar gesture – the impossibility of community. A community is not a project of fusion, or in some general way a productive or operative project – nor is it a *project* at all . . . A community is the presentation to its members of their mortal truth. . . . It is the presentation of the finitude and the irredeemable excess that make up finite being. . . .[12]

When theorists nostalgic for an assumed bygone immanence argue that society is a falling off from community, a falling off generated by "the dissociating association of forces, needs, and signs," they say more than they know.[13] From a Latourian perspective, such dissociating of association is *crucial* for the establishment of any communication/community whatsoever. The world of social ties depends not upon perfect – immanent – communion but rather upon the imperfections of communication, a function of the excess that attends signification. For no communication is possible without signs, and signs by definition work by being appropriated, that is, taken up in new contexts to produce new meanings. The excess necessary for signification *enables* associations by *dissolving* previous associations: without such dissolution, the link between signifier and signified would ossify and signification would be impossible. So, if we understand "society" to refer to a realm of contested needs and contested meanings, if it is formed of fluctuating bonds and imperfect communication, then society is not the impediment to community, it is the only possible basis of community. As Nancy puts it: "community, far from being what society has crushed or lost, is *what happens to us . . . in the wake of society.*"[14]

Here and throughout the rest of the book, we will be working towards an understanding of the "social" as a term describing the "un-working" and "re-assembling" that Nancy and Latour describe as the signature of the social realm. Coming to grips with the fact that the "social" does not refer to some special capacity or force or medium means accepting that it neither enables the fullness of community nor registers an unfortunate loss of that ideal. Only in this sense is the social the pre-condition of all political, economic, ethical activity: each of those spheres offers different ways of grappling with the reality of *excess*, that is, with the impossibility of immanent communion and with the appropriability of the signifier.

At the same time, this picture of a fluctuating social field is incomplete insofar as it does not clarify how power is generated, accumulated, channeled, directed, or exercised. It does not explain the mechanisms by which individuals become groups, how and why institutions, ideas, and arrangements perdure, or how apparently autonomous activities may be linked. If we are interested in social change, all of these issues must be addressed from within the framework of this alternative picture of the social field. Latour's empirical project of describing these forms and the activities which sustain them may not provide all the answers to the question of the nature of the social, but it serves as a useful corrective to the dominant paradigms of social thought in contemporary academic discourse. At the level of the empirical, however, one must make choices about which variables to consider and how to rank their importance, a task that requires some model of the causal relations operating in the social field. What is more, an empirical focus on particular pathways and networks that develop, as Latour describes, to knit together actors at specifiable historical junctures may easily leave out of account macro- and micro-processes that transpire at different scales to those observable within the empirical study. So, empirical work such as Latour's can tell us what happened – who and what was woven together in the trajectory of the "fact" – but may have no way to account for why it happened. The value of conceptualizing the social realm in terms of fluctuating social bonds and dissociating significations may dwindle unless we also articulate the means for finding and differentiating forms of mediation with varying degrees of staying power (such as relatively perduring insti- tutions) and multiple modalities of relationality (such as instantiations of power relations). Talking about social change requires a conception of the social that either explains phenomena in terms of underlying causes or establishes why it is impossible to do so.

This need to find the cause of social phenomena drives the return to the assumption that the social realm is composed by *a priori* forces. Given that this assumption is flawed, each effort to theorize the cause of the social will necessarily reveal its own limitations. If our approach is guided by the insights furnished by Latour, Sewell, and Nancy, we will be able to identify these limitations in a way that leads us to a new understanding of the properties of the social field and its causes. It will be useful, therefore, to take a quick look at the problems that the notion of the social as a special domain or governing force creates for theories of social change before tackling the difficult issue of social causality based on other premises.

Some of the problems that result from the assumption of a special "social" force are well known. For example, when we seek to explain individuals by their social conditioning we assume that this conditioning stems from forces that stand "behind" the individuals, inculcating them with just those properties which facilitate their alignment with each other and positioning them within a social medium that transmits whatever is necessary to coordinate them. This presumed force of inculcation, transmission, and coordination appears to give the individuals within it access to something fundamental about the way the society works: as a consequence, or so it is said, these conditioned individuals are able to assess problems at their source and address them.

But the explanatory advantage conferred by recourse to this metaphor of a common medium (conditioning forces, disciplinary regimes, or discursive channeling) is immediately lost when we realize that conditioned individuals are also those least likely to be able to act against the society that conditions them. How can individuals be conditioned by these forces and still retain sufficient agency to discern and change them? And how will they know whether their analyses of these social forces are expressions of their agency or of their conditioning? This question – and others related to its primary assumption about the independent existence of a "social" property – takes up a considerable amount of discursive space in academic circles.

Contemporary social change theory has told a number of stories to mitigate the problems created by its reliance on an *a priori* social glue. These stories have wide circulation in the academy. Fortunately for us, however, these debates expose the problematic nature of this generally shared assumption. The lapses in these stories are especially valuable because they point to the need for an alternative framework for addressing causality in the social world as well as the process by which subjects come to be forged in a social realm characterized by "re-assemblage." For our purposes, the stories told about the problem of whether subjects are determined by social forces or vice versa provide the most useful introduction to the importance of extimate causality for the formation of social subjects.

The In-determinate Social Subject

How should we understand the nature and formation of the subject as a social phenomenon? We have just rehearsed a brief version of the story that approaches this question by assuming the existence of some special force – the social – that shapes individuals to act in the service of larger societal goals. This story of the harnessing of individual agency by "social" forces has been around for a long time, but it has undergone some interesting mutations in the past century and a half. So, for example, the problem of distinguishing individual motive from social conditioning, frequently noted by Victorian philosophers, finds succinct expression in

J. S. Mill's *On Liberty*: "A person whose desires and impulses are his own – are the expression of his own nature, as it has been developed and modified by his own culture – is said to have a character. One whose desires and impulses are not his own, has no character, no more than a steam-engine has a character."[15] Although Mill seems to acknowledge that desire and impulses may be inculcated by external forces and so rob individuals of their character, the alternative – that character is the "expression" of an inherent "nature" – compromises the distinction. Whether we understand "his own culture" to mean cultural influences or the individual's self-cultivation, nonetheless desires and impulses (those most personal and idiosyncratic of all mental phenomena) turn out to be compounded of social dictate and individual predilection. If all desires and impulses are culturally fashioned, then there is finally no way to distinguish the man of natural but cultivated character from the mechanical man.

Seen in this light, human beings are complex amalgams of social patterning, unconscious motivation, and autonomy. As a result, actions cannot be read off their determinants, be they drive, ideology, normative conditioning, or calculation of self-interest. Instead, volitionality itself, rather than signaling individual intentionality and autonomy, must be understood as a function of the interaction of social conditioning and individual purposes. Not only are social determinants inculcated into individual psyches, making it impossible to distinguish idiosyncratic motivation from socially directed activity, but the inmixing of individual intentions with social determinants is further complicated by the ways in which the purposes and actions of one person come in conflict with those of others. Actions transpire in a social sphere in which interior motivations are thoroughly entangled with external determinations, not governed by some power behind the scenes. The ability of others to re-shape the meaning of one's actions makes it impossible to reliably link outcomes to initial purposes. When this activity is taken into account, it calls into question long-accepted modes for claiming agency and assigning responsibility. For if actions cannot be traced securely back to their determinants, and if those determinants are a mix of inner and outer forces, then consequentialist moralizing loses its suasive power, and assigning responsibility on the basis of intention or outcome becomes an extremely vexed matter.

Contemporary theories of subject formation have sought to acknowledge the co-implication of interior and exterior determinants of subjectivity by "building in" a social dimension to the subject from the start, as in the case of the "de-centered subject" of post-Freudian and post-Derridean theory and the de-individualized subject of post-Marxist theory. The advantages and disadvantages of these theories direct our

attention to the need for a more robust explication of subject formation sensitive to the "un-working" of the social in any theory of social
change.

The relatively rapid "dissolution" of the individual subject of liberal
thought reached its modern forms by way of the Marxist propound-
ing of the subject-as-class, the Freudian revolution of the subject of the
unconscious, and the Nietzschean genealogical exposure of the rhetorical foundation of the subject. These challenges to the individual subject
opened up new theoretical possibilities for understanding the subject as
agent of social change. At the same time, this transformation of the agen-
cies responsible for social change has created new problems for theories
that assume that the "social" refers to special properties or forces that
hold individuals together. Absent recourse to meta-actors such as History
or *Geist*, any theory of agency has to offer some way to link purpose to
outcome, else the changes it promotes would be indistinguishable from
chance effects. That is, in order to distinguish intended changes from
aleatory processes, a theory has to account for the generation of purposes and the means by which they can be matched to specific results.
Traditionally, such accounts have assigned this role to individual motives
and actions. What can take the place of individual motives and actions in
theories of a de-centered and de-individualized subject?

The "subject in question" of poststructuralist thought, which extends
and reworks these earlier radicalizations of the subject, takes two related
but ultimately opposed forms in theories about the subject's role in social
change. The first form is historicist and goes by various names, such as
"cultural studies" or "multiculturalism," in the United States: by these
lights, the subject, discursively constructed and policed, is construed as a
function of external determinants. Its power to change those conditions
is figured in terms of group identities based on differences, the specification of positions relative to power immanent in those discursive regimes,
and the ability to appropriate the signifying tools of their determinations.
The second form is avowedly psychoanalytic: while it does not appear
under one label, due primarily to its relatively small representation in the
United States, its various theoreticians have in common their reliance on
a (broadly) Lacanian understanding of the split subject as a retroversive
effect and their sense that any agency with cultural and/or political effects
must be thought in universal terms rather than in terms of particularist
cultural identities.

For better or worse, the symbiosis of cultural studies and identitarian
concerns has politicized the humanities in the US for at least the past two
decades. Apart from its effects on institutional policies and practices,
this convergence has stimulated work devoted largely to studying the
means and opportunities for the deliberate transformation of society.

After poststructuralist theory had, it seemed, failed to engage the question of social change in any politically relevant way, theorists struggled to find a guide for praxis in the theoretical tradition. These efforts responded to a double demand. In order to locate the proper place for effective intervention, theory not only had to analyze social structure in terms of fundamental causal relationships, it had also to explain the means of subjectification, the way a society conditions its subjects to its requirements.

Of course, it was Marx who most forcefully articulated this double demand. However, classical Marxist theory in the US depended on a relatively simple understanding of economic determinism and its allied models of superstructural reflection. Insofar as Marxism proposes that the economic laws of history necessarily and autonomously transform productive forces, it seems to offer no way for individuals or groups to take up the challenge of social change. Change in this model occurs in impersonal if knowable ways. Cultural theory after poststructuralism turned instead to the theorist who had made explicit the role that superstructural activity could play in social change – Louis Althusser. Althusser argued that only by theorizing the relative autonomy of the superstructure in terms of "a 'reciprocal action' of the superstructure on the base" as a function of ideology is it possible to make a place for agency.[16] He reconceived the duality of the Marxist dynamic of base–superstructure relations through an encounter with Lacanian psychoanalysis in order to emphasize the importance of subject formation for any viable theory of social change: "This is a *crucial question* for the Marxist theory of the mode of production. To let it pass would be a theoretical omission – worse, a serious political error."[17] Coming to grips with the "reproduction of the conditions of production," as Althusser succinctly expresses it, means not only understanding how society is organized to replicate productive forces but also entails theorizing how the existing relations of subjects to those forces are replicated by reproducing subjects.[18] Ideology, in Althusser's famous formulation, constitutes subjects to take their appropriate place in the relations of production which are, as he reminds us, "in the last resort *relations of exploitation*."[19] But how is it possible for exploitation to continue without resistance? If exploitation remains the rule, it is because ideology parcels out subjects into antagonistic economic relations and, at the same time, interpellates them in such a way that they misrecognize the exploitation at the heart of the social structure.

Contemporary scholarship has leaned heavily on this conception of ideological interpellation to explain the continued efficacy of innumerable unfair and damaging power relationships. Patriarchy, racism, heterosexism, and colonialism, it is argued, sustain and reproduce themselves by generating subjects in their own image who are incapable of recognizing the fundamental reality structuring their lives. Yet if subjects are so produced by interpellation, nonetheless the theory seems to promise some tool for intervention: by analyzing the modes of ideological operation, it ought to be possible to locate the place from which new subjects, free in some measure from ideological determination, might arise and begin the work of liberation.

The Problem with Interpellation

Activist social theory encounters a problem here, however. Despite appearances, the theory of ideological interpellation cannot deliver on its promise to orient social change. In its efforts to account for social reproduction, the theory presents subjects as thoroughly conditioned by ideology: subjects who are positioned sufficiently inside a social structure to register its oppressive effects are determined by it in such a way as to consistently misrecognize their oppression. Yet, if they are to bring about social change, at least some of these subjects have to be capable of recognizing and acting independently of ideological operations. They have to transcend their ideological determinations somehow and lift the veil of misrecognition, even though they themselves are nothing other than the expression of ideology and thoroughly blinded by it. Althusser's famous solution to this problem – that there is an "outside" of ideology – simply repeats the problem in another register. The question is precisely how a subject of ideology finds or recognizes this "outside."[20]

One instructive attempt to address this difficulty emerges in feminist, queer, and postcolonial studies which argue that certain subjects – precisely those most dominated or marginalized by social power – are in a position to know the workings of power better than other subjects, simply by virtue of their marginal status, and are therefore uniquely situated to propagate resistance. Acceding to the Althusserian analysis of hegemonic interpellation, the theory depends on the counterintuitive assumption that those most deprived of the benefits of power would be least susceptible to ideological misrecognition.[21] Somehow, for these subjects, hegemony works by domination rather than by interpellation. But the theory cannot explain how this difference between types of subject is produced without risking repeating the essentializing gestures it is designed to combat, or without relying on precisely the stability of the social system it is supposed to transform. How is it that a hegemonic force fails to interpellate precisely those subjects who are most oppressed? What makes these subjects different in their encounter with power? What comes first – the subject's difference or the subject's subjection? If the former, these subjects embody some difference prior to their encounter with power, which means that they are not subjected by cultural power but by nature or God. If that is so, analyses of the social distribution of power are beside the point. On the other hand, if power in fact constitutes these subjects differentially, then how do they acquire their margin of freedom from ideology even as they are so completely dominated? What is it that interferes with the mechanism of interpellation? The same questions haunt the return of exceptional individual agency in Marxian thought insofar as it relies on the "intellectual" as agent of change in the otherwise unconscious movement of class history.

I return to these questions in later chapters, but for now we can simply note that the problems with this "exceptionalist" theory demonstrate the crucial role that the theoretical link between subject formation and social forces must play in any viable theory of social change with political aspirations. The exceptionalist account is unsatisfactory because the agency that emerges from breaking the link between interpellation and social forces has no purchase on social power. Correlatively, the Althusserian account is unsatisfactory because it seals social forces so tightly to subject formation that agency never arises. An activist social theory must be able to provide, in a non-contradictory way, not only a credible analysis of the link between power and subjectification but also a plausible locus of resistance.

The most popular contender for displacing ideological interpellation in recent times, Foucault's model of power as proposed in the *History of Sexuality*, fails to meet either criterion. If Foucault's picture of a social structure pervaded by mobile and fluctuating power relations seems to capture the complexity of social interactions, it indicates no tool for distinguishing causes from effects in a politically useful way. At the same time, subjects produced within that mode of power have no effective autonomous agency, subsisting as nothing other than the intersection of various discursive determinants. As purely external (and discursive) productions, subject positions have no interiority from which they might mount resistance to their own conditions of determination. Where Althusser conceives of subjects as mis-recognizing (and therefore in principle capable of recognizing) the truth about their relations to real conditions of their production, Foucault conceives of subjects as nothing more than the conditions of their production and so as incapable of mis-recognition or recognition. So, even though some theorists have tried to introduce Althusserian interpellation into a Foucaultian framework, the theories themselves are fundamentally incompatible in their assumptions about subject formation.

In the preceding discussion, I have already begun to sketch a second problem that the Althusserian model of ideological interpellation poses for activist social theory. If ideology functions by installing a fundamental misrecognition of the subject's place, it would seem that that misrecognition could be countered by acquiring a certain knowledge. In the case of exceptionalist agency, this knowledge derives from the subject's "marginal" position, a premise that seems unlikely at best. But let us stipulate that a subject could come to recognize the truth about her interpellation, even if we reject the positional explanation of the exceptionalist account or the Althusserian "scientific" explanation of this possibility. Even so, as Žižek (following Peter Sloterdijk) has argued, such knowledge does not necessarily interfere with ideological operation at all. Žižek explains the difference as that between the Marxist statement of the ideological effect – "they do not know it but they are doing it" – and the cynical position – "they know very well what they are doing, but still, they are doing it."[22] When the emphasis is placed on the question of truth and knowledge, as it is in the exceptionalist and Althusserian models, the material level at which ideology operates, i.e. the level of *doing*, seems to cease to be a factor. Knowledge seems to trump practice. Still, as Žižek points out, there is a "distortion already at work in the social reality itself, at the level of what the individuals are *doing*, and not only what they *think* or *know* they are doing . . . even if we keep an ironical distance, *we are still doing them*."[23] The Althusserian model of interpellation fails to take into account this "doing"; that is, the question of ideological resistance remains at the level of knowledge. While it is true that Althusser asserts in his second thesis that ideology is materialized through practices, it is implicit in his theory that these practices can endure only so long as the subject is ignorant of the ideology they instantiate; when knowledge of ideology replaces ignorance, new practices will emerge. For Althusser, lack of knowledge supports the materiality of ideology in practice.

According to Žižek, resistance to ideology cannot be mounted at the level of knowledge. In his view, the interpellative account of ideology does not provide a sufficient theory for understanding how the internalization of ideology gains an authoritative effect on the subject. As he puts it: "how does the Ideological State Apparatus . . . 'internalize' itself; how does it produce the effect of ideological belief in a Cause and the interconnecting effect of subjectivation?"[24] Althusserian interpellation makes the psyche (inside) match the ideology (outside). This adequation of inside to outside not only vitiates agency, but also, from a psychoanalytic point of view, misrepresents the nature and function of the unconscious, presenting it as a space of "unknowing" which could become known by an act of will – a reservoir of thinking/thought that the subject could consciously assume or with which she could identify. So, Althusser's apparent innovation on Marx, the turn to psychoanalysis to supply the missing account of subject formation, implies a decidedly non-psychoanalytic account of an unconscious wholly at the disposal of consciousness.

If Althusser's quasi-psychoanalytic thesis on ideological interpellation fails to provide a much more substantial tool for drafting subjects into politically effective resistance to their interpellations than Foucault's psychologically-bereft subjects, we might well ask what psychoanalysis could contribute to the project of a usable theory of social change. But should we abandon psychoanalytic tools simply because Foucault fails to theorize the subject or because Althusser turns out to be a poor Lacanian? Instead of trying to cobble together a theory of social structure with a theory of subjectivity to account for the ways that societies bend their members to social purposes, I argue throughout this book that we should turn to those thinkers who, in using psychoanalytic concepts, persistently if unwittingly uncover the *excessive* dimension of the subject as the foundation of the social itself. I call this type of subject the "Möbius" subject, for reasons that will become clear in the next chapter.

Let's take an example of such an excess with which we are all intimately familiar: the fact that we can never know for certain what others think of us. We know that we have some meaning for some others, and we may wish that we had a specific kind of meaning for them. But we do not have the power to ensure that others will think of us in precisely the ways that we wish. Each of us develops characteristic ways of handling this uncertainty. Some will seek constant reassurance from others; others will disengage. Some will turn to the limited but stabilizing power of stereotypes and social coding; others will find joy in the shared enterprise of creating and circulating social meanings. The nondeterminacy and ungovernability of meaning is what makes possible this variety of social interaction. From this perspective, the social field itself is a function of nondeterminate meaning, for the social field is the only place in which we can even try to find out what we mean to others. We could say that the excess produced by the extimate cause of subjectivity is both the obstacle to our knowing our meaning as social beings and the necessary ingredient of the social field within which we obtain the only meaning that we will ever have, however nondeterminately excessive.

As I pointed out in the introduction, other theories of social change, subject formation, and political alliance may acknowledge this excess, but they invariably conceive its *elimination* as being necessary to their projects because it seems to them that the excess of each subject stands in the way of secure self-knowledge, solidarity, or stable political regimes. We are familiar with these dreams of perfect communion, often arising, as Nancy says, in the form of nostalgia for an imagined lost community from which we are exiled. From this perspective, modern social bonds are conceived to be poor substitutes for a communal immanence, for a more intimate communication. In this view, society is a space of discord and competition, all we have left of that communal existence which (so we imagine) connected us to everything human and transcendent to the human.

In contrast to fantasies of immanent meaning and perfect communion, theorists of extimate causality make it clear that the excess which marks and makes the social field is ineradicable. Any theory of social change must therefore either find a way to account for it or else condemn itself to recapitulating the same problems repeatedly. Extimate causality allows us to grasp how excess is generated, how it gives rise to the excessive social subject, and how it structures the social field in specific culturo-historic circumstances, a prerequisite for a historicizing cultural analysis that seeks to understand or promote social change. Let's turn, then, to the elucidation of the extimate cause and its production of the social subject of excess – the Möbius subject.

2

Extimate Causality and the
Social Subject of Excess

How to Add Nothing and Get Excess

We can now begin to develop the definitions, principles, and advantages of extimate causality and its product, the excessive subject, for thinking through subject formation and social causality. I have argued that neither external causality nor immanent causality alone can offer a satisfactory account of how subjects can be both conditioned by and free from their social determinants. Neither provides a plausible model for causal analysis. So how does extimate causality operate?

Let me give an initial idea of what extimate causality involves and point towards its relevance for social change by focusing on the spatial relations involved in external and immanent causation. On one hand, external causation presents the space of causes (e.g., economic forces) as being outside and exceptional to the space of its effects (superstructural elements, e.g., law, education, art, mass media). In this model, the field being analyzed is divided into two, such that the arena of causes is separated from the arena of effects by a boundary that, in theory, is impermeable. Yet, this boundary must be crossed in order for a causal force to generate its effect, that is, in order for a cause to "touch" what it brings about. Theories of external causation typically have a difficult time addressing the nature of this boundary with its contradictory properties of impermeability and porosity.

On the other hand, immanent causation renders causes too close to their effects. Causes and their effects mutually condition one another, making it impossible ultimately to distinguish one from the other. The focus of critical attention is the *unified* field of reciprocal causes and effects, but the boundary that forms the space *around* this unified field is ignored. That is, whatever generates this infinite field of dynamic forces – whatever serves as the cause, so to speak, of social causes and effects – goes untheorized.

In contrast to both of these, the extimate causal model presents the social space as a special *unbounded* yet finite spatial object – what is known in topology as a "non-orientable" object. Bear with me while I sketch the nature of these objects before I talk about their relevance for theorizing extimate causality and subjectivity. In non-orientable objects, an apparently distinct surface, such as the inside, imperceptibly transforms into its opposite without crossing a discontinuity (an edge or a hole). The most familiar object with such a topology is the Möbius band, which is formed by twisting a rectangular strip of paper or cloth 180 degrees and gluing the two ends together. If you start on the outside of the band and then trace around to your starting point without lifting your finger, you will end up on the inside of the band even though your finger never crossed an edge or poked a hole in the paper. An apparently two-sided band turns out to have only one side. It will seem from your point of view that, while your finger is always on one side of the band, it is impossible to say whether it is on the "inside" or the "outside" of the band at any given point. Unlike the spatial relations between cause and effect in external causation, the Möbius strip is "unbounded" (which is to say that there is no boundary between inside and outside). But unlike the infinite space of immanent causation, it is finite.

Let's see how the spatiality of the Möbius band helps us to think about causality in the social field. One can define each point on the band as *here* or *there*, but each point is *excessive* with respect to the determination of its "sidedness." The Möbius band suggests a field in which both the paradoxical boundary of external causation and the infinite mutual implication of cause and effect of immanentism cease to be problematic. We can define points of contact that are not so discrete as to become uncoupled, thanks to the nondetermination or excess embodied in the band. This excess alters the apparently rigid boundary between sides (or between cause and effect): nondeterminate sidedness means that causes are not quarantined from their effects because the excess brings them into contiguity. At the same time, these points and their relations have a certain specifiability; they do not merge into one another as they do in the infinite flux of immanentism.

Now imagine that something in the social field produces an analogous excess or nondeterminacy that serves as the switchpoint between inside and outside. The theory of extimate causality accounts for the generation of just this kind of excess by way of an operation we will call the formal negation. Subjects created in the social field, through the operation of the formal negation, as we will see below, inevitably carry with them a kind of excess or nondeterminacy analogous to the points on the Möbius band. We can say, then, that each subject is a Möbius subject, a site of nondeterminate "sidedness" or switchpoint, if you will, which lends to the social field its character as non-orientable object. Extimate causality, as the alternative to both external and immanent causation, produces the excess that links subject to social field.

Although Lacan mentions the *extime* only a few times in his work, the principle of extimacy can be found throughout his writings.[1] Far from being the paradoxically impossible entity that it seems to be, in Lacan's view the extimate cause turns out to be necessary to explain the advent and structure of the subject. Because standard philosophical perspectives on causality do not capture the phenomenon of the unconscious, Lacan had to turn to other disciplines such as set theory, topology, and symbolic logic for help in fleshing out his ideas. But rather than begin with the difficult task of elucidating subjectivity, which we will take up later, we can approach extimacy from a simpler direction.

Imagine that you walk into your dimly lit garage and discover a mess. The place is so jumbled that you cannot even distinguish one thing from another. Now, let's say that, suddenly, the walls of the garage disappear, and you discover that this jumbled mass stretches in all directions. One final gesture: remove yourself from the scene, so that you cannot serve as a reference point or means of orientation. No up nor down, no inside nor outside. No spaces between things, no background against which they stand out, no standpoint from which to assess their relationships. It is as though everything is glued to everything else in what Copjec calls the "realtight." I will follow Alain Badiou in calling this state of affairs "being," where things have no particular identity or relationship to one another, where there is no subject, and where orientation is impossible. In this state, no thing is determined because no thing has any *relation* to anything else.

Obviously, this is not the world in which we live. In discussion of his latest work, *Logics of Worlds*, Badiou puts it this way:

> We can speak of an object in the world. We can distinguish it in the world by its properties or predicates. In fact, we can experience the complex network of identities and differences by which this object is clearly not identical to another object of the same world. But a thing is not an object . . . We must think of the thing before its objectivation in a precise world. The Thing is: *das Ding*, maybe *das Ur-Ding*. That is this form of being which certainly is after the indifference of nothingness, but also before the qualitative difference of object.[2]

We could say that, at the level of being described by Badiou, nothing exists *for us, in our particular world.* In order for objects in our world to emerge, at least one operation must occur, a simple yet somewhat mysterious function. If the "things" of being are to become "objects" for us, with identity and relationality, something about the state of affairs of being has to be *nullified.* That is, before being-things can become objects of experience for us, before they can exist *qua objects* for us, their status as *sheer being* first has to be cancelled. If it is not, then we can never "take up" these things: we can never come into relation with them. Remember, in the state of being, there are no relations and no orientations by which to grasp things.

So, to transform a being-thing into an object, something must be nullified or negated – the state of *mere being.* This negation, however, does not act on the "whole" state of affairs; that is, after the negation, we are not left with *nothing.* We are not speaking here of some science fiction scenario when matter encounters anti-matter and – Boom! – the whole universe disappears. Rather, we are speaking of a type of negation with certain formal properties. We get a handle on being-things, so to speak, by *adding a formal negation* to the state of being-things. What does this mean?

As it turns out, we learn from set theory that such a formal negation, strictly speaking, is the same as the null set or *empty* set. The empty set is simply that – a set that does not contain anything. Yet there is a bit more to be said. To invoke the empty set is to say something like "there exists a set": it speaks to the *set-ness* of sets.

Now, in order for undetermined things to become determinate objects, they must have a minimum of relationality, a minimal order, within which to establish vectors of identity and difference. One way to approach the nature of that minimum formally is to think of it in terms of gathering things into a set. Obviously, gathering things into a set requires "setness," or the simple possibility of a set without anything in it – the *empty set.* We can write the empty set in two ways: by using the brackets denoting a set, with nothing inside them, {}, or by using the formal notation of set theory, ø. The simple addition of a formal property, the empty set, which has no substance in and of itself, *negates* the state of sheer being that attends each thing-as-such. It does so by establishing a minimal point of orientation – like making a small cut in a sheet of paper. Once this cut is added, then "things" can bear some minimal relation to each other – they all have a relation to this minimal point of orientation. The "cut" of the empty set creates a vector, and with this stroke, things precipitate into a world of identities, properties, and relationships – as *objects.*

The empty set is a good metaphor for the addition of a negation because it has no substantive properties in itself. Contrary to what our customary usage of "set" implies, gathering things together within the brackets of the empty set does not mean that the things so gathered share any properties *other than the fact that they are together in the set.* The empty set subsists as a mere function, and yet at the same time it has a substantial effect, establishing a minimal relationship of difference among all the things it brings together in relationship to itself.

The empty set's lack of properties qualifies it to remedy the defects in Foucault's one-tier model of social cause. That is, the addition of the negation does not simply add another positive (particular) element to the causal field, to be swallowed up in the flux of cause and effect among particularized determinants. At the same time, its effect of establishing relations among the things in the field in which it operates qualifies it to remedy the flaw in the Marxian two-tier model of social cause. In other words, it provides a "link" between the cause and its effects that the external Marxian cause cannot.

This addition of the negation through the operation of the empty set upon things generates a set full of these former "things" that can now be registered in relation to one another, "things" that now have some minimal determination as objects. If it seems unlikely that the empty set can produce this effect, that is because the empty set itself is nothing substantial: it has no positive properties. Yet this tiny operation is sufficient to transform a thing into an object. The empty set "unglues" things; it cuts into the state of being, adding (so to speak) its own emptiness, creating a space. Formally speaking, the addition of the negation of the empty set gets the whole process off the ground. Bring in this null set, and it nullifies the being-ness of things, simply by adding a space or a kind of cut around each thing. That cut, formalized in the brackets of the set, "holds" the thing within a void or hollow, creating an invisible shadow that cleaves (to) the border of the thing.[3]

Speaking logically, the empty set, as set-ness, must be added before any other sets can be formed. Without the empty set, no further specification of relations, predicates, properties, or identities is possible. We cannot go from the state of being to the state of objective determinations like "twenty apples" or "Rome" or "people with gray hair" or anything else that exists for us in the phenomenal world without the first step, the addition of the empty set. But having added the empty set, having created from *thing plus empty set* a set of objects (we can call it set *A*), the empty set *remains* present as one of the possible subsets of this new set. As the set-ness of sets, as the addition of a negation, as the necessary cut in sheer being, the empty set persists in the determination of the object. The object precipitated from the conjunction of empty set and thing always carries with it this "cut" – or space or shadow – that cleaves to its lineaments precisely. It is as if the empty set creates a hole exactly the same size, shape, and volume of the thing, cradling the thing within its own void. The empty set hollows out a place in being, creates a *void place of the thing*, like a negative space, and in so doing, precipitates out the thing-in-its-hole as object. The thing-in-its-hole is equivalent to the thing joined to the empty set.[4]

As a result, this conjunction generates the new set, *A*, which contains two subsets. One subset is the "thing-to-become-objectified" and the other subset is the empty set itself. Taken together, the set of these subsets is the object. Using set notation, we would write *A* = object: {{thing}, ø}, where the brackets {} refer to set-ness and ø stands for the empty set as subset.[5] The empty set, then, is the irreducible persistent remainder of all sets as well as the very condition of their existence. As *set-ness* (the outer brackets, or external {}), it is *constitutive* of the set; as inevitable remainder (ø, or internal {}), it is *excessive* to it.

In effect, the empty set, the addition of a negation, is a cause that is both immanent to and external to the field of its effects (in this case, the "field" is the world in which objects emerge).[6] Alenka Zupančič has found an analogous function described by Nietzsche, expressing

> the miraculous power of the Symbolic to transform the Nothing itself into something, to transform the lack itself into an object. Instead of the lack of an object itself becoming an object, the lack exists solely in the form of the inherent difference of an object, that is to say, in the form of the object not fully coinciding with *itself*.[7]

Putting this in the terms we have been using, we could say that adding the minimal difference to a *thing* (adding a "lack") keeps it from fully coinciding with itself, which is what *makes it an object* – and this minimal difference is produced by the operation of the formal negation. The minimal difference – the empty set – persists after the object is precipitated from the thing. It persists as the object's minimal difference from itself: in bringing the thing into the empty set, the empty set forces the thing to lose its self-coincidence, while the empty set itself persists as this minimal self-difference in the object. The thing becomes joined to the empty set, which is nothing other than the operator of this minimal difference, and this operation makes of the thing an object. In effect, the object is generated from the conjunction of being and minimal difference, or being and the addition of a negation. As we have seen, the empty set persists as *both* the container of the set, its set-ness, *and* a subset of the set, inside the set as a subset of itself, that is, as the minimal difference adhering to the thing that transforms it into an object.

This "neither purely inside nor purely outside" structure is what we mean by extimacy, and, as we will see, it is the function that produces non-orientability in the social field. The extimate cause functions like the empty set: it provides the cut necessary to bring an object into our world from sheer being, and so acts as external cause. At the same time, the minimal difference that makes an object non-self-coincident (and therefore not a sheer "being-thing") adheres to the object as an internal cause. Taken together (as they must be, because they are the same function), they form the extimate cause.

The extimate cause, functioning by way of the specific mechanism of the formal negation, engenders a structured field or system (with its concomitant objects, properties, and relationships) out of what would otherwise be a state of undifferentiation or monadic unrelatedness. At the same time, it inevitably gives rise to an element of nondeterminacy, surplus, or excess. Speaking in terms of the social arena, we could put it this way: the operation that bestows identities, properties, and relationships also leaves a residue, so that every subject bears some excess. At every point in the social field, then, an irreducible excess attends social relations. In fact, although it seems paradoxical, this excess is what makes the social field itself possible and makes its structure potentially analyzable.

More Than One, But Not Quite Two

The apparently spontaneous generation of excess from the extimate cause, as the previous discussion demonstrates, arises from the addition of a negation. The addition of the empty set results in its appearance in *two places at once*, that is, in the outer brackets of the set and as one of the inner elements of the set.[8] It is important, however, to be clear that these "two" empty sets do not exist at different levels, even though it might seem so. Neither is more important than the other; and neither superintends the other. They are merely two faces of the same operation, analogous to the in-differentiation of inside and outside of the Möbius strip. Lacan created a similar effect with the so-called "internal 8" (*huit intérieur*), a figure of eight that is twisted back on itself, so that it looks like a small circle within a large circle, with one point of connection. In figure 1 opposite, I have exaggerated the point of contact between the two circles as a large black dot. This dot corresponds in our discussion to the excess that, in all two-dimensional non-orientable objects, exists at every point.

Trace the inside circle and at the point of intersection you can switch to the outer circle, until you arrive again at the point of intersection; from

Figure 1

Figure 2

here, you can make your trip back around the inner circle. More importantly, every point on the smaller inner circle can be this switchpoint: imagine that the small circle is rolling around the inside of the large circle, so that the point of contact of the inner circle changes as it rolls to every new point on the outer circle (figure 2). The dotted circles represent the positions of the previous point of contact on each of the circles after the inner circle rotates. This means, of course, that every point on the outer circle is also nondeterminately "sided."

Charles Sanders Peirce has a dynamic version of this excessive effect. In one of his more inventive logical notations, which uses planes and lines, he postulates a figure in which a line intersects a plane. At this place of intersection, two things happen simultaneously that would be mutually exclusive in our commonsense way of thinking. Where the line crosses the plane, it pierces a hole in the plane. *At the same time*, where the plane crosses the line, it cuts the line. Of course, it seems logical to us to say that either the line is whole, in which case the plane isn't, or that the plane is whole, in which case the line isn't. But Peirce has a use in his logical system for this neither-nor/both-and structure.[9]

Lacan's *huit intérieur*, Peirce's figure, and the Möbius band appear to violate traditional logical presuppositions. An entire system of logic, known as "nonclassical logic" or "paraconsistent logic" (for convenience, I will call this "paralogic"), has arisen which interrogates the accepted rules of classical logic. One group of these classical rules which govern the valid procedures for assigning the values of true and false is expressed in the Aristotelian idea that the negation of the negation of A (not not-A) yields A. However, for paralogicians, it is possible that the negation of the negation of A *does not* yield A, or rather that it could yield A and something else.[10] Double negations have strange properties in paralogic, but we have some familiar examples of their effects in our ordinary linguistic usage. For example, one of the characteristic rhetorical tropes of Wordsworth's poems is *litotes* or understatement, which often makes use of the double negation, as in "I am not unwilling." We know what it means to be willing and unwilling, but we also know that to say "I am not unwilling" is nowhere near the same thing as saying "I am willing." The Greimasian semiotic square produces an excessive term at the place of double negation, and Žižek's oft-repeated example of the "undead" is another case of it.[11] In his criticism of Hegel, Adorno notes that double negation never returns us to a state of unalloyed positivity.[12] Lacanians will immediately think of the *vel*. In these examples, the double negation of A does not return us to A but rather yields an excess, a nondeterminacy.

It will be convenient if we use a more formal notation to show the generation of excess from a double negation. Using the letter **P** to stand for a proposition, we can set up some typographical definitions. The negation of **P**, or not-P, will be written as **~P**. The negation of **~P**, or **not not-P**, will be written as **~~P**. Now, in classical logic, **~~P = P**. But in paralogic, **~~P = P and some nondeterminate remainder**. This remainder will be written as *****. Let's say that **P** corresponds to **<dog>**. The negation of **P**, or **~P**, is equivalent to **not <dog>** or, in our notation, **~<dog>**. What happens when we negate the negation, **~~<dog>**? Surely one result is that we return to **P**, **<dog>**. But that is not all that happens, because to say something is not not-dog, does not actually specify what it *is*. "Not not-dog" doesn't necessarily point us to the determination "dog": it could point to something nondeterminate, in the same way that "not not-willing" points to something besides "willing." So "not not-dog" remains as a nondeterminate result of the double negation. Using our notation, we would say that **~~<dog>** yields **<dog>** *and*, surprisingly, **~~<dog>** (i.e., yields both dog and not not-dog). Suddenly, we find the same kind of spontaneous generation as in the operation of the empty set, since **~~<dog>** gives rise to **<dog>** and to *itself* as a nondeterminate remainder or excess. Using an asterisk to signal the presence of this excess, we can write this result as **~~<dog> = <dog>***, or **~~P = P***.

It is this emergence of a nondeterminate residue after the double negation that will be important for us. The operation of the double negation is homologous to the operation of the empty set: it "spontaneously generates" an excess. In the action of the empty set upon the thing, it is as though the thing is doubly negated, once from the outside (the cut or hollowing that unglues the thing from being) and once from the inside

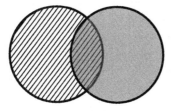

Figure 3

(the minimal difference from itself). Thanks to this operation, the doubly negated thing yields an object to which adheres a nondeterminate excess: for the sake of homology, we could say that an object is really an **object***. The object is always itself and a nondeterminate something else. This "something else" is not some other, second object standing over against the first; it is merely that minimal difference inscribed within the object, that difference from itself which is excessive to it – **object***.

For this reason, the **object*** cannot be said to be a unity. It does not "count for one." The **object*** – whether material object, linguistic object, or subject – is always *more than one, but not quite two*.[13]

Excess and the Social Subject

Psychoanalytic discourse has a name for what we've been discussing – Symbolic inscription. What appears in the Symbolic is the result of an operation of the formal cause – the addition of a negation – to the state of being. In a well-known example, Lacan describes the subject as just such an effect, emerging where Being and Meaning come together; at the point, that is, where the subject is produced through its entry into the field of signification (Meaning) by way of a formal negation of Being (what we will discuss later as the *Non/Nom-du-Père*).[14] But it is easy to be led astray by this example, because when Lacan presents it schematically, he appears to be using a Venn diagram, showing two overlapping circles with the emergence of the subject at the point of intersection. For us, it will be more useful to reconsider the figure of two overlapping circles from the standpoint of the principles of paralogic (figure 3).

The area of overlap between the two circles, marked as *, is shown as a dotted black space (figure 4).

Unlike a true Venn diagram, however, this figure does not represent the intersection of the two circles. The overlapping area does not indicate what the two circles share in common. Nor should we regard this figure as one circle "taking a bite" out of the other, or as supplying the missing

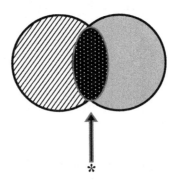

Figure 4

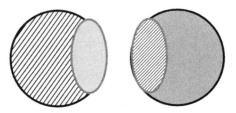

Figure 5

element that will make the other whole. Rather, it represents a *mutual interference*, and the overlapping area contains both what they each lose by the encounter and what they each gain. Let's look at each of the circles independently of each other (figure 5).

Each circle has an element of the other added to it, which is to say as well that each negates some aspect of the other. We encountered this figure in our discussion of paralogic as "neither-nor/both-and." It corresponds very nicely to the Peircean schematic of a line cutting into a plane while at the same time the plane bisects the line. This is the figure of double negation, and like all such operations in paralogic, it results in an excess: where each circle infringes on the other, "taking away" its area, so to speak, each circle also gains an additional element. As a result of their mutual interference, each circle is "more than one, but not quite two."

Žižek has described this structure throughout his work, perhaps most clearly in the following long passage, where he recalls the role of extimate causality in producing the subject:

> The two series [signifier and signified] can, therefore, also be described as the "empty" formal structure (signifier) and the series of elements filling out the empty places in the structure (signified). From this perspective, the

paradox consists in the fact that the two series never overlap: we always encounter an entity that is simultaneously – with regard to the structure – an empty, unoccupied place and – with regard to the elements – a rapidly moving, elusive object, an occupant without a place. We have thereby produced Lacan's formula of fantasy ($\$-a$), since the matheme for the subject is $\$$, an empty place in the structure, an elided signifier, while *objet a* is, by definition, an excessive object, an object that lacks its place in the structure. Consequently, the point is not that there is simply the surplus of an element over the places available in the structure or the surplus of a place that has no element to fill it out. An empty place in the structure would still sustain the fantasy of an element that will emerge and fill out this place; an excessive element lacking its place would still sustain the fantasy of some yet unknown place waiting for it. The point is, rather, that the empty place in the structure is strictly correlative to the errant element lacking its place. They are not two different entities but the front and back of one and the same entity, that is, one and the same entity inscribed onto the two surfaces of a Moebius strip. In short, the subject qua $\$$ does not belong to the depth: it emerges from a topological twist of the surface itself.[15]

For Lacanians, the excessive dimension (*) is the little bit of the Real that intervenes in the Imaginary regime of self-coincidence (and vice versa) to create the minimal self-difference, the excess, necessary for Symbolic registration. Žižek refers to the point where, as in figures 1 and 2, the two series cross each other to produce both lack and excess, as the "short circuit." This is the same structure that appears in the *huit intérieur* and in Peirce's line–plane interference. It corresponds, as we have seen, with the double inscription of the empty set, both the formal apparatus of set-ness itself and an element within the set. Here Žižek is describing the production of the subject as an effect of the extimate cause at the crossing of two series, the signifier (formal apparatus) and the signified (material element). But why choose to describe the extimate cause of the subject in terms relevant to signification?

The subject occupies this position because it is produced by the materiality of the signifier as a speaking/spoken being, what Lacan calls *parlêtre*. Language comes to prominence in this account not simply because it is itself symbolic, but also because of the special structure of spoken language as dependent upon an excess of signification. We must be careful here, however. The "excess" attending signification is not merely the fact that the signifying system never closes in on a signified, as Derrida would have it. Rather, Lacan is working out the consequences of the fact that every utterance has two parts. One part consists of the content of what is said, what is usually referred to as the level of the enunciated. The other part consists of the fact *that* something is being said, what is usually referred to as the level of the enunciation. It is as though every statement of enunciated content contains an unspoken excess that nonetheless must be there, to wit, *the fact that it is being enunciated*. The gap between these two levels is where the subject as excess is located.

So, for example, if we take the utterance "I love you," at the level of the enunciated, the utterance also includes a level of enunciation, i.e., "(I am saying that) I love you" or "(It is true that) I love you." Of course, the utterance doesn't have to capture the truth: in fact, I might not love you. But the utterance *asserts as true* that I love you. And precisely because this assertion adheres to the enunciated content, it makes the status of the truth of what is enunciated questionable. We have all encountered the maddening person (the older sibling, the classroom smartass, the teenage child, the insecure lover) who, when confronted with some simple assertion, challenges us with a direct "So you say." One's instinctive retort is to re-assert the utterance by incorporating the level of enunciation into the level of the enunciated: "No, it's not what *I say*. It is *true* that I love you." Unfortunately, this rejoinder cannot forestall the inevitable retort, "So you say." The incorporation of the level of enunciation into the level of the enunciated does not remove the unspoken excess; it merely shifts it back a step: "(I am saying that) it is true that I love you." No matter how hard we try to eliminate it by adding clarifying prefixes to our utterances, an excess persists. Such a challenge to our attempts to communicate arises not because we have not said enough but because we cannot help but say *more* than what we are saying, even though we don't know precisely what that "more" is.[16] As Žižek puts it in his Foreword to this book, it is impossible to take "into account the way our own intervention will transform the field. The speaking subject cannot take into account the way it is itself 'counted' in the signifying series."

In other words, excess arises not because the signifier does not have a stable signified, nor because the signifier as materiality can be taken up and used (even nonsensically) in ever-changing contexts. Rather, the excess is located at the point where the subject is split between the level of enunciation and the level of the enunciated. Where excess emerges in the utterance is also the point at which the speaking subject appears. The excess in the utterance corresponds to the excess in the subject, that minimal self-difference that makes a subject (which, after all, is a meaningful object), emerge from the state of being. Although in the chapters that follow I will have much more to say about the emergence of the subject as non-self-coincident, here I want to focus on how the excessive dimension of the utterance links up with the excess of the subject.

We are accustomed to hearing a great deal about the "subject of lack" in contemporary theory, yet the argument I have been exploring suggests that the subject of lack should be understood as a subject of excess, that is, as a subject to which an excess ineradicably adheres.[17] The fact that one has become meaningful to others – i.e. been registered in the Symbolic – does not mean that one actually knows what one means to others. On the contrary, to enter the Symbolic register is to fall under the regime of signification as a signifier, that is, as capable of transmitting meaning, but not capable of coinciding precisely with one's meaning. A gap remains between the subject who is *referred to* in the utterance at the level of enunciated ("I am a woman") and the subject who is *making the utterance* at the level of enunciation. This gap marks the locus of the minimal difference that keeps the subject from coinciding with itself. It is as though one were constantly uttering, simply by virtue of being a subject, "Here I am," without, however, knowing what others make of that message. The subject does not know what message it is sending, because the subject cannot eliminate the excessive dimension from its utterance. The subject cannot make the subject of which it speaks ("I am a woman") coincide with the subject which is speaking ("[Here I am saying that]. . ."). That difference, that excess, is irreducible. So, the inability to control the meaning of oneself for others, this consequence of the difference between the level of the enunciated and the level of enunciation, is the way in which the subject becomes aware of its own non-self-coincidence. It is the way that the subject experiences its excessiveness with respect to itself, its existence as **subject***.[18]

The subject, as Lacan announces, is a signifier for another, which is to say that the subject does not control its own message. The behavior of all subjects is motivated in part by the (often unpleasant, but sometimes – as in love – wonderful) discovery that one's meaning for others is neither a function of what one "utters" about oneself nor knowable in any final way. In this situation of not knowing the nature of the message I am sending about myself, it does no good for me to ask someone else to disambiguate my meaning. No matter what the reply, I will still face the residue of excess that necessarily sticks to the statement. This excess is not a function of a misinterpretation. Rather, it is a function of the fact that interpretation cannot be stabilized, so that even if I sense that I am meaningful to another, I do not know *what* my meaning is for that person, no matter how hard either of us try to clarify the matter.

Of course, this excess which causes the uncertainty about the subject's meaning is also what permits the subject to become meaningful to others at all: both the uncertainty and the meaningfulness arise from the effects generated by the added formal negation. Lacan explains that when one is submitted to Symbolic registration, one has to make a compromise. In return for becoming a subject – for becoming meaningful to others – one has to lose one's own immediacy to oneself, one's self-coincidence. And, as Lacan points out, you don't have much choice in the matter: either you enter the Symbolic or you cannot even be a "you," for there is no such thing as a *subject* that is self-coincident.[19] As we have seen, Žižek emphasizes that the excess in the subject is produced by the addition of a particular form of the extimate cause, just as it is produced in the object. You have only two choices: either subjectivity with loss of immediacy, or non-subjecthood. Again, the loss of immediacy does not result in a lack: it generates an excess, an excess of meaningfulness that is not in the control of the subject.

As may be obvious, the problem for the subject in its social relation to other subjects is that an excess of meaning sticks to *every* subject. The excessive dimension of a subject, which is a function of her minimal self-difference from herself, means that her very meaning *for herself* is routed through the defiles of signification, a function of the vicissitudes of excess. At the same time, no appeal to another subject to stabilize her meaning, to eliminate her excess, can have the desired effect, because the other subject also has his own excessive dimension, which shadows every attempt to arrive at a final determination of the subject's meaning. Consequently, the excessive dimension sticks to all the subjects in the field – even collective action cannot get rid of excess.

These excesses have a dual role. On the one hand, they make it possible for the subject to become meaningful to others, for all meaning depends upon the opening of a space of signification from the "realtight" by way of the extimate cause. However, the price to be paid for becoming meaningful is being stuck to/with this excess. So, on the other hand, this excessive dimension prevents any final determination of the subject, fating it to remain uncertain of its place among others.[20] The excess sticking to subjects is like a handle by which subjects can "grasp" each other, but it is also a barrier preventing them from knowing what it is that they are grasping. What makes it possible for subjects to recognize each other *as subjects* is precisely what keeps them apart. As Badiou formulates it, in a paraphrase of Lacan's conception of the sexual relation, "the only social relation is the relation of nonrelation."[21]

The "relation of nonrelation" encapsulates the dynamics of excess generated by the extimate cause. Each subject is stuck to an excess, but subjects react to this excess in a variety of ways. Some imagine that their excess of meaning is solely their deficiency, one not shared by others. Accordingly, many think that another person can remedy the deficiency, like the romantic tales of one person "completing" another person or Plato's story of the original human, severed in half, perpetually seeking its complement. But the excess is irremediable. Two subjects who find each other do not make a "whole." We do not have a "less than one" subject joining to another "less than one" to make a "one." Nor is it the case that one subject has a lack and the other a corresponding excess, so that they fit together like lock and key. Rather, because each subject is a subject*, a more-than-one-but-not-quite two, there is no comfortable fit between them: the excess gets in the way. Put another way, adding a more-than-one-but-not-quite-two to another more-than-one-but-not-quite-two never results in a completion or a unity. In fact, adding a subject* with another subject* makes *neither* one nor two!

Plato's story in *The Symposium* of sexed beings created from an eight-limbed spheroidal creature is one of humankind's innumerable attempts to account for the lack of perfect social harmony through a utopian fantasy. We can make sense of such tales as defenses against the reality that all subjects are Möbius subjects, subjects whose meanings are not in their own control, who will always be in contention for the right to define themselves, and who will always be vulnerable to the appropriation of their meaning by others. Möbius subjects are therefore forced to live with uncertainty about their status and security among others. This uncertainty and its consequent anxiety somehow has to be managed (the list of psychic attributes suggests the range of such management tactics: aggression, humor, paranoia, depression, narcissism, love, etc.). The excess that cannot be eradicated means that subjects can never live in absolute peace and harmony: some form of social discord is inevitable.

The history of political thought, seen from this perspective, reads as a long series of efforts to deny or dismiss the Möbius subject as a politically relevant figure. On the other hand, if we understand the social field as shot through with the excesses stuck to each subject, we will have a picture by which to evaluate the various models of social relations and systems on offer in the various theories of change and political action explored in this book. Later we will see how the failure to conceptualize the "relation of nonrelation" generated by this dynamics of excess results in a disavowal of the very nature of the social field itself. In the following chapters, I will discuss how extimate causality produces social subjects with the Möbius form as well as how such subjects can intervene in the social field. We will then arrive at the point where it will be possible to theorize the implications of the specific properties of Möbius subjects for participation in group politics and democratic interactions. A number of fantasies about the social field and subjects' relations to each other underwrite the political claims of these theories, fantasies that can be recognized if we are attentive to the operations of the extimate cause.

From Many, One – or Möbius?

If social discord is the primary problem addressed by politics, then politics must offer some program, however fantasmatic, for creating unity out of multiplicity. How does the heterogeneous "many" become unified and capable of concerted action? What should we name the political subject in its collective aspect? Traditionally, political philosophy that seeks to capture this collective subject speaks of the *demos* or the people. Marx urges "the class-less class." Michael Hardt and Antonio Negri suggest "the multitude." Each name carries a penumbra of presuppositions about the properties of subjects who can effect group solidarity, exercise collective agency, and promote democratic outcomes. So that my reader does not have to wait to see the usefulness of the Möbius subject, let me prepare the ground for our later investigations on this topic by discussing two philosophers, Jacques Rancière and Giorgio Agamben, who unwittingly demonstrate the utility of the Möbius subject for political thought.

In his reading of Aristotle's *Politics*, Rancière locates what he calls "an original duplicity" in the relationship between politics and philosophy: Aristotle proposes two contradictory origins of politics, each deriving from a different conception of the political subject (OSP 12ff). On the one hand, politics is "the organization of the human community in accordance with the *telos* of the reasonable being"; on the other, politics is "a remedy for the sheer fact of social division" (OSP 13). If subjects are reasonable beings, as Aristotle conceives, then something like a rational organization of the community is possible. But if the *demos* is divided into *euporoi* and *aporoi* – haves and have-nots – then the best we can hope for, Aristotle says, is an "art of politics" that mitigates the danger to social harmony that the have-nots would pose if they gained power. In Aristotle's view, the societal division into rich and poor is both inevitable and irremediable. Following the logic of contradiction, Aristotle recommends adapting to the contingent fact that we will just have to put up with the existence of these two groups by, as Rancière puts it, "regulat[ing] the intermittency of the *demos* by imposing intervals which place its strength at a distance from its turbulence, at a distance from itself" (OSP 15).

This Aristotelian solution of putting obstacles in the way of radical democratic politics (e.g. poll taxes, property requirements) consists of disqualifications backed by law but intended to disengage the populace from its own political power. In this way, even democracy depoliticizes the political itself. As Rancière points out, it is impossible on the face of it to distinguish this depoliticization from tyranny. In fact, it is a time-honored strategy of all politics.

Rancière draws our attention to a peculiarity in Aristotle's argument. If the members of the society are reasonable beings, social harmony can result. If the society is composed of passionate actors, regulation of disruptive affects through education or force can be achieved. If the society is split between rich and poor, then depoliticizing mechanisms can bring about some measure of peaceful coexistence. A "realistic utopia" is possible, even if the ultimate dream of social unity is not. From whence, then, does war arise? In Aristotle's view, there are only two possibilities: either from the conflict between rich and poor (i.e., the failure of depoliticization), or – and here Aristotle introduces a new actor – from the apolitical man, an *azux*, a non-cooperator.

What is the *azux*? If the human being is a political animal by definition, then the apolitical man necessarily departs from the human in some way: in having "neither hearth nor home [he] is either 'above humanity' or else abject (*phaulos*)" (OSP 27). Rancière confirms that the *azux* cannot be a political actor in Aristotelian terms: as extra-human, the *azux* is not only solitary but inexplicable, insofar as we would have to assume a nature other than human to understand the kind of war the *azux* would bring about.

In Rancière's view, Aristotle's analysis has led him to miss another possible source of war – what he calls the "rallying power of hatred" (OSP 26). What if there were a form of social unity that is supported by hatred rather than, say, consensus, common interest, social regulation, or sympathy? What if there were, as Rancière puts it, a "being-together which could be a conductor of hate, a contributor to war" (OSP 27)? This particular source of unity has been overlooked in political philosophy, he argues, because philosophy persists in regarding "war as division and hatred as envy, whereas in fact hatred is a rallying force in its own right and rallies for no reason but the precise fact that for each individual it is simply there" (OSP 28).

At this point, Rancière characterizes the nature of the political subject and the motivation for collective action in a figure that barely holds together, so contradictory are its parts. He presents the rallying by hate as the "excluded middle" of Aristotle's two poles – on the one hand, "the solitary state" of the *azux*; on the other, "a collective struggle for what the other group possesses." This "middle" term borrows asocial discord from one side and solidarity from the other, producing the apparently paradoxical prospect of a group of mutually hating subjects becoming united by that very hatred, even as hatred works to destabilize its bonds.

Rancière claims that the modern world's rejection of the dualism on which Greek political discourse is based has led it to ignore the production of unity through hatred:

> This is an area that philosophy has trouble approaching, whether its relationship to the ignorant mass be patient (Spinoza) or impatient (Plato): that point where the order of the pack becomes clearly distinct from the

> disorder of popular movements; that junction of the one and the many
> which is neither the union of the discordant many nor the resolution of the
> contradiction, but the place where the terrors of the One meet the terrors
> of the many, where the dread of the disarmed subject . . . becomes the face
> of a mobilizing hatred, where the cure for separation turns into radical evil.
> (OSP 28)

He implicitly asks us to re-think the desire for unity from the standpoint
of the nature of the subject. For Rancière, political philosophy's failure
to recognize the form of unity achieved by rallying through hatred marks
a dangerous point in modern thinking, which amounts to a failure to
maintain a proper sense of duality in the political register:

> By positing a single essence of domination as the unified principle of our
> time, it prohibits the giving of meaning to the *Two* of politics in whatever
> form (Nazism and social democracy, bourgeoisie and proletariat, democ-
> racy and totalitarianism) . . . And what disappears in this account is the
> singularity of rallying-to-exclude, along with its most radical, extermina-
> tory, expression. (OSP 29)

Yet while Rancière approves a philosophical approach that keeps dualism
to the forefront, he himself projects his dualisms (bourgeois/proletariat;
democracy/totalitarianism) out of the excess attending the subject, the
"more than one, not quite two," without ever acknowledging his doing
so. Let's follow this track.

What motivates the passion for political unity when, in Rancière's
view, duality is the cornerstone of politics? Although he does not continue with this analysis, Rancière's account is suggestive. The relevant
motivation is not a utopian wish for brotherhood and harmony – the
dissolution of the self in the group – but rather a hatred composed of a
narcissistic intolerance for others and a fear of weakness. Such hatred is
inherently conflictual, simultaneously promoting and destabilizing alli-
ances. I think of it this way: through hatred, the members of the pack act
together but remain lone wolves at heart. If the resultant pack mentality
gathers into a crushing force, it nonetheless does not guarantee solidarity.
It is always liable to disintegration. After all, members of the pack can
turn on each other.

Although Rancière himself does not, we can take up this track with the
Möbius subject as our guide. From this point of view, Aristotle's origins
of politics depend upon a rhetorical trope, the presentation of an essential *self*-division of the subject as if it were a division at the level of the
social – the split between rich and poor, for example. But in fact this riven
state drives the subject: all of the subject's emotional characteristics are
functions of its fundamental lack of self-cohesion. The dream of politics

is that there is a remedy for social division – a dream of unity – but this dream is motivated by the subject's own division. To avoid encountering its own excess with respect to itself – its non-self-coincidence registered as angst, anxiety, and anger – the subject projects the source of its problems onto other people. So, the defensive projection of self-division from the level of the subject to the level of the socius means that every person in the society can be targeted as the source of discord for every other person. The logical consequence of this projection is social chaos, which creates a strong incentive for avoiding this outcome by turning the hatred of all against all into a hatred of all against one. And then another one. And then another.

While Rancière does not make this argument explicitly, he does imply that something like a riven subject, a subject at odds with itself, must be taken into account in the political domain. So, for example, he contrasts Aristotle's diagnosis of the source of social division in the *demos* (*euporoi/aporoi*) and its concomitant pragmatics of an art of depoliticized politics with Plato's darker vision of a *demos* that threatens always to dissolve into heterogeneity. We can go further: whereas Aristotle is forced to consider the *azux* as apolitical (because for him politics is the management of social division, not the coming to grips with self-division), Plato's worry is that the entire *demos* is in fact composed of subjects each of which is an *azux*, that is, fundamentally self-riven and therefore merely one of the rabble, *ochlos*. Plato attributes the inevitability and irremediality of social division to the character of the *demos* as *ochlos*, or as Rancière puts it, to "the infinite turbulence of collections of individuals who are always at odds with themselves, living rent by passion and at the mercy of desire." But if the subject is "rent by passion," then its self-division as cause of social division would not be resolvable through political means.[22]

Rancière's discussion brings to light for us the possibility of a crucial link among the *azux*, the *ochlos*, and the rallying by hate. We now know the name of this link: it is the excess attending every social subject, the fundament of the "relation of nonrelation." When he describes the *ochlos* as a collection of subjects at odds with themselves and the *azux* as both more and less than human, Rancière willy-nilly brings to the fore the non-self-coincidence and excess of the Möbius subject. The *azux*, then, is only apolitical in the sense that his politics are not regulatory, depoliticizing, or dispossessive – that is, they do not lead to the eradication of an excess that (presumably) disrupts social harmony.

But consider that the *azux* can stand as easily for the subject ready to be rallied by hatred ("above the human") as he can for the one on whom the pack turns ("*phaulos*"). As unassimilable surplus, as extra-human, he is the exemplum of the subject bearing the Möbius conditions of subjectivity. Both proto-pack member and scapegoat, we might say that the *azux* serves as a switchpoint in the political field, the undecidable point of excess that turns the rabble of the *ochlos* (that congeries of heterogeneous and uncoordinated subjects) into the *demos* (that temporary alliance of interests capable of concerted action) and back again. If he is not the Aristotelian political subject, nonetheless, he is one of the figures by which political subjectivity must be thought.

In his call for a thinking of the "singularity of rallying-to-exclude," Rancière lays the groundwork for conceiving the excessive dimension of the pack member. We have noted that hatred is the link that works against linkage, the relation that destroys relationality, the excess that distances the subject from himself and forces him to detour through others, however unsatisfactorily, to find himself. The mechanism of the pack works no better than any other to eradicate excess, but it is a telling symptom of its presence. In its recognition of the excess that founds the subject, the concept of the pack rallied by hate represents a fundamental truth of the political subject without invoking the utopian fantasy of social unity or the regulative depoliticization that Aristotle's rational organization requires.

We could say that what Rancière leaves unacknowledged in this discussion is the necessity of the *azux* as Möbius subject – the elemental cell of politics that exemplifies the basis of the relation of nonrelation. It is significant that in his discussion of the need for dualism, Rancière reproduces the "more than one, not quite two" structure of the Möbius subject: the proletariat is always necessarily excessive to itself, non-self-coincident, because it is at once a particular class and the condition of class-lessness. If the proletariat is the "agent of declassification," Rancière asks, how shall we name it "if not still by the class name?" (OSP 33). The *azux* shows us one way that groups form without individuals being subsumed in a group identity. In this sense, the *azux* figures forth one possibility for the articulation of a group out of heterogeneous, even opposed elements, while preserving the possibility of the kinds of disarticulations and re-articulations crucial for democratic interaction. The question of the means by which groups form, become stabilized, and undergo reconfiguration is central to the problem of democracy, a question we will take up again in chapter 5 with Laclau's work.

Refugees and the Face: The Politics and Ethics of Agamben's Möbius Topology

Many other contemporary writers addressing social change offer examples of explorations that can be understood in Möbius terms. In Agamben's work, for instance, the refugee becomes one of the limit-figures for think-ing the political for the same reasons as does Aristotle's *azux*: both have a Möbius topology. Before turning to larger ethical and political impulses in Agamben's work, let me take a moment to review his discussion of the refugee to provide a brief example of the utility of the Möbius figure for addressing longstanding deadlocks in political thought. Agamben argues that the refugee brings to light the scandal that the principle of sover-eignty is bound to the nation through a fiction of nativity:

> the refugee represents such a disquieting element in the order of the nation-state . . . because, by breaking the identity between the human and the citizen and that between nativity and nationality, it brings the originary fiction of sovereignty to crisis. . . . Inasmuch as the refugee, an appar-ently marginal figure, unhinges the old trinity of state-nation-territory, it deserves instead to be regarded as the central figure of our political history. . . . The concept of refugee must be resolutely separated from the concept of the "human rights," and the right of asylum . . . must no longer be con-sidered as the conceptual category in which to inscribe the phenomenon of refugees. . . . The refugee should be considered for what it is, namely, nothing less than a limit-concept that at once brings a radical crisis to the principles of the nation-state and clears the way for a renewal of categories that can no longer be delayed. (MWE 21–3)

Agamben points to the transformation of the economic and political realms of the European states created by the "permanently resident mass of noncitizens who do not want to be and cannot be either naturalized or repatriated" (MWE 23). Agamben chooses Tomas Hammar's neologism "denizen" to describe these people, comparing them to their *frères-semblants*, the mass of citizens who no longer take part in the political processes of their own states: "citizens and denizens – at least in certain social strata – are entering an area of potential indistinction" (MWE 23). Denizens, born elsewhere, live within the territorial confines of another nation without being of it in a political sense; while increasing numbers of modern-day citizens, born within their own nation, attenuate their participation in the political life of the nation and in this way become more like denizens.

    Guided by these reflections on the exposure of the fiction that sovereignty depends upon nativity – the dismantling of the "trinity of state-nation-territory" – he sees a possibility for a new "model of international relations" based on the figure of the refugee (MWE 24). The example of Jerusalem gives concreteness to the model. Currently a locus of competing territorial claims based on nativity and religion, the fact that Jerusalem can belong wholly to no single group becomes in Agamben's view an opening to a solution, in which the conflictual site becomes "simultaneously and without any territorial partition . . . the capital of two different states" (MWE 24). The figure Agamben implies in this passage is the same as that of Lacan's pseudo-Venn diagram. Each of two entities – say, Israel and Palestine – has added to it something extraneous from the other, the "Jerusalem" that is not its own capital. This external "Jerusalem" both coincides with the internal "Jerusalem" and exceeds it.

This figure of a double negation or reciprocal exclusion results in the Möbius condition, where inside and outside become "in-determinate": "This space would coincide neither with any of the homogeneous national territories nor with their *topographical* sum, but would rather act on them by articulating and perforating them *topologically* as in the Klein bottle or in the Möbius strip, where exterior and interior in-determine each other" (MWE 25). What is useful for us here is Agamben's description of the solution in *topological* terms, as he makes explicit when discussing Europe as a similar kind of extraterritorial space:

> Instead of two national states separated by uncertain and threatening boundaries, it might be possible to imagine two political communities insisting on the same region and in a condition of exodus from each other – communities that would articulate each other via a series of reciprocal extraterritorialities in which the guiding concept would no longer be the *ius* (right) of the citizen but rather the *refugium* (refuge) of the singular. (MWE 24)

I would argue that this is an instance of the way that conceiving of an addition of a negation in order to produce an excess transforms political thought. I do not pretend to know what the consequence of "reciprocal extraterritoriality" might be in any given situation. To my knowledge, Agamben has not attempted to work out the practicalities of this plan. One might ask how a Palestinian or an Israeli person would be protected, absent citizenship rights, in such a Jerusalem: how might the provision of refuge to the two "denizen" populations actually be realized politically and juridically? Yet even if we may have no answers to these questions, nonetheless, by resorting to Möbius topology to describe the social space, Agamben's thought opens up a new way of thinking about a situation that has appeared insoluble. Taken together with similar insights from other philosophers and social change theorists, this description helps us to flesh out the map of possibilities that appears when we consider the social space as a non-orientable object.

These reflections are part of Agamben's larger philosophical project, which includes an exploration of the nature of the human. As is well-known, Agamben conceives of human beings – at least in their political dimension – as belonging to two registers simultaneously: on the one hand, in relation to the sovereign power over life and death, which reduces the human being to "naked life" (*homo sacer*); and on the other hand, in relation to "forms of life," in which "what is at stake in its way of living is living itself" (MWE 4). He conceives of political power as always founded on the (unconscionable) separation of these two registers, or, rather, on the extraction of a "sphere of naked life from the context of the forms of life." This reduction of human beings to naked life excludes what is most valuable and essential to the human. The term "forms of life"

> defines a life – human life – in which the single ways, acts, and processes of living are never simply *facts* but always and above all *possibilities* of life. . . . Each behavior and each form of human living is never prescribed by a specific biological vocation, nor is it assigned by whatever necessity; instead, no matter how customary, repeated, and socially compulsory, it always retains the character of a possibility; that is, it always puts at stake living itself. That is why human beings – as beings of power who can do or not do, succeed or fail, lose themselves or find themselves – are the only beings for whom happiness is always at stake in their living, the only beings whose life is irremediably and painfully assigned to happiness. But this immediately constitutes the form-of-life as political life. (MWE 4)

Here Agamben is emphasizing a particular ethical modality of human life: the value of the human is the means of putting at stake "living itself," where living is also a means, the means of putting at stake what is "human itself." In this way, Agamben argues, humans are "means without end." Not being limited to what he calls their "social-juridical" identities ("the voter, the worker, the journalist, the student, but also the HIV-positive, the transvestite, the porno star, the elderly, the parent, the woman"), which are founded ultimately on naked life, human beings ought to be conceived not as "always already and solely enacted, but rather [as] delivered to a possibility and a power" (MWE 6–7, 9).

We can hear in these reflections issues similar to those involved in our discussion of the operation of the formal negation. Agamben rejects the definition of human beings in terms of their social identities, as possessing this or that particular property, as firmly as he rejects as a pernicious universality definitions of the human that depend on the mere fact of our being alive, that most basic of positive properties. Yes, humans have those identities and that bare life, but they are also something more. It is important to insist that this something more does not belong to the realm of metaphysics: what is properly human concerns an excess generated through a kind of reflexivity that both founds genuine (but not immanent) community and is founded on the fact of our being linguistic beings:

> Among beings who would always already be enacted, who would always already be this or that thing, this or that identity, and who would have entirely exhausted their power in these things and identities – among such beings there could not be any community but only coincidences and factual partitions. We can communicate with others only through what in us – as much as in others – has remained potential, and any communication (as Benjamin perceives for language) is first of all communication not of something in common but of communicability itself. After all, if there existed one and only one being, it would be absolutely impotent. . . . And there where I am capable, we are always already many (just as when, if there is a language, that is a power of speech, there cannot then be one and only one being who speaks it.) (MWE 10)

Agamben repeatedly makes explicit the political valence of this argument, as when he points out that "what the state cannot tolerate in any way is that singularities form a community without claiming an identity; that human beings co-belong without a representable condition of belonging (being Italian, working-class, Catholic, terrorist, etc.)" (MWE 87). Agamben is not arguing for some kind of immanent community in which communication is perfectly achieved without excess – just the opposite. An immanent community would be no community at all, equivalent in its perfect communication to a single member. Rather, he is describing the only actual basis of community, the only genuine social bond, in terms of what humans have in common: Agamben calls this common element "communicability." His description makes it clear that what he is describing without naming is the excess attending signification, the excess that founds subjects in their social dimension ("always already many"). This is the excess that both makes community (and communication) possible and prevents its immanence to itself.

Understanding "communicability" as the excess of signification opens Agamben's thought to us in another way. As he grapples with the ethical import of understanding the human in terms of communicability, he proposes a term that captures exceedingly well the phenomenon of exposure to interpretation that inheres in our social life. As I pointed out earlier in this chapter, the uncertainties created by our inability to control how others interpret us not only promote our entry into the social field as the only place in which we can be meaningful, they also foster characteristic modes of defense against those uncertainties. Agamben's term "face" seizes on both of these emphases:

> What the face exposes and reveals is not *something* that could be formulated as a signifying proposition of sorts, nor is it a secret doomed to remain forever incommunicable. The face's revelation is revelation of language itself. Such a revelation, therefore, does not have any real content

and does not tell the truth about this or that state of being, about this or that aspect of human beings and of the world: it is *only* opening, *only* communicability. To walk in the light of the face means *to be* this opening – and to suffer it, and to endure it. . . . Nature acquires a face precisely in the moment it feels that it is being revealed by language. And nature's being exposed and betrayed by the word, its veiling itself behind the impossibility of having a secret, appears on its face as either chastity or perturbation, as either shamelessness or modesty. (MWE 92)

Agamben doesn't use my terminology to describe the problem of signification from the point of view of the subject as signifier; he doesn't refer to significative excess or to the Möbius subject. But I think we must understand this passage in those terms if we are to grasp both his ethical reflections and his political project. By virtue of the fact that human beings are exposed to communicability, they seek to grasp their meaning through their interactions with others, which, as Agamben puts it, means that "they want to recognize themselves, that is, they want to take possession of their own very appearance" (MWE 93), an impossible yet utterly compelling quest. From his perspective, this attempt (what we would describe as trying to find the truth of one's own meaning for others) transforms the world "into the battlefield of a political struggle without quarter . . . whose object is truth [and] goes by the name of History" (MWE 93). Humans' "own proper truth" is "not something of which we can take possession" because it is nothing other than the excess attending signification – "pure communicability" (MWE 97). From Agamben's point of view, the proper political task is to expose this pure communicability – which the politicians and media apparatuses of the society of the spectacle seek to control.

It would take a sustained investigation to see whether Agamben's political thought ultimately accords with our description of Möbius subjectivity and extimate causality. His argument in "The Face," that capitalism alienates the communicative nature of human beings, while seeming to verge on suggesting that capitalism can somehow abolish excess (a suggestion that our analysis of social signification would dispute), captures the exhortations of modern political discourse to "total self-possession," or what he calls a "grotesque counterfeit of the face" (MWE 97). But rather than venture into these deeper waters, we can simply note that Agamben's ethical and political project engages the same analysis and topology as does our discussion of Möbius subjectivity and the excess of social signification.

With these tools and examples in mind, we can begin our journey through the terrain of social change theory, guided by thinkers who highlight the inadequacy of traditional models of social causality and subjectification. Each has a unique way of trying to solve the problem of external/immanent causation. Their explorations lead them to posit the need for what we are calling the extimate cause and the Möbius subject, in order to remedy deficits in contemporary theories of social change. We will find that when they revise or reject such theories through the application of psychoanalytic principles, they develop promising tools advancing theories of social change in a historicist key. And we will also discover that their specific *disavowals* of excess have a great deal to teach us about the value of the Möbius subject for the politics and ethics of social change.

3
The Social Structures of Bourdieu and de Certeau

What Determines the Subject's Freedom?

Let's start with a problem that we've already begun to discuss: in order to understand how subjects in a society connect to one another and coordinate their actions sufficiently to produce that society, many theorists operate with the assumption that mechanisms of inculcation fashion subjects to conform with social dictates. Ideological interpellation is one such mechanism. But if we are fashioned by our social world, how can we gain sufficient difference and distance from it to resist or change that fashioning? We might have more agency to bring about social change if we were not embedded so profoundly *within* the social universe. If we could only find a way to detach ourselves from the very world that fashions us, it would not seem so natural; alternatives to the status quo would become apparent, and we could see our way clear to making needed changes. But how can we bring about such disengagement if we ourselves are social products? How do products of social forces take a stand against their producer? Theories of how social change takes place have to provide a story that links individuals sufficiently to their social world to enable their actions to count within it (and to be coordinated with one another) without subsuming them entirely to social determination.

Two eminent theorists, Pierre Bourdieu and Michel de Certeau, were dissatisfied with the predominating theories of their day which purported to explain the "fit" between subject and socius in a way that accounts for how the subject could be simultaneously a product of the social structure and free enough to act against its dictates. Bourdieu and de Certeau begin with the obvious: social structures have the power to align individuals with systemic rather than personal interests. Social structures somehow have the power to forge subjects in their own image. Individuals manifestly are not always aware of those alignments and, as a result, frequently misrecognize their own interests and overestimate their agency. For this reason, it is not possible to found a theory of social change on intentionality or individual agency alone.

Acknowledging the limitations of the individual's apprehension of its own determinants, the twentieth-century French social scientists in the group to which Bourdieu and de Certeau belong, including Luce Giard, Marcel Detienne, and Michel Foucault, regard the individual as "a locus in which an incoherent (and often contradictory) plurality of . . . relational determinations interact" rather than as an integral site of intentional activity (de Certeau, PEL xi).[1] Both Bourdieu and de Certeau look to patterned repetitive behaviors, or *practices*, as the central example of a type of non-intentional, supraindividual, and politically relevant agency (Bourdieu, LP 25). They conceive of themselves as carrying out the work of a new kind of social science that, in taking seriously the decentralization of the subject, critiques both liberalism and Marxism while retaining a progressive political engagement. For them, psychoanalysis – and in particular, Lacan's work – provides the seminal terms for understanding how this decentralization should be theorized. De Certeau was a member of the (Lacanian) Freudian School of Paris; Bourdieu acknowledges the importance of Lacan's seminars and makes explicit use of psychoanalytic terminology and concepts, especially the concept of *Verneinung* (denegation) that figures so prominently in Lacan's work and in our discussion of the genesis of the Möbius subject. The psychoanalytic dimension of both Bourdieu's and de Certeau's thought is at once more significant and more pervasive than commentators have acknowledged: in fact, the strengths and weaknesses of their theories cannot be assessed without taking this dimension into account. Both Bourdieu and de Certeau make use of the psychoanalytic account of subjectification to open up the possibility of a subject that cannot be reduced to its structural determinants, introducing a margin of contingency, but without severing the subject from its social moorings. Unlike American cultural studies scholars (many of whom rely on Bourdieu and de Certeau), who routinely champion the historicizing impulse of cultural studies against the "universalizing" program of psychoanalysis, Bourdieu and de Certeau, each in his own way, explicitly derive the historicizing dimension of their theories of social change from psychoanalysis.

In their efforts to avoid the Scylla of inescapable social determination and the Charybdis of unanchored individual freedom, they unwittingly reveal the centrality of extimate causality and Möbius subjectivity for any theory of the subject's nondeterminacy. To understand precisely how the Möbius subject affords such a theoretical foundation, we will begin by exploring this French tradition of social change theory that draws from Marxist and psychoanalytic traditions alike as it seeks to accommodate the twin demands of autonomous and heteronomous subjectivity. Beginning with Bourdieu's contribution before tracing how de Certeau follows his own line of departure, I show how each theorist seeks to establish the historical status of practices through a re-imagining of the subject's relation to the social field.

The "Ruinous" Opposition of Subjectivism and Objectivism

Bourdieu argues that past philosophizing about social relations and social change has fallen into two extreme positions: on the one hand, the subjectivist view (exemplified by Sartre) which accords absolute and unconditioned freedom to the individual to will the terms of her existence; on the other, the objectivist view (exemplified by Levi-Strauss) which regards individuals as mere counters in the play of external forces. Bourdieu takes it as a sign of their mutual insufficiency that any given exponent of one of these positions inevitably if unintentionally imports the other's arguments. Accordingly, his project is not to synthesize objectivist and subjectivist solutions to the problems of the genesis of society and the efficacy of practical action but rather to "make explicit the presuppositions that they have in common as theoretical modes of knowledge, both equally opposed to the practical mode of knowledge which is the basis of ordinary experience of the social world" (LP 25). He seeks to chart an alternative course

> between an objectivist vision that subjects freedoms and wills to an external, mechanical determinism or [what amounts to the same thing] an internal, intellectual determinism and a subjectivist, finalist vision that substitutes the future ends of the project and of intentional action . . . for the antecedents of causal explanation. (LP 46)

If individuals are conditioned by social structures, their actions are as likely to reflect that determination as to challenge it: conditioned by externals, individuals have no means to see alternatives outside the status quo or will have no power that is not already co-opted by those external forces in advance. By the same token, if individuals are not conditioned by social structures, if they are radically free in the Sartrean sense, then their actions become "a kind of antecedent-less confrontation between the subject and the world . . . dependent on the decrees of the consciousness that creates [them] and therefore entirely devoid of objectivity," a situation that renders them meaningless to others, making collective action impossible or irrelevant to the structures in question (LP 42).

It is relatively easy to see why the objectivist position is uncongenial to theorists of social change. If external determinants make individuals, then how can individuals re-make those determinants? On this account, individuals have no purchase on the systems that govern them, which means that the ability to initiate change is taken out of the individual's hands.

Choosing Sartre as his example of the "ultra-subjectivist" position allows Bourdieu to clarify how the objectivist insistence on external determinations appears as impotence to the advocates of the subjectivist position, among whom Bourdieu includes the "rational actor" theorists of contemporary economics (LP 46).[2] According to Bourdieu, Sartre refuses to define social class "as a class of conditions and conditionings," which he views as "class reduced to a thing, 'congealed' in an essence, reduced to inertia and impotence" (LP 43). Such descriptions of class-as-thing seem to Sartre "designed to contain, even push back, the working class into what it is and so distance it from what it has to be, the mobilized class" (LP 44). Thus, from within the subjectivist stance, rejection of the external conditions that determine subjects (and class qua class) as they are now – that is, as the past – is the only way to bring to the fore the subject (or class) as they must be – that is, as the future. Only by transcending the past and its determinations can individuals make change take place, first in themselves and then by that means in the outer world. In other words, the weight of the past instanced in social conditioning is felt to be positively deadening, a form of inertia so extreme that it can admit of no movement whatsoever.

As Bourdieu points out, the Sartrean solution is an imaginary one: from its perspective, the actual world is the world of a "congealed" past, while the world of "transcendence" that is to come into being exists only in the mind – and for that reason offers no resistance to the desires and plans of the subject. Bourdieu refers to this "imaginary anthropology of subjectivism" as a "tyrannical desire" (quoting Durkheim) "to construct – or rather reconstruct – the world through its own power" (LP 42, 44). Yet in this account, this all-powerful subject loses its links to the very world it would change. Somehow, the past will be left behind: having no influence on the present or future, it can be ignored. The conditions by which change transpires, then, do not conform to the actualities of any given situation, which means that, in effect, the individual undertaking change loses all connection to the very locus of change itself. Thus the desired and imagined changes have no purchase on the real world, ironically vitiating the agency of this omnipotent subject. In psychoanalytic terms, we could say that a fantasy of omnipotent narcissism haunts both the subjectivist and the objectivist accounts. Easier to see in the subjectivist version, where this pure, unattached individual is posited as having no limits to his freedom or power beyond those of his will, it is nonetheless also present in the objectivist version, insofar as the theorist identifies with the system of external constraints precisely in his project to model the totality of that system. The dynamic of an all-powerful entity (the Sartrean subject; the world of socio-cultural forces) dominating a helpless object (the world as "worked-upon matter"; the socialized individual) is inscribed in the fantasy of narcissistic omnipotence, a defense against its own enraged helplessness (LP 44).

The *Habitus* and the Temporality of Conditioning

Bourdieu's solution to this problem resides in the particular way in which he conceptualizes practices. The notion of practices as change mechanisms seems odd at first glance. After all, a practice is something that is repeated – like a golf swing or a piano scale – to produce a faithful reproduction rather than a transformation. But Bourdieu and de Certeau take their cue from Maurice Merleau-Ponty's *Phenomenology of Perception*, which explains how repeated actions, in the form of habits, signify the capacity to change: "The grasping of a habit is indeed the grasping of a significance, but it is the motor grasping of a motor significance . . . Habit expresses our power of . . . changing our existence by appropriating fresh instruments."[3] For Merleau-Ponty, no matter how the habit is acquired – by conscious self-discipline, for example – it represents *non-intentional* agency as it re-shapes us and by extension the world around us. When we obtain new bodily knowledge, our ability to transform our lives and our circumstances grows, no matter what our conscious intentions.

Bourdieu agrees that habits represent non-conscious acquired bodily knowledge, but he expands Merleau-Ponty's concept by emphasizing that such habitual actions are embodiments of an external field of social forces which structure perception and experience as "durable transposable predispositions," installed at the non-conscious level by patterns of daily life. He gives the name *habitus* to systems of these "structured structures predisposed to function as structuring structures" (LP 53). Here is a representative excerpt that indicates the flexibility and nuances of Bourdieu's concept:

> the structures characterizing a determinate class of conditions of existence produce the structures of the *habitus*, which in their turn are the basis of the perception and appreciation of all subsequent experiences. The *habitus*

. . . ensures the active presence of past experiences, which, deposited in each organism in the form of schemes of perception, thought and action, tend to guarantee the "correctness" of practices and their constancy over time, more reliably than all formal rules and explicit norms. . . . the conditioned and conditional freedom it provides is as remote from creation of unpredictable novelty as it is from simple mechanical reproduction of the original conditioning. (LP 54–5)

In this formulation, distinctions among unconscious habits, socially patterned behaviors, and freely willed actions disappear, leaving a nonconscious and non-intentional basis for purposeful action. The *habitus*, an internalized form of the social structure, serves as a *collectivized* and *unconscious* motive and guide for actions, a paradigmatic system (like a language system) that enables the generation of diverse practices (like sentences), each of which, however various, conforms in some way to the internalized rules of the social structure. Bourdieu calls it a "structuring structure" to emphasize that its work is never done although its work is always in some sense the same (LP 53).

What is the problem Bourdieu is trying to solve with the concept of *habitus*? If the subjectivist route to social change begins and ends in delusion because the rootless subject loses its links to the place where it would exercise its powers, then, similarly, the objectivist route implicitly demands quietism because the individual is so firmly entrenched in social constraints that she can effect no changes that are not already immanent in the status quo. What does the *habitus* offer by contrast? After all, given that the internalized *habitus* serves as the conduit for social patterning, if the freedom to choose in the Bourdieusian account is merely the freedom to choose among behaviors to which one is already predisposed at the level of the body by the inculcation of social forces, as though no other possible behaviors exist, then it is difficult to see how any such actions could provide the impetus or the means for bringing about change to the social structure.

Against this objection, Bourdieu theorizes the *habitus* precisely in order to explain how individuals acquire some freedom from determination, a modicum of unconditioned – and therefore potentially transformative – action. What matters most to Bourdieu is the fact that the *habitus* brings the past and the future into a conjunction (unlike the Sartrean position) in a way that offers sufficient disjuncture to provide a measure of freedom from determinations. His solution is that the *habitus* frees the individual – by means of these durable inculcations of the *past* – from the determinations of *immediate* externalities in the *present*:

The *habitus* – embodied history, internalized as a second nature and so forgotten as history – is the active presence of the whole past of which it is the product. As such, it is what gives practices their relative autonomy with respect to external determinations of the immediate present. This autonomy is that of the past, enacted and acting, which, functioning as accumulated capital, produces history on the basis of history and so ensures the permanence in change that makes the individual agent a world within the world. (LP 56)

In other words, the *habitus* retains the imprint of a past structure, so that when the structure changes, the *habitus* no longer matches it. Capitalizing on this slim margin of release from immediate determination, the individual may not be able to create new state forms or act in unpredictably novel ways, but then again, neither will she be doomed to live in conformity with her original social conditioning. Contrary to the Sartrean analysis, which makes the past the source of unfreedom, Bourdieu makes the past-as-structuring-structure the source of individual autonomy, the means by which the individual escapes (some) determinations in the present.

Bourdieu's use of *habitus* is an ingenious way to solve the problem created for an account of agency when we assume that subjects are produced by society to advance its own purposes. How do such "forged" individuals adjust themselves to changing conditions, and what independent capacities do they have for affecting or changing those conditions? How do they know when they are acting in accordance with systemic dictates or behaving freely in order to direct their actions either in conformity with or against the social system? These questions can be summarized in terms of the degree of determination the social system imposes on the individual: without some social determination, the individual would be disconnected from the social structures in which he lives and would therefore have no opportunity to affect the system through his actions; too much determination, however, will only subsume individual behavior under systemic control, affording no space for relatively independent action. By deconstructing the opposition between social determination and individual freedom, Bourdieu arrives at an account of individual determination within and by social systems that at the same time allows for some individual freedom.

Political Ploys and the Incomplete Social Structure

No one understands the stakes of Bourdieu's theory, takes its contributions more seriously, or criticizes it more rigorously, than Michel de Certeau. Being as committed as Bourdieu to finding a non-individualized, non-intentionalized theory of agency, through an analysis of practices or "ways of operating," de Certeau says that

> [an] examination of such practices does not imply a return to individuality. The social atomism which over the past three centuries has served as the historical axiom of social analysis posits an elementary unit – the individual – on the basis of which groups are supposed to be formed and to which they are supposed to be always reducible. This axiom . . . plays no part in this study. (PEL xi)

And like Bourdieu, de Certeau acknowledges the conditioning of some "structuring structure" while recognizing that individual practices vary within it. Yet from the first, in large part because his purposes are avowedly more political than Bourdieu's, he is dissatisfied with the portrait of individual action that Bourdieu draws. Where Bourdieu proposes a theory that applies to everyone in a society in order to account for individual variation within social constraints, variation which may lead to social change, de Certeau announces from the outset that his theory focuses on a special group of people – consumers – whose weakness in relation to power structures defines their modes of operating within them. His purpose is to "bring to light the models of action characteristic of users whose status as the dominated element in society (a status that does not mean that they are either passive or docile) is concealed by the euphemistic term 'consumers'" (PEL xi–xii). He approves the ingenuity of Bourdieu's solution to the problem of how a conditioned individual nonetheless obtains some freedom from conditioning – through the very structures that condition her. Yet he objects to the passive role in which this account casts the individual and to the lack of a genuine mechanism of social change.

Let's return to Bourdieu for a moment to clarify the role that individual action and individual intention have in his scheme. Even as he emphasizes the governing and regularizing effects of the *habitus*, he doesn't deny that the individual has the ability to consciously decide on a course of action:

> It is, of course, never ruled out that the responses of the *habitus* may be accompanied by a strategic calculation tending to perform in a conscious mode the operation that the *habitus* performs quite differently, namely an estimation of chances presupposing transformation of the past effect into an expected objective. But these responses are first defined, *without any calculation*, in relation to objective potentialities, immediately inscribed in the present . . . in relation to a probable, "upcoming" future (*un à venir*), which . . . puts itself forward with an urgency and a claim to existence that excludes all deliberation. . . . The practical world that is constituted in the

relationship with the *habitus*, acting as a system of cognitive and motivating structures, is a world of *already realized ends*. (LP 53, my emphasis)

For Bourdieu, the deliberate action always takes place within a "structuring structure" or framework of defined potentialities and procedures. Alternatives to this framework simply do not appear because the framework is what makes perception and cognition possible in the first place: "the regularities inherent in an arbitrary condition ('arbitrary' in Saussure's and Mauss's sense) tend to appear as necessary, even natural, since they are the basis of the schemes of perception and appreciation through which they are apprehended" (LP 53–4). Even when the individual's conscious action "performs quite differently" an operation the *habitus* already performs, that difference emerges within the horizon defined by the structuring structure:

In short, being the product of a particular class of objective regularities, the *habitus* tends to generate all the "reasonable", "common-sense", behaviours (and only these) which are possible within the limits of these regularities, and which are likely to be positively sanctioned because they are objectively adjusted to the logic characteristic of a particular field, whose objective future they anticipate. (LP 53, 55–6)

The possibilities the individual seeks to calculate are given in advance, i.e., the future that she tries to bring into being through conscious choice has its properties inscribed already in the non-intentionalized adjustments the *habitus* makes to the field in which it operates.

In order to insert a politically relevant agency into this model, de Certeau retains Bourdieu's notion that structures provide a framework within which any number of actions may be generated, but he argues that individuals actively choose which actions to take. So, when it come to Bourdieu's idea that "practices give an adequate response to contingent situations" in the absence of any intentionality on the part of the agent, de Certeau accuses Bourdieu of expounding a "*[d]octa ignorantia* . . . a cleverness that does not recognize itself as such" (PEL 56). De Certeau, unlike Bourdieu, emphasizes the individual's conscious choices among this infinite if limited set of options, stressing that individuals seize on opportunities which their immediate circumstances afford them in order to respond creatively or in an unpredictable but self-interested way within the larger circumscribed social framework. Just as someone may choose to wander through city streets, vary his pace, stop here or there, return or not, so in daily life the individual has many choices to make that inscribe a kind of singularity within a larger pattern. Most importantly, "[t]he tactics of consumption, the ingenious ways in which the weak make use of the strong, thus lend a political dimension to everyday practices" (PEL xvii).

This political dimension arises because, de Certeau argues, the singularities produced by these ingenious ways of maneuvering within structured constraints constitute a *resistance* to the system, not just variations enabled by it. However, it is important to understand that de Certeau is *not* claiming that this resistance is an *intended* product of the individual's practice. Rather, individuals who try to achieve their own self-interested goals unwittingly locate the "gaps" in the structure, places where the structure has failed to determine individual behavior in advance, and thus individual practices can be formally resistant to the structure, whatever the individual's own perceived relationship to and intentional uses of the structure may be. Individuals have a connection to the determining system, and therefore the opportunity to act to change it, by virtue of the structures and patterns the system installs in their lives, but they can escape total determination by the system not because the system changes but because the system is not total. Repetitive patterned actions or practices will eventually and in the aggregate reveal the incompleteness of the system.

Where Bourdieu relies on the temporal discontinuity between the past incorporated in the *habitus* and the conditions of the present structure to establish the individual's relative *autonomy* from (immediate) structuring determinants, de Certeau regards this discontinuity as producing the individual's complete *subsumption* to structural power, undermining any possible basis for social change. De Certeau puts it this way:

> Bourdieu has to find *something* that can adjust practices to structures and yet also explain the gaps remaining between them. He needs a supplementary category. . . . an interiorization of structures (through learning) and an exteriorization of achievements (what Bourdieu calls the *habitus*) in practices. A temporal dimension is thus introduced: practices (expressing the experience) correspond adequately to situations (manifesting the structure) if, and only if, the structure remains stable for the duration of the process of interiorization/exteriorization; if not, practices lag behind, thus resembling the structure at the preceding point, the point at which it was interiorized by the *habitus*. (PEL 57)

De Certeau points out that, in Bourdieu's theory, only structures change (somehow): "achievements" cannot change, being nothing other than "the place in which structures are inscribed, the marble on which their history is engraved" (PEL 57). The principle by which structures change is attributed, mysteriously, to the structures themselves, so de Certeau, objecting to Bourdieu's implicit apoliticism, finds the theory totalizing and dogmatic – what he calls "the affirmation of a 'reality'" (PEL 59).[4] The "knowledge" of social structures incarnated in the body turns out to provide no special means for accessing the system or altering it. The fact that the *habitus* incorporates a past merely insures that 1) if a structure changes, the individual will lose his connection to the (new) structure and so lose the opportunity to manipulate it or transform it; and 2) if a structure doesn't change, the individual who is so determined by that structure must always act in conformity with it. He notes that the temporal mismatch which Bourdieu proposes as providing a measure of freedom from determination takes place when the structure changes, but that this change is itself mysteriously motivated. Structures change as a matter of course, but in Bourdieu's account individual practices do not change structures. In effect, then, from de Certeau's perspective, Bourdieu's theory can do nothing other than describe a status quo; it cannot provide a theory of social change.

In de Certeau's model, the agency that creates a "singularity," finding an occasion to play creatively with the opportunities afforded by the system, does not in and of itself constitute political agency. He grants intentionality to the individual to use and innovate on practices that seem to her to be likely to achieve her goals, but he makes no claims that such intentions will actually result in those achievements, or change social structures. Rather, the aggregation of such singularities, the combined effect of the "art" of these practitioners, emerges as "culture": culture itself will reveal the "cracks" in the system, in an evolutionary way:

> Similar strategic deployments, when acting on different relationships of force, do not produce identical effects. Hence the necessity of differentiating both the "actions" or "engagements" (in the military sense) that the system of products effects within the consumer grid, *and* the various kinds of room to maneuver left for consumers by the situations in which they exercise their "art" . . . . [Culture] develops in an atmosphere of tensions, and often of violence, for which it provides symbolic balances, contracts of compatibility and compromises, all more or less *temporary*. (PEL xvii, last emphasis mine)

Although at some points in his exposition de Certeau explicitly abjures the role of the scientific expert as the "master" of an (illusory) totalizing system, he appeals in the final analysis to observers of culture, like social science researchers, who will be in a (supraindividual) position to judge which practices foster progressive social change and to promote them as political action: "These ways of reappropriating the product-system, ways created by consumers, have as their goal a *therapeutics for deteriorating social relations*. . . . A politics of such ploys should be developed" (PEL xxiv, original emphasis).

Holding conflict in tension, the "culture" described by de Certeau seems to belong to the tradition of formalist theory. In fact, de Certeau values a kind of aesthetic formalism, in which elements are sustained in a *"formal harmony"* found in "everyday know-how" (PEL 75, 74), but his descriptions of this kind of formalism apply to a perpetually mobile situation that requires constant adjustment – as in the above description of the elements of culture or, to take his favored example, like Kant's tightrope walker who has to achieve a new equilibrium at each moment. What makes this discussion of culture as formal harmony suspect is the nature of its political turn, with its appeal to the special powers of the politically motivated social science researcher, who will apparently survey a field of cultural effects as a *totality*. This theoretical vantage point would then provide a reliable, because empirically validated, guide to political action – as though the "gaps" or incompletenesses revealed in the past would persist in the same way, and as though our intention to make use of those gaps in a particular way would bring about that desired outcome.

In this respect, perhaps as a result of his residual Marxism (and in particular, the vexed role of the intellectual in Marxist theory), de Certeau contravenes his own insistence on the temporary nature of culture's formal compromises.[5] For the development of a politics of "ploys" depends upon finding some method for distinguishing among practices to find those that are politically useful: how is it possible to separate out practices that "the system of products effects within the consumer grid" from those that are "art" or maneuvers by consumers in the room left to them by the system – a task made even more difficult if, as de Certeau admits, all the practices that count as "art" or "culture" aggregate to legitimize the system some of the time and displace it at other times (PEL xvii)? In that case, we would not be able to distinguish among practices on the basis of their effects: as de Certeau explains, "[s]imilar strategic deployments . . . do not produce identical effects" (PEL xvii). So which features will mark out "culture" from the system? How to separate the system of capitalism from the "culture" of creative consumption that takes place only in and through capitalism? It seems that no bright line divides complicitous practices from resistant ones.

Let me draw out the implications of this a bit further. If culture both develops in response to the system and takes only temporary shapes, as de Certeau observes, then the system must be changing somehow, or the culture would not be temporary. In other words, if cultures are temporary, there will be a temporal mismatch between social system and culture that precludes political application: the lessons learned from a culture derived from resistances to a given social structure may not apply at a later time to the state of affairs that will obtain when the social structure changes. Thus, the mechanism of social change in de Certeau is no less mysterious than it is in Bourdieu, for where Bourdieu explicitly approves the mismatch (as a source of limited freedom), de Certeau disavows it, in effect positing as a condition of tactical efficacy social structures that do not change in response to cultural innovations. In this case, it is not clear what political effects the art of maneuvering actually has or could have.

The Tactics of Complicit Resistance

In order to provide a more secure basis for distinguishing culture from social structure, de Certeau embarks on a theoretical path that only exacerbates his problems and risks reintroducing both intentionalism and exceptionalism into the bargain. He distinguishes between strategies, which are operations enabled by and adequated to social patterning, and *tactics*, which are individual practices that resist social patterning:

> By contrast with a strategy. . . a *tactic* is a calculated action determined by the absence of a proper locus. . . . It takes advantage of "opportunities" and depends on them, being without any base where it could stockpile its winnings, build up its own position, and plan raids. What it wins it cannot keep. This nowhere gives a tactic mobility, to be sure, but a mobility that must accept the chance offerings of the moment, and seize on the wing the possibilities that offer themselves at any given moment. It must vigilantly make use of the cracks that particular conjunctions open in the surveillance of the proprietary powers. . . . In short, a tactic is an art of the weak. (PEL 36–7)

Following his initial promise to champion the "dominated element" of society, and using the *position* of the individual vis-à-vis the system as his guide for separating tactics from strategies, de Certeau risks replicating the problems of all exceptionalist arguments: only the weak, those who are not aligned with the dominant reward structures of the system, are in a position to reveal the vulnerabilities of the system. At the same time, as we have seen, he re-imports a volitional account of political efficacy into his theory, for he regards the mass effect of multiple, unwitting practices of working in and through the dominant system as providing a potential resource, at the epiphenomenal level, for the researcher or theoretician, who would analyze and promote those practices that have proven to have political utility. As he says, a "politics of such ploys should be developed" (PEL xxiv).

In addition to the problems posed by his invocation of intentionalized subversion (as a function of the theoretician's assumed meta-position relative to the system), de Certeau creates another difficulty by offering two different accounts of the relationship between strategy and tactic. Even though he draws a line between the two – such that strategies always pattern structurally complicitous individual actions while tactics always challenge social structures – his first discussions of practice as creative consumption, or the devious and deviant uses the weak make of the strong, indicate that the two cannot be distinguished *a priori*, either by reference to descriptions of actions or to their outcomes. Individual consumers, for their own reasons and in contingent circumstances, make use of opportunities provided by the system's strengths as well as its gaps. But because "[s]imilar strategic deployments, when acting on different relationships of force, do not produce identical effects," the effects of individual consumers *per se* do not necessarily undermine or challenge the system (PEL xvii). The net effect of their "art," what de Certeau calls "culture," can both confirm as well as challenge, align with or evade, systemic forces – and always only *temporarily*.

The second account emerges in de Certeau's insistence on this distinction (despite the above-mentioned difficulties) when he relegates some practices to strategic action because they are formed, like the *habitus*, in accord with social dictates, while describing others as tactical. These tactics are calculated, volitional practices, which, whether intended to or not, have politically resistant effects. In this account, de Certeau ignores his own insight that practices do not have *a priori* or inherent meanings, but only temporary significances. His original analysis of the *co-implication of complicity with resistance* as well as his insistence on the *temporary* nature of tactics disappears, which is to say that de Certeau's theory, like Bourdieu's, also has a flaw in its reasoning about the temporality that links individual action to social structure.[6]

When de Certeau faults Bourdieu's concept of a temporal mismatch for dissociating the individual from the structure in such a way as to vitiate agency completely, he in turn, and despite his nod to the temporary, tacitly assumes that political resistance from the weak depends upon the structure *never* changing. In his model, the ploys of consumers-as-culture which provide some resistance against the dominant system at one moment somehow remain effective at another, even when new circumstances arise. If only the weak have no "proper place," and so are the only people in a position to be tactical, they must remain weak vis-à-vis the system (paradoxically) to have any agency whatsoever. Correlatively, in order for them to remain weak and *therefore most effective*, the system itself must remain the same. So, either the structures are proof against change *tout court* (i.e., new circumstances cannot dislodge the same old structure), which makes politically relevant agency impossible, or any changes that do transpire do so in some mysterious way, making politically relevant agency unnecessary, because the changes are not susceptible to calculation or direction. Thus, de Certeau retails a picture of the temporality of the relations between systemic determinations and individual agency such that it is difficult to see where, how, or why politically relevant agency would emerge.

In addition, while he initially acknowledges that both tactics and strategies may be both complicitous and resistant at the same time, de Certeau's theory treats these as mutually exclusive states. In effect, his distinction between strategy and tactic is simply another way of trying to ground an inherent distinction between complicitous and resistant actions, as though the meanings of actions could be ascertained independently of the contexts in which they are interpreted. Even if we were to try to grant such stability, problems arise. By what means and from what standpoint shall we learn enough about a system to locate its weak spots? De Certeau assumes that the constant testing by many individuals over time will locate these weaknesses evolutionarily and change the system perforce. But how will we know which actions changed the system, or whether the system would have changed without those actions? How and when will we know if an action is resistant or complicitous? When de Certeau labels practices as strategic or tactical, he is assuming a meta-objective point of view that stabilizes and spatializes this temporal flux. Even if we assume that, as researchers, we can in fact stand somewhere from which we can conceive a structure sufficiently comprehensively to be able, in principle, to compare the resistant action to the structure's dictates, we must still address when the comparison should take place and under what conditions. Unless we have a crystal ball in which to see the concatenation of effects from this action, clearly some time must pass before such a comparison can be attempted. But when will we know whether enough time has passed? Perhaps the more immediate effects will seem to challenge the structure but then, later, systemic forces will marshal sufficient counter-measures to return the structure to its initial state. Should we then consider this action to be resistant or complicitous? Resistant at first, complicitous later? Simultaneously complicit and resistant? When do we stop attributing effects to the action as cause? How are we to factor in other actions as concomitant or overriding causes?

Furthermore, de Certeau's proposal that resistant and complicitous actions can be disimplicated or parsed into separate moments not only fails to acknowledge that these actions have no inherent meaning – because the assignment of their meaning as subjected or subversive depends upon the changing contexts from which they are interpreted – it also neglects to discuss how we are to recognize structures themselves. For in order to grant an action strategic or tactical status it must be compared to the system, judged as conforming or evasive. Yet the system to which these actions are compared is itself deduced necessarily from those same actions by attributing complicity or resistance to them. Supporters of his position argue that de Certeau's explicit analogizing to linguistic theory offers a solution.[7] For example, de Certeau points out that "in linguistics, 'performance' and 'competence' are different: the act of speaking (with all the enunciative strategies that implies) is not reducible to a knowledge of the language" (PEL xiii).

But this analogy between everyday practices and utterances that operationalize language rules in innovative and productive ways bears investigating: how useful is it for discerning the rule-governing system, or for distinguishing categories of "utterance" that more or less follow those rules? De Certeau himself rejects the notion that the *langue* is somehow there to be known independently of the *paroles*. Rather, it is deduced from a selection of actual speech acts, in an operation he calls the "cut out," a first step of theorizing (PEL 62).[8] If it is the case that the system exists nowhere but in the *paroles*, or actions, then determining the relative conformity or non-conformity of an utterance to its "governing system" has a tautological feel. In other words, the analogy suggests that de Certeau is saying something equivalent to: "Language has a structure, such that there are two kinds of utterance, those that function in harmony with the structure, i.e., reflect the rules of the structure, and those that do not." Strategies would reflect the rules of the structure, tactics would not. But the linguistic category under which the latter would fall, according to this analogy, is "meaninglessness" (significantly, not non-sense, which obeys the rules of a given language), which means that, in the case of de Certeau's distinction, tactics would not be relevant to the structure at all – they would look like idiosyncratic, meaningless behaviors. While they might indeed be unusually creative, they would not link up with the structure sufficiently to constitute a counter to it.

Nonetheless, such "meaningless" actions might still have productive effects, in the sense of gumming up the works or providing inspiration to others. Commentators on de Certeau's work frequently admonish readers not to take "resistance" in the politically strong sense of revolutionary activity, but rather to see such actions as "confirming the unsutured nature of the social . . . and the ubiquitous eruption of the heterogeneous,"[9] or as having a "deeply ambivalent character" – not necessarily "oppositional" or "progressive" but fundamentally "conservative."[10] Apart from the fact that de Certeau's own argument for the development of a "politics of such ploys" is here being denied, is this not simply another way of saying that resistance and complicity cannot be distinguished *a priori*? An action that gums up the works or is highly idiosyncratic, and in this way constitutes a drag on the system (whether to progressive or conservative effect makes no difference), is by definition being distinguished from that system. But it cannot be specified *as* a drag on a system, as opposed to a support for it, simply by reference to its own qualities. It must be compared, over time, to the larger system which, again, is deduced from the actions that seem to transpire "within" it but in fact are the only material out of which the system is made in the first place.

Some commentators (e.g., Highmore) have suggested that de Certeau avoids this difficulty by postulating a plurality of systems. Let me offer an example: a large number of people attending extended church services every day might slow down the advance of a dominant impulse toward modernization under capitalism. Church-going practices would be strategies within a religious system, yet function like tactics within the capitalist system. This solution returns us to Bourdieu's *habitus*, for "resistance" here indexes the degree to which a given practice from an old structure is out of step with a new structure. But in this case, nothing would remain of de Certeau's emphasis on the individual creative deployment of "chance offerings of the moment," the "seiz[ing] on the wing the possibilities that offer themselves at any given moment," still less of the political urgency he gives to "vigilantly mak[ing] use of the cracks that particular conjunctions open in the surveillance of the proprietary powers" (PEL 37).[11]

In any case, de Certeau provides no story sufficient to account for structural change. Because tactics never shift positionally weak people into a position of strength (at least not without the help of the all-seeing research scientist), the structures seem to be proof against change, making tactical practitioners politically irrelevant.[12] De Certeau more or less admits as much when he describes folk tales as the repositories of tactical knowledge:

> The formality of everyday practices is indicated in these tales, which frequently reverse the relationships of power and, like the stories of miracles, ensure the victory of the unfortunate in a fabulous, utopian space. This space protects the weapons of the weak against the reality of the established order . . . [T]hese "fabulous" stories offer their audience a repertory of tactics for future use. (PEL 23)

But the "weapons of the weak" hidden in these stories are only weapons *in the stories*, in "a fabulous, utopian space." If the tactics actually work, we have no way of knowing it, and de Certeau provides no means for distinguishing between the wishes of the unfortunate to overcome their oppressors and a "knowledge" that could actually change their circumstances. What is more, as noted above, in his model there is no guarantee that a tactic developed in the past will work under future circumstances, unless the structure to which it is addressed remains the same, in which case we might just as well say that the *tactic didn't work in the first place*, so why bother to memorialize it in the "hidden" recesses of folk tales? Or if it did "work," then what exactly did it accomplish if the structure remains intact? If it works in the realm of "culture," but not in the realm of social structures, as de Certeau's descriptions suggest, then what value do these tactics have for the oppressed? Aren't they simply a form of adaptation to the status quo?

De Certeau even concedes that unless practices are "regulated by stable local units" tactics will go "off their tracks," that is, be indistinguishable from strategies (PEL 40). So tactics can only be recognized as such so long as the system is stable and in force; otherwise they do not engage the system at all or become complicitous with it, making political agency impossible. But because the "culture" that is made up (solely) of "artful" practices sometimes reinforces structures, that criterion for distinguishing tactic from strategy cannot be applied.

Overdetermination, Internalization, and the Politics of Stable Structures

We can detect the source of de Certeau's difficulties by returning to the idea of practices. It is impossible to distinguish tactic from strategy – or complicit from resistant action – in any *a priori* way, as de Certeau concedes, because it is not possible to read backwards from an action to its regulating force. In arguing for a space of relatively *undetermined* action, de Certeau (unlike Bourdieu) makes the mistake of assuming that something in the action itself will reveal its source and degree of determination. But practices are *overdetermined*. Bourdieu puts it this way:

> practices cannot be deduced either from the present conditions which may seem to have provoked them or from the past conditions which have produced the *habitus*, the durable principle of their production. . . . [but only] through the scientific work of performing the interrelationship of these two states of the social world. . . (LP 56)

What is more, given that "culture" is in flux, as de Certeau so rigorously describes, how will we compare any given action to a "structure" which itself exists nowhere but in this flux of practices? How will we know which practices reveal the determinations of the structure and which reveal resistance to the structure? Bourdieu avoids this circularity when he resists dividing actions into categories: all actions are evidence of the system and all origins of actions (intentions, desires, social patterning) point back to that overarching system. Thus, de Certeau is right to say that Bourdieu's procedure gives us no information about the operation of the system, that it amounts to "an affirmation of reality" rather than an analysis of how a state of affairs gets generated and controlled. But

Bourdieu is right to avoid the *petitio principii* that haunts de Certeau's model.

French social change theory inflected by the work of Bourdieu and de Certeau shows despite itself that the thought-lessness of practices does not make them more likely to reinforce dominant culture (e.g. excessive drinking) nor does becoming conscious of a practice (say, a gender practice) make it easy to choose to act otherwise. Because practices are observed regularities, they constitute evidence of a regulating force, like a social structure. Yet because, like habits, they arise from diverse sources (e.g. a self-conscious decision to discipline one's mind and body, or a socially-directed regimen, or a psychodynamically generated compulsion) and from complicated forces (including the intersection of peer pressures, familial routines, occupational requirement, generational acculturation, psychological predilection, and so forth), they become entrenched in ways that make it impossible to separate out, simply by reference to the behaviors themselves, conscious from unconscious motives, external from internal determinants, individual from social factors, and oppressive from liberatory effects. The *overdetermination* of these sources and the co-implication of their effects mean that those actions do not reveal the nature of the regulation. De Certeau's own observation that a system does not have univocal effects points to this overdetermination, to the impossibility of deciding whether a given action's "departure" from systemic dictates is a legitimate expression of a multivocality inherent in the system or evidence of creative transgression from that system. Just as we cannot read off directly from performative intention to political effect, neither can we read off directly from practices to the source, degree, or univocity of their regulation.

The indeterminacy of the status of practices derives from this overdetermination, which has a different origin in each of the theories. In the case of Bourdieu, the indeterminacy is due to the unpredictable variety of ways that the *habitus*, an internalized version of a past structure, will interact with present conditions. In the case of de Certeau, the indeterminacy is due to the impossibility of distinguishing strategies from tactics at any given point in time. In effect, the functions Bourdieu assigns to the *habitus* as internalized "past structure" appear in de Certeau as "strategy," whereas the functions Bourdieu assigns to the *habitus* as taking up contingent present conditions appear in de Certeau as "tactic." Each author asserts the possibility of disambiguating one from the other, and each assigns science this role, even though, as we have seen, each also concedes the serious difficulty, if not impossibility, of actually doing so. That is, each regards this indeterminacy of practices – evidenced by their overdetermination – as the obstacle to the scientific and political value of the theory.

In my view, however, this indeterminacy not only renders the empirical scientific project dubious while compromising its political utility, it also marks the point at which an alternative formulation becomes possible, as we will see in a moment. But first it will be useful to look a little more closely at the crucial supposition for both theories – the origin of the regularity of practices. Both theorists postulate that the observed regularity is due to structural constraints (rather than, say, to human nature), but in Bourdieu these constraints are internalized, whereas in de Certeau they remain external to the individual. We find only these two options for how such regularities arise: either they derive from the *internalization* of a structure (Bourdieu), or they are due to the potency of an *external* constraint, from which all behavior, whether in conformity or in reaction, derives a certain regulation. In other words, both Bourdieu and de Certeau posit the presence of a rigid or invariant structure which functions in fundamentally the same way for whole groups of individuals. Whether this structure is internalized, as in Bourdieu, or remains purely external, as in de Certeau, the structure is conceived as indifferent to any individual's encounter with it, as perduring no matter what individual or aggregate behaviors occur within it, and as deducible from the responses to it.

It is perhaps more difficult to see this point in de Certeau. Recall that tactics require the presence of a stable social structure without which they "go off their tracks." But even when they are on their tracks, tactics have no particular purchase on the social structures within which they maneuver, forming rather a "culture" that exists side by side with – rather than articulating with or transforming – the social structure. Because de Certeau resists the idea of internalized or inculcated dispositions, we may ask in what manner do the strategist or the tactician encounter the structure within which they move? If the structure is not internalized, then it can only be encountered as an externality: individuals bump up against these externalities as they go about their lives, behaving like automatic pool cleaners or Roomba vacuuming robots that turn when they hit a wall. In this way, both strategists and tacticians learn (some of) the parameters in which they live (or they can learn practices which they adopt without entering into their own "experiments" with the limitations). The regularities observed in the tactics or the strategies are a tracing of the regularities of those limitations: because the structure remains the same, different people will bump up against the same limitations, collectively marking the boundaries, so to speak, of the structure by their own "independent" activities. Whether they follow the structure or depart from it, whether strategic or tactical, these behaviors are a function of encounters with the structure and so inevitably trace out its contours, its limitations, and its enabling properties. Thus, both tactics and strategies are governed by and are evidence of the presence of the same social structure.

Both Bourdieu and de Certeau, then, conceive of a social structure as invariant and perdurable with respect to the behavior of human beings. Inside or outside, the social structure is unaffected by the actions of individuals – or groups of individuals. Paradoxically, it is the perduring quality of the social structure that provides each theorist with the grounds for his political claims for social change. In Bourdieu, the social structure pre-exists the internalization; the structure remains unchanged in the encounter with the individual, and it persists in and through the process of internalization. Bourdieu depends on the social structure inside the individual *matching* the social structure outside the individual, such that all individuals in a group contain the same social structure inside them in the form of a shared *habitus*. Because Bourdieu imagines that the social structure remains stable and is internalized *in the same way* by everyone in the group, this internalization serves as the linchpin of Bourdieu's claims for a nonindividual and nonintentional, politically relevant agency. De Certeau agrees that this picture of internalization amounts to the preservation of the social structure *per se*: for this reason, he rejects internalization because it subordinates individual autonomy to structural dictates. From his perspective, if individuals internalize the social structure as is, then they will not be able to act creatively or autonomously. Yet, as we have seen, in de Certeau's model, the structure perdures *outside* the individual; only if it *remains the same*, can tactics remain "on their tracks" and de Certeau gain political traction for his theory.

Both de Certeau and Bourdieu make the same mistake when they conceive internalization: each imagines that internalization inculcates the social structure more or less *as is*. As a result, both theories suffer at crucial junctures from a failure of historicization, in the one case because the invariant social structure superintends action from inside the individual, and in the other case because the invariant social structure superintends action from outside the individual. In such models, meaningful change is not only vitiated but the very basis for conceiving historicity also disappears. In relying on the unchanging nature of the social structure, these theorists counterproductively position ahistoricity squarely at the center of their theories. Neither admits the possibility of another alternative to internalizing or externalizing an invariant social structure, to wit, that the social structure could be internalized *differently*. I will be arguing that these theorists disavow this alternative: they deploy this possibility when they seek to ground the historicizing capacity in their theories, but they implicitly or explicitly deny these insights when they turn to finding a basis for their political valence. In the next section, I will show that both

Bourdieu and de Certeau rely explicitly on psychoanalysis as a prime example of a properly historicizing theory, before going on to show how psychoanalysis functions for them in a disavowed form.

Psychoanalysis as Historicizing Theory

The group of French social scientists to which Bourdieu and de Certeau belonged has strong ties to the psychoanalytic movement in France. De Certeau, as mentioned, was a member of the Freudian School of Paris. For his part, Bourdieu relied increasingly heavily on psychoanalytic concepts, such as *Verneinung* and *Spaltung*, and he wrote *Questions de sociologie* (in 1980, the same year he published *The Logic of Practice*) to explore the relationship between sociology and psychoanalysis, without, however, rejecting one in favor of the other.[13] The foregoing discussion has suggested some of the ways in which psychoanalysis affects the thinking of both theorists. Internalization, predispositions, over-determination, condensation – all these psychoanalytic concepts serve important functions, even if they appear in attenuated form. But more importantly, although each theorist has expressed reservations about, even hostility towards, some aspects of psychoanalysis, both regard it as an exemplary *historicizing* discourse, albeit for different reasons. Because psychoanalysis has been rejected by American cultural studies scholars as unacceptably "universalizing," it is worth noting that both Bourdieu and de Certeau dissent from this view. Indeed, it is the means by which each makes his argument on a *historical* basis.

For his part, Bourdieu relies on the psychoanalytic conception of the unconscious as the support for his theory of *habitus* as internalized structures. The influence of psychoanalysis on this theory appears in its stress both on a nonconscious knowledge or significance and on a nonintentional purposiveness:

> [B]eing produced by a *modus operandi* which is not consciously mastered, the discourse contains an "objective intention," as the Scholastics put it, which outruns the conscious intentions of its apparent author and constantly offers new pertinent stimuli to the *modus operandi* of which it is the product and which functions as a kind of "spiritual automaton." (LP 57)

Any student of psychoanalysis will recognize in this a portrait of the unconscious, here represented by the *"modus operandi."* In this passage, Bourdieu relies on the fundamental principle of psychoanalysis – the unconscious as the reservoir of idiosyncratically associated

Vorstellungrepräsentanzen and *Darstellungrepräsentanzen*. In other words, Bourdieu takes the psychoanalytic position that the unconscious is a product of an individual's contingent experience of a world that is structured in ways beyond her ken.

Because practices originate both in objective structures and in the *habitus*, some additional operation is required to distinguish the two types of history encoded in practices, an operation provided by science. Bourdieu's reliance on the concept of *overdetermination* develops in a psychoanalytic rather than a Marxian key:

> Because they tend to reproduce the regularities immanent in the conditions in which their generative principle was produced while adjusting to the demands inscribed as objective potentialities in the situation as defined by the cognitive and motivating structures that constitute the *habitus*, *practices cannot be deduced either from the present conditions which may seem to have provoked them or from the past conditions which have produced the habitus, the durable principle of their production.* They can therefore only be accounted for . . . through the scientific work of performing the interrelationship of these two states of the social world that the *habitus* performs, while concealing it, in and through practice. (LP 56, my emphasis)[14]

Here practices are doubly conditioned – by the *habitus*, itself an internalization of past social conditions, and by the current social conditions which provide the "raw material," so to speak, that the *habitus* sifts for meaning. The *habitus*, as we have seen, provides the perceptual and conceptual framework for seizing the current social conditions as opportunities for action. This double conditioning, this overdetermination of practices, makes it impossible to tell what the contributions of past versus present social conditions may have been in the production of the practices. In effect, the *habitus* crystallizes the past in a way that makes the present "take shape" in accord with its dispositions. The structures embodied in the *habitus* do not "show" themselves as such, because the *habitus* does the work of adjusting past to present, in effect making the present over in the image of the past.

Let us leave aside for the moment the question as to whether a scientific study so conceived could be based on anything other than circular reasoning (where, for example, does the past structure exist for scientific study separate from these overdetermined practices?) in order to focus on Bourdieu's conception of the unconscious as crucial to his understanding of the *habitus*. In the adjustment between past and present, in the taking up of the present situation by reference to past meanings internalized and operating without our knowledge, Bourdieu recovers one aspect of the functioning of the unconscious as it is understood psychoanalytically – its appropriation of the present by way of past experience that is psychically significant. The unconscious records a past made meaningful by its experience with others, and it grasps the present by reference to those meanings. In this way, the *habitus* functions like the unconscious: it serves as the framework through which all perception and cognition take place. Bourdieu also equates the unconscious with the *habitus* in that neither recognizes the past *as past* (in this passage he says that the unconscious "is never anything other than the forgetting of history") even as it memorializes the past and lifts it to the principle by which all present situations will be understood (LP 56). Like the unconscious, the *habitus* operates automatically ("a modus operandi which is not consciously mastered"):

> the *habitus*, which is constituted in the course of an individual history, imposing its particular logic on incorporation, and through which agents partake of the history objectified in institutions, is what makes it possible to inhabit institutions, to appropriate them practically, and so to keep them in activity, continuously pulling them from the state of dead letters, reviving the sense deposited in them, but at the same time imposing the revisions and transformations that reactivation entails. (LP 57)

In this way, the unconscious serves as the example *par excellence* of the way that individuals are articulated with history: the unconscious is itself historical. Finally, while it seems that a signal difference between the *habitus* and the unconscious is that one is collectivized and the other individual, Bourdieu himself has drawn the conclusion that the unconscious itself is somehow both.[15]

Where Bourdieu uses psychoanalysis to ground his scientific project, de Certeau uses it to critique the privileging of science, by tracing a path in Freud's work from the discourse of the "Expert" to the discourse of the common man. In his view, the later Freudian writings accord due weight to the "ordinary" and embody a properly historicizing approach. Speaking of *Civilization and Its Discontents*, de Certeau notes that Freud "is in the same boat as everyone else and begins to laugh":

> An ironic and wise madness is linked to the fact that he has lost the singularity of a competence and found himself, anyone or no one, in the common history. In the philosophical tale that is *Civilization and Its Discontents*, the ordinary man is the speaker. He is the point in the discourse where the scientist and the common man come together – the return of the other (everyone and no one) into the place which had been so carefully set apart from him. . . . The approach to culture begins when the ordinary man *becomes* the narrator, when it is he who defines the (common) place of discourse and the (anonymous) space of its development. This place is no more given to the speaker of the discourse than to anyone else. (PEL 4–5)

Here de Certeau is not making a minor exception with respect to psycho-analytic discourse: what he finds so appealing in Freud's later practices as a writer and as a psychoanalyst are the insights into the importance of the ordinary as crucial in human history. Additionally, psychoanalytic practice is exemplary of what de Certeau calls a "contemporary historic-ity" (PEL 12). Drawing a parallel between Freud's ceding of the role of expert and Wittgenstein's descriptions of the role of the philosopher of ordinary language, de Certeau paints an accurate picture of psychoana-lytic practice:[16]

> By being "caught" within ordinary language, the philosopher no longer has his own (propre) appropriable place. Any position of mastery is denied him. The analyzing discourse and the analyzed "object" are in the same situation: both are organized by the practical activity with which they are concerned, both are determined by rules they neither establish nor see clearly. . . . Philosophical or scientific privilege disappears into the ordi-nary. (PEL 11)

The psychoanalyst and the ordinary language philosopher engage in a his-torical process, and the "object" of their investigation is the very historical process that engages them, a process which grants no special privilege to the expert/master/psychoanalyst/philosopher, for these are "in the same boat as everyone else." Under these conditions, universalizing gestures come undone. As de Certeau puts it, "from what privileged place could they be signified? There [are] *facts* that are no longer *truths*" (PEL 11).

In drawing out the implications of this lack of a privileged place from which to interpret the historicity of our existence, so to speak, de Certeau strengthens the connection between Wittgenstein and Freud, to the point of arguing that Wittgenstein has a fundamentally psychoanalytic concep-tion of the subject's "foreignness": "we are *foreigners* on the inside – *but there is no outside* . . . a situation close to the Freudian position except that Wittgenstein does not allow himself an unconscious referent to name this foreignness-at-home" (PEL 13–14). So, like Bourdieu, de Certeau also uses psychoanalysis as the fulcrum on which he bases the historical dimension of his work.

If it will be a surprise to American cultural studies scholars, who have rejected psychoanalytic theory as dehistoricizing, to learn that both theorists (each of whom has a strong following in cultural studies) regard psychoanalysis as the historicist discourse *par excellence*, and depend upon it as the crucial tool to enable theories of agency in a historical key, it may be even more surprising to find that, as I will now argue, the weak-nesses in precisely *the historicist aspirations* of these French theorists are due to their suppression of the historicizing properties of psychoanalysis in favor of bolstering their claims for political agency.

Retroversively Articulating the Subject with History

Bourdieu and de Certeau offer two options for the historical articulation of individual to social structure in order to account for social change: while in both cases, the past persists in an unchanged form to govern activity or changes mysteriously, in Bourdieu's case it persists (as the out-dated *habitus* in new conditions) by means of an internalized structure and in de Certeau's as the external determinant of tactics, as we have seen. But these options do not exhaust the possibilities for a properly historical articulation of individual to social structure. It is on this question of how the past conditions the present that a psychoanalytic conceptual framework can be brought to bear.

The crux for these theories with respect to agency turns precisely on the question of historicity: how does the theory find regularities that make behaviors intelligible without de-historicizing the individual's responses to new contingencies? How to conceive the articulation of individual activities with particular social spaces without lapsing into determinism or radical subjectivism? How to "read out" the history embedded in practices that have multiple determinants? We have already seen how Bourdieu's and de Certeau's answers to these questions include both individuals appropriating elements in historically contingent situations and stable social structures that somehow guide those appropriations into cultural channels (by internalization or by external constraint). We have also seen how psychoanalytic theory serves as a prime example of historicized theory for each theorist. The question before us now is to what extent these theorists take up psychoanalytic tools in building historicity into their theories. As we will see, each tacitly disavows the psychoanalytic tools he has found so useful, a disavowal undertaken for the purpose of salvaging political agency.

Let us begin with Bourdieu. Given the close relationship between the functions of the *habitus* and the functions of the unconscious, we might wonder why Bourdieu bothers to invent the *habitus* at all. I believe there are two related reasons, the first of which we have already touched on. Like the unconscious, the *habitus* preserves external structures in an interiorized form, the advantages of which we have seen. But unlike the unconscious, which internalizes these structures in idiosyncratic ways (more on this in a moment), the *habitus* preserves them in the same way for everyone in the group. This move allows Bourdieu to collectivize the unconscious, so to speak, in order to create a politically relevant dimension to his theory. Because a group shares the same *habitus*, individual behaviors will show the same regularities, and then, theoretically, the researcher would be in a position to assess the effects of structures for political purposes (a conclusion considerably complicated by Bourdieu's admission that the relationship between structure and practice cannot be read off directly from practices).

The second reason gets us to the heart of Bourdieu's disavowal of psychoanalysis. Like the unconscious, the *habitus* finds in present circumstances some "incitement," some galvanic element that puts to work the mechanism of "snatching" or appropriating the present by means of the past, an "incitement" that is not a function of some quality *inherent* in that element but simply serves the purposes of the *habitus* as it articulates the past with the present. In Bourdieu's formulation, the *habitus* moderates a ratio of past to present conditions, a ratio manifested in the form of practices. It is at this point that overdetermination, in the psychoanalytic sense, enters the Bourdieusian scheme, where it threatens to render the theory as problematic as it does for de Certeau's distinction between strategies and tactics. To mitigate the effects of this overdetermination, Bourdieu has to posit that any given *habitus* remains essentially unchanged: the component parts of past and present that it articulates retain their discrete identities, ready to be parsed by scientific research. Without the perdurability of the *habitus*, and the unchanging nature of the past structure embodied in it, Bourdieu's claims to discover (scientifically) the properties of governing structures (even in their historical dimension) lose their persuasiveness. With respect to its internalized function of articulating past and present, the *habitus* operates like the unconscious, but with respect to the way it leaves unchanged the elements of past and present (so that they can be disarticulated by the scientist) and its own unchanging nature, it is singularly *unlike* the unconscious: in the unconscious, the appropriation of the present by the past works a transformation on both past and present, such that no disentanglement of the scientific sort envisioned by Bourdieu can take place. Like the *habitus*, the unconscious acts creatively to preserve and rework the past with the materials furnished in the present, but with a crucial difference, the difference provided by retroversion: when the unconscious seizes these present materials, they in turn structure and illuminate the past as *different*. The past is not forgotten or replaced by a "different" past, but, as Žižek puts it, the coordinates by which it is known and valued change as a result of this appropriation. Retroversion produces a change in perspective on the past.

In psychoanalytic parlance, this retroversive mechanism is known as *Nachträglichkeit* or *après-coup*. Without some such mechanism, the psychic structures preserving the past would be overwhelmed by the multifarious contingencies of the present, or the past would completely transform the present back into itself. In other words, without the retroversive effect, *there is no history qua history*. It is in the work of knitting up present contingencies (by way of overdetermination, condensation, displacement, and so forth) into the fabric of past structuration that the past comes to be something *different* than what it was, while the present comes to be something familiar. It is indeed in this unconscious activity that the subject (and agency) itself exists – and nowhere else. But in Bourdieu's model, because the structure is internalized *in its original form*, all individual variation is lost, which, while a bonus for the collectivizing side of the theory, means that nothing can ever really change:

> The *habitus* which, at every moment, structures new experiences in accordance with the structures produced by past experiences, which are modified by the new experiences within the limits defined by their power of selection, brings about a unique integration, dominated by the earliest experiences, of the experiences statistically common to members of the same class. . . . the *habitus* tends to ensure its own constancy and its defence against change through the selection it makes within new information by rejecting information capable of calling into question its accumulated information. (LP 60–1)

The *habitus*, unlike the unconscious, is not *itself* transformed by the encounter with the present; neither are past and present transformed by their combination in practices. The *habitus* merely enables a variety of practices, each of which incorporates past and present in ways that do not alter their meanings.

It is not difficult, therefore, to see why Bourdieu recasts the unconscious as the *habitus*: not only would the retroversive transformation of an internalized structure make impossible the scientific project of disentangling the past from present in practices, a project on which the political valence of his theory rides, it would also mean that any analysis of such transformed interiorities would have to move away from the sociological level in order to take account of the highly personal ways in which individuals internalize the "same" social structures. Yet without something like a *nachträglich* mechanism, the theory loses its historicizing capability, which is to say that the failure to press the psychoanalytic concept of the unconscious is at the root of the de-historicization compromising Bourdieu's theory.

A similar de-historicizing effect occurs in de Certeau's disavowal of psychoanalysis. Just as the *habitus* recapitulates the key functions of the unconscious – articulating past with present in a purposive but nonconscious way – so does the tactic. De Certeau, as we have seen, has a more nuanced understanding of the relationship of past to present in this articulation, as he indicates when he says that both the "analyzing discourse and the analyzed 'object' are in the same situation: both are organized by the practical activity with which they are concerned" (PEL 11). Here he seems to recognize that practices do not merely bring past and present together in forms unchanged sufficiently for scientific research to disentangle them, as in Bourdieu, but rather that each element acts upon the other, a mutual conditioning that gets us closer to the retroversive action of the unconscious. Only if the meaning of the past can change for the present will the present have its own distinctive status. And if the present escapes the determinations of the past to any extent, the past itself will change as a result. It is in this retroversive articulation of past and present, as present contingencies are read in light of the past, and the past is re-interpreted in light of present contingencies, that history – moving time – can take place. But de Certeau immediately falls away from this insight in the very next moment, for "both [past and present] are determined by rules they neither establish nor see clearly" (PEL 11). At this point, the historical dimension is fatally compromised, for the structures themselves exist independently of the individuals, while the rules (presumably) are felt in the same way by everyone under their regulation.

What is at stake here? In the operation of the unconscious, at every moment, the individual seizes on some particular feature of a present situation because and by means of past meaningful experience. This ongoing adjustment to the present by way of the past – the way in which the present's failure to conform explicitly to the past is marked through (the necessity of) the work of practices, or the work it takes to make the present meaningful in light of the past – is the process by which history is both engaged (as that which precedes the subject) and made (as that which the subject brings into being). In this sense, the taking up of present contingencies in inventive ways that re-make them into personally mean-ingful devices for getting along within the "tracks" laid down by a social structure provides a fair analogy to unconscious workings. This work is like the dream-work that grasps a congeries of elements and re-fashions them through functions like displacement and condensation for present purposes. And the temporary cultural space is like the dream space – a space of florid creativity that always moves within the same limitations, tethered to the same preoccupations. But the difference is that the materi-als on which the unconscious works are internal psychic materials with internal psychic effects, while the materials taken up by Certeauesque individuals are external materials with external social effects. While this model does not rule out the possibility that each individual may have his or her own, more or less unique, way of appropriating these materials, de Certeau postulates that the social structure must provide a large-scale regularity for these practices as a group, else they would not appear as practices or "culture."

It is on this point that de Certeau comes closest to a properly his-toricized account – and then disavows it. For if the taking up of present contingencies is a more individualized matter in de Certeau than Bourdieu (for whom individuals are "forged" by the internalization of the social constraints) and so underwrites the investigation of historically particular significances, nonetheless the social structure, as de Certeau presents it, perdures with its "content" intact, just as it does in the case of Bourdieu. The social structure makes specific rules, it operates in particular locations under such-and-such conditions, it orients power into discrete channels but, as we have seen, in the same way over time for everyone in the group. It must do so, as we saw above, in order to provide the regularities from which de Certeau seeks to fashion the political charge of his theory. In short, it is a structure of *materiality*, the durability of which underwrites the theory's political dimension: all individuals encounter the same structure, with its set of meanings, proscriptions, and forces. The perduring "content" of the structure is precisely what vitiates the possibility of historicity in his account.

The Extimate Cause of the Symbolic

But what alternative could there be? Could there be such a thing as a content-free operation linking subjects to the social field? As we have seen, the genesis of the Möbius subject occurs by way of a formal, content-less function, the extimate cause. At the psychic level, the operation necessary to bring a subject into being – through retroversion – is Symbolic inscription by way of the formal negation. The striking difference between social structures and the Symbolic is that the former are content-full, collectively shared, stable structures of meaning, whereas the latter is a psychic register originating from a formal (content-free) negation that comes to have an idiosyncratic – not collective – meaning for the individual. The tendency in theoretical discourse today to conflate given social structures (a gender system, an economic system, a class system) with the Symbolic is both pervasive and incorrect. Social structures themselves are not the Symbolic or its equivalents. When Bourdieu (or Althusser, for that matter) talk about the internalization of the social structure as part of the production of subjectivity (e.g. interpellation), they miscognize the relationship between the Symbolic and social structures. The move, which has its origin in the pre-psychoanalytic discourse of Marxism, is tempting, but it is a temptation that has to be resisted in order to preserve a conception of the subject that is both minimally free from external determinants and historicized.

Thanks to the Symbolic (although this is not something about which individuals may feel grateful), what makes a person a person is not the internalization of social systems (Bourdieu) nor an encounter with the same social system as the rest of the group, even if they live in the same society (de Certeau). We might say that Bourdieu and de Certeau posit an "Imaginary" Symbolic, to use Lacan's idiom – one that has the same structure throughout and produces mirror-relations between people – as opposed to a genuine Symbolic. The Lacanian Symbolic is not a universal or even a collective system, nor is it a system that precedes or generates the subject. In fact, it is not a system at all: it is a psychic register that arises with the emergence of the subject. In the psychoanalytic formulation, the network of signifiers available to the child for making meaning may be the same as those used by others, but for each child, the meanings attached to those signifiers will have a dimension of idiosyncratic, particularized value.

How does the extimate cause bring this idiosyncratic Symbolic into being? When the child encounters the world of meaning (whether this is in language, or more frequently, in bodily practices), she does so by way of her primary caregiver. There is no way at that stage for the child to sort out which are the *caregiver's* idiosyncratic meanings (fear of frogs, for example), which are fantasms of the *child's* own making (the picture on the wall of Mrs. Piggle-Wiggle reminds her of her Nana), which are *familial* practices ("brush your teeth after you put on your pajamas"), and which are a function of larger *social worlds* (always, of course, interpreted through parents, teachers, friends, and so forth). As a result, the child lives in a claustrophobic world wherein all meaningfulness is linked to the primary caregiver and associated with the pleasures and fears that accompany the demand for love.[17]

In order for the child to become subjectified, capable of functioning outside the dyad, the child must somehow come to understand that the caregiver is not the source of meaning. That is, the child has to learn *both* that the caregiver doesn't establish the child's meaning once and for all *and* that the caregiver's meaning also comes from elsewhere. It is the function of the formal negation (which, because the mother is so often the primary caregiver, Lacan denominates the *Non/Nom-du-Père*) to open up this possibility. By negating, or crossing-out, the meaning world of the primary caregiver (as experienced and construed by the child), the negation does not replace it with a new world of meanings with pre-existing significance. It does not install a different set of contents *per se*, but rather merely opens a place of nondeterminacy. When the negation says "not that," it does not specify instead a "this." It merely leaves open the possibility of something else.[18] Thanks to this nondeterminacy, the apparently stable meanings of the dyad become more fluid: signification can circulate, signifiers can be appropriated and take on new resonance, and the child can become a Möbius subject, a subject that embodies excess for other subjects and for itself. This process is the process by which any subject enters the field as a *social subject*.

We can now turn to my earlier claim that the efforts Bourdieu and de Certeau make to dissolve the nondeterminacy of practices actually undermines their theories. Despite their efforts to believe the contrary, this nondeterminacy is irremediable, rendering the scientific project dubious and the political project futile. So, each is right to regard the excess of signification as an obstacle to completing their scientific and political projects, even though they are mistaken in thinking that the excess could be eradicated. They also fail to accord this excess its proper role: it is absolutely essential for subjectification itself. Only the encounter with significative excess produces the subject as a *social* subject, serving as the means for freeing the child from the closed world of dyadic meanings and ushering him into the world of circulating (not completely stable) meanings available for appropriation and re-signification.

Here is the crucial point. Thanks to this excess, the social world of meanings – the Symbolic world in which the child learns that its meaning as signifier is subject to perpetual negotiation and appropriation – is not a *content-full structure*. The Symbolic is not a systematic set of proscriptions, rules, practices, or any other substantively specifiable content shared alike by everyone else in the social field: it is not a system of stable meanings, even though it may seem that way at times and even though one might fervently wish or imagine it to be so. Rather, the Symbolic is a psychic register, the register of significative excess and appropriability. In this register, in the mind of the individual, resides a collocation of meanings that have significance for that person, meanings which are always to some extent *fantasmatically* shared with others. These meanings come from the world of bodily experience, parental behaviors and dicta, extended familial practices and beliefs, the school environment, and the larger social world. Of course, people sometimes overlap in their habitation of these worlds: siblings, schoolmates, neighbors, party members, fellow religionists, countrymen, and conlinguists may share signifiers and contexts. Yet the significance invested in even the most closely overlapping elements may be radically different from person to person – and from time to time for the same person. Even children raised in the same house have different experiences and attach different meanings to the same events, parental actions, family narratives, and emotional states taking place in their home environments.

Once the child fully "enters the Symbolic" (again, a function of adding a formal negation rather than installing a systematic content), then the first meanings from the primary caregiver take on new significance. (We will return in a later chapter to the stages of separation and alienation through which the child becomes subjectified.) The child moves from the world of the Real (where what is given is absolute) through the Imaginary (where what is meaningful is a function of the equivalence between self and other) to the Symbolic (where what is given can stand for something else that is not present).[19] Contradictory ideas, old and new experiences, meanings from diverse and conflictual loci, exist side by side. The Symbolic is neither *externally* (de Certeau) nor *internally* (Bourdieu) the same for all members in the social field.

Neither does the past perdure in a stable form in the Symbolic, although elements of the past persist associated to new meanings. This is the operation of the *après-coup*, or retroversive re-signification. Let's take as an example the closeness a child feels when his mother sits on his bed and tells him stories at night. Suppose that the mother has her own reasons for this ritual: suppose that she is trying to minimize the time she spends alone with her husband. The child who experiences the mother's closeness as comforting before the intervention of the paternal negation may come to feel that the mother is *too* close afterwards. The pleasure may remain, but if the meaning of the act is understood as the mother's desire for the child to return to the meaning-world of the dyad, the child may begin to feel anxious. This retroversive movement of re-signification, as we have seen, is required for historicity itself – for the past to be sufficiently transformable for present contingencies to take on new meanings.

When Bourdieu and de Certeau tacitly rely on an invariant social structure to regulate individual appropriations in order for them to appear as a collective form (the *habitus* or the culture of tactics), they deny the particularity, the fluidity, and retroversivity of the Symbolic even as they rely on these properties for their descriptions of appropriability. The consequence is that the temporality of historicity that they claim to respect vanishes. As we have seen, each performs this disavowal because the same unconscious operations in the Symbolic register that historicize the subject also undermine the conditions (stabilization of meaning) necessary for making political claims. The very assumption that causes Bourdieu and de Certeau difficulty in promoting historicity – the pervasive dominance of a set of structured meanings that regulate practices – is what they choose as necessary for the political valence of their theories. At the same time, the very psychic operation that makes it possible to think historicity and to create a margin of freedom from social determination, a margin necessary for political action – the entry into an idiosyncratic Symbolic with its particular appropriations – compromises the regularization that makes the action susceptible to empirical study and then political application.[20] It seems we have to choose between a dream of political agency that is paradoxically founded on the premise of systematic social determination and a description of a social subject

excessive to its determinants stuck to the temporality of retroversive signification in a way that obviates its political purchase.

This crux brings us to the work of Judith Butler, who has made it her
mission to think through the problem of how to derive political agency
from the temporality of retroversion and the excessive dimension of the
subject. While acknowledging the need to incorporate psychoanalytic
principles, as we have seen, Butler nonetheless argues against what she
regards as the illegitimately universalizing propensity of psychoanalysis.
As a consequence, she tries to build a theory of subjectification that ties
the subject to the social world in ways that respect subjective particularity. In this regard, she has a more nuanced approach to the determinants
of the social field than do Bourdieu and de Certeau, although she leans on
their work at crucial moments. As we will see, the arguments she adduces
for her version of social change theory thoroughly engage the question of
the extimate cause of the Möbius subject.

4
Butler's Embodied Agency

Agency and the Cause of the Subject

Perhaps more than any other contemporary theorist, Judith Butler has grappled with the problem of how the subject's social determinants disable or enable agency. Like Bourdieu, she begins with a model of subject formation that assumes the internalization of social dictates. Taking direction from Althusser and Foucault, she postulates the subject's interpellation by the contents and strategies of social discourse – its categories, exclusions, and judgments. However, this approach has the obvious disadvantage that it conceives of the subject as a mere product of social discourse. Accordingly, Butler's early work tried to inject a measure of unconditioned agency into this model by deploying Derridean iterability to argue that the appropriability of the signifier provides a mechanism for intentional re-signification of the discourse producing the subject. In this way, she imagined that the subject could intervene in the conditions of its own formation.

The critical flaw in this model, emphasized by critics of Butler's *Gender Trouble*, is its assumption that an individual can control the *social* meaning of these re-significations: Butler failed to see that, whatever meanings the subject intends by re-signifying, others still retain the power of appropriability. Consequently, she has drawn upon a wide variety of theories to help her figure out how the unconditioned dimension of the subject necessary for enacting social change might arise from a subject of discursive regulation without simply relying on intentionalized meanings. As we shall see, by the time of writing *Excitable Speech*, Butler comes to lean heavily not only upon Bourdieu and Derrida, but also on psychoanalytic thinkers – notably Lacan, Shoshana Felman, and Žižek

– to arrive at a model of an embodied subject, excessive to its linguistic determinants, with political agency.

That Butler would cast in her lot with psychoanalysis might come as a surprise to readers of *Gender Trouble*, with its excoriation of psychoanalytic discourse as universalizing, de-historicizing, and (hetero) sexist. However, in her second major volume, *Bodies That Matter*, she acknowledges the cogency of the psychoanalytic critique of Foucaultian historicism, conceding that "Žižek is surely right that the subject is not a unilateral effect of prior discourses, and that the process of subjectivation outlined by Foucault is in need of a psychoanalytic rethinking" (BTM 189). Following Žižek, she then explains that the subject is never wholly determined by the positivities of the social field, for "any effort of discursive interpellation or constitution is subject to failure, haunted by contingency, to the extent that discourse invariably fails to totalize the social field" (BTM 191–2). The incomplete totalization of the social field both renders the field susceptible to transformation and makes causal analysis difficult. Only psychoanalytic theory, in her view, explains the failure of totalization in a way that accounts for a subject who is both determined by and to some extent free from external determination. It seems that Butler is here arguing for the conditions of extimate causality and Möbius subjectivity.

In the psychoanalytic account, as Butler rehearses it, the Lacanian conception of the Real serves as the example of the kind of "external" which nonetheless can *never* appear as a positivity – a good approximation to the extimate cause. She relies on Žižek's work to explain how this kind of cause has political valence insofar as it offers a margin of indetermination that destabilizes the link between intention and outcome:

> . . . any attempt to totalize the social field is to be read as a symptom, the effect and remainder of a trauma that itself cannot be directly symbolized in language. This trauma subsists as the permanent possibility of disrupting and rendering contingent any discursive formation that lays claim to a coherent or seamless account of reality. It persists as the real, where the real is always that which any account of "reality" fails to include. The real constitutes the contingency or lack in any discursive formation. As such, it stands theoretically as a counter both to Foucaultian linguisticism, construed as a kind of discursive monism whereby language effectively brings into being that which it names, and to Habermasian rationalism which presumes a transparency of intention in the speech act that is itself symptomatic of a refusal of the psyche, the unconscious, that which resists and yet structures language prior to and beyond any "intention." (BTM 191–2)

We will return to Butler's interest in the speech act as offering an alternative theoretical route to this non-positive externality, but for now I want to note that Butler approves psychoanalytic theory's refusal of intentionality and applauds psychoanalytic critiques of both the external, meta-principle of explanation (itself exempt from the workings of history) and the immanentist "causality" that reduces all determinants to positivities (such that no resistance to the status quo is possible).

What Butler finds so promising in the notion of the Real, then, is that it serves as a cause of the social field without reducing to a positivity within that field, insofar as it has no determinate content itself – the key principle of extimate causality. Throughout her work, Butler continues to rely on Lacanian psychoanalysis as a warrant for her theory of subject formation. Yet, even as she approves the principles of extimate causality, she rejects the Real as a candidate for this type of cause. Her quarrel with Žižek in the chapter "Arguing with the Real" from *Bodies That Matter* as well as in her later work seems not to recognize that the very concept she is using has the same properties Žižek describes as crucial to subjectification. Butler's rejection of his formulation comes down to her sense that Žižek conceives of the Real as a lack or trauma which is the same for every contingency which it secures. By relying on such universalist conceptions, she argues, Žižek is precluded from being able to "respond to the pressure to theorize the historical specificity of trauma" (BTM 202). She believes that she is agreeing with Žižek when she claims that the social field is produced through acts of exclusion (as we will see below, she has misconceived this point), but maintains that Žižek reduces all such founding exclusions to the same trauma (of castration):

> to supply the character and content to a law that secures the borders between the "inside" and the "outside" of symbolic intelligibility is to preempt the specific social and historical analysis that is required, to conflate into "one" law the effect of a convergence of many, and to preclude the very possibility of a future rearticulation of that boundary which is central to the democratic project that Žižek, Laclau, and Mouffe promote. (BTM 206–7)

We can understand her complaint as charging Žižek with committing both of the errors of causation described above. First, the Žižekian Real seems to Butler to be a historical contingency masquerading as a universal or unchanging meta-principle, unaffected by history. Second, she believes Žižek's Real to be "filled up" with a specific "character and content" and so, in effect, reduced to positive determinants immanent within the social field. That is, while she rejects the Žižekian solution, she does so in the name of the very principles that the theorists of extimacy apply against external and immanent causation. But despite this avowal of psychoanalysis, Butler also continues to reaffirm Foucault's immanentist paradigm when it suits her purposes, repositioning herself in alliance with that theory so cogently critiqued by Copjec. For example, when Butler conceptualizes censorship, she notes the usefulness of the Foucaultian conception of power as productive, as "formative of subjects" (ES 133), rather than as juridical prohibition. She is surely right to distinguish, as Foucault does, between juridical and productive power, but her use of the concept indicates that she has returned to the immanentist position on the reduction of subjects to their determinants:

> Censorship is a productive form of power: it is not merely privative, but formative as well. I propose that censorship seeks to produce subjects according to explicit and implicit norms, and that the production of the subject has everything to do with the regulation of speech. The subject's production takes place not only through the regulation of that subject's speech, but through the regulation of the social domain of speakable discourse . . . To become a subject means to be subjected to a set of implicit and explicit norms that govern the kind of speech that will be legible as the speech of a subject. (ES 133)

By drawing on this fundamentally Althusserian formulation of interpellation, Butler makes clear that she regards the subject *qua* subject to be a function of internalized discourse. She explicitly invokes the Foucaultian model of immanent power – as productive rather than prohibitive.

Let us take note of a point to which I will return below. In this quotation, Butler moves from a specific social phenomenon – censorship – to a general theory of subject formation. To say that censorship seeks to produce the subject according to explicit and implicit norms is to say that censorship of speech is the mechanism of subject formation. Whether or not subjects are formed by censorship or some analogous type of prohibition on speech is a crucial point, as we will see, but what I want to emphasize here is that asserting this point contradicts Foucault's "anti-repressive" theory, which abjures such a notion of the constitutive role of repression. So, even as she is invoking Foucault in her reference to his model of power and to his notion of the discursive constitution of subjects, she is importing a non-Foucaultian – and equally non-psychoanalytic element – into her theory, that is, the constitution of subjects by way of exclusion.

What is most important to remark here, however, is that even as she presses a quasi-Foucaultian conception of the discursively constituted subject and the immanentist model of power into service for her theory of political agency, Butler conveniently forgets that these carry problematic baggage along with them, in particular the problem that the Foucaultian theory is "resistant to resistance" (as Copjec puts it), when she argues that subjects must "exploit the presuppositions of speech to produce a future of language that is nowhere implied by those presuppositions"

(ES 140). Obviously, the one-tier model of immanent causation has great attractions, given that it enables one to find causes (power) everywhere one looks, but Butler neglects to take into account, in contrast to her earlier critique, that that is also its great weakness.

This apparent oscillation between psychoanalysis and a Foucaultian position, as I discuss below, has its uses for Butler: she supplements the Foucaultian and the psychoanalytic theories of subject formation with each other. Unfortunately, she chooses as supplements exactly those elements of each theory that cost her theoretical consistency and the ability to analyze historically. At her most theoretically rigorous, she acknowledges the need for the particular type of cause offered by psychoanalytic theory, but she always brings back precisely what is prohibited by the psychoanalytic framework – that is, the immanentist reduction of the social field to positivities – and in this way she ultimately disavows psychoanalysis. Yet Butler will also use (her version of) psychoanalytic theory to argue that the subject is formed by exclusionary operations, the argument precisely prohibited by a Foucaultian model of power (and by psychoanalysis as well), and in this way she disavows Foucaultianism.

Butler's *Excitable Speech* (subtitled *A Politics of the Performative*) provides a useful case study of her use of psychoanalysis to revise the Foucaultian account of subject formation. At the same time, both her rejection of psychoanalysis as a historicizing discourse and her disavowal of the very psychoanalytic precepts on which she claims to be relying, albeit without acknowledging doing so, opens an opportunity for reviewing the way that extimate causality and Möbius subjectivity enable historical specificity. Although the critical commentary on *Excitable Speech* focuses primarily on her use of speech-act theory for political purposes, Butler draws on other theoretical resources to support her claims for performative political agency.[1] In a tacit admission of the limitations of J. L. Austin's work for her purposes, she introduces an extended supplement to her linguistically based performative theory – a discussion of embodied subjectivity presented in ways never before instanced in her work. Even while she continues to use speech-act theory (as usual, articulated with Derridean iterability) to ground performativity, she also presents a version of embodiment newly derived from psychoanalysis to establish the political efficacy of the subject. She treats this psychoanalytic dimension as animating her entire argument in this volume. Nonetheless, this psychoanalytic addition to her previous theory of the discursive cause of the subject has gone unexamined in the scholarship, so that to date we have no evaluation of its contribution to performativity or political agency.[2]

The complicated argumentative structure of *Excitable Speech* merits close attention. Butler is an engaging but demanding writer whose work does not reduce easily to propositional statements. In this chapter, I closely follow the rhetorical and logical pathways Butler traces in her efforts to connect historicism, deconstruction, and psychoanalysis. I focus on the introduction, "On Linguistic Vulnerability," and the final chapter, "Implicit Censorship and Discursive Agency," because it is here that Butler lays out her most sophisticated discussions of political agency and proposes her new theory of a nonlinguistic, embodied political performative most directly.

I begin by summarizing Butler's anti-censorship position in order to showcase the role and limits of linguistic performativity that impel her to offer a new account of the embodied political performative – in effect, a turn from the immanentist version of discursive subjectivity to a recognition of the need for the extimate cause. In subsequent sections, I explore the embodied performative to assess its foundations, its functions, and the derivation of its explicitly political force. I conclude by discussing how her effort to accommodate the Foucaultian historicist account of subject formation to what she considers to be the more theoretically rigorous psychoanalytic account both grounds and creates problems for her new theory. My purpose here is to provide an evaluation of Butler's revision in its psychoanalytic key that moves beyond the criticisms of psychoanalysis currently on offer in social philosophy, feminist studies, and queer theory and, through that assessment, to show the value of the psychoanalytic conception of the extimate cause of the Möbius subject for a historicizing theory.[3]

The Limits of Linguistic Performativity

In the final chapter of *Excitable Speech*, "Implicit Censorship and Discursive Agency," Butler lays out her argument against censorship as a prelude to theorizing the embodied performative. She interrogates the meaning of the term censorship to uncover not only its effects – censorship is constitutive as well as prohibitive – but also its status as performativity: how does censorship achieve its effects in the social field and how does political agency emerge in relation to it? Surprisingly, she uses the example of hate speech to oppose censorship on the grounds that it is based on the incorrect view that injurious speech does not also include the possibility of its own subversion. In what is by now her characteristic appropriation of Derridean iterability, she reasons that the effects of speech can exceed the context of its utterance – speech is "excitable" – and so any given speech act has the performative power to institute as well as to close off meanings. Concerned that censorship will limit the means by which the injured can redress their wrongs through the *re-appropriation* of the very speech that harmed them, Butler forges an argument for the performative as politically relevant agency. In pursuit of that goal, she attempts to transcend the limitations of linguistic performativity while retaining its advantages.

As her readers well know, the performative as theorized by Austin sits at the heart of Butler's work, and *Excitable Speech* continues her long-standing love affair with speech-act theory. Yet in relying on Austin's formulations, she remains vulnerable to her critics' charges both that her theory speaks only to individual rather than social transformation and that she is ignoring the social embeddedness of speech acts, the power relations that constitute and enable them.[4] Under pressure to revise Austin, she sees in "[t]he disjuncture between utterance and meaning . . . the condition of possibility for revising the performative" (ES 87). We have identified this disjuncture as the excess of signification, and Butler outlines its features in both Austinian ("infelicity") and Derridean ("iterability") terms, remarking that the fact "that performative utterances can go wrong, be misapplied or misinvoked, is essential to their proper functioning" (ES 151). When contemporary arguments for the censorship of hate speech, pornography, and obscenity ignore this requirement, conceiving instead that speech can act as conduct – which is to say that its intention is realized univocally in the effect on the addressee – they rely on a "phantasy of sovereign action . . . one that immediately does what it says" (ES 12). However, as we will see, despite having made this criticism, Butler goes on to garner support for this very "phantasy" as she articulates the political valence of her theory.[5]

Although she admits that in the world of reality "the teleology of action . . . is disruptible by various kinds of infelicities," she wants to sustain the distinction between "sovereign" *illocutionary* acts and other *perlocutionary* acts that, in her view, are more susceptible to infelicity and therefore to intentional re-signification (ES 12). In this respect, Butler foregoes the Derridean critique of Austin, which shows that such a distinction between illocution and perlocution is untenable. At first it looks as though Butler wants to retain the category of perlocutionary acts because such speech acts, she argues, are inherently "ungovernable" and therefore acquire political pertinence, challenging and even destroying the sovereignty of an utterance, thanks to the iterability inherent in perlocution: "[t]he interval between instances of utterance not only makes the repetition and resignification of the utterance possible, but shows how words might, through time, become disjoined from their power to injure and recontextualized in more affirmative modes" (ES 15). The iterable quality of speech acts thus can undermine the power of the "illocutionary" performative to realize its intentions, enacting a nonvoluntarist yet subversive form of agency: "I hope to make clear that by affirmative, I mean 'opening up the possibility of agency,' where agency is *not* the restoration of a sovereign autonomy in speech, a replication of conventional notions of mastery" (ES 15, my emphasis). But the appropriately cautious tone she strikes here with regard to the subversive potential of resignification frequently gets lost, as in her example of "the revaluation of terms such as 'queer,'" which, she says, "suggest [sic] that speech can be 'returned' to its speaker in a different form, that it can be cited against its originary purposes, and perform a reversal of effects" (ES 14). In this case, and throughout the volume, Butler treats this "resignification" as though it can have *predictable* effects, re-describing the contingent contextual appropriation of the speech act as if it had all the intentionalist force of an illocutionary act, a move which is strictly precluded by the theory of iterability. For example, she argues that "the word that wounds becomes an *instrument* of resistance in the redeployment that *destroys* the prior territory of its operation" (ES 163, my emphases). Or, to take another example, at times she urges "misappropriating the force of injurious language to counter its injurious operations" (ES 41). Yet to speak of "misappropriation" is to imply that there are two kinds of appropriation, those that simply repeat ("re-enacting") an original intention and those (in her words, "misappropriations" and "expropriations") that intentionally break with that origin: "the re-signification of speech requires opening new contexts, speaking in ways that have never yet been legitimated, and hence producing legitimation in new and future forms" (ES 41).

To make the transition from the "possibility of agency" to political agency seem credible, she divides iterability's "repetition with a difference" into discrete temporal moments, as though iterability means oscillating between sameness (repetition without slippage) at one moment and difference (resignification without normative reinscription) at another.[6] When it comes to certain performances, she forgets about the slippage, the opening for re-interpretation, that iterability confers on *every* repetition. As she describes it, iterability ceases to operate in the special case of performers who *intend* to appropriate the speech act for subversive purposes. Significantly, Butler reserves the power of such insurrectionary speech for those who have been the objects of injurious speech, the marginalized or abjected: "agency is derived from injury, and injury countered through that very derivation" (ES 41). For such specially empowered yet abjected subjects, the performative engagement with the convention is described as producing calculable effects (commensurate with the intention of the performer) upon a given social context.[7]

In other words, in the political parts of her exposition, iterability functions only *initially* to make it possible for the addressee to appropriate the original utterance. It then *ceases* to operate when the addressee brings about her subversive intentions through resignification. In fact, her final sentence – "Insurrectionary speech becomes the necessary response to injurious language . . . a repetition in language that forces change" – indicates this excision of iterability's nonvoluntarist function in two ways: "insurrectionary speech" is speech that realizes its subversive intentions, and a repetition in language that "forces change" is one that has exercised sovereign autonomy (ES 163). What Butler fails to respect in these formulations is that *all* signification is iterable, working by *simultaneously and unpredictably* repeating and breaking with prior contexts (ES 41). Iterability (as she sometimes acknowledges in her more tempered moments) does not confer on the speaker the sovereign power of opening or closing contexts, legitimating or de-legitimating meanings.

This unacknowledged gliding between a more cautious formulation and a full-blown claim for agency as control makes it possible for Butler to complain that her critics misread her when they charge her with voluntarism. Yet to uphold the promise of her subtitle, she must and does argue for a theory of special performativity that reinscribes sovereign action. Although she has disclaimed this voluntarist form of agency since charged with it by critics of *Gender Trouble*, she nonetheless continues to resurrect it, along with its positional claims, as the political warrant of her theorizing about agency. To take just one example from *Excitable Speech*, but one that Butler emphasizes as the most telling, she attributes to Rosa Parks a freely chosen, unilateral, and creative act of (previously unavailable) counterperformativity, the subversive political results of which devolve from Parks' purposes and her marginal status: "she had no prior authorization, [yet] she endowed a certain authority on the act, and began the insurrectionary process of overthrowing those established codes of legitimacy" (ES 147).[8] For all of her temperate reasoning about the impossibility of governing speech, then, Butler repeatedly returns to the more politically useful, if less theoretically valid, formulation of special performative agency.

Indeed, in order for her theory to have any political traction, she must advance this stronger version of agency. If agency is not the same as control, as she sometimes notes, then the possibility of a politically subversive or progressive action arises in every act but in an *ungovernable* way: relying on iterability offers no way to guarantee a politically positive outcome (ES 8). Unless iterability can be applied selectively to acquire sovereign force when the intentions of the addressee of hate speech are politically subversive – that is, unless there is special performative agency – Butler's argument loses its political force, as the 1980s debate over the political valence of iterability rehearsed *ad nauseam*. The theoretical import of iterability precludes precisely the type of politics for which Butler has become famous.[9]

Butler utilizes a number of strategies to maintain the distance between the parts of her theory that depend upon the weak form of "possible" agency enabled by iterability and those that claim the strong form of political agency for special subjects. Chief among these strategies is her theory of the embodied performative, which retains the advantages of linguistic performativity but serves to render her less vulnerable to criticisms of linguisticism, voluntarism, and neglect of social determinants: "If agency is not derived from the sovereignty of the speaker, then the force of the speech act is not sovereign force. The 'force' of the speech act is, however incongruously, related to the body whose force is deflected and conveyed through speech" (ES 39). Butler here begins her investigation into the source of a speech that has a "sovereign force" derived from the body rather than from language. What authorizes this move to the embodied speech act, what advantages does it have, and what challenges does it present for a theory of political agency?

The Performative Force of the Embodied Speech Act

Responding to the problems the linguistic performative causes, Butler wonders how performative force could work to give her the political valence she needs. In a section of her final chapter entitled, appropriately enough, "Speech Acts Politically," she asks "in what does the 'force' of the performative consist, and how can it be understood as part of politics?" (ES 141). She suggests that "[t]he performative needs to be rethought not only as an act that an official language-user wields in order to implement already authorized effects, but precisely as a social ritual" (ES 159). With this comment, she signals her project of bringing together historicist constructivism with deconstruction and, ultimately, psychoanalysis into a theory of the embodied political performative. She begins by surveying three different explanations of performative force.

She draws first on a psychoanalytically inflected objection to Austin's linguistic formalism. Taking refuge from those who charge her with linguisticism, Butler makes use of Bourdieu's *habitus* – the embodied product of inculcated durable dispositions that operate unconsciously to make the subject's practices conform to institutional authority – to suggest that interpellation constitutes "the social life of the body . . . discursively and socially at once" (ES 155).[10] Thus, she gets her revision underway by retaining the linguistic performative as part of the subject's interpellation, while deploying Bourdieu's formulation that embodied practices channel and reproduce social authority.

Still, Butler remains dissatisfied with Bourdieu's emphasis on the determining function of social institutions because it avoids linguisticism "at the expense of . . . transformability" (ES 151). The *habitus* conforms to social power: only those who have the prior authorization given by their relation to social power will be able to work the performative "social magic: that derives from and reproduces official authority" (ES 156). From a political perspective, then, the Bourdieusian performative works to sustain rather than subvert the status quo.[11] She contrasts Bourdieu's notion that performative force comes from *outside* language with Derrida's position that performative force resides *inside* the very structurality of language itself: there is, he says, "a certain conventionality intrinsic to what constitutes the speech act (locution) itself, all that might be summarized rapidly under the problematical rubric of 'the arbitrary nature of the sign' . . . 'Ritual' is not a possible occurrence (*éventualité*), but rather *as* iterability, a structural characteristic of every mark" (Derrida quoted ES 149).[12] Although Butler does not highlight the universal application of iterability to every utterance, she still references the Derridean critique in order to establish that performatives can liberate subjects from the conditions that have formed them: "Derrida's formulation offers a way to think performativity in relation to transformation, to the break with prior contexts, with the possibility of inaugurating contexts yet to come" (ES 151–2).[13]

Suddenly, at this point in her argument, Butler decides to reject both Bourdieu's theory of performative force derived from social authority, on the grounds of its political quietism, and Derrida's theory of performative force derived from the structure of language, on the grounds of its "excessively formal interpretation of the performative" (ES 151). Each lacks some component of the "social iterability" she desires (ES 150). She initially tries to resolve this problem by marrying Bourdieu with Derrida, arguing that interpellation functions by way of iteration – calling subjects into being, but never perfectly reproducing them, so that interpellation has to be continually, iteratively, performed.[14] Bringing iterability together with the *habitus*, she reasons that if the subject is formed in and through continual social interpellation, then the very speech acts which interpellate the subject themselves must be limited (else they would not need to be repeated), which opens a space for resistance and subversive agency. In order to make her case, Butler specifies the body as the site of resistance:

> The body, however, is not simply the sedimentation of speech acts by which it has been constituted. If that constitution fails, a resistance meets

interpellation at the moment it exerts its demand; then something exceeds the interpellation and this excess is lived as the outside of intelligibility. This becomes clear in the way the body rhetorically exceeds the speech act it also performs. This excess is what Bourdieu's account appears to miss or, perhaps, to suppress: the abiding incongruity of the speaking body, the way in which it exceeds its interpellation, and remains uncontained by any of its acts of speech. (ES 155)

Leaving aside for now the question of how a body 'rhetorically exceeds the speech act it also performs' (and ignoring the unnecessary and unexceptionable claim that a body is more than its acts of speaking), we can see that here Butler is taking on the task of theorizing the embodied performative to demonstrate its resistant capacities.

In a characteristic logical chiasmus, Butler defines speech as having a bodily component – speech is produced by people with bodies – in order to make the more problematic argument that interpellating speech has corporeal effects – speech acts have such profound determinative effects that they can literally, corporeally, wound people: "words enter the limbs . . . bend the spine . . . live and thrive in and as the flesh of the addressee" (ES 159). This logic not only allows her to claim a certain agential force for speech acts but also an exceptional status for the body as that which is both vulnerable to hate speech's wounding force and capable of escaping the intentions of those who seek to regulate the subject. In fact, for Butler, the speaking body, by virtue of its "excessive" quality, can subvert and resist its interpellation in ways that the Bourdieusian bodily *habitus* cannot. We must follow Butler further in her thinking to understand the basis for this unexpected conclusion.

The Excessive, Expressive Body

To set up this stage of her new theory of embodied performativity, Butler turns to a psychoanalytic account of the bodily speech act, one which she had discussed in her introduction: "the 'force' of the speech act, as it was articulated by . . . Shoshana Felman, has everything to do with the status of speech as a bodily act" (ES 152). She finds in Felman the psychoanalyst an argument against the exclusive focus on linguistics in Austinian (and, by her lights, Derridean) speech-act theory, an argument which helps her claim that speech acts have bodily consequences. Butler reads Felman as saying that "the speech act is a bodily act, and . . . the 'force' of the performative is never fully separable from bodily force . . . the speech act [is] at once bodily and linguistic" (ES 141). At this juncture in her final chapter, it would be reasonable to expect Butler to elaborate on Felman's theory as providing the "social iterability" missing in Bourdieu's and Derrida's accounts of performative force (ES 150). She does not do so. But in order to understand why Butler's argument for the embodied performative takes this turn we have to follow it from its first appropriation of Felman in the introduction, "On Linguistic Vulnerability." There Butler references the psychoanalytic reading of Austinian speech-act theory in which Felman proposes that the speech act always exceeds its intended meaning thanks to unconscious motivations. In Felman's own words (words, by the way, that are not quoted in context in Butler's text):

> if the theory of the performance of the speaking body – of speech acts proper – lies in the realm of the performative, the theory of the scandal of this performance falls in the domain of psychoanalysis. The scandal consists in the fact that the act *cannot know what it is doing*, that the act (of language) subverts both consciousness and knowledge (of language).[15]

To Butler this means that "the body becomes a sign of unknowingness precisely because its actions are never fully consciously directed or volitional . . . that unknowing body marks the limit of intentionality in the speech act" (ES 10). Felman herself does not regard the body as a "sign of unknowingness," but to the extent that Butler is trying to capture the sense that intentionality is always disrupted, she is on the same track as Felman. Still, Felman seems an odd choice, for her point that all speech exceeds its intentions by virtue of unconscious determinants runs counter to Butler's goal of finding a performative force in the speaking body. So, in this introductory chapter, Butler adds a twist to the idea of the speaking body: people not only use their bodies to articulate speech but also to express intentions with gestures, even intentions that are unconsciously motivated. Using a threat as her example of a performative effect, Butler argues that

> a statement may be made that, on the basis of a grammatical analysis alone, appears to be no threat. But the threat emerges precisely through the act that the body performs in the speaking act. Or the threat emerges as the apparent effect of a performative act only to be rendered harmless through the bodily demeanor of the act. . . (ES 10–11)

In this analysis of the threat, she argues that the true significance of the speech act is guaranteed by what the speaker's body expresses nonverbally. Consonant as this account may be with a psychoanalytic conception of the unconscious, in the sense that "body language" may reveal unconscious motivations unacknowledged in the speaker's words, Butler's view here departs from psychoanalytic theory, and Felman's insight, in assuming that the body's language gives access directly to intentions while the spoken language does not. In Butler's account, even though a speaker may not have access to the unconscious meaning of his message, his auditor can tell what he really means by watching his body language. That is, in Butler's account, the body does not *exceed* the speaker's intentions; instead, it transparently *expresses* them, even if the speaker is "unknowing" about what his true intentions are. The truth of the speaker's intentions is not to be found in his verbal articulations but in his bodily significations. In this move, Butler completely (and without acknowledging it) contradicts Felman's criticism of Austinian intentionalism by offering a theory of the embodied speech act that *reinstates* intentionality at the level of the body. The speaking body as sign of unintended expression becomes the body speaking its expressed intentions.[16]

Butler abruptly drops Felman's work at this point in the introduction and does not return to it until her final chapter, in which she stresses its foundational importance to her theory of the embodied performative. She briefly mentions Felman's notion that "speech is not fully governed by intentions," but then devotes her attention to the picture of the body as expressing its own intentions in a readily available way (ES 155). She claims to find in Felman her warrant for the notion that the body provides the true gauge of the meaning of the speech act: "the bearing of the body as rhetorical instrument of expression . . . makes plain the incongruous interrelatedness of body and speech to which Felman refers, the excess in speech that *must be read along with, and often against,* the propositional content of what is said" (ES 152, my emphasis). Here again, the body ceases to stand for the exceeding or disrupting of intentionalized meaning, as Felman theorizes, to serve instead as the vehicle and guarantor of intentionality. The impossibility of securely recovering intentions turns into a demand – "must be read along with, and often against" – that assumes their ready transparency.

Recall that Butler embarks on her discussion of the embodied performative in order to explain how speech powerful enough to interpellate (and harm) subjects can be resisted by those same subjects. If speech-act theory will not suffice, then a theory of a speaking body expressing intentions different than those inculcated during subject formation might. Butler attempts to create this theory by doubling the site of articulation for the same reason that she divides iterability into discrete temporal moments: it allows her to appear faithful to the theory's constraints while creating (unfounded) special exemptions. In this case, Butler applies the principles of disrupted intentionality and linguistic interpellation to the speaker while resuscitating readable intentionality and an interpellation-free zone for the special case of bodily gesture. Her argument runs like this: 1) subjects are interpellated through language, which even affects their bodily existence, but 2) language is by nature excessive, so something escapes the interpellative intentions, and 3) bodies are the signs of that excess; 4) at the same time, bodies do not simply *stand for* the excess that disrupts intentionalized meaning but also *enact* that excess by escaping the determinations of interpellation (bodies are excessive to the intentions of other speakers), so 5) bodies themselves, not determined by interpellation, can articulate their own intentions (bodies are expressive of the intentions of their own speakers) in order to disrupt interpellative intentions (bodies are subversive). There are several weak links here, especially the slide from the body's "exceeding" its own speaker's intentions to the body "exceeding" society's intentions to interpellate the subject. What is more, Butler never answers the question, if interpellation follows iterability, and therefore is always incomplete, how does the body escape interpellation while the mind does not? Why distinguish two sites of articulation, if interpellations act on both mind and body iteratively?

Recapping this logic allows us to see that Butler is playing word games with the concept of "excess." In some cases, the body's "excessive" dimension simply refers to the fact that the body is not the same as language: the body is the instrument by which language is articulated. In some cases, the excess refers to a body language that reveals motivations other than those acknowledged by the person who is using that body to speak. In still other cases, the body somehow "exceeds" the intentions of other speakers (who have their own bodies).

Just as importantly, Butler's "excess" is not Felman's. For Felman (and psychoanalysts), every signification (whether in articulated speech, written text, or bodily gesture) produces and leans on an excess inherent to signification itself, an excess that makes it impossible for the subject's intentions to govern the reader's interpretation. Yet for Butler, the failure of intentionalized meaning only applies to spoken articulations, while the body escapes that stricture. If in her model the body is outside or "excessive" to speech, still its intentionalized meanings have no excessive dimension, for they are readable and recoverable. In Felman, excess is irreducible; in Butler, it is not.

The Social Dimension of Performative Agency

Butler's inversion of Felman's critique of Austinian intentionality answers directly to the crucial elision in her theory of performativity as agency, an elision apparent from the inception of her work. Having lamented others' failure to "give an account of the power that such [offensive] words are said to exercise," she herself fails to expound with any rigor the *reason why* speech acts exceed their speaker's intentions (ES 13). This reason has nothing to do with the body's ability to express unconscious motivation or to resist interpellation. Rather, speech acts exceed the intentions of the speaker because other people interpret them according to their own lights in ways that are not predictable or governable in advance. By consistently sidestepping the role of the auditor in the "exceeding of intentionality," Butler seeks to preserve for her theory of political agency the very sovereign force that she has disallowed to the speakers of hate speech and would-be censors.[17] Because in all cases of signification, not only those that injure or marginalize, the auditor or reader has a role in the production of signification, Butler's pleading on behalf of special embodied performativity takes on an ironic cast. In essence, by failing to recognize the true status of the "excess" in signification, Butler elides the very dimension of meaning which any theory with political ambitions must engage – the social dimension. That is, in her efforts to eliminate excess, Butler throws out any conception of the social field as a product of signification and responsiveness to the Möbius condition of the subject. In effect, she leaves herself with no theory of the social whatsoever.

Butler employs iterability to acknowledge the limits to intentionality, but she mislocates these limits, finding them not in the audience's reception but rather in the *body*, which she misdescribes as being capable of its own sovereign speech, "confounding the performative power of the threat" (ES 12). In this way, she can use iterability to argue for the re-appropriation of a speech act, as we have seen, in a "repetition that *forces* change," as though the person appropriating the speech – thanks to iterability – has the capacity to close off *her* auditor's ability to make that speech meaningful according to his own lights and as though the audience can somehow be prevented from making use of iterability (ES 163, my emphasis).[18] In this scenario, in order for the repetition to force change, that is, in order for iterability to cease to operate, speaker and auditor must either have the same mind already, or the one must be capable of dominating the other's mental processes in some mysterious way. Whether Butler is arguing for such special cases of iterability or locating sovereign force in the body, she covertly relies on this invariance between the speaker's intentions and the audience's construals for the performative force she needs in her account of political agency. The perfect match between intender and auditor disposes of any excess and with it the social dimension of language.[19]

This theorizing of an excess that sticks to and flows from all signification (whether in speech or in bodily gesture) is the hallmark of a psychoanalytic approach. The excess is inescapable, irremediable, and unsymbolizable: in Lacanian parlance it subsists in the register of the

Real. So, when Butler transforms Felman's insistence on the *inaccessibility* of the speaker's intentions into a guarantee for the *recovery* of the force of those intentions by "reading" meanings, even those that are covert or unconscious, she uses the trappings and terminology of psychoanalysis but spectacularly fails to appreciate precisely what distinguishes psychoanalysis from Foucaultianism – the theorization of the dimension of excess inherent in every speech act. This failure inflects her version of subject formation: in disavowing the extimate cause, Butler leaves herself with no way to theorize the subject as a site of excess, as a Möbius subject.

Subjects of Exclusion

When Butler imagines circumstances in which the speaker's desire can be disambiguated by reading the truth of bodily gestures, she fantasizes that *some* special utterances do not generate this excess. Powerful purposes drive her: in this text as elsewhere, she proposes that society produces abjected subjects who, while apparently rendered powerless, nonetheless can at times bring about a change in their own status. Her commitment to this vision makes her touchy about any theoretical proposition that regards such subjects as victims ("Those who argue that hate speech produces a 'victim class' deny critical agency" [ES 41]). Having accepted the reasonable proposition that subjects are formed through language, she makes her theoretical missteps when she tries to figure out how to confer power on marginalized subjects by imagining that they can control the surplus attending all utterances. Time and again she gets tripped up by an inadequate conception of the source and role of signification in subject formation, relying continually on a belief that somehow, the excess attending signification can be eradicated. In this persistent gesture, Butler reveals that she does not understand the subject as itself a site of excess. Let's take a closer look to see how her argument for subject formation develops as a disavowal of excess. We'll begin with Butler's unique version of the constitution of the subject through exclusion.

For a generation of theorists, Foucault's description of the subject as a discursive effect has served as the exemplary model for the project of theorizing the relationship between the subject and language. In his formulation, discursive power is always everywhere creating subjects by a process of contestation and reformulation, working independently of the intentions of the "singular subject." His elaboration of a non-prohibitive power leads Foucault to specify that every performance of power includes its own resistance. While the nonintentionalist and resistive dimensions of this theory suit Butler's purposes, she worries that the Foucaultian model reduces the subject to a set of positive determinants supplied by discourse. As we have noted, she turns to psychoanalysis to bring contingency into that model of subject formation: "any effort of discursive interpellation or constitution is subject to failure, haunted by contingency, to the extent that discourse invariably fails to totalize the social field" (BTM 191–2).

But in this appeal to psychoanalysis, Butler has not forgotten her past criticism that psychoanalysis is ahistorical, a charge she bases on her belief that psychoanalysis presents castration as a universal form of lack (BTM 202). So, in order to benefit from the psychoanalytic model of subjectification, she proposes in *Excitable Speech* that subjects are formed by the installation of a lack that can be historicized. She conceives of this lack in her final chapter in terms of *exclusion*, an exclusion that produces a realm of "unspeakability" as the condition of the emergence and sustenance of the subject proper, but the "contents" of which are determined historically. This account of subject formation supports her argument that censorship is the founding gesture for subjectivity:

> Although the subject enters the normativity of language, the subject exists only as a grammatical fiction prior to that very entrance. Moreover, as Lacan and Lacanians have argued, that entrance into language comes at a price: the norms that govern the inception of the speaking subject differentiate the subject from the unspeakable, that is, produce an unspeakability as the condition of subject formation. (ES 135)

She finds that the Lacanian term "foreclosure" best covers the operation of subjectification as she conceives it: "The psychoanalysts Jean Laplanche and J.-B. Pontalis have distinguished the censorious act of repression from a preemptive operation of a norm, and offered the term 'foreclosure' as a way of designating preemptive action, one that is not performed by a subject but, rather, whose operation makes possible the formation of the subject" (ES 138). Citing the *OED* to define foreclosure as "to bar, exclude, shut out completely," Butler goes on to explain how the subject born of foreclosure encounters the limits of speakability as the condition of its continued existence:

> The condition for the subject's survival is precisely the foreclosure of what threatens the subject most fundamentally; thus, the "bar" produces the threat and defends against it at the same time. Such a primary foreclosure is approximated by those traumatic political occasions in which the subject who would speak is constrained precisely by the power that seeks to protect the subject from its own dissolution . . . Acting one's place in language continues the subject's viability, where that viability is held in place

by a threat both produced and defended against, the threat of a certain dissolution of the subject. If the subject speaks impossibly, speaks in ways that cannot be regarded as speech or as the speech of a subject, then that speech is discounted and the viability of the subject called into question. . . (ES 135–6)

In a nod to the centrality of iterability for her model, Butler argues that this constitutive "foreclosure does not take place once and for all," which means that it must be "repeated to reconsolidate its power and efficacy." In this way, she imagines that the subject could appropriate speech by "redrawing the distinction between what is and is not speakable" (ES 139).

By this route, she also creates an analogy between her notion of an exclusion constitutive of subjectivity and the exclusion of people from the polity, arguing that the political act of appropriating the "unspeakable" can lead to the political inclusion of dispossessed or marginalized people.[20] Here she explicitly proposes that the subject can access the realm excluded by foreclosure by "speaking impossibly" or by "redrawing the distinction" (ES 139). From her perspective, the politically motivated subject has to take the "risk" of accessing this realm, even at the cost of being seen as something other than a subject. Butler's argument is nothing less than the claim that the subject can transform the very conditions of (its own and others') subject formation through special speech acts that control their own reception. What has been excluded can be included, the marginal can take center stage, and formerly unspeakable acts will have normative force: "The appropriation of such norms to oppose their historically sedimented effect constitutes the *insurrectionary* moment of that history, the moment that founds a future through a *break* with that past" (ES 159, my emphases).

Exclusion or Foreclosure?

Wagering her own theory's political value on this exclusionary model of subject formation, she marshals resources from psychoanalysis to bolster her view that foreclosure founds the subject. She believes that the excluded element would dissolve the Symbolic (and the subject with it) if foreclosure were to fail and the "unspeakable" were given a hearing. By casting foreclosure as the guarantor of symbolic and subjective integrity, she imagines that this excluded material remains a permanent, if historically specific, threat to the status quo – and hence a reservoir of politically subversive materials:

In the *Vocabulaire de la psychanalyse*, Jean Laplanche and J.-B. Pontalis refer to foreclosure as a primordial rejection of that which remains outside of the symbolic universe of the subject . . . what is set outside or repudiated from the symbolic universe in question is precisely what binds that universe together *through its exclusion* . . . [They] argue that what is foreclosed is to be distinguished from what is repressed . . . What is foreclosed . . . does not belong to the realm of neurosis, but to that of psychosis; indeed, its entry into the symbolic universe threatens psychosis, which is to say that its exclusion guarantees symbolic coherence. (ES 180 n. 17)

It is important to note that in her references to psychoanalysis in the final chapter of *Excitable Speech*, Butler is neither criticizing nor rewriting psychoanalytic theory: she is claiming to represent the theory adequately and to use it on its own terms. Yet if we look again at Butler's deployment of psychoanalytic theory here, we will find, unfortunately, that her construal could not be further from the position she purports to be summarizing. Contrary to her interpretation, psychoanalytic theory does not propose that subjects are formed by foreclosure nor that foreclosure prevents psychosis.

The definition for foreclosure (*forclusion du Nom-du-Père*) offered by Laplanche and Pontalis is: a "term introduced by Jacques Lacan denoting a specific mechanism felt to lie at the origin of the psychotic phenomenon and to consist in a primordial expulsion of a fundamental 'signifier' (e.g. the phallus as signifier of the castration complex) from the subject's symbolic universe."[21] In Lacan, and Laplanche and Pontalis, foreclosure is the *cause* of psychosis, not the means by which the subject is protected from psychosis, as Butler would have it. Moreover, *what* is foreclosed does not "belong to the realm of psychosis" (and Laplanche and Pontalis never say that it does); rather, what is foreclosed (the phallus as signifier, or *Non/Nom-du-Père*) in psychosis belongs precisely to the realm of the nonpsychotic – it is the *addition* of a negation. Far from an exclusion, the Name-of-the-Father is what is *included* in order for the nonpsychotic subject to form. Similarly, it is not the *exclusion* from the Symbolic of this foreclosed element that creates "symbolic coherence," but rather the *inclusion* of the *Nom-du-Père* that makes it possible for the subject to enter the Symbolic at all, that is, for the Symbolic to develop as a coherent psychic register.

Nor is it the case that the price of the entry into language is that "the norms that govern the inception of the speaking subject differentiate the subject from the unspeakable." No one properly versed in Lacanian theory would talk about "the norms that govern the inception of the speaking subject," because what governs the subject's inception as subject has no specific social content: it is nothing more than the addition of a negation to the realm of the Real.[22] Butler's mistaken formulation conforms to her belief that subjects are formed in and through a primary exclusion.

In fact, without this formulation of "unspeakability," her argument that subject formation transpires by way of censorship disappears, as does the glue binding the various strands of her argument in *Excitable Speech*.

In order to understand the psychoanalytic conception of foreclosure, it is necessary to realize that the *Non/Nom-du-Père* has no content, much less normative content. The addition of the negation, the *Non/Nom-du-Père*, makes the subject a signifier, which means that the subject does not control what s/he means to others any more than s/he can know for certain what others mean. In effect, the "paternal metaphor" places a "minus sign," so to speak, on the immediacy of the presence of the individual, raising the question as to the meaning of the individual, and in this way makes of the individual a signifier, bringing the individual into the realm of signification from the realm of the Real. That is, the *Non/Nom-du-Père* is a metaphor for the process by which anything, including the child, ceases to simply *be* and comes to *mean*, which is to say that it enters into the defiles of linguistic mediation and social appropriation.[23] No object simply means what it is; every object becomes a site of excessive meaning. To be a signifier – and a subject – is to be stuck to an irreducible excess of meaning. In other words, this form of internalization is very different from what Butler imagines to be the process of subject formation: at its core is the social dimension of language, an unsymbolizable *excess* (not an unsymbolizable *exclusion*) produced by the conditions in which meaning arises as perpetually ungovernable.

In this sense, the paternal metaphor *causes* the subject without adding any content to the subject's determinants. This cause "comes from" outside the subject – in fact, its purpose is to bring the subject into contact with the external social world – and it must be internalized to become operative, but it does not provide any substantive positivities in the process. The subject is not formed by the *exclusion* of signification but by the *excess* of signification that irremediably adheres to the *subject* as signifier. Butler's effort to re-write the extimate cause as an exclusionary gesture based on symbolic *contents* repositions her squarely in the Foucaultian register. Butler simply does not understand that the subject is a signifier, with all of the properties of appropriability and significatory excess that attend its Möbius condition. As a result, the "subject" she proposes instantiates neurotic defenses against excess: Butler's subject is nothing but a symptom.

Between Neurosis and Psychosis

This psychoanalytic theory of subject formation directly contradicts Butler's assertion that the paternal metaphor creates a realm of "unspeakability" that could somehow be accessed through willed speech acts, no matter how risky. Instead, the addition of the paternal metaphor creates the illusion that something has been lost, a world of perfect understanding with no possibility of slippage. Pace Butler, this "loss" never actually happened; it is simply an after-effect of Symbolic registration. And because this world never existed, it can never be recovered. The subject has not been "barred" from this world, and she is not "excluded." Rather, the subject is structured around this imaginary loss produced by the addition of the *Non/Nom-du-Père*. Butler's project of "redrawing the distinction between what is and is not speakable" presupposes that somehow one does gain access to the "barred" remainder (ES 139). In principle, then, for Butler, the loss can be remedied – by an appropriation of speech acts that will lead to the opening of previously "closed" contexts, resulting in the inclusion of the politically oppressed.

Psychoanalysis has a name for the position Butler adopts: the neurotic.

> The neurotic does believe that the lost object can be recovered . . . The neurotic can only accept the lack to the extent that she can also believe that it can in principle be remedied . . . [T]he neurotic understands her suffering in terms of frustration – she has been denied or deprived of something that she should have (and could have) had in order to lead a successful life.[24]

When she accounts for the formation of the subject along exclusionary lines, then, Butler not only signals her demand for the loss to be remedied, she also shifts from a psychoanalytic to a Foucaultian register. If the loss is a fact, then it must be the loss of a determinate something: the loss should be remediable by the addition of a positivity.

Imagining that subjects are formed through foreclosure, Butler *herself* endows all subjects with the attributes of psychotics, relying on these very attributes to make her argument plausible.[25] Defined in psychoanalytic terms, the psychotic

> does not recognize the lack in the Other, and thus has no grasp of the constant sliding of meaning under or along the chain of signifiers. The psychotic lives, on the contrary, in a world of fixed and clear meanings, which he encounters, or which even impose themselves upon him, both in words and in reality . . . [she] does not really inhabit her own body . . . this body is not her own. The sensations that appear in the body, and the ideas that arise there, do not belong to the subject – they are the thoughts of an anonymous Other that has taken possession of the body.[26]

Not recognizing the lack in the Other means not recognizing the Other's desire – or, we could say, not recognizing the capability of the hearer to have desires different from those of the subject, which is a convenient feature for an implicitly sovereign theory of the performative speech act. Butler does postulate that her subject lives in "a world of fixed and clear meanings": she fosters the fantasy that the listener's interpretations will conform to the speaker's intentions. What is more, the capability of the speech act to wound "bodily" in this "literalization of metaphor," as Butler has it, conforms to the properties of language as experienced by the psychotic. And her version of interpellation is tantamount to the infestation of the subject by the discourse of the social, the taking over of the subject's body and mind by an anonymous and omnipotent external power. Given these imputed qualities, it is indeed difficult to imagine how this (psychotic) subject could deploy her paltry resources against such a powerful force. In Butler's theory of the political performative, the neurotic speaker seeking to reclaim the lost and forbidden realm of "unspeakability" can only acquire (imagined) efficacy by way of a fantasized psychotic interlocutor – one whose body is literally vulnerable to the words of the performative politician, someone whose mind is taken over by the desires of the performative politician, whose very inclusion is the sign of its subjection to the force of the performative politician.

Historicizing Desire

In effect, Butler's conception of an exclusionary mode of subjectification implicitly disavows the psychoanalytic account (the addition of an indeterminate negation) in favor of the Foucaultian one (the determination of subjects by positive elements; the "norms that govern the inception of the speaking subject"). Yet by this action Butler leaves herself in a theoretical no-man's land: the psychoanalytic account abjures *positivities*, and the Foucaultian model abjures *exclusion*, yet these are the very elements on which she must rely for her theory of the political performative. We can put it this way: in her disavowal of psychoanalysis, she has also given up the one useful aspect of Foucault's work for a historicizing theory – the refusal to think power in terms of exclusion and prohibition. So, her version of psychoanalysis resupplies Foucaultianism with the one tool Foucault most forcefully rejects. That she is wrong about psychoanalysis does not alter the fact that she tries to forge an account based on exclusion as well as on positive determinants. Without a remediable exclusion (say, of non-normative discourse) and the reinstatement of excluded positivities (say, of marginalized subjects), Butler's whole project of transforming norms and including marginal peoples through the appropriation of speech acts falls apart, and with it, any possibility of historicizing the subject. Ultimately, Butler's inept use of psychoanalysis creates a mangled version of historicism that completely vitiates her political project: her misguided reliance on exclusion effectively reduces the subject to positive determinants – that is, to a mere expression of the social structure itself – and thereby eradicates the subject *as such*, destroying any possibility of resistance.

In order to see how the extimate cause of the Möbius subject supplies an alternative account of an historicized subject, we can return to the example of the paternal metaphor as cause of the subject. Unlike the Foucaultian cause, it is not simply one positive determinant among others. Even though, by virtue of its internalization, it belongs to the field in which it works its effects, it nonetheless remains distinct from the other elements of the field in that it has no content. Instead of becoming just another positive determinant, the *Non/Nom-du-Père* works a transformation on the entire field to add another dimension to it, that of signification. The value of this cause, this excess, for theory can be seen when we consider not only how it addresses the dilemma of social change by supplying to the psyche the minimal necessary contingency from which resistance can be staged, but also, by virtue of that contingency, how it meets Butler's charge that it is ahistorical. As we noted in the previous chapter, this cause enables the child to enter history as a *subject* in a particular relation to a particular historical field (a relation that has both conventional/systemic and arbitrary/idiosyncratic aspects). In failing to see that the Law itself consists only of a *content-less*, formal negation, Butler becomes blind to the fact that the Symbolic, and the Law, are not the same for everyone in the social field, nor could they be: castration does not, no matter what she says, have a universal meaning or form. The conditions of subjectification – that is, the ability to substitute one signifier for another; the stricture that meaning is always elsewhere; the fact that the contents supplied under symbolization emerge as functions of contingent experiences with all manner of people idiosyncratically regarded as meaningful – preclude the emergence of "one law." That this is so is demonstrated by the varieties of desire, for if the Law were the hegemonic and unitary "one law" of Butler's imagination, then all subjects would be constrained to the same desire, and the charge of ahistoricity would be fair.[27] But desire, installed through the negation of the paternal metaphor, moves within the order of the signifier, not the signified. To imagine otherwise is to be trapped always within the Imaginary. Precisely because the Law is formally empty, its action nothing more than a function of the addition of a negation that makes signification possible, it *activates* desire in unforeseen and ungovernable ways, fleshed out on contingent circumstances and properties, driving a particular individual history while seizing social history for its signifiers. Strange as it may seem, the Law and contingency are two sides of the same moving coin.[28] Far from being ahistorical or politically quietistic, a Möbius theory of subject formation provides the only account of causality capable of putting historicism on a firm footing, that is, in its proper relation to the excess that mobilizes desire.

5

Laclau's Radical Democracy

What is the Source of Solidarity?

Does a political regime with the power to cast its subjects in its own image somehow bring about its own demise? Is the common genesis of subjects by social forces a way for them to bond together against the power that produces them? In their own ways, Bourdieu, de Certeau, and Butler set up the problem of social change as a function of the social origins of individual subjectification, oscillating between what I have called the external and the immanentist models of social causation. A brief recap may be in order. In the immanentist model made famous by Foucault, causes and effects transpire in the same field and so become indistinguishable: in this story, individuals are heteronomous, so molded and constrained by social systems that they cannot act independently from those systems sufficiently to change them.[1] In the external model made famous by Marx, causes are so radically sequestered from effects that the mechanism by which social constraint can be inculcated disappears from view: if individuals are autonomous, then how do social systems that don't rely on the naked use of force constrain them? In the theorists we've discussed so far, psychoanalysis seems to offer a solution by splitting this difference to offer a portrait of a divided individual, part idiosyncrasy, part social conformity. Problem solved: individuals are unconsciously formed by social systems, but something idiosyncratic remains, from which political agency can arise. But attempting to theorize the *source* of this idiosyncratic agency leads these writers into difficulties, for while idiosyncrasy and contingency may suggest that individuals have the agency to resist social forces, they are not particularly useful attributes for *collective* or coordinated action. Emphasizing social determination vitiates individual *agency*, but emphasizing individual idiosyncrasy as the fundament of resistance vitiates *political* practice. So, if psychoanalytic concepts (such as unconscious internalization and identification) are used to explain the vigor of social forces to cast subjects in their own mold, in order to posit a source of solidarity, then these concepts get jettisoned when an explanation of agency is required. By the same token, if psychoanalytic concepts (such as unconscious desire and contingent appropriations) are used to promote a version of the subject relatively free from social determination, these concepts disappear when the question of coordinated political practice is at issue.

The problematic consequences for historicism of this disavowed and flimsy version of psychoanalysis cannot be overstated. True historicism requires the modulation of individual particularity with more general social trends. If individuals simply mirror social forces, or if individuals freely escape them, such modulation disappears. Understanding a historical phenomenon as expressed by individuals or groups in its own time and in relation to what comes before and after requires a more supple comprehension of the links of individuals to their social worlds and to each other, one that permits the question of significance to rise to the surface. In the critiques of Bourdieu, de Certeau, and Butler offered in the preceding chapters, I have sketched a more robust version of psychoanalysis that emphasizes the role of the extimate cause of the subject, the excess of signification as a condition of the Möbius subject, and the retroversive temporality attending it. These concepts address the problem of how subjects produced in and by a structured system can achieve a margin of freedom to bring about something new, neither simply repeating the past nor departing entirely from it.

I turn now to a theorist noted for developing the political potential of Lacanian thought – Ernesto Laclau. Laclau finds Lacan's work useful for a theory of "democratic interaction"; in particular, he argues that the Lacanian concept of the formal negation or extimate cause helps him develop a concept of a limit to the social system that both fosters equivalence among particular groups and destabilizes hegemony (E 35). We will see how his reliance on this concept provides his theory with great force, as compared, say, to Butler's or de Certeau's, not only because Laclau works with a full complement of poststructuralist tools, including Derridean iterability, but also because he has a more expert understanding of the psychoanalytic cause as a response to the deadlock of external and immanent causality. Correlatively, his disavowal appears in a more sophisticated way – as a disavowal of fantasy as a key component of the social bond. It is this lapse in Laclau's theoretical stance that hampers his ability to theorize egalitarian democracy in ways that respect the particularity and historicity of the parties involved.

Laclau keys his theory of political change to a criticism of a traditional binary – the universal versus the particular. It is relatively easy to understand the importance to social change theory of a conception of subject formation that neither reduces the subject to a mere function of its external determinants nor detaches the subject completely from its social world in an excess of autonomy. And it is reasonably straightforward to connect that theory to one that makes of history neither a sheer repetition of past meanings nor the free re-signification in the present of meanings with no moorings in the past. However, it may be more difficult to see what the opposition between the universal and the particular has to offer in the way of benefits to or problems for considerations of social change. Perhaps this difficulty arises from the current success of particularism over universalism in contemporary political and academic discourse. But this circumstance offers a clue to the significance of thinking the universal and the particular in a political key: a historicizing theory of social change must account for the emergence of particular identities in a form that permits their *coordination* with each other. If universalism is distasteful in its dominative implications, as particularist discourse would have it, particularism alone cannot provide a principle by which conflicts among particulars may be resolved, except by the assertion of might. This significant weakness helps account for the difficulty in generating collective actions. By contrast, Laclau proposes a theory that explains how the universal and the particular condition one another while retaining their own specific functions: he wagers that this re-thinking of the binary will make it possible to theorize a radical form of democratic interaction that sustains identities within a coherent political arena.[2] For Laclau, getting the relationship between the universal and the particular right is essential to creating a viable theory of social change which will explain the particular kinds of collective identifications that support a generalized form of radical democracy. In effect, he is working out a theory of the social bond that does not sacrifice historicity but works from a principle of extimate causality operating to produce the social field.

The Political Potential of the Universal Place-Holder

In *Emancipations*, a collection of some of his most important essays, Laclau lays out the problem caused by the universal/particular binary for democratically minded historicists. He notes that the success of the critique of the universalism of Enlightenment political philosophy posed by the proliferation of incommensurable particularisms attending today's cultural identity politics, far from undermining universalism, in fact highlights the need for *political* identities to partake of both. Laclau arrives at this position by noting that neither particularism nor universalism alone can describe the political landscape. Given that we must start with "social and cultural particularisms . . . defining the central imaginary of a group," doesn't that imaginary identification preclude identification with universal values (E vii)? By the same token doesn't the "very proliferation of antagonisms . . . require a language of 'rights' which must include the universalist reference" (E vii–viii)? The task is to find some way to appeal to a larger principle of unity and group identification without unduly constraining the heterogeneity necessary to democratic interaction. The competing claims of particularist interests lose their specificity – and even the grounds for taking them into account – if they are accommodated to or held together in a larger field that focuses on commonalities rather than differences. But if universalizing gestures court dominative politics, it is difficult to see how to compose the field within which these competing claims could be recognized or adjudicated in the absence of universals. If every group has a "differential, non-antagonistic relation to all the other identities," no principle can be articulated by which current power and status arrangements could be challenged (E 27). Respecting particularity at all costs can only bring about the separate and uneven developments of particular groups under status quo power conditions at best (which Laclau likens to a self-produced apartheid) or, at worst, institute a group version of the Hobbesian war of all against all. Correlatively, an abstract universal would have to find some embodiment by way of a concrete particular within the social field itself. We are confronted, apparently, with a Hobson's choice: when the particulars in the social arena do not belong to the same field, anarchy looms, but when some particular arrogates to itself the mantle of universality, totalitarianism threatens.

In the face of this seemingly intractable antagonism, Laclau proposes a "logic of a possible mediation" which "modifies the identities of both the particular and universal" (E viii). He begins the work of reconceiving the relationship of particular to universal by surveying the three historical forms in which that relationship has been imagined. In the first case, classical philosophy considers universality to be "graspable by reason" and distinguished absolutely from particularity (E 22). If the two come into contact, one disappears: either the particular realizes the universal in itself, thereby dissolving its own particularity, or it contaminates the universal. What remains unavailable to thought in ancient philosophy is the status of the line dividing the two: is it universal or particular?

In the second case, which Laclau associates with Christianity, the pole of universality is not graspable by reason: it is "only accessible to us through revelation," in which case the relation between particular and universal is incommensurable. Eschatological realization requires that in some unfathomable way, the infinite embodies itself in the finitude of concrete reality, a mysterious process called "incarnation." With God serving as the "only and absolute mediator" in some way inconceivable to us, a new logic began to make itself felt, "that of the *privileged agent of history*, the agent whose particular body was the expression of a universality transcending it" (E 23). When the Enlightenment adapted this logic by replacing God's function of universal guarantor with reason, the mystery of incarnation, which had linked the incommensurable realms of particular and universal, was transformed into a rational, *commensurable* connection between universality and particularity. Some body, in and of itself, has to realize the universal.

While in the abstract, this concrete universal body seems to cancel the distinction between particularity and universality – and in this way eliminates the incarnational moment (as Hegel asserts) – the problem at the level of the political is that some actual particular has to serve as the embodiment of the universal, providing the rationale and impetus for imperialist expansion. As Laclau puts it, "[t]he resistances of other cultures were, as a result, presented not as struggles between particular identities and cultures, but as part of an all-embracing and epochal struggle between universality and particularisms – the notion of peoples without history expressing precisely their incapacity to represent the universal" (E 24). This third type of relation between the universal and the particular grants an ontological privilege to certain agents of historical change, anointing some particulars with the mantle of universality in the name of reason but in fact merely reproducing the lines of force extant in the political sphere.

Arguing that the inherent opposition between universal and particular must be resolved but not dissolved in order to promote democratic interaction and positive social change, Laclau turns to Saussure's description of language as a system of signification in order to represent the political sphere as a system of differences. This move allows him to explore the constitution of particular identities in terms of their *relations* to one another and to the system rather than in terms of *positive qualities*. In a repetition of Lacan's formal negation as the cause of the subject, Laclau conceives of the universal not as a substantive element with positive qualities but rather as a content-less place-holder – what he calls an "empty signifier" (E 36).

Laclau begins by noting that the particulars within such a system have their identity only by virtue of their differences from one another. Yet, at the same time, something has to hold these particulars together in relation to one another as a system: some "limit" has to serve the function of "systematicity" (E 39). Two possible modes of this limit present themselves. On a first approach, the limit might be "neutral" with respect to the differences it sustains (E 37). One could imagine something like a fence that runs around the system and corrals each particular. Such a limit, however, is just another difference: particular A is different from particular B and each is different from the fence. In this case, the limit ceases to function as a condition of systematicity itself and joins the field of the system.

In perhaps his most Derridean and anti-Foucaultian moment, Laclau points out that one more difference cannot establish the ground of differences. To theorize a limit that actually produces systematicity as such, we must conceive of the limit to the system as completely other to the system itself. He proposes to think of the systematizing limit as "exclusionary," that is, as a limit that remains radically other to the contents of the system (E 38). In order to prevent the collapse into mere difference, this limit would have to be content-free, an empty place. Or, to put it another way, the limit of a system of signification cannot itself be signified, because were it susceptible of being signified, it would simply revert to being one of the differences *within* the system itself, rather than the system's limit and condition of existence.

Following his initial analogy to systems of signification, Laclau proposes that the exclusionary limit of political systems be thought in terms of the "empty signifier":

> [i]f democracy is possible, it is because the universal has no necessary body and no necessary content; different groups, instead, compete between themselves to temporarily give to their particularisms a function of universal representation. Society generates a whole vocabulary of empty signifiers whose temporary signifieds are the result of a political competition. (E 35)

By bringing in the empty signifier, Laclau seeks to avoid the problems that attend the exclusionary model as it operates in Butler, for example, where what is excluded has a historically determinate content which the one who "speaks impossibly" endeavors to regain. He explicitly rejects Butler's conception of exclusion in order to argue for the radical historicizing function of the kind of limit he conceives, one that can *"expand the relation of representation (as a failed representation, of course) beyond all limitation."*[3] Over the course of the major essays in *Emancipations*, Laclau works towards a conception of the universal as this kind of "empty place" or as a place-holder for a "missing fullness" in order to avoid giving any positive substance to the universal while maintaining its cohesive properties.

How does Laclau conceive of the function of the universal? According to him, the universal sets up a *system* of differences by functioning as a negation to cancel some dimension of particularity of each element in order to make all part of the same system. From this perspective, every element has the same relationship to the limit; every element is the equivalent to every other element, for each is held in the system by the limit. But this system is a system of *differences*: the action of the universal does not homogenize the social field. Their equivalence with respect to the limiting universal leaves in place other differences they have from each other. The equivalence among elements stands in tension with the differences that mark them out. For this reason, Laclau claims that the presence of the exclusionary limit constitutively splits each particular: "on the one hand, each difference expresses itself *as* difference; on the other hand, each of them *cancels* itself as such by entering into a relation of equivalence with all the other differences of the system" (E 38, original emphases). The identity of each particular is established by two dimensions, its connection to the system – in which dimension it is equivalent to other particulars in the same system – and its difference from those other particulars. In other words, particular identity is not a mere function of external differences, as it is in the particularist model where identity and difference amount to the same thing, as Laclau points out ("difference = identity" in particularism, he says) (E 38). Rather, identities emerge by way of a split within the particular, such that identity is always self-different, split *between* an equivalence and a difference.

This self-difference marks the failure of the field to cohere fully – to form one harmonious whole. But because this self-difference is *necessary* for the field's emergence as such, it must be the case that the divisions internal to the field, like the splits within the particulars, are irremediable. Social antagonism, then, has to be understood not as some element of the social field disturbing its integrity but as the very constitutive dimension of the field itself.[4] The self-difference of the particulars – a function of the constitution of the field – cannot be healed through the addition or exclusion of some other element. The field and its own self-difference, its inner antagonism, are two sides of the same coin.

In psychoanalysis, the split subject imagines that it is possible to be a subject (exist in the world of meanings as a signifier) while returning from the universe of meaning to the state of mere being or "eternal life" from which it feels it has been ejected. The neurotic position, as we have seen, involves precisely this fantasy that the subject is unjustly but *remediably* barred from something which will allow it to obtain this "lost" state. Psychoanalysis conceives of this fantasy as the split subject's attempt to acquire an impossible object, *objet a*, in order to recover this "lost" state of affairs. The fact that it is structurally impossible to be simultaneously a subject and a mere being does not register, or rather, it registers in the fantasmatic transformation of impossibility into prohibition – for what is merely *prohibited* (rather than impossible) might be attained.

Now Laclau gives this neurotic desire its due (without, however, describing it as neurotic) by positing that every particular in the social realm seeks to achieve a "lost" state of harmony, the "absent fullness of the community" (E 42). For Laclau, the political move *par excellence* is the re-figuration of antagonism – the impossibility of the social system to cohere fully – in terms of a fantasmatic "absent fullness of the community." The desire for this impossible state of affairs drives a contest to present the political agendas of particular groups as bringing about this ideal of the "fullness" of community. Other participants identify with this version of the ideal, recasting their own agendas in and through that particular version. At the same time, the contest for hegemony over the social field can have only provisional equilibria. Because antagonism is irremediable, any particular occupying this position will fail to represent the community adequately and therefore will not have a firm grasp on its hegemony.

Laclau designates the social antagonism instantiated in both the split identities and the unstable hegemony "which makes the distance between the universal and the particular unbridgeable" as the "very precondition of democracy" (E 35). This part of the logic has been clear since *Hegemony and Socialist Strategy*, and it is reiterated in these essays. If the universal in fact did have content, difference would disappear and the impossible and horrifying dream of social homogenization would be realized. Democracy depends upon minimal particular differences. By the same token, the constitution of "difference as difference" is equally impossible and horrifying: radical difference means no ground of inter-action whatsoever. Fortunately for the future promise of democratic interaction, as poststructuralist thought has abundantly shown, differ-ence and identity can no more be unalterably separated and opposed than can universality and particularity.

Laclau makes a final refinement to his theory. In proposing that democratic interaction emerges because the particular identities are split and in flux, he realizes that the hegemonic instance, the object of their identification, is also split: "no particularity can be constituted except by maintaining an internal reference to universality as that which is missing. But in that case, the identity of the oppressor will equally be split: on the one hand, he will represent a particular system of oppres-sion; on the other, he will symbolize the *form* of oppression as such" (E 31, original emphasis). That is, the object of identification does not exist in any objective or *a priori* way: it depends for its efficacy on its relation to the particulars it marshals. But in that case, it would seem that the theory cannot promise a *democratic* relation among particular political identities: an oppressor's identity may be split but the split itself doesn't guarantee that it won't be oppressive. How does Laclau handle this apparent refutation of his own proposition that democracy flows from the generation of split particulars?

The Criteria of Democratic Interaction

Perhaps more than any other political thinker, Laclau has insisted on our conceiving political identity from the standpoint of the subject *qua* self-different subject. He takes as his main focus the specific political question as to whether such subjects can participate in, promote, or even guarantee democratic interaction. He addresses this question by recasting the question in both psychoanalytic and semiotic terms. Like the identity of the subject, the object of identification (in political terms, the particular occupying the place of the content-less universal) does not pre-exist the identification in some *a priori* way, but comes into being as a stabilized set of characteristics only on account of the act of identification by the others. In semiotic terms, both the subject and the object of identification are signifiers held in multiple relations of resemblance and difference that are a function of their participation in (or their production of) a non-foundational, differential system. But why does Laclau link democracy to the impossibility of society, the failure to constitute difference as *pure* difference? In other words, given that all identities, including political ones, are necessarily split – not to mention in flux – how can we conclude that "democratic interaction [is] achievable"? What makes the prospect of these interactions "democratic" per se?

As we have seen, Laclau's answer conforms to rigorous antifoundationalist principles. The type of universality he proposes is, he says, "very different . . . from an underlying essence or an unconditioned *a priori* principle"; it has no content of its own (E 55). It is precisely because it lacks all positive content (because any positive content would inevitably reveal itself to be inadequate to the task of universalization) that it can function as a place-holder for the "transient articulation of equivalential demands" (E 56). The parties to the social interaction achieve a "democratic" relation on account of their equivalence with respect to this "absent fullness of the community, which lacks . . . any direct form of representation and expresses itself through the equivalence of the differential terms" (E 57). The place-holder *negates* some aspect of the particularity of each to bring it into equivalence with the others. In other words, the democratic relation is established by creating an equivalence among otherwise heterogeneous particularities as a consequence of the fact that all of these identities share *the same relationship of exclusion from and representation by* the absent and content-free, place-holding universal.

The crucial feature of this theory for democratic interaction, Laclau goes on to argue, is that the chain of equivalences so established must remain *open*: were it to close, this would mean that some method had been found to actually (not symbolically) realize the "fullness of the community," that some particular difference had somehow achieved the status of true universality, which is an impossibility. For although the chain of equivalences must express the universal, not the particular, in order to do so the universal must be represented by some particular – which necessarily fails in its task as universal, opening the way to its overthrow. Nonetheless, as a consequence of "hegemonic aggregation and articulation," the hegemonic instance still succeeds in establishing a kind of democratic relation of equivalence among the non-hegemonic particularities by virtue of their exclusion from the position of the "universal" (E 57).

Laclau's conception of *democratic* interaction has several features, then. First, he articulates the principle that any particular group could serve the hegemonic function as well as any other, that is, that no particular group has any given innate properties suiting it better to hegemony than any other particular. Second, all the groups are "equivalent" thanks to the sameness of their relationship to the limit marking the field, and each is equally split by that relationship into two parts – its identity as different from its counterpart particulars in the field (and different from the limit itself), and its sameness to them in their relationship to the "exclusionary" limit. These conditions, according to Laclau, ensure that the chain of equivalences will remain open and mobile. The equivalence ensures that no group will have any more "right" to the hegemonic position than any other, promoting continued competition for that place, and the differential identities, the identities-formed-through-relationships with others, ensure that the hegemonic instance will depend for its identity upon the other groups and therefore remain unstably positioned. Democratic interaction depends upon unstable hegemony (the split identity of the hegemonic instance ensuring its failure to achieve transcendental status), a system of differential identities (all groups affect each other), and an equivalence produced by the universal (equality of "right" to the hegemonic position ensuring continued competition). We will return to Laclau's analysis of these fundamental requirements of democratic interaction, but first let's take a look at the theory in action.

The Problem with the Hegemonic Instance

Laclau translates his conception of the universal as place-holder into political terms by positing that, under any given hegemonic regime, different particular groups will be oppressed and in this way achieve a kind of equivalence. To the extent that each particular group's identity is in some way negated by the regime, it becomes like its counterpart oppressed groups. Recognizing their similarities as oppressed by that regime will, he says, galvanize the collective identification of each particular group with a larger goal – liberation from the regime – as instantiated or expressed by one of the particular groups. The hegemonic instance will be conditioned by its relationship to the other groups in the chain of equivalence and therefore fail to achieve the fullness of community, resulting in a hegemonic instability. Laclau offers as an example of this process a worker's movement that

> succeeds in presenting its own objectives as a signifier of "liberation" in general. (This, as we have seen, is possible because the workers' mobilization, taking place under a repressive regime, is also seen as an anti-system struggle.) In one sense this is a hegemonic victory, because the objectives of a particular group are identified with society at large. But, in another sense, this is a dangerous victory. If "workers' struggle" becomes the signifier of liberation as such, it also becomes the surface of inscription through which *all* liberating struggles will be expressed, so that the chain of equivalences which are unified around this signifier tend to empty it, and to blur its connection with the actual content with which it was originally associated. Thus, as a result of its very success, the hegemonic operation tends to break its links with the force which was its original promoter and beneficiary . . . As society changes over time this process of identification will be always precarious and reversible and, as the identification is no longer automatic, different projects or wills will try to hegemonize the empty signifiers of the absent community. The recognition of the constitutive nature of this gap and its political institutionalization is the starting point of modern democracy. (E 44–6)

In this example, the workers' group stands in for the aspirations of liberation of all the other particular groups, who identify with the workers in common. Laclau finds the democratic potential here in the fact that the hegemonic group always has a precarious hold on power: because oppressor and oppressed alike are split in their relationship to each other, the "absent fullness" of the community can never arrive – and the democratic potential is preserved. The more the workers' group approximates the *purity* of the signifier of liberation, or is seen to do so, the less it retains its *particular* identity, and the more likely it is to "negate" the particular groups with which it had been allied, creating equivalences among them.

At first glance, this scenario meets Laclau's criteria for democratic interaction. First, the particular groups become equivalent under the initial hegemonic regime: they are all oppressed (or negated) by it and so seek deliverance from it. Each has an equal share, we might say, in this negating process and an equal stake in being freed from it. Second, each of the particular groups is "represented" in the common goal of liberation and therefore by the workers' group. In fact, each particular group identifies with the workers' group and finds the representation of its goal of liberation through that identification. Finally, the hegemonic group has a retroversively split identity – split between its functions as the representative of the absent fullness of community and its own particular interests and concerns, creating an instability that can lead to its dislodging.

In theorizing this split, Laclau relies on a distinction between "empty" signifiers and "floating" signifiers which have no fixed or proper signifieds ("either an overdetermination or an underdetermination of signifieds prevents [them] from being fully fixed"), but pass from one state of signification to another, in "an excess or deficiency of signification." But how could there be an empty signifier – a signifier without a signified? As Laclau explains it: "The only possibility for a stream of sounds being detached from any particular signified while still remaining a signifier is if . . . something is achieved which is internal to significations as such" (E 36). Laclau canvasses some "pseudo answers" to this enigma, but finally settles on the notion that the empty signifier emerges "if there is a structural impossibility in signification as such, and only if this impossibility can signify itself as an interruption (subversion, distortion, etcetera) of the structure of the sign" (E 36–7). The empty signifier, we learn, has two functions: it "constitutes the condition of possibility of a signifying system" and serves as that system's "condition of impossibility – a blockage of the continuous expansion of the process of signification" (E 37).

We have seen these functions before, in the extimate cause. The extimate cause constitutes the system of signification by producing a lack or space within it: without this lack, signification is not possible. The lack of a proper signified for one signifier injects a slippage between signifier and signified for all signifiers, allowing them to circulate and to refer to one another. This is the subversion of the structure of the sign and the establishment of the system of signification per se. The second function is the function of stopping the circulation, at least provisionally, by providing a reference for all the other signifiers, what Lacan calls the *point de capiton*. The empty signifier plays both roles by first unfettering the signifier/signified bond, setting up a signifying system composed of "floating signifiers," and then providing the conditions by which such bonds can be re-established provisionally.

Laclau likens these functions to the dual role of the hegemonic instance: the particular establishes the relationships among the other groups' properties, securing new meanings for them by reference to itself, a process which detaches them from their own prior meanings. However, it is hard to see how the particular that achieves hegemonic status conforms to the desiderata of the empty signifier, for by Laclau's own reckoning, the empty signifier has no signified at all, whereas the workers' group discharges its hegemonic obligations only because it has particular properties with which the other groups can identify. While the very presence of the "empty signifier" reveals (but does not signify), Laclau says, the limits to the system "as the *interruption* or *breakdown* of the process of signification" (E 37), the hegemonic group seems to correspond to the "floating signifier" with an excess *and* a deficiency of signification that arises from the other groups' identifications with it (relying on its particular properties and emptying it of them at the same time). In fact, it starts to sound more like the other groups are functioning as "empty signifiers" for the hegemonic instance, detaching and attaching its meanings at will. So, where the theory stipulates that the content-free place-holder produces the equivalence so that the groups can become equivalent, the example proposes that the groups, functioning as equivalent in their desire for liberation and their identification with the workers' group, produce the emptiness in the workers' group. In other words, the mechanism supposed to create the equivalence of the other groups (the emptiness of the universal), so that they can then identify with the workers, is here itself generated by an equivalence that seems always already to be in effect.

Of course, Laclau might say that there are three temporal moments here: first, the oppression by an earlier hegemonic instance forms the equivalences among the groups, which then compete for hegemony; in a second moment, one group emerges with which the others identify, thereby emptying it of its particular properties so that it can hold them in continued equivalence; finally, the emptying de-links the worker's group from the force of its particular properties, the very properties that enabled it to become a focus for identification. That explanation accords with Laclau's theory, but it has two disadvantages. In the first place, it sets up a *mise-en-abîme*. If the initial hegemonic instance acquires such repressive force that it produces equivalences, how does it do so? In the same way as the workers' group, by virtue of the identifications of some other equivalent groups which empty it out? If so, how did the equivalences that promoted the group identifications occur? And if not, how does the instability of the initial hegemonic group transpire?

In the second place, this explanation urges a distinctly different source of and route to hegemony than that proposed in the theory. In the theory, the hegemonic operator gains force by becoming a mere empty place-holder. But in the example, the hegemonic operator breaks with "the force which was its original promoter and beneficiary [i.e., the workers' group]" (E 45). Here Laclau tacitly endorses a theory of hegemony that derives its force not from the operation of the empty place-holder but from particular groups' identifications with specific content-full objectives. This endorsement becomes obvious when we note that hegemony is weakened to the extent that those specific objectives are obscured. In effect, Laclau proposes both that the hegemonic instance becomes hegemonic because it is *emptied* of its particular properties by the chain of equivalents and that the hegemonic instance becomes hegemonic because it is *full* of particular properties with which the chain of equivalents identify.

How could Laclau address this problem? At this point in his exposition, he seems most concerned to explain why the hegemonic particular has an unstable position. For the workers' group, as a group with specific and possibly unique concerns, interests, and political agendas, the conditioning by the identificatory actions of the other groups could indeed undermine the particularity of its identity. The danger for the workers' group that it might lose its specificity as it gains power may well be a boon to democratic interaction. But while it might seem that Laclau is holding fast to his insight that the "universal" and the "chain of equivalences" mutually condition one another, in fact, in the example he gives only the hegemonic instance is conditioned by the chain: the conditioning is one-way. In theory, "the process of representation itself creates retroactively the entity to be represented," which would mean that the process of representing the demands of the equivalent groups creates the identity of those groups.[5] Yet, in the example, the objectives of the workers' group focalize the identifications of the particular groups. It is the persistence of the particular concerns of these groups that causes the "emptying" of the particularity of the workers' group.

This outcome contradicts Laclau's exposition in two ways. First, the other groups have acquired the ability to act in solidarity, but evidently not because they were subjected to the operation of the universal placeholder. Rather, the workers' group becomes the universal place-holder – and therefore the (unnecessary) operator of an equivalence that has *already* taken place – because the particular groups identify with it. One might say that this result is simply a function of the retroversive relationship of one to the other, except that the particular identities of the groups remain tied to their original signifiers. It is on account of this retention of a "proper signified" – one not transformed by the hegemonic instance – that the workers' group itself becomes emptied of its particular content. And this is the second way in which Laclau departs from his initial premises, for the example abrogates the principle of self-difference in its implicit rejection of retroversion: the force of the groups' effects on the workers is due to their particularity, not their self-difference, and the force of the workers' group is due to its emptiness, not its split identity.

Another problem with Laclau's model can now be seen more clearly.

By his own lights, the most favorable conditions for fostering equivalence are produced by the most repressive regimes. In fact, the greater the repression, the greater the equivalence, according to Laclau, and (here is the twist) therefore the greater the chance of democratic interaction:

> the repressive power . . . will count less as the instrument of particular differential repressions and will express pure anti-community, pure evil and negation. The community created by this equivalential expansion will be, thus, the pure idea of a communitarian fullness which is absent – as a result of the presence of the repressive power. (E 42)

Under these conditions the negating power of the exclusionary limit will be at its most concentrated, generating in turn the highest degree of empowering unanimity among the interests and perspectives of the parties of resistance. Apparently, repression is sufficient for democracy to take hold, and, paradoxically, democracy will be the logical outcome of repression. But if we are to take seriously Laclau's other "concrete" example, Peronism, interaction among disparate groups itself leads to the emergence of a repressive regime – not, as one might have thought, to the emergence of a democratic one (E 54–6). Laclau offers no actual analysis of the circumstances under which democracy emerges (or flourishes) nor of the requisites for stabilizing or destabilizing democratic interaction. Rather, in his model, the transformation of democratic interaction into repressive power – and vice versa – transpires automatically.

Laclau's initial conditions for "democratic interaction" indicate how this unlooked-for result comes about. His reliance on the place-holding universal derives from his analysis of the need for some operator that will account for social antagonism (as indicated by the irremediable necessity of split identities to the production of the social field) at the same time as it creates some system within which those split particulars can interact. In its function of splitting the identities of the particulars, the universal place-holder corresponds to a description of social antagonism. But social antagonism, by Laclau's own lights, is always already present. It is always in force no matter what the particular political form (it is as true for dictatorships as for parliamentary democracies). Social antagonism is not *produced*. In effect, Laclau uses the same terms to describe democratic interaction as he uses to describe social antagonism. The sleight-of-hand that makes them seem separate depends upon the slippage we have already indicated: the universal place-holder as content-less negation of "hard-shelled" particularity is implicitly equated with the universal fantasy of an absent but recoverable "fullness of community." When Laclau wants to stress democracy, he highlights the fact that no hegemonic instance can fully instantiate that fantasy, opining that any other split particular would have the same problems – and the same chances of – embodying it. Hence "democratic interaction," which means here continual transformation of the hegemonic instance among a set of equivalent groups, as though the only requirement for holding power is having the capacity to present oneself as – or having the fortune to be taken as representing – the locus of group identifications. But like split identities, the incapacity of any given particular to bring about the fullness of community has nothing to do with democratic interaction, because it is simply a function of the irremediability of social antagonism. It is, in fact, one way to describe the fact of social antagonism. And, as Laclau's examples demonstrate, there is nothing about social antagonism *per se* that leads to democratic interaction. What is "democratic" in Laclau's theory – split identities, hegemonic instability, competition among particular groups – is merely another way to describe the fact of social antagonism. In effect, Laclau has substituted sufficiency for necessity, as though social antagonism, a necessary pre-condition of all social systems including democratic ones, is also sufficient for democracy to arise.

Laclau's Incomplete Psychoanalytic Theory

How, exactly, does Laclau run into trouble? I will be arguing that even though Laclau borrows from Lacanian psychoanalysis to derive the function of the extimate cause as empty place-holder, his difficulties arise from its incomplete application just when it could do him the most good. Obviously, Laclau makes use of psychoanalytic concepts, including the self-different or split subject and its recourse in fantasy to an imaginary object that promises to rectify social antagonism and restore wholeness. He also gives weight to the principle of retroversion by which the meanings of particulars change with every new arrangement of the social field. He emphasizes the crucial action of identification as a constituent of both group and collective identities.[6]

Most importantly, his elaboration of the universal as place-holder owes a large debt to Lacan's exposition of the formal negation that brings the subject into the Symbolic. Laclau himself comments on the utility of Lacanian precepts for his project. He draws special attention to the Lacanian conception of retroversion in the relation of the signifier to the signified:

> Hegemony requires, as we have seen, a generalization of the relations of representation, but in such a way that the process of representation itself

creates retroactively the entity to be represented. . . . This "liberation" of the signifier *vis-à-vis* the signified – the very precondition of hegemony – is what the Lacanian bar attempts to express. The other side of the coin, the contingent imposition of limits or partial fixations – without which we would be living in a psychotic universe – is what the notion of "point de capiton" brings about.[7]

Conceived along Lacanian lines, the empty place-holder has two dimensions, both of which Laclau references here. First, it functions to subvert particular sedimented signifier/signified complexes, "liberating" them, as Laclau puts it. But this is just a first step in making it possible for the signifier to be appropriated for new purposes in new contexts. A system of signification emerges not simply because signifier/signified relationships have been dislocated but also because signifiers can be linked up with new signifieds, however provisionally. This provisional linking occurs thanks to the second dimension of the place-holder, which Laclau calls by its Lacanian name – the *point de capiton*.

To make clear what is at stake in invoking these Lacanian concepts, it is useful to return to the process by which the child becomes a subject in Lacan's theory. In the process of subject-formation, the child encounters sedimented meanings in the mother's universe – a world of apparently fixed, immutable meanings. Each signifier appears to have its own proper signified; each signifier/signified dyad is a "hard-shelled" particularity, bearing no systematic relationship to any other. These are not the "dictionary" meanings of words: rather, in addition to the private words developed between mother and child ("binkie" for blanket, "passie" for pacifier, "baba" for bottle), even standard language takes on an extra significance, installed by way of the mother's desire. In speaking the mother's tongue, the child is not participating in a larger social world so much as he is reestablishing his connection to the mother. In order for the child to enter the Symbolic and the wider social uses of language to establish connections to others, the formal cause has to intervene to "liberate" these sedimented meanings. (We might note here that this "liberation" in no way *equates* these meanings: they do not become equivalent just because they are subjected to the formal negation.)

Fortunately for most children, the *Non/Nom-du-Père* accomplishes this task, releasing the signifiers to the mobile operations of signification. The negation of the particularity of each fixed signifier/signified brings them all into the realm of signification, where meaning is a function of signifier-to-signifier relations in a differential system. In this way, too, the child can become a signifier and a subject, as Lacan describes: "My definition of a signifier (there is no other) is that which represents the subject for another signifier."[8] The institution of the *bar*, which is the mark of negation of these fixed relations between signifier and signified, makes possible the transition to subjecthood by way of the signifier. After this "liberation" of the signifier by means of the formal negation, the second operation takes place: what Laclau calls "the other side of the coin, the contingent imposition of limits or partial fixations – without which we would be living in a psychotic universe – is what the notion of 'point de capiton' brings about."[9] The *point de capiton* restabilizes the unmoored signifiers with provisional signifieds, allowing them to acquire specific properties of identity. The extimate cause – here equated with the paternal function – encompasses both operations, for not only does it supply the requisite negation of sedimented meaning, freeing the signifying chain, but it also serves as the anchoring point by which the "partial fixations" occur.

Paradoxical as it may seem, the signifier serving as *point de capiton* has no signified of its own. It only acquires some stability and partial fixation as a result of its association by reference to other (chains of) signifiers. This is the moment of retroversion, when the quilting signifier takes on its signified, which turns out to be nothing other than the group of signifiers held together in the signifying chain by the quilting signifier. As a result, the quilting signifier has a paradoxical function with respect to these signifiers. On the one hand, it is added as a purely formal negation to the previous state of affairs: in this sense it is completely unlike the other signifiers and apparently exceptional to the signifying system of differences. On the other hand, it is the absolutely necessary element of the system, establishing the system through its addition: in this sense, it *is* a part of the system. As we have seen, the extimate cause always has this paradoxical inside/outside structure.

Lacan uses two symbols to articulate this paradox. The first, S1, is the *point de capiton*, the quilting signifier, while the second, S2, is the chain of signifiers so quilted. The temporality of their relations is complex. But speaking logically, we can posit three moments by returning to the discussion of extimacy outlined in chapter 2. The first is a state of affairs Copjec refers to as the "realtight," where there are no signifiers, only entities without identity or relation, as in our example of the messy garage.[10] Neither S1 nor S2 has emerged as a signifier at this point. These hard-shelled particulars do not have identities, properly speaking, because identity is always a function of relation. In order for identities-in-relation to arise to constitute a system of signification, something different from this initial state of affairs somehow has to be distinguished. This "exception" cannot be another hard-shelled particular, obviously; adding one such particular after another, on to infinity, can never change the state of affairs. (It is convenient to use Žižek's Hegelian term, "bad infinity," for this form of the infinite.) Rather, the "exception" can consist of nothing positive: as we have seen, it is no more than the formal addition of a negation to the state of affairs. The entities affected by the formal negation initially have no relation to one another, which means that they do not have identities properly speaking, because identity is a function of both difference and sameness: it is *self*-different.

Prior to the addition of the negation, entities in the "realtight" exist in the mode of sheer being, unrelated to anything else. They have no *identities*, because identity only emerges when that entity enters into some relationship, which is what the "liberation" of the negation produces. When the formal negation is added to the "mere being-ness" of the entity, it acts like the brackets of the set, as a kind of outline or container for the entity, doubling it like a shadow.[11] This "outline" is the connection between an inside (the entity) and an outside (the space around it, other entities), both part of and not part of the entity. The split achieved by this doubling cancels out the "mere being" of the particular, putting it into a relationship with itself as well as with others. In chapter 2, we described these as its *set-ness* and the *elements of the set*. Thus, in the first step from being to meaning, the entity becomes a particular identity-in-relation by way of the negation.

With the addition of the negation, the conditions for identity are established. The formal negation establishes a system of differential relations that confer identity, which allows them to be grouped together. But this grouping does not take place on the basis of some common or shared property. Rather, the elements in the field are held together by the fact that they have been negated in such a way as to be able to be identified in relation to something else – they have become signifiers. In this second (logically speaking) moment, the particulars form a differential *and incomplete* (nontotalizable) system of signifiers, in which each signifies through its relationship to all the others as well as to the function – the addition of a negation – that has cancelled their "mere being." This addition prevents the system from becoming complete because it does not simply contain the elements, like a corral, but rather injects into their relationship a void – the *empty set*, which is nothing other than the function of "set-ness" in the relations among the elements, what keeps them distinct yet connected to one another within the external brackets, so to speak. It is important to keep in mind that the two modes of the negation – set-ness and empty set – are merely two faces of the same function. The relations among the elements, thanks to this void, remain fluid: no signifier gains a final signified because each signifier's link to any signified depends upon its relation to the other signifiers.

Viewed from a perspective *within* the system, the operator of this function of negation appears to be both excessive and necessary to the system. In its excessive dimension, S1 appears to be radically unlike the signifiers of S2, because it does not enter into the relations of identity and difference of the system. Nonetheless, S1 is necessary for the system to emerge with the specific property of incompleteness, for if the system were to be totalizable, we would be back in the Imaginary world of the dyad's sedimented meanings. In adding a negation rather than another element to the system, S1 "infinitizes" the system: its incompleteness means that signifieds are always provisional and stability is endlessly deferred. This form of infinity (Žižek's "good infinity") makes the interior of the system infinite in its possible interrelationships – and therefore untotalizable.

Now, S1 is paradoxical in another way. Because S1 is necessary to the system's emergence and because the system itself is composed of signifiers, it seems that S1 must be some kind of signifier. Lacan has described S1 in various ways, most frequently as a signifier without a signified or as a signifier whose signified is "primordially repressed." Yet insofar as S1 has no signified within the system of signifiers, it can only gain an identity as a signifier *retroactively* from its action of generating S2. In this third logical moment, S1 retroversively acquires S2 as its signified, so that S1's status as signifier (it has a signified) seems assured. So, S1 is a peculiar kind of signifier. Consider that S2 is an assemblage that operates as a system and that systems function only to the extent that they are not total or complete. S2 coheres as a system because S1 adds a lack to it: that lack both generates the system and prevents its signifier/signified relations from becoming sedimented. Then from one angle, it looks like S1 is *necessary* to the system, but from another angle is looks like S1 is precisely what *stands in the way* of S2 completely cohering, the obstacle to its achieving stability. Consequently, S1 as signifier comes to stand both for that which is necessary to the system and for that which obstructs its totality. Because the system is constituted by the lack that S1 adds, and because S1 is also excessive to S2, it seems as though S1 could remediate that lack, creating what is in fact impossible – a system without a surplus. When S1 plays this role, Lacan denominates it as the phallic function (Φ) – an Imaginary function of totalization, the opposite of (and complement to) the function of the addition of a negation (or castration).

At this point, we can put our finger on at least one way in which Laclau's appropriation of psychoanalysis diverges from Lacan's theory, even as he attempts to deploy it. The Phallus, for Lacan, is the most basic signifier: "For the phallus is the signifier intended to *designate as a whole the effects of the signified*, in that the signifier conditions them by its presence as a signifier."[12] In other words, the S1-as-Phallus is the signifier of the totality of the signifieds of S2 insofar as they Imaginarily constitute a whole. At the same time, S1 is *also* the extimate cause in its paradoxically dual status as set-ness and empty set, the addition of *nothing* that generates the system and the operator of the system's incompleteness.

This dual nature of S1 is precisely what Laclau omits in his example of the hegemonic instance: in representing the absent fullness of the community as the goal of all the other groups, S1 seems to operate like the Imaginary phallic function. Laclau's hegemonic instance does not acquire its split identity in the same way as Lacan's S1 does. The hegemonic instance, we recall, becomes *emptier* retroactively by reference to the other groups' interests or properties (which Laclau treats as analogs of the signifieds of S2), a relation that splits the hegemonic instance between emptiness and *its own* particular interests or properties. In Lacan's theory, by contrast, S1 is split between its two functions as formal negation and its Imaginary role of the Phallus signifying S2 as a sedimented totality. Unlike the hegemonic instance in Laclau's model, S1 does not have its own particular interests or properties, but arises as a signifier with a provisional signified as an epiphenomenon of the very system of signifiers it generates.

Why should this matter? Why couldn't we just say that Laclau is using Lacan for his own purposes, perhaps even making a positive innovation on the Lacanian conception of the signifier? One answer to that question is that by his own lights, Laclau has turned the hegemonic instance into "just another difference" – which means it is incapable of serving the function he assigns to it. So, for example, insofar as the workers' group has its own particular interests, it cannot function as an S1 to bring the others into relation to one another (not to mention, make them equivalent with one another). And if the workers' group did *not* have its own particular interests, it could not serve as a point of identification for these groups in the way that Laclau suggests. So, in order for Laclau to derive a political valence from the operation of the extimate cause, he has to forsake its true theoretical status as content-free. But once he has done so, he gives up extimate causality and with it any way to avoid the immanentism he is at such pains to renounce.

Counting Versus Unifying Identifications

In fact, no matter what he says, the political mechanism Laclau describes in the workers' group example relies far more on identification than it does on the formal negation as cause of the system. On one hand, this is good news for Laclau: it will help release his theory from the strange result that the greater the repression, the greater the democracy. On the other hand, it is bad news, because his reliance on the particular type of identificatory mechanisms he describes places his theory squarely in the Imaginary register of narcissistic/rivalrous relations with de-historicizing consequences. In order to see the consequences of Laclau's conflation of two distinct modes of identification, as psychoanalysis defines them, it will be helpful to take another look at the cause of the subject.

In the Lacanian story, the child becomes a subject by way of two modes of identification, one Imaginary, the other Symbolic. Imaginary identification produces the conditions under which desire emerges during the renowned mirror stage: the split, the longing for an illusory wholeness, the *objet a* presumed to restore that wholeness. This form of identification involves the imitation of an image of an other as a totality (turning it into an Other who holds the secret to the subject's meaning). In Imaginary identification, the ego comes into being by internalizing an image of an other as a complete entity: this image could be the mirror image of the child itself. The child experiences itself as less whole than the image: the image provides both a wished-for, anticipatory form of the subject (which, in fact, could never be realized), and a standard against which the subject measures itself and finds itself wanting, incomplete. The image of totality serves as a support for the subject as an *ideal ego,* but at the same time, it makes the subject believe that it lacks something to make it complete, a mysterious *objet a.* As Lacan is at pains to point out, in Imaginary identification the subject attempts to achieve a fantasmatic *unity* by means of the illusory *objet a* that fills out the subject's lack. This identification is the means by which the subject contemplates itself as a whole.

Imaginary identification, predicated as it is upon a relationship to an image of wholeness and routed through an *other*, involves a dynamic of emulation and rivalry. The subject's attempts to imitate the other as a global entity inevitably pit the subject against the other. In effect, this identification attempts to put the subject in the place where the other stands – but there is only room for one in that position. The more closely the subject emulates the other, the more closely the subject comes to usurping the place of the other or feeling that the other is likely to take the subject's place. Through this mode of identification, the subject seeks to be the "unifying one" – a narcissistic relation of complete self-sufficiency. Far from establishing a basis for collective identification, it promotes antagonism and ultimately provides the rationale for the annihilation of rivals.

Unfortunately, Imaginary identification cannot support the kind of social interactions that enable groups to form, because this form of identification eradicates others. In order to ameliorate the kinds of rivalrous emulation generated by Imaginary identification, the subject must learn to identify with the other in a nontotalizing mode. Freud describes this form of identification in *Group Psychology and the Analysis of the Ego:* "The identification is a partial and extremely limited one, and only borrows a single trait from the person who is its object."[13] This single or *unary* trait (*traite unaire*, in Lacan's terminology) anchors the subject in the Symbolic without embroiling it in the rivalries of Imaginary identification. The anchoring point most often chosen is some arbitrary *paternal* trait – the trait that for the child places the father in reach of identification, although the person filling the bill need not be the father or even male. Lacan calls this the unary trait not only because it is a specific trait but because, by analogy with the unary signifier, S1, it is the trait that, *from the child's point of view*, makes the person so chosen appear to embody that wished-for self-coincidence as the Phallus. From the point of view of others, this trait might not seem to be a noteworthy feature of that person's qualities; it might be a wholly contingent object or characteristic (a certain posture; a pitch of voice). The actual relationship of this trait to this person's ability to command respect or the centrality of this trait to the person is, however, not what gives it its importance. In effect, the child is "struck" by this trait unconsciously for idiosyncratic reasons; the trait which seems to confer the status of law-giver, focus of mother's desire, and source of signification is purely contingent.

In this fantasmatic role, the chosen person is the exception to the rule of castration, superintending the system of signification and conferring signification on everything else. The child unconsciously identifies with this trait as the basis for its own sense of significance, but the child does not confuse himself with the person he has chosen: each retains a particular identity. Still, the child's sense of its own meaning depends on its internalizing as its own the concrete property that – for the child – embodies a power of self-particularization, the capacity to acquire both position and meaning by one's own efforts. In this way, the unary trait will become the basis of all transferential identifications for the subject.

In Freudian terms, this identification produces the *ego ideal* within the child's psychic economy, and Lacan follows Freud in distinguishing this form of identification from that of the *ideal ego*, the internalized picture of the self that (if it were possible) is imagined to repair the split in the subject. If Imaginary identification were the only dynamic at play in the subjectification of the child, the child would forever be trapped in the dangerous world of narcissistic rivalry. And, of course, this can happen. But because the child can become a subject through the function of the extimate cause, it can partake of another dynamic with another destiny.

Within the Lacanian system, the unary trait is some signifier in S2 that stands in for the phallic quality or access to missing *jouissance*. The unary trait, in other words, is a signifier, like any other signifier. But because it serves the phallic function for the subject, it emerges in the role of S1. In effect, the particular trait loses its "everyday" signified (gray sweater, deep voice) and takes on the generalized function of S1. Any signifier could fill this function, because it requires no special properties, including "emptiness": it is a contingent choice on the part of the child. In this account, then, we find revealed the true status of S1: *any* signifier can take on the role of the Imaginary Phallus (so much for Laclau's attempted distinction between "empty" and "floating" signifiers), because *every* signifier necessarily re-marks the paradoxical functions of the extimate cause.

Identification via the unary trait, by which the child gains a toe-hold in the Symbolic, does not produce a "whole," however illusory. It does not depend upon some comprehensive identification. Rather, the unary trait is a limited, specific trait which the child grasps in order to establish his own particular identity among the identities of others. The unary trait keeps the subject afloat as a particular signifier in the sea of signifiers, anchored to the father, and hence apportioned some small if provisional stake in the Symbolic as *one among others*, enumerable. In this way, the subject becomes not a "unifying one" but a countable one, "as one more among subjects, capable of being named and differentiated."[14] From the point of view of Laclau's needs, we can see that it is this countability derived from the unary trait, not the unifiability derived from the *objet a*, that could promote democratic interaction: only identification in the mode of the unary trait provides equivalence rather than rivalry.

The crucial point to keep in mind is that the unary trait is not *objet a*: they have two completely different functions. *Objet a* is a fantasmatic object that fills in for the lack (of *jouissance*) for the subject, the lack which precipitates the individual from being into meaning, to repair (in fantasy) the split that makes it a subject. Were the subject able to acquire *objet a* in actuality, it would cease to be a subject: *objet a* is the cause of desire, and the fulfillment of desire, were it possible, would spell the end of the subject. The unary trait by contrast gives the signifier/subject a contingently determinate place in the chain of signifiers, allowing the signifier to attach provisionally to a signified. The *objet a* represents the Phallus insofar as it is *lacking*, while the unary trait stands in for the Phallus insofar as it seems to be *present*: "The object a is something from which the subject, in order to constitute itself, has separated itself off as organ. This serves as symbol of the lack, that is to say, of the phallus, not as such, but insofar as it is lacking."[15]

Why stress this distinction between Symbolic and Imaginary identification? Because Laclau's unwitting collapsing of identification by way of the unary trait (Symbolic identification) with identification by way of *objet a* (Imaginary identification) leads him to the predictable result that his model becomes mired in the dynamics of imitation and rivalry. In his example, for instance, the workers' group initially struggles with all the other groups. Then, when the other groups identify with it, the workers' group gains hegemony but only by losing its particularity vis-à-vis these other groups. Thus, the working group is either one among many atomized particularities in rivalry for hegemony, or it is an undifferentiated part of a solidary block taking hegemony as its own. Laclau proposes that the hegemonic instance affords the other particulars with a global site of identification: in this capacity, the hegemonic instance plays the part of the entity that has *objet a*. When other groups emulate the hegemonic group, they both imitate and rival it, the situation Laclau invokes as the "dangerous" quality of the workers' "victory."[16] In his substitution of a fantasy of global identification for the reality of split identities, he describes the type of identity in play in the political process not as permanently self-different but rather as always perfectly identical with itself.

Why Equivalence is not Democratic

Laclau's reliance upon Imaginary identification not only forces him to describe social interactions predicated on rivalry – which renders them unable to fulfill the mission of political solidarity he assigns them – it also fails to provide him with a way of describing the true nature of groups formed by identification. We can see these problems when he explains that the collective identifications of the groups propel one of their own into hegemony by virtue of their equivalent desire for the "absent fullness of community." In Lacanian terms, this desire corresponds to the neurotic's desire for the apparently prohibited "lost" world of immersion in *jouissance*, the universe of being that is sacrificed in order to become a subject. The focus on lost or prohibited wholeness, the fantasy of a remediated split by way of imitation of the entity presumed to have *objet a*, and the ensuing rivalrous interrelations promoted by this global form of emulation, mark Laclau's model as Imaginary. Clearly what is missing in his account is a theorization of group formation by way of Symbolic identification.

To get at this missing piece of the theoretical puzzle, we can begin by focusing on Laclau's insistence that groups in the political arena are mobilized by a desire for the "absent fullness of community." We might well ask, what would make any particular group believe that access to *jouissance* could be attained by way of the fullness of community? That is, why would the fullness of community be the particular fantasy driving each and every group in the social arena? Laclau's answer to this question is that the fullness of community is the opposite of social antagonism: the desire to remedy social antagonism would necessarily correspond to some fantasy of social cohesion.

The problem with this line of reasoning is that social antagonism doesn't appear *as such*: rather, its effects are always attributed to some specific element in the subject's world or, in this case, the social system. Some particular element is conceived as an obstacle to the *jouissance* of the subject or the group. Racism is a good example of this phenomenon. The effects of social antagonism are registered – but not in terms of a constitutive antagonism affecting all parties all the time. Rather, they are imagined to be a function of a particular group's way of enjoying: that group is thought to be too seduced by pleasure to participate in the work of the social project, or too enamored of money to concern itself with the general welfare, or too violent to be tolerated, and so forth. In effect, the hated group seems have misappropriated *objet a*. In order to return *objet a* to its "proper" owners that group must be deprived of it somehow – by exclusion, deprivation, punishment, servitude, and so on.

On this analogy, were the groups in the Laclauian social arena to regard the hegemonic instance as having access to *objet a*, they would be in competitive rivalry with it, not recognizing their common goals through it, as we have just seen. But this theoretical error is not the only one lurking in Laclau's exposition. The groups under discussion in his model seem to be both unusually similar to one another in their actual properties – sharing the same ideals, for example – and unusually self-consistent. In other words, in Laclau's story, the cancellation of their particularity produced by the negating limit serves to make the groups at once more like each other and increasingly internally consistent. For Laclau, all of the groups share the same relation to the absent fullness of community, and everyone in each group shares this relation as well. This global emulation within and between groups also bears the mark of Imaginary identification. By contrast, in psychoanalytic theory, groups are composed of individuals who identify with the group's aims in their own ways and for their own reasons. Similarly, any group as a whole might identify with another group's political agenda in its own way and for its own reasons. In theoretical terms, we are speaking of the modes of transference: any given individual identifies by way of an internalized unary trait idiosyncratic *to itself*. Once we understand that the unary trait is at issue, we can see that the identification with the Phallus can take place – is likely to take place – by way of quite different and even mutually contradictory signifiers for individuals, even when they are members of a group.

Every group identity, then, is formed through identifications with *something* but that something is only nominally the same for each member of the group, for each member identifies *differently*, by way of a unary trait significant to itself. The public identifying characteristics of the object of identification for members of the group need not be – and typically are not – the characteristics on which the identification with that object is based. Thus, at the Symbolic level, the "group-ness" of the group depends upon a fantasy: each imagines the others to identify in the same way. So long as the group sustains its identity by way of its difference from an other – that is, in the Imaginary register, where the struggle for a given place is paramount and minute differences have ultimate narcissistic value – the fantasmatic nature of this presumption will remain masked, and the group will appear more cohesive than it really is. The well-known phenomenon of groups undergoing internal strife immediately after they succeed in securing the coveted position against all opposition, evinces the fantasy that serves to disguise the actual heterogeneous nature of Symbolic identifications within the group. The differences among the group members rise to the surface, making visible the illusory quality of the group's prior solidarity.

We can recall that the child seizes on the unary trait in a *contingent* way.[17] What counts as the phallic trait for one person will have no effect on another. In other words, different groups identify with distinct traits of the hegemonic group, just as different members of a group anchor themselves to it by way of unique points of identification. These traits can be so different as to be inconsistent or even in conflict, which accounts for the internal lability of groups. The result of different groups identifying with the same hegemonic instance by way of different traits would be as likely to create fragmentation and contestation as (even provisional) solidarity.

Of course, in the discourse of democratic values that arises in the cultural studies milieu, the polity and the groups within it often pride themselves on tolerating, accommodating, or welcoming differences. But these are differences that are assumed *not to make a difference* to the larger group identity. The members are conceived as being the same at some level – they are all women or members of the same cultural subgroup or victims of the same oppression, and so forth. However, from a psychoanalytic perspective, the only truly democratic mode of group formation, one that does not reduce the members to a sameness conceived in positive terms, involves Symbolic identification wherein each member's *difference* or unique choice of unary trait is its route to inclusion in the group. The point which must be emphasized is that the "object" of identification is *not the same* for the members: the America in which I am a citizen is not the same for me as it is for other people. The traits of the US government which are excoriated by libertarians as too oppressive are not the same traits that a liberal group will deem unacceptable: so while both may object to the "same" government, neither conceives of the government in the same way.

The "universal" is always a particular universal for each of the particulars it holds together: what Laclau calls the "universal" is nothing more than a fantasy that the aggregate of the points of identification seized upon by each subject cohere as the same object. When he speaks of the hegemonic instance being split, he verges on recognizing the irreducibility of its inflection by the particulars in its field. But, as we have seen, for Laclau the hegemonic instance's own specific identity remains throughout, which means that he relies on a positive trait to establish the grounds of the group's cohesion. In his model, S1 has discrete, proper, positive qualities, which is to say that he presents the universal under the guise of the mystification of the Phallus.

This theoretical error makes it impossible for Laclau's model to distinguish between repressive and democratic regimes. Laclau himself stipulates that groups might choose order over democratic interaction (E 62). Here Laclau vitiates his ideal of egalitarian participation in favor of a scene of equal oppression. Particular entities within a political arena, Laclau tells us, cannot engage in democratic interaction unless they find some universal through which to mediate their differences. The empty signifier is supposed to supply sufficient tension between the universal and the particulars to maintain separate individual and collective identities and to allow for that equivalence among them necessary to competitive and concerted action alike. The apparently democratic goal of equality among differences derives, then, from the negating action of the exclusionary limit. But the so-called "universal" can never be empty (or particular) in the way that Laclau thinks because it exists nowhere except in the relations of other particulars, each of which gives it its own inflection, each of which "hooks" onto it in its own way, by means of a specific trait that appears significant only for that particular.

The Political Valence of the Veiled Phallus

Although he tries to describe it as such, the "empty signifier" of Laclau's theory is not the extimate cause which generates S1/S2, because the "empty signifier" functions outside the system that it creates and superintends. What is the difference? When the extimate cause quilts the concrete particulars of any political arena, it establishes specific relationships between them and itself, but those relationships are inflected differently by each particular: for each signifier in S2, a different kind of relation, a different point of connection, to (an) S1 is generated. Why? Because S1 exists nowhere except in these particular relations. In the quilting function, there are as many points of connection – and therefore as many versions of – S1 as there are S2. So, just as S1 brings all the other signifiers in relation to each other, and in this way crosses each signifier with every other, bringing each into relationship with all (forming the system), so there is a retroversive conditioning between S1 and any given signifier in S2, such that S1 is criss-crossed by a set of different relations. It is the different inflections of the relationships between S1 and each of these other signifiers that makes it possible for these signifiers to sustain their differences from each other, just as it is the fact of the relationship to S1 in each case that makes it possible for S1 to serve as a kind of referent for all of the signifiers in S2. S1 becomes the Phallus only when these inflections appear to be "ejected" as signifieds, so that S1 in its multiform identity *appears to have no signified of its own but rather stands over, as external cause, a system of which it is no part.* Lacan describes this function as "veiling": insofar as the inflections of S2 are curtained off (which is to say, that the splits in S1 are ignored), the Phallus appears to be outside the system of signifiers, conditioning them as its stable and permanent signifier and immune to their individual retroversive conditioning of itself.

S1 appears as the Phallus when the inflected relationships to S2, which split S1 in infinite ways, are shuttered. The Phallus then appears to be the "solution" to the splits in each signifier in S2, because it doesn't seem to be split and doesn't seem to be the cause of the splits in the signifiers in S2, even though, as S1, it is both. The Phallus is an illusory aspect of S1, an epiphenomenon of its serving as a relay for the S2s to each other. Only in fantasy, however, does the "same" S1 serve as relay for all S2s: no signifier is a signifier except insofar as it is in relationship with another signifier, which means that the relationship necessarily inflects both signifiers. In the fantasy that S1 can serve in the same way for all the other signifiers, S1 emerges as an illusory entity – as the Phallus – as though the actual inflections were somehow put out of play.

At the same time, the phallic mode is crucial: it is what halts the slide of the signifiers along S2 to give them provisional signifieds. This Imaginary function serves as the necessary complement in the operation of signification to the operation of splitting or liberating the signifier from a signified, detaching it so that signification proper can take place. What is more, this Imaginary function is what prevents S1 from becoming just another difference in the system of differences. In effect, the system has to "except" some signifier – the one that serves as Phallus – in order to constitute itself. Or rather, at every moment of signification, some signifier seems to be an exception to the splitting of all the other signifiers and outside the system. Calling this a fantasy is another way of saying that the extimate signifier is a floating signifier like all the others in S2 but that its own splits appear to be occulted. *Quilting, excepting,* and *occulting* are just different descriptions of the fantasy of the Phallus, a way of designating the Imaginary pole of signification.

By contrast, Laclau describes the "empty signifier" in terms that make it clear that it has nothing other than this Imaginary function. While he says that the empty signifier splits all the others and that it obtains its own split identity from the others, his examples show that this in fact is not the mode of operation that he attributes to the "empty signifier," as we have seen. In his examples, the "empty signifier" has the same relationship to each of the signifiers in the system; it has an exceptional status; and it superintends the relationships among all the others, from outside, without entering into the system of signification. As confirmation of his misrecognition of the empty signifier/phallic mode of signification for the extimate signifier, we can turn to his acknowledgment that the emptier the signifier, the more detached it is from the other signifiers, the less likely a democratic result: "precisely because the universal place is empty, it can be occupied by any force, not necessarily democratic" (E 65).

Laclau goes on to surmise that if, on the contrary, the "place of power is not unique," there may be some protection from totalitarianism, but the status quo would be favored, and no social change would come about (E 65). But the situation cannot be the one Laclau describes here. The universal place is never empty – the signifier producing the system, with its own split identity, is given its signifieds by the other signifiers. This does not mean that totalitarianism or quietism can be eliminated as possible outcomes: it means that if there were such a thing as an empty (or a full) signifier, totalitarianism would be inescapable, not simply one among many options. In other words, Laclau's own reliance on the empty signifier as Phallus rather than the signifier as extimate cause produces the very result that he is trying to avoid.

Repressive Consequences of Imaginary Identification

The premise (not the fact) that groups are formed by way of total emulation rather than contingent identifications serves the interest of repressive social groups, such as the army. Why? Because the differences in identification (different unary traits) are occulted by the fantasy that the different members of the group lose their differences. That is, the members of the group are enjoined to become identical (the unifying-one), when in fact the mechanism of identification at work serves to particularize them (the countable-one): this gap is crucial to the ongoing function of repression. Because Symbolic identification constitutes the subject as particularized, the fantasy of group homogenization can never be realized, which means that the inevitable failure of every individual to perfectly match the ego ideal gives the disciplinary apparatus abundant and constant reasons to operate. The necessary fact of the differences between individuals, and their unconscious diversity of choice of unary traits, gives the repressive authority ammunition for discipline and punishment for deviations from the fantasized sameness of the group members. In fact, to the extent that the authorities desire to hold on to their position, they will be at pains to seek out the most minor of differences for punishment, ensuring that efforts to do the impossible – perfectly emulate the standard of identification – continue and necessarily continue to fail, making the "need" for their intervention apparent. This is the totalitarian procedure in all its reliance on superegoic logic: nothing in this scenario undermines hegemony or promotes democracy. On the contrary, its adoption energizes repression.

As we saw in chapter 4, even so vociferous a proponent of the democratic potential of iterability as Butler admits that the failure to repeat can just as easily be the means for the reinscription of the norm as a liberation from it. Laclau is not unaware that the mechanism of rivalry and imitation on which he relies serves the hegemonic imperative to repeat (and fail to repeat) the norms. But he makes the same mistake as Butler in arguing that the fact of social antagonism (and the kinds of failed iterations to which it necessarily gives rise) is sufficient to promote democratic interaction. His remedy also follows Butler's lead in her turn to intentionalism and for precisely the same reason – to assign a political task of opening or closing signification:

> Difference and particularisms are the necessary starting point, but out of it, it is possible to open the way to a relative universalization of values which can be the basis for a popular hegemony. This universalization and its open character certainly condemns all identity to an unavoidable hybridization, but hybridization . . . can also mean *empowering existing identities through the opening of new possibilities* . . . But this democratico-hegemonic possibility has to recognize the constitutive contextualized/decontextualized terrain of its constitution and *take full advantage* of the political possibilities that this undecidability opens. All this finally amounts to saying is that *the particular can only fully realize itself if it constantly keeps open, and constantly redefines, its relation to the universal.* (E 65, my emphases)

Intentionalism shows up in two places in this statement. First, Laclau implies – contrary to his own express theory of political identity as always already, irrevocably split – that "hybridization" of identity is an effect of a process of "relative universalization." Second, Laclau as good as states that the particular, concrete historical identity has it *in its own power* to redefine its relation to the universal. Such a power would amount to control over the entire field of political signification. But since, according to Laclau, what constitutes the identity as hybrid in the first place is its position as one among many differential elements held in some relation to an absent factor, no single particular identity can in fact control its own relation to the universal. This is standard semiotic theory: the signified is not a function of the signifier but of the field in which the signifier moves, as Laclau himself has pointed out (E 37). Indeed, it is precisely from this point that Laclau was able to ground his theory of the absent presence of the universal in the first place. In his implicit disavowal of his originating premises, Laclau forecloses on both the social and the unconscious dimensions of political identities. Indeed, we must understand these foreclosures to be the same act inasmuch as the unconscious has to be formulated as fundamentally social if we are to make sense of the subject as split.

Laclau's theory seems to focus primarily on the need to destabilize the hegemonic instance in order to foster "democratic interaction" by keeping the chain of significations "open." The same criticism applies here as in the preceding chapter: opening and closing are integral operations of signification, and are not at the disposal of intentionalized activity, which in any case would be both unnecessary and impossible. Furthermore, because contingent identifications enter the picture, the whole apparatus of "splitting" the hegemonic instance as a way of keeping "democratic" potential (i.e. particular differences) alive is a red herring. There is no need for any special action to keep these groups from becoming one homogeneous block: they are not homogeneous in themselves, on account of their Möbius subjectivity, which involves a diversity of points of identification within the group. Nor could they be homogeneous with each other, on account of their Möbius subjectivity, which (also) involves a diversity of points of identification with the hegemonic instance. Laclau's explanation of groups joining together on account of some particular signifier of the fullness of community would require that social antagonism and the excess attending signification had *already* been overcome in *reality* in order for groups to coordinate to overcome it in *fantasy*.

The Hysterical Social Bond and Phallic Politics

The underlying problem in Laclau's theory is not how to explain the instability of hegemony – which after all may be attributed to the impossibility of the totalization of the social field, due to the excess of the social subject – but rather how any social bond amenable to coordinated collective action can be established at all, given the constitutive operation of social antagonism. The view of this problem offered by psychoanalysis is that *no such social bond would be necessary if subjects were not Möbius subjects to begin with* – not only would no subjects as such exist, but no social field in which they could operate would exist either. So, what we call "social bonds" are merely the forms of discourse by which Möbius subjects that make up the social field enlist others to remedy the excess that makes them subjects. No social bond *remediates* this excess. Rather, a social bond is nothing other than a *necessarily* failed attempt to eradicate excess: the motivation to try to establish the bond and the failure to do so generate the social field within which subjects can be subjects. The impossibility of such remediation does not deter anyone from imagining its realization or attempting to recruit others to effect it. Lacan describes this impossibility and its galvanizing social effects as the "relation of nonrelation," in a precise homology to his famous "there is no sexual relation" ("il n'y a pas de rapport sexuelle"). In the absence of the sexual or the social relation, we try to get others to fill our lack, even though it is impossible for them to do so.

As Lacan sees it, the fact of this nonrelation is defended against by certain forms of discourse, which also express the only forms of social bond we have.[18] One discourse, the discourse of the Master, presents itself as an absolute authority that guarantees the truth of the knowledge it produces. The Master takes on the functions of the Phallus: exempt from the conditions it describes in the knowledge it generates, transcendent to any system over which it has authority, and pretending to an absolute self-integrity not shared by anything else in the universe it superintends. Contemporary philosophy has unmasked what supports this discourse – a denial of the subject's non-self-coincidence. But it has taken Lacan to demonstrate that this discourse always misses what it aims at with its knowledge – *jouissance*, which exceeds the known by definition.

A second discourse, University discourse, presents itself as the nonsubjective source of a knowledge that purports to give access to *jouissance* directly, but in fact depends upon the support of a "Master" who hides beneath it. Again, contemporary philosophy has exposed this secret support. Derrida, for example, shows the way that this discourse occludes its reliance upon an impossible, transcendent presence. But Lacan goes on to explain how University discourse creates a greater sense of the subject's lack/excess: the more you know of University knowledge, the more you will feel "that is not it," intensifying the sense of loss of *jouissance*, and galvanizing a vicious circle in a search for even more knowledge to make up for this loss, knowledge which must fail to satisfy.

We come now to a third form of social discourse, what Lacan calls the discourse of the Hysteric. Here the subject confronts an authority and demands that this authority live up to its promises to deliver on *jouissance*. The Master has no special ability to remedy the subject's split, so his only recourse is to produce more knowledge. But, as we have just noted, more and more knowledge only intensifies the loss of *objet a*. The Hysteric's demands, therefore, in effect seek to castrate the Master, or rather expose the fact of his castration, his inability to deliver. In this respect, the Hysteric offers a "progression" from the discourse of the Master. Yet, despite her demands and her castrating effect, the Hysteric does not come to any realization about the impossibility of *objet a*. Rather, because she imagines that some obstacle stands in her way, that some master *could* deliver, she *insists* on a Master.[19] Her discourse does have a political value insofar as she exposes the falsity of the Master's claims to self-sufficiency and the insufficiency of knowledge. Her castrating effect, her exposure of the Master's failure to be the Phallus, can only be defended against by the production of S2, as though the Master is saying, "Look what I can do, look what I know, I can endlessly generate this stuff: how could I be lacking?" But the production of this kind of add-on infinity is not what the Hysteric wants. She wants to become "infinite" in the sense that she would become immortal, gain eternal life through the eradication of her excess, her Möbius subjectivity, and in this way accede to Being and *jouissance*.

None of these discourses could undo the excess created in the formation of the subject, but each establishes a distinctive fantasy of how to transform the relation of nonrelation into a relation of union. Only in the fourth discourse, the discourse of the Analyst, does the subject acquire a knowledge (by the signifiers produced in the analysis) that tells the truth about the impossibility of *objet a* and the uniqueness of the master-signifier that governs the subject's life. This is the only social bond that is not based on the Master's presumed totality, or on the "bad" infinity of University knowledge as a substitute for *jouissance*, or on the Hysterical demand for and castration of a Master. Its purpose is to help the subject recognize and work through its own idiosyncratic fantasy that someone, some Other, knows the truth about the world and the subject, and for that reason deserves to be in a position of mastery.

Laclau understands the dynamics of the Master's discourse: he is careful to deprive the hegemonic instance of any *a priori* properties that would legitimate its authoritative position. When he proposes that groups will compete among themselves to produce the hegemonic instance and then, by virtue of their identification with it, find it wanting and destabilize it, he casts them in the role of the Hysteric. Groups repeatedly install and unseat the hegemonic instance which they have charged with the task of delivering the "fullness of community." The political path that Laclau denominates as "democratic" is in fact a perpetual search for the phallic Master. In the absence of (the possibility of) an ultimate Master eternally occupying the place of hegemony,

Laclau posits that that place will be emptied and re-filled over and over. It is this continual proposal, rejection, and re-erection of candidates for the top spot that marks Laclau's model as a version of the Hysteric's discourse in the service of repressive politics. The unmasking of the hegemonic instance's failure to deliver on its promise does not undermine hegemony per se, but rather establishes the conditions of "bad infinity," as one group after another occupies the site of power. The constant sliding from one group to another is a macro version of S2 as the agent of the social bond, both occulting the master-signifier on which it depends and substituting itself for *jouissance*. No wonder that Laclau's theory obsessively reinscribes an implicit equation between democracy and repression, as it oscillates between multiplicity and mastery as two sides of the same coin.

Disavowed Psychoanalysis, Forfeited Historicity

The Hysteric disavows the subject's lack of self-coincidence: somehow, the wholeness that has been "lost" can be found. She thinks that, surely, it is merely prohibited and not impossible to grasp that missing part. Her discourse demands that the Master be both an integral whole (the aspect in which he has the power to remedy the hysteric's complaint) and subverted lack (his weakness is exposed by her continued "loss"). She needs the Master both as the warrant for the possibility of remedying her deficit and as incapable of doing so: without him, the impossibility of recapturing what in fact has never truly been lost – the fantasmatic *objet a* – would no longer appear in the guise of prohibition, so that the truth of its impossibility would stand revealed. The explanations generated by the relation between the Hysteric and the Master – the signifiers of knowledge, or S2 – don't give access to *jouissance*, but serve as "positive" attributes that both screen the impossibility of filling her lack and, in their failure to be *objet a*, intensify the sense of its loss.

Let us focus for a moment on this knowledge, for it will give us the clue to the dimension of historicity at stake in Laclau's work.

Laclau's unwitting turn to this discourse derives from his neglect of the retroversive action of the signifier. The "master-signifier" obtains its split identity from its aspect as the Phallus, the fantasy of an external, exceptional cause of a totalized signifying system, which is the retroversive effect of the quilting of S2, by means of which it acquires its status as signifier. Laclau's implicit positing of the Phallus as the linchpin for democratic interaction means that the retroversive dimension, which is to say, S1's criss-crossing by the signifying system itself, falls out of consideration. As we have seen, the hegemonic instance, which is supposed to be split in Laclau's account, turns out to be self-identical.

But that's not the only way in which retroversion disappears. The particular groups that identify with the hegemonic instance, we can recall, never lose their initial particular properties at the time of hegemonic consolidation. The theory calls for them to acquire new meanings as they enter into new relations in the system, but the theory doesn't address their idiosyncratic relations via the unary trait to the hegemonic instance and the retroversive individual inflection of their initial identities as a consequence. Laclau's failure to respect the contingency of these unary traits is of a piece with his failure to respect the retroversive emergence of the fantasmatic Phallus.

I have been arguing that these problems render Laclau's theory nonpsychoanalytic. But why should that matter? What difference does it make if, at the end of the day, Laclau disavows the psychoanalytic precepts on which he claims to rely? After all, perhaps that is merely a sign that psychoanalysis cannot do the job that needs doing. My answer is Laclau's own: only by incorporating the extimate cause, retroversive signification, and the specific nature of identification as split relationality can his theory achieve "radical historicism." It is Laclau's failure to persist in adhering to these precepts that renders his theory dehistoricizing. Why?

At bottom, what is missing in Laclau's considerations is the operation of fantasy as a screen for the lack in the subject. True, he gives lack a place of prominence when he points out the crucial function of the constitutive split in the subject and of the instability of the hegemonic instance. But in his description of particular groups seeking the fullness of community he misrepresents the function of fantasy in the transferential relation. As we have seen, the groups installing the hegemonic group do not share the same relationship to that group: each group has its own point of identification with the hegemonic group, because each experiences social antagonism in a specific way, and so every group has a unique fantasy about the way the hegemonic group can remedy its particular lack (not the lack in the social field per se) or is stealing its *jouissance*. If the specificity of these transferential relations is not taken into account, we have no way to analyze the historical forms that the attribution of the loss of *objet a* takes. It is not, as Laclau would have it, that a specific group loses its particularity in its rejection or elevation of the hegemonic group. Rather, it relates transferentially to the hegemonic group in its own way. The fact that a group takes another group as its transferential object makes it possible to analyze the specificity of that group's fantasies about what is missing in the social field from the point of view of that group. The group's specificity, rather than its equivalence, is the key to this historical dimension, but not in the same way that multicultural-ist historicism imagines. We need not attribute any positive properties to these groups, no essential identities, and no perduring qualities. The "groupness" of the group is a function of its retroversive relations to the other groups and its relationship to its own split. More importantly, we do not take the group "at its word": we accord no special knowledge of itself to the group, nor do we accept that group's analysis of the reasons for its dissatisfaction. The unconscious (Real) register is our concern. The historicist dimension enters into the analysis when retroversion and fantasmatic identifications take center stage.

The politics of group interactions takes place on the terrain of fantasy. Whether or not it is possible to traverse a group fantasy – to discover its particular screen for encountering the lack in the subject – is at present not known. As Freud points out in *Civilization and Its Discontents*, we do not have a procedure for the psychoanalysis of societies, although in chapter 7 we will consider one possibility for a transformational psy-choanalysis of groups. What we do know, however, is that the historicity of political action can only be approached by considering group identi-fications in both their Imaginary and their Symbolic dimensions and in terms of the particular discourse of the social bond it articulates. What demands does the group address to a "master" as a way of redressing its lack and how does it imagine that this master operates? Where does the group locate the lack and what story does it tell about how it came to be lacking? What "knowledge" does the group generate as a means of accounting for its lack of *jouissance*? What fantasy does it articulate about who possesses *jouissance*, or how to recover *jouissance*, and what effects does it imagine that recovery will have? Every answer to these questions will be historically specific – constructed from the materials at hand – because the unary trait founding Symbolic identification in each case is not itself ahistorical but historically contingent. Unless these ques-tions are articulated – that is, unless the role of unconsciously motivated identifications and fantasies is given due weight – political activity desir-ing to effect truly relevant change will be likely to foster repressive rather than democratic interaction.

6
Žižek's Political Act

The Temporality of the Political

Bourdieu, de Certeau, Butler, Laclau – these theorists present themselves as promoting radical social change, but their theories of political action have some strange properties. So, for example, Butler exhorts readers to undertake actions that are simultaneously impossible and irrelevant, such as "keeping signification open." And Laclau proposes that automatic mechanisms – such as the generation of equivalence from repression – will produce desired progressive outcomes. Given the Marxist heritage of most radical social change theory, it is no real surprise to find this reliance on automaticity (History is on the march) or superfluous intentionalism (if History has its own laws, then why must the proletariat work to achieve class consciousness?), because the irrelevant operations and the automatic ones are closely linked. The business of political discourse is to convince people to take or endorse actions that are supposed to bring about desired outcomes, despite the fact that no one controls the direction of change or could foresee all of the consequences of an action. Consequently, the political discourse of social change must make its appeal as wish-fulfilling dreams of omnipotent intentions or destined futures. From this perspective, every political program is not only inherently fatalistic, but also mired in fantasy and narcissism from its inception. The discourse of social change takes place on the terrain of the Imaginary.

Of course, we do act without knowing all the consequences of our actions – we simply hope for our preferred results. Precisely because the meanings and consequences of our actions are not at our disposal, it is consoling, even enlivening, to imagine that we have the power to match intention to outcome: we have to believe that our desires are potent enough to create a reality that conforms to them, so we convince ourselves that we know how to create groups that persistently cohere or that we can foresee all relevant consequences. Our lack of foreknowledge and our complex motivations don't mean that we give up prudent efforts to assess likely outcomes. Still, the fantasmatic nature of the powers political leaders assign to themselves must rely on mass (self-)deception, charisma, or threats of force to convince their audiences to act without reservation.

Under these conditions, we might regard the difference between quietism and activism as virtually nil: act, don't act – no one knows what will happen anyway, and anyone who says differently is lying. We seem to have returned to the conclusions drawn from our exploration of Bourdieu and de Certeau: the considerations of historicity are at odds with those of politics, insofar as politics proposes a relationship of fulfillment between present and future. Political discourse seeking to persuade us to take action to produce social change presumes that some perspicacious politician can pick out just those elements of a desired future which lie dormant in our present in order to bring that future into being. As we anticipate that future, our present becomes merely the means to the future's realization. If the purpose of the present is to realize that future, then the advent of the future exhausts the meaning of the present. Such a view of history in which past, present, and future coexist along an unbroken line, the old perpetually folding seamlessly and without remainder into the new, is itself de-historicized. Elements of the present that don't affect the future either simply persist without becoming meaningful or disappear as so much waste. Contingency, being incalculable, is treated as negligible. Each past moment merely mirrors the present moment from which it is seen, while each present fits the bill of the anticipated future.

A truly historicist theory must reject this relationship of past, present, and future in order to retain a sense of the distinctiveness of the past's relationship to the present – and to sustain an orientation that can recognize opportunities for change. Historicizing the past involves presenting a version that makes sense of it in the context of the present without claiming to exhaust its meaningfulness. But such a vision implies that every transition from one moment to another carries along with it a kind of excess, a potential for changed meaning – and for the exercise of *judgment*. The temporal fulfillment promised by politically charged social change discourse cannot serve as the basis of a historicist approach because it admits of no excess: the value of each present moment is exhausted in the future it births. So, it is difficult to see how to reconcile the requirements of a political program based on temporal fulfillment with those of a historicism based on the excess attending deferred signification. What kind of political theory could direct us to shared goals reliably enough to take action, given the impossibility of calculating all the consequences, without disavowing that excess? Is it possible to escape the deadlock of the Imaginary in political theory?

In this chapter, I focus on the work Žižek has published since 2001, with particular attention to the "Afterword: Lenin's Choice" from *Revolution at the Gates: Žižek on Lenin – the 1917 Writings* (2002), *Welcome to the Desert of the Real* (2002), *Organs Without Bodies: On Deleuze and Consequences* (2004), *Iraq: The Broken Kettle* (2004), and *The Parallax View* (2007). Žižek's exposition in these books always circles around criticisms of proponents of democracy and liberalism who disallow the utopian revolutionary gesture. He makes a case against their fears that revolutionary action always risks devolving into chaotic violence. In the process, he canvasses a number of alternative theories to show the importance of the excess, generated by the mechanism of extimate causality, that produces Möbius subjects. In his efforts to put revolutionary acts on a sound theoretical basis, Žižek expounds on these concepts as essential ingredients for a theory of social change that refuses the illusory gratifications of fantasmatic social relations. Put in Lacanian terms, we can read his work as a running commentary on the "relation of nonrelation" structuring the social field.

But explicating Žižek's theory of social change is no easy task. When it comes to his ideas on politics and social change, there is both too much and too little to choose from. Too much, because everything he writes has a political edge, and too little, because he does not lay out his theory in any straightforward way.[1] Other hazards await the would-be expositor. As anyone who reads much Žižek knows, he uses the same examples and arguments in different texts, while changing the purport of the examples from text to text. The argumentative line is sometimes difficult to follow. A reconstructed argument will always be subject to the charge that it ignores a statement elsewhere in his corpus that contradicts it.

In this chapter, I follow the red thread of Žižek's definition of revolutionary acts in order to extract his argument that such acts comprise the sole route to significant social change. I explore his underlying assumptions about the nature of the political act, the means for achieving solidarity, and the temporality of the revolutionary event. He emphasizes retroversive temporality as he seeks to take into account the excess attending signification. At the same time, because retroversion is a condition of the signification of *every* act, he is under some pressure to define the political Act inherently. His efforts to establish the nature of the political Act take place by way of an engagement with Badiou's philosophy, as we will see. One important facet of his argument depends upon defining the revolutionary act in terms of a particular kind of subject

– the "acephalous subject of the drive," while another concerns the definition of a particular kind of violence as the revolutionary act's crucial criterion. In order to make sense of the twists and turns of his argument, I begin with Žižek's criticisms of the de-historicizing effects of the fulfillment model of political action.

What is a Political Act?

Time is of the essence in Žižek's approach: his delineation of the temporality proper to the political Act takes shape after reading Badiou on the *event*. To use the parlance of historiography for a moment, Badiou's work points up the distinction between an *occurrence* and an *event*. An occurrence is what happens in the course of the activities attending any situation, grasped at any scale (family, ethnic culture, corporate structure, nation, global economy), which leaves *intact* the crucial determinative elements of the situation (structure, ideology, social relations, cultural formations, systems of circulation, hierarchies of value). By contrast, when an event takes place, it brings something new into the world that changes the determinants and significance of the very terms by which we had previously comprehended the situation. Žižek puts it succinctly when he says that an event *changes the coordinates by which we grasp the situation*. It transforms what *counts* as significant in the framing of the situation. Given this insight, Žižek argues that the only way to bring about an event is by means of the revolutionary political Act.

The exemplar of an event for historians and philosophers alike is the French Revolution. Only after the events of 1789 did the concept of revolution come to mean the overthrowing of a despotic government by the people, by violence if necessary, as legitimated by a theory of popular sovereignty. At the time of the various occurrences of which it is now considered to consist, the "French Revolution" had no reality for the participants. The king's capitulated agreement to call the Estates General in 1788; the refusal of the Third Estate to accept its status as the lowest body of the three-part legislature in May 1789; Louis XVI's dismissal of Necker and the encircling of Paris and Versailles with royal troops in July; the higgledy-piggledy emergence of the popular militia that broke into Les Invalides; the taking of the Bastille and the public execution of its governors; the king's order to pull back the royal troops from Paris and his acceptance of the National Assembly – each of these makes up a crucial part of what we call the French Revolution and none of them, including the Bastille (which for us is the emblem of the Revolution) was conceived at the time as effecting revolution in the modern sense.[2] In fact, the assault on the Bastille and the executions of de Launay and Flesselles, were initially considered by the Assembly to be "disastrous news."[3]

Although prior to the French Revolution, people used the term "revolution" to refer to any number of occurrences in which power changed hands, only after 1789 does "popular sovereignty" serve as the legitimation for the overthrow of a despotic government, even by violent means, a legitimation that comes into being as a new politico-theoretical entity.[4] The "durable articulation of popular violence and popular sovereignty" brings into being a new political concept of revolution.[5] To be sure, the Enlightenment provided the terms on which the Assembly, and Buzot in particular, drew to formulate retroactively the meaning and justification of those occurrences. And, of course, the idea of "popular sovereignty" has its own history. But only after the Assembly's debates did the term revolution acquire its modern meaning which was applied retroactively to the events we now call the French Revolution. In effect, this after-the-fact signification is the decisive moment – the "event-ifying" moment – of the French Revolution. From that point on, the people involved understood their own actions in a completely different way, orienting themselves to the new coordinates for understanding their own situation. Since then popular movements have had at their disposal a recognizably authorized philosophy and a rhetorical tool for political change.

In Žižek's terms, the occurrences of the French Revolution generate a "Truth-Event," that is, the inauguration of an innovation that transforms the very terms by which we understand what has happened. Although he claims to derive the fundamentals of this idea from Badiou, as we will see, his version is not precisely what Badiou means by an event. In the discussion that follows, I will be using Žižek's capitalized form "Event" when I elaborate the political dimension of his usage. For Žižek, bringing about a Truth-Event is the defining criterion for a political Act (which he capitalizes, again, to distinguish it from run of the mill actions). And while he leans heavily on Badiou – explicitly and implicitly – the differences between them will be instructive.

Žižek pegs his concept of the political Act to a particular temporal logic, explicitly rejecting the discourse of political fulfillment in which the future exhausts the possibilities of the present and the outcome justifies the means:

> . . . what is the criterion of a political act proper? Success as such clearly does not count, even if we define it in the dialectical terms of Merleau-Ponty: as the wager that the future will retroactively redeem our present horrible acts (this is how Merleau-Ponty, in *Humanism and Terror*, provided one of the more intelligent justifications of the Stalinist terror: retroactively, it will become justified if its final outcome is true freedom). . . Revolution is not a Merleau-Pontyan wager, an act suspended in the *futur*

antérieur, to be legitimized or de-legitimized by the long-term outcome of present acts. . . (RG 259–60)

Having rejected the successful matching of intention to outcome as the criterion of the political Act, Žižek presents two alternative definitions. The first, drawn from Eric Santner's readings of Benjamin's *Theses on the Philosophy of History*, offers the concept of redemptive revolutionary time, in which a present political action brings to light the unrealized promise of the past, the opportunities that failed to materialize. The second is based on a Badiouan description of the hidden dimension of a situation which can only be brought to light retroversively. Although these two approaches seem to have little in common, Žižek brings them together in a novel analysis of the conditions of social change.

His commentary takes its start from Benjamin's third thesis in which the redemptive model of history is adumbrated:

> A chronicler who recites events without distinguishing between major and minor ones acts in accordance with the following truth: nothing that has ever happened should be regarded as lost for history. To be sure, only a redeemed mankind receives the fullness of its past – which is to say, only for a redeemed mankind has its past become citable in all its moments.[6]

Žižek particularly approves Santner's reading of this thesis. For Santner, the past not only contains major and minor deeds – or recorded and unrecorded acts which, in the fullness of time, will be recognized in their proper aspect – but also serves as a reservoir of unrealized potential action. The past sustains our sense that there have been omissions or failures to act, even "failures to respond to calls for action" (RG 255, quoting Santner). The revolutionary intervention redeems these omissions; it makes visible and brings to realization the ignored potentials of the past. In contrast to Merleau-Ponty, for whom the present serves as a standard by which we judge the necessity (or wrongheadedness) of past action, this model proposes that present revolutionary action makes up for the omissions of the past, redeeming those failures: as Benjamin puts it in the fifth thesis, "every image of the past that is not recognized by the present as one of its own concerns threatens to disappear irretrievably."[7]

But Žižek runs a risk here, because Benjamin's position looks a lot like de-historicized political fulfillment. The excess in the redemptive model is a function of the perpetual retaining of multiple possibilities from the past for the present and future. In theory, nothing of the past is lost: all of the political potentials of the past can be realized. The appeal of this model is that the past remains permanently available, in what Benjamin calls redemption – "nothing that has ever happened should be regarded as lost for history. . . . only a redeemed mankind receives the fullness of its past."[8] When seen from the perspective of redeemed futurity, however, the "excess" carried along from past to present is not an excess at all. Rather, the present appears to be impoverished only by reference to a past full of resources that will be realized completely in the future. In effect, the apparently privative present can be remediated by recourse to the fullness of a past that realizes itself in the redeemed future, a future which swallows up all the available "excess" of meaning of the past.

So, whether we are talking about a political outcome that matches its promised intention, or a future situation that legitimizes acts which seemed irresponsible in their time, or the political potentials of the past that are redeemed in the future, we are implicitly relying upon the *futur antérieur* as the justification of our present actions. This temporality is fundamentally eschatological, for which the term "redemptive" is quite appropriate. As eschatology, it is de-historicized: the excess attending the Möbius condition of subjects is imagined to disappear.

Perhaps because he recognizes this risk, Žižek turns to an alternative temporality for the political Act, one that traces its filiation to Badiou's theory of the event. Žižek follows Badiou in arguing that every situation has a hidden dimension structuring the situation, a dimension that never appears as such. Žižek has different ways of articulating the nature and function of this hidden dimension. Sometimes it is a fundamental social antagonism, i.e., "class struggle." Sometimes it is "the double-bind inherent" in any ideological injunction, the "point of inconsistency of the big Other" (RG 224, 242). Sometimes, as in Lacan, it is the Real as absent cause. In any case, the properly political Act orients itself to this hidden dimension, like (to use another Žižekian example) a strange attractor in chaos theory. In this way, the political Act brings the presence of this hidden dimension to light – but only retroversively. How does this model avoid the temporality of the fulfillment model? Here we need to take a brief detour through this landscape of hidden dimensions.

Universality and the Strange Attractor

This invocation of a hidden dimension helps make sense of some of Žižek's most contradictory passages about the nature of the Act. Let me take just one illustrative example from the discussion of the "redefinition of coordinates" in *Iraq: The Broken Kettle* (published two years after *Revolution at the Gates*). Relying on Bernard Williams' distinction between *ought* and *must* (in his *Truth and Truthfulness*), Žižek proposes:

it is not only that, within the limits that our situation sets on our deliberation, we "cannot do otherwise": the character of a person is revealed not
only in the fact that he does what he must do, but also "in the location
of those limits, and in the very fact that one can determine, sometimes
through deliberation itself, that one cannot do certain things, and must do
others". And I am responsible for my character – that is, for the choice of
coordinates which prevent me from doing some things and impel me to do
others. This brings us to the Lacanian notion of the act: in an act, I precisely
redefine the very co-ordinates of what I cannot and must do. (IBK 121)

This passage gives some context for the more abstract proposition that a
proper act retroversively changes the very framework by which a situation is grasped. Yet something seems amiss here, in that the invocation of
choice implies that a particular result is being sought, one that cannot be
articulated from within a given set of coordinates but which can be articulated once one (sees it and) *chooses* to redefine those coordinates. Apart
from the (discredited) intentionalism he resuscitates here (how can "I precisely redefine the very co-ordinates of what I cannot and must do?") with
its implied control of re-signification, Žižek also contradicts this emphasis
on choice immediately, when he proposes that a proper act is undertaken
because of some underlying hard reality to which one must conform:
"when you 'must' do something, it means you have no choice but to do
it, even if it is terrible" (IBK 122). The language of choice disappears in a
flash, and we are left with the impression that there is some reality in the
situation which compels our acts, no matter how distasteful or horrific.[9]

It is this impression of the dictates of a reality, whether in the present
(I must bow to the pressures of this reality) or in the future (I choose the
coordinates that will permit me to bring a particular reality into being),
that emerges as crucial in this discussion. Why would we choose one
set of coordinates over another unless we were trying to find a way to
bring about a specific outcome or emphasize an extant (if heretofore
unrecognized) condition? Žižek seems to be saying that either we choose
the coordinates that permit us to realize the future reality we seek, or we
accede to a present reality as compelling us to act in a certain way. In
either case, some occulted condition serves as the guide or limit to action.
So, one way to resolve his apparently contradictory emphasis on both
chosen acts and dictated ones is to note that each alternative actually
refers to a hidden dimension of the situation, one to which we are either
compelled unconsciously to conform or by which we consciously choose
to orient our actions. It is in keeping with Žižek's psychoanalytic com-
mitments that this picture of the subject as both determined and as free
to choose its character is consonant with the psychic structure of Möbius
subjects, both constrained by the drive and able to transform the meanings of their symptoms.

How does Žižek use this idea of the hidden dimension to further articulate the nature of the political Act? He takes up the challenge of theorizing political action in terms we have explored in our discussion of Laclau concerning the mutual conditioning of universality and particularity:

> Lenin's premiss – which today, in our era of postmodern relativism, is more pertinent than ever – is that universal truth and partisanship, the gesture of taking sides, are not only not mutually exclusive, but condition each other: the *universal* truth of a concrete situation can be articulated only from a thoroughly *partisan* position; truth is, by definition, one-sided. (RG 177; original emphases)

When Žižek speaks of universality and particularity here, he implicitly invokes the theoretical position that meanings are not at the disposal of the speaker but change with the auditor. If there were such a thing as a universal unaffected by the particular positions from which it is engaged, then meanings would be stabilized once and for all, and the fulfillment of political promises would be an easy task. So far, so good. Yet Žižek's conclusion that "the universal truth of a concrete situation can be articulated only from a thoroughly partisan position" is not so easy to deduce. If the universal is conditioned by the particular, how does Žižek argue for something like a universal truth rather than a merely relativized one?

He clarifies this point in his discussion of the difference between form understood as a neutral container of content and form understood as an inherent bias determining the entire field:

> Form is not the neutral frame of particular contents, but the very principle of concretion, that is, the "strange attractor" which distorts, biases, confers a specific colour on every element of the totality. . . [W]e should not confuse this properly dialectical notion of Form with the liberal-multiculturalist notion of Form as the neutral framework of the multitude of "narratives" – not only literature, but also politics, religion, science, are all different narratives, stories we are telling ourselves about ourselves, and the ultimate goal of ethics is to guarantee the neutral space in which this multitude of narratives can coexist peacefully – in which everyone, from ethnic to sexual minorities, will have the right and opportunity to tell their story. . . The properly dialectical notion of Form signals precisely the *impossibility* of this liberal notion of Form: Form has nothing to do with "formalism", with the idea of a neutral Form, independent of its contingent, particular content; it stands, rather, for the traumatic kernel of the Real, for the antagonism which "colours" the entire field in question. In this precise sense, class struggle is the Form of the Social: every social phenomenon is overdetermined by it, so that it is not possible to remain neutral towards it. (RG 190, original emphasis)

In this distinction, Žižek exemplifies the utility of "partisanship" when it comes to truth, for if form is a specific function that shapes the ground of reality itself, then there can be no "objective" place from which to view reality. Rather, one is always taking sides, whether one knows it or not. And while this may seem at first glance to recapitulate the liberal-multiculturalist position Žižek is at pains to decry – in that it seems to validate the multiplicity of subjective positions – the difference is that the liberal position results in diverse narratives all existing on a par with one another because they all share the same relation to the neutral frame (as in Laclau's theory of the production of equivalence), whereas the Žižekian position affirms that every element has its own relationship to the determining frame. The coloring that the overdetermining kernel of the Real gives to one element is different from that produced on other elements. Imagine a blue light shining from an invisible source on a room full of differently colored materials: the blue light has no visible presence in the air, but a white curtain will appear blue, a red wall will appear purple, and so forth. The *same* invisible force creates *different effects*. This is why Žižek can say that every element in the situation (which is itself shaped by some determining but hidden Real) "takes its own side" with respect to it. Because the shaping force does not exist independently of these particularized relationships – because it comes into view only by means of the particular elements (which, in the case of the social field, are historical contingencies) – it has no single or stable configuration. (We can recognize here an analogy to the way that S1 emerges as a function of the multiple particular relations of S2, as we saw in the previous chapter, in the operation of the unary trait.)

Žižek's thinking about the political Act in this way is influenced by Badiou. Despite his criticisms of Badiou in *The Ticklish Subject* and in some recent works such as *Organs Without Bodies*, Žižek shares the Badiouan emphasis on the revolutionary dimension of political acts based on "partisanship." Badiou argues that in any "situation" there is a truth, but *one that does not pre-exist the situation*. It only comes into being through the partisan fidelity to its emergence: one-sided truth is the only truth possible. So, truth has to be produced by a choice, and those who make that choice become the subjects of that truth. The "event" is the discerning of the possibility of becoming the partisan of a truth-process. If what Badiou calls "fidelity" occurs – if the subject so generated continues to work to make that truth emerge – then the elements which were not "counted" in the situation before the event takes place will have a chance to come to light. In this way, the situation comes to be seen to have a quite different configuration than was initially supposed (the invisible blue light is revealed as the single source of the different "coloration" of diverse elements), or, to use Žižek's phrasing, the coordinates by which we grasp the situation itself change.[10] Although Badiou posits four different types of truth – politics, art, science (in the form of mathematics), and love, each with its distinct processes by which a subject is constructed in fidelity to the truth – we can focus here on the political type. In Badiou's schema, constructing the political truth of a situation depends upon discerning an egalitarian position within it, that is, a position from which everyone can become not only the subject of address but also the subject of the truth-process itself.[11]

The retroversion in Badiou's model concerns the construction of a space and a vocabulary that could make visible what was overlooked in the original situation – an occulted egalitarian dimension – but this dimension is posited (and glimpsed in the event) rather than achieved. To take an example from Badiou's own political efforts, the *sans-papiers*, foreign workers in France, are recognized in the current political situation only as "immigrants," not as productive workers. The "encyclopedia" of the French (and arguably Western) situation has no term for these people that would bring to light their status as workers, that is, as having the same properties, necessary to France, as any other worker. The specifically *political* nature of the Badiouan act is a function of *working towards* realizing this occulted egalitarian dimension, a dimension which we prescribe.[12] Badiou emphasizes repeatedly that one's efforts to work to reveal equality should continue regardless of any apparent lack of success. In this way, his thought accords with the Žižekian desideratum of eschewing the *futur antérieur*.

Žižek does not always approve Badiou's egalitarianism, pointing out that capitalism too treats everyone as equal.[13] However, when it comes to Žižek's fundamental adherence to the concepts of extimacy and minimal self-difference, he finds Badiou's universalizing approach to politics congenial and particularly useful against the multiculturalist particularist discourse of the past quarter century. The way in which Badiou's universalism approaches Laclau's is one of Žižek's reasons for supporting Laclau, despite reservations. In a significant passage, Žižek brings Laclau together with Badiou to explain the kind of universalism which, in his view, enables proper political action:

> True universality can be best captured through Laclau's opposition of antagonism and difference: when we are dealing with a system of differences (a structured social body), its "universality" is not the encompassing totality which includes all parts, or some feature shared by all of them, but its "antagonism" as a certain difference which cuts diagonally across all parts of the system of difference (the social body). This is what Badiou attributes to Saint Paul, as his great invention: the invention of a "militant universalism." The position of universality is not simply one which floats above differences mediating or encompassing them all, but the position of

knowing how to traverse the field with an additional, more radical difference, a difference which cuts each particular part from within. This is how
the "universality" of Christianity functions in Saint Paul's work: when he
wrote, "there are no Jews or Greeks, no men or women", this suspension
of differences is not achieved through an all-encompassing shared universal
feature ("they are all human"). . . (IBK 88–9)

The essential point in this passage is the contrast between two forms
of egalitarian thinking: one that establishes equality through the neu-
tralizing of difference by way of some shared trait versus one that
establishes equality through the addition of a negation which establishes
the self-difference within each element. So, here, Žižek reiterates the
basic assumptions of extimate causality as the function installing self-
difference. Universality based on the excess generated by the formal
negation does not depend upon finding a common ontic property, that
is a property which is just one more difference within the situation. All
such properties can be used to name differences that are mobilized in
the game of hegemony, empty spaces, and master-signifiers, as we have
seen in the discussion of Laclau's political thought. Only the minimal
self-difference (described as the radical antagonism cutting across every
element) escapes this play of signifiers, existing in an extimate relation
to the situation, rather than in its encyclopedia. This self-difference or
(self-)antagonism subsists (ex-sists, Lacan would say, to emphasize its
extimacy) as the hidden dimension. Accordingly, Žižek goes on to argue
for Badiou as the exemplar of the philosopher of extimate causality,
while admonishing Laclau, who seems so promising in this passage, for
ultimately recasting antagonism as agonism, that is, as differences among
self-same elements in the social field (IBK 90).

   Thus, to continue the analogy proposed by Žižek, we could say
that every situation giving rise to a political event contains a hidden
dimension, the dimension of egalitarianism. In a moment, we will
interrogate this appropriation of Badiou, but for now let us simply
note that, by reading Benjamin with Santner to highlight the importance of the "omissions" or "symptoms" of the past, Žižek is making
an effort to bring Benjamin's ideas into line with those of Badiou (and
Lacan). If the past contains "omissions," this must be because the
present can discern something in the past that was indiscernible at the
time. The past, therefore, contains a hidden dimension that is always
already there, one that is invisibly shaping the situation, just as the
(inexistent) objet a gives shape to the circuit of the drive. Given Žižek's
commitment to defining the political Act without relying on a Merleau-
Pontyan eschatological wager, we could say that what he approves in
Benjamin is the aspect of the hidden dimension (expressed by Santner

as the "omissions" or unknown potentials of the past) rather than the redemptive political fulfillment Benjamin describes. In this way, Badiou's egalitarianism, linked as it is to this hidden dimension, helps Žižek avoid the trap of redemptive temporality by providing the retroversivity he wants to emphasize. In Badiou, the event of discerning the hidden dimension of the situation is a precondition for constructing the truth that will retroversively allow us to grasp the situation in a new way. Insofar as Žižek and Badiou agree that the situation appears to have radically different elements (elements that were uncognizable although present) only *after* the Event takes place, they share a reliance on retroversion.

Retroversive Politicization?

As we have just seen in his deployment of Williams' must/ought distinction, Žižek sometimes seems to neglect the criterion of retroversivity he promotes, falling back on intentions or future success to define the Act, even while he is appealing to retroversive temporality. It seems that he is always in danger of reverting to the discredited intentional agency that the discourse of the political Imaginary so cavalierly disseminates. So let's look more carefully at an example of an Act in which Žižek explicitly argues for the importance of retroversion:

> The Act occurs in an emergency when one has to take the risk and act without any legitimization, engaging oneself into a kind of Pascalean wager that the Act itself will create the conditions of its retroactive "democratic" legitimization. Say, when, in 1940, after the French defeat, de Gaulle called for the continuation of warfare against the Germans, his gesture was without "democratic legitimization" . . . However, in spite of this lack of "democratic legitimization", the truth was on de Gaulle's side, and he effectively was speaking on behalf of France, of the French people "as such". This also enables us to answer the ultimate democratic reproach: the absolute (self-referential) act is deprived of any external control which would prevent terrifying excesses. . . . The answer is clear: as [this case] demonstrates, democracy itself cannot provide such a guarantee; there is no guarantee against the possibility of the excess – the risk has to be assumed, it is part of the very field of the political. (WDR 153–4)

Here Žižek tries on the proposal that an act becomes a properly political Act when it leads to its own politicization/legitimation *after the fact*. Explaining that the "Act occurs in an emergency when one has to take the risk and act without any legitimization," Žižek adheres to his sense that strategizing for success or making claims about being able to foresee and bring about a desired future – in short, the whole apparatus of political fulfillment – are illusory routes to political practice. It is a fantasy to imagine that a procedure or political form could guarantee a promised result – or, perhaps more importantly, guarantee that no unforeseen, horrible consequences will occur. Such people want "an Act without an Act" (WDR 153). Žižek is decisive on this point: "there is no guarantee against the possibility of the excess – the risk has to be assumed, it is part of the very field of the political" (WDR 153–4). Not even democracy can furnish such a guarantee. Since we cannot know in advance what will happen, our only criterion for the Act must come after the fact, in a retroversive movement of politicization.

But Žižek has gotten himself into some tricky waters. He is implying that de Gaulle's statement counts as an Act because he had truth on his side and/or subsequent events gave (democratic?) legitimacy to his pronouncement after the fact. Each of these propositions is problematic. Not only is there no way of knowing where the "truth" of that situation lay at the time (although one may speak with the benefit of hindsight), but it is also misleading to propose that the authority of de Gaulle's statement derived from that "truth" and not from any prior authorization. Having fled France for London after the German invasion and Pétain's armistice, de Gaulle was the only remaining French military leader not subjected to German authority. If he had no right to assume the authority to speak for the French as a free people, then who else could have? So, the example doesn't seem to correspond very well to the criterion of a purely *post hoc* legitimation which Žižek has proposed, given that de Gaulle was already invested with authority for the audience he addressed.

What is more, Žižek doesn't indicate what after-effects of politicization he has in mind, and it is difficult to imagine how the occurrences that followed on the London speech could be seen as consequences attributable to it. Certainly, there was no immediate "legitimation": France would not have a legitimate self-government for years to come. And who can say that de Gaulle's speech – rather than, say, US military intervention or Germany's economic and military fiasco – was the key factor when it did occur? Apart from the fact of de Gaulle's becoming a politician after the war, some of the more notable happenings were that the Vichy government was installed, the French Resistance undertook efforts against the Germans independently of any political legitimation, and de Gaulle himself organized a short-lived, right-wing political party after leaving the Presidency of the Fifth Republic. Which of these counts as "proper politicization"?

Why then does Žižek insist on the criterion of retroactive politicization or (in his equation) legitimation? It seems that he is trying to remain faithful to the insight that no claim to prior knowledge of the outcome of an act can be used to legitimate it, the same issue that he takes up in his discrediting of Merleau-Ponty's "wager." This emphasis appears consistent with the theoretical framework he is developing. But is the "Pascalean wager" really so different from the one Žižek attributes to Merleau-Ponty? Doesn't Merleau-Ponty also make the point that a risk has to be assumed that present violence will result in a better way of life?

A more serious problem arises in this example. By making "any legitimization" refer to "democratic" legitimization, Žižek gives the reader a false choice. He goes further than this faulty syllogism (if neither democracy nor emergencies can provide the external control necessary to prevent excesses, then we are to assume that all political acts are *equally* unauthorized) when he argues that we should *prefer* acts undertaken in emergency situations because these do not pretend that legitimation in itself confers any special foreknowledge or ability to control outcomes. It is hard to escape the conclusion that Žižek is sometimes at greater pains to discredit the possibility of democratic legitimation than he is to make his claims consistent.

The phrase "the risk has to be assumed" is just ambiguous enough to impart a flavor of intentional fulfillment to Žižek's model without explicitly committing him to it. Yes, the risk must be assumed, in the sense that one must simply take for granted the possibility that the act will not bring about the conditions of its politicization, but the risk cannot be assumed in the sense of deliberately taking on the risk, as though some acts are risky and others are not. In fact, any act can be appropriated, and any act, no matter how small, can become the occasion for politicization. Žižek considers de Gaulle's call to arms an Act, but it's hard to see how this speech act qualifies as an Act for Žižek by the criteria we have already discussed. It didn't change the coordinates of the situation. It didn't result in subsequent politicization. But more importantly, offering *any* example of an act that becomes an Act after the fact simply begs the question as to what it was about the act that *enabled* it to become politicized. Otherwise, the entire discussion is purely tautological: every act that becomes politicized is a political Act, and every act that doesn't, is not. Let's leave aside the problem of how far into the future we have to go to find these effects of politicization (or how far into the past we have to go to single out some act that we can nominate as the Cause of the transformation). No matter what, we will be beholden to the future anterior tense in the short or the long run under these terms.

What is more, we can endlessly recite examples of acts that became politicized after the fact and those that did not – but to what end? We would be saying only that we have no idea what enables some acts to become politically effective: without foreknowledge of all consequences or the power to bring the future into alignment with desire, we must regard every act as *inherently* the same as any other. Exhortations to "act" in an emergency (or at any other time), as well as urgings to assume the risk of acting without legitimation, cannot be used to fence off some acts from others: every single act that anyone might undertake, whether the act is large or small and whether it is enacted by someone authoritative (for example, de Gaulle) or not (for example, Rosa Parks), carries with it a significative excess – that is, a potential for appropriation, misunderstanding, and causing unforeseen consequences. We can recall here that Butler makes the error of proposing a distinction among types of actions on the basis of some imagined ability to assume a risk (for example, taking a risk in order to keep signification open). The risk is part and parcel of *all* signification, not just "the political field itself." Does Žižek think that there is some quality that makes an Act inherently political or not?

We can sharpen our discussion by noting how Žižek's thinking on this point comports with Badiou's. In his allusions to the Badiouan event and his references to a shared Lacanian framework of a Symbolic space shaped by an invisible force, Žižek depends upon Badiou. In his notion of a *post hoc* legitimation of an Act, Žižek is echoing – but with a crucial difference in temporality – Badiou's ideas about the retroversive element in political events. That is, for Žižek, the Act brings about the Event: when we "assume the risk" and act without any prior legitimation, we may bring about a political Event . . . if politicization takes place. For Badiou, by contrast, when an event takes place (the discerning of a hidden dimension of political equality in which everyone may stand as an equal), the work of political activity just begins. Badiou carefully explains that this work proceeds in the absence of any guarantee that it will result in an effective change.[14] In the patient process of the day-to-day working out of the insight into the egalitarian dimension of a situation – a bringing to awareness of elements of the situation that were never expressly recognized within it ("absent from the encyclopedia of the situation" is Badiou's way of putting it) – the individuals so engaged become "subjects" of truth procedures, processes by which the political truth of egalitarianism comes into being (or not) in the practical work of political activity. But by putting the cart before the horse (Act leads to Event), Žižek transposes the terms of Badiou's thought (event leads to acts). So long as Žižek conceives of the Event as a function of (dependent upon) the Act, he will have difficulty avoiding the *futur antérieur*, for he will always be judging the efficacy of the Act by reference to its outcomes.

The Politics of *Schadenfreude*

Throughout the texts we are considering, Žižek struggles to define the political Act in the temporal terms he has set up. As he expounds his version of a political Act that is not mortgaged to the future fulfillment of a present intention, he has to contend with the problem of finding a criterion *in the present* that will distinguish a specifically political Act from any garden-variety act. As he points out, we can't know in advance whether an act will achieve its proper politicization. But does that mean that we should simply regard all acts as fundamentally the same at the time of their enactment?

In order to address this difficulty, Žižek floats several other definitions that may invoke retroversion but which turn out to be independent of this temporal criterion. For example, he contrasts "the way of the act" with "the way of the superego" – in the latter, the subject makes itself "an instrument of the big Other's *jouissance*," and in the process covertly satisfies its own sadistic urges (RG 249). This way resorts to violence as the only means of propping up the symbolic gap – the inherent impotence of the big Other. Of course, in this perverse economy of supporting the (illusory) power of the Other, such acts often serve to promote the status quo rather than political change. By contrast, the political Act rejects the "cover" provided by the big Other. It will "authorize itself only in itself" in order to "interven[e] in the very rational order of the Real, changing-restructuring its co-ordinates – an act is not irrational; rather, it creates its own (new) rationality" (RG 243). We hear in this statement echoes of the de Gaulle example: legitimation comes after the fact; the coordinates by which the act will be judged are created by the act itself. When Žižek points out that the effects of the Act cannot be known in advance, which means that "we have to take a risk, a step into the open, with no big Other to return our message to us," he could be setting up the conditions for future legitimation or coordinate re-calibration. (RG 243). But having staked his definition of the Act on the question of whether the subject adopts the perverse position vis-à-vis the big Other or whether the act is complicitous with superego aggression, he now relies on a subjective experience to distinguish one kind of act from another.

In another text published in the same year as *Revolution at the Gates*, he concedes that "the same gesture can be an Act or a ridiculous empty posture" depending on the "specific socio-symbolic context." But this criticism, he claims, is not the true focus of those who are disturbed by the "Lacanian notion of Act" (WDR 152). Rather, precisely because its effects cannot be calculated in advance, these critics shrink from the Act because it carries with it no guarantee that it will not lead to "terrifying excesses" (WDR 153). The Act may be ethical or it may be monstrous; as Žižek puts it in another text: "in a truly radical political act, the opposition between a 'crazy' destructive gesture and a strategic political decision momentarily breaks down" (OWB 204). We cannot ignore the risk that violence may fail to achieve any positive political outcome. For this reason, he argues, the authentic political Act cannot be opposed in any straightforward way to what psychoanalysis calls the *passage à l'acte*, an outburst of destructive behavior that follows when the subject is confronted with an apparent deadlock or double bind.[15] "We simply have to accept the risk that a blind violent outburst will be followed by its proper politicization – there is no short cut here, and no guarantee of a successful outcome either" (RG 225). So, on the one hand, Žižek acknowledges that an act's true significance cannot be ascertained until after the fact, when politicization either emerges or does not. On the other hand, he insists that an "authentic revolutionary intervention" necessarily abjures its complicity with the aggression of the superego. This point suggests that it is possible to intend a revolutionary act and to know in advance whether the act is revolutionary, that is, before politicization. In that case, the subjective experience of *Schadenfreude* or superego complicity would signal a *non*revolutionary act. But how will we know in advance how sadistic we will feel once we undertake the act?

If it is not possible to foretell the status of the act as revolutionary rather than as sadistic, then the distinction between the authentic intervention and the complicit one must depend on the outcome (successful or failed politicization); in which case it is just as difficult to see why any appeal to a precedent subjective experience of superego complicity is necessary as it is to see how Žižek avoids the future anterior tense. An "authentic" act would be one that is followed by politicization, while a complicit act would merely mean one that failed to elicit politicization. In order to be consistent, he would have to argue that the subjective experience of *Schadenfreude* accompanying superego complicity would emerge retroactively, rather than supplying a motive. But this subjectivist approach to distinguishing the two kinds of acts would be irrelevant if the Act only emerges as such after the fact anyway, as a function of its subsequent politicization.

I can see only one way to make sense of Žižek's definitional maneuvering: because he cannot legitimately offer future justification, subjective feeling, or a specifically political nature as the criterion for the Act, he is left asserting the necessity, if not sufficiency, of violence for social change. That is, while violence in itself cannot guarantee that an act will bring about social change, only a violent act has the ability to do so. Only violent acts qualify as revolutionary Acts, even if some of these eligible acts ultimately fail to become revolutionary. Everything else, everything after the violence, is a matter of chance. As Žižek puts it:

> we cannot provide in advance an unambiguous criterion which will allow us to distinguish 'false' violent outburst [sic] from the 'miracle' of the authentic revolutionary breakthrough. The ambiguity is irreducible here, since the 'miracle' can occur only through the repetition of previous failures. And this is why violence is a necessary ingredient of a revolutionary political act. (RG 259)

Žižek offers different reasons for elevating violence to the level of the criterion. For example, in *The Parallax View*, he argues that "pure" revolutionary violence is "a goal in itself, an act which changes the very concept of what a 'good life' is, and a different (higher, eventually) standard of living is a by-product of a revolutionary process, not its goal" (PV 380). In this case, the criterion of "purity" is Kantian in its disinterestedness: we don't engage in revolutionary violence to make the world better. We engage in revolutionary violence "as a liberating end in itself" (PV 380). Žižek refers to Jameson's idea that violence is a sign that existing power relations are under attack as a warrant for his own claims that violence is necessary for revolution:

> Violence plays in revolutionary process the same role as worldly wealth plays in the Calvinist logic of predestination: although it has no intrinsic value, it is a sign of the authenticity of the revolutionary process, of the fact that this process is actually disturbing the existing power relations – the dream of a revolution without violence is precisely the dream of a "revolution without revolution" (Robespierre). (PV 381)

Žižek accurately portrays Jameson's views up to the dash in this passage. But the rest of the quotation forces us to ask whether Žižek and Jameson are really on the same page. Jameson seems to be saying that, when political change actually challenges the powers-that-be, then those powers will react with violence. Žižek, by contrast, makes violence not the sign that revolution is taking place but rather the *sine qua non* of the revolutionary act. Yet, surely, not all violence signals that a revolution is taking place. Jameson's analogy to Calvinism brings in all the difficulties of foreknowledge which attend the temporality defining the political act according to Žižek, as we have already seen.

Of course, there is good historical reason to link revolution with violence. As Sewell reminds us, the invention of the term revolution itself was a novel yoking of two concepts previously held apart – popular violence and popular sovereignty (we may wonder why someone committed to the notion of establishing new coordinates by which to judge events would hold on to a potentially outmoded version of revolution). Yet, it seems not to occur to Žižek, at least not in these contexts, that the retroactively conferred status of revolutionary Act could befall a nonviolent act, such as Rosa Parks' refusal. Despite his avowed commitment to the idea of *post hoc* politicization, Žižek's preferred example of an Act is not Parks' nonviolent refusal to take a seat at the back of the bus, an act which was prepared for in advance by political organizing and a discourse of legitimation, and which resulted in further politicization and ultimately changes in laws and social institutions. Instead he nominates the heroic action of the "famous Jewish ballerina" who shot the Nazi guards for whom she was forced to dance, effectively committing suicide in the process. The difference between these two incidents is striking: a nonviolent act that achieves politicization in Parks' case versus a violent one that does not. Nonetheless, Žižek specifically designates the example of the ballerina as "the way of the act" (RG 249).

A similar if more muted defense of violence appears in his appropriation of Badiou. Žižek collapses two temporally distinct phases in Badiou's theory.[16] For Badiou, the event occurs in a flash, at the time of the discernment of the hidden dimension of equality, but the truth procedures through which the event comes to have its effects take place over time and with no certainty of success. In conflating these two steps, Žižek can make use of the elements of Badiou's theory that support the politics of rupture rather than the politics of process. It seems to be Žižek's opinion that any political *process* represents an accommodation to the status quo and as such is merely an excuse to take action in order to change nothing. Nothing other than a sudden eruption of violence will produce social change.

Žižek is not blind to the difficulties this line of argument creates. So, for example, when he meditates on utopia as the key to the political nature of the Act, he seems to be trying to make this naked assertion of the critical function of violence more palatable:

> The only criterion is the absolutely inherent one: that of the enacted utopia. In a genuine revolutionary breakthrough, the utopian future is neither simply fully realized, present, nor simply evoked as a distant promise which justifies present violence – it is rather as if, in a unique suspension of temporality, in the short circuit between the present and the future, we are – as if by Grace – briefly allowed to act as if the utopian future is (not yet fully here, but) already at hand, there to be seized. Revolution is experienced not as a present hardship we have to endure for the sake of the happiness and freedom of future generations, but as the present hardship over which this future happiness and freedom already cast their shadow – in it, we are already free even as we fight for freedom; we are already happy even as we fight for happiness, no matter how difficult the circumstances. (RG 259–60)

Remarkably, he once again stakes his definition on *feelings*: we are happy to imagine that utopia is just at hand, even if we are not yet enjoying its fruits; we are happy to undergo difficulties, even if we are suffering. It is difficult to see how happy feelings or certainty about one's acts could be sufficient to determine what counts as a political Act. But Žižek has indemnified himself against this criticism by conceding that no one can know in advance how it will all turn out. In these circumstances, feelings are as good (or bad) a criterion as anything else. We are faced once more with the notion that all acts are on a par with one another, that mere chance turns an act into an Act of social change.

Why, then, the turn to utopia? For one thing, the promise of a better state of affairs (however near or far) dilutes the negativity and potential sadism of the use of violence. Hence Žižek's deployment of a religious vocabulary of "Grace" and "miracles." However, the false distinction between a "distant promise" and a utopia not yet present does not alter the fact that we are back in the realm of eschatology – of the Merleau-Pontyan wager. The theoretical value of this feeling of happiness in the "utopia to come" is dubious.

However, another passage published two years later gives us a different sense of the significance of utopia and may return Žižek to more secure theoretical ground. Against arguments which link twentieth-century utopian appeals to totalitarian terror, he urges us to think of utopia as a crucial political category, without which no authentic political Act can take place. In contrast to the idea that utopia concerns a promise of a better life, as in the passage we have just discussed, he proposes that "utopia has nothing to do with idle dreaming about ideal society in total abstraction from real life: 'utopia' is a matter of innermost urgency, something we are pushed into as a matter of survival, when it is no longer possible to go on within the parameters of the 'possible'" (IBK 124). He summarizes his approach to utopia in stating that "[t]he 'utopian' gesture is the gesture which changes the co-ordinates of the possible" (IBK 123). We have already seen that he does not have in mind here the constructivist approach to equivalent narratives; rather, when he invokes the transformation of the very coordinates by which a situation can be grasped, he is implicitly invoking the presence of the strange attractor. If we can change the coordinates by which a situation is framed, it is because the original framing is fantasmatic, an illusion that hides a certain level of the Real. Referring to Lenin's "utopia" as the "imperative to smash the bourgeois state . . . and invent a new communal social form . . . in which all could take part in the administration of social affairs," Žižek argues that for Lenin

this was no theoretical project for some distant future . . . *This urge of the moment is the true utopia. . . .* This utopia has to be opposed both to the standard notion of political utopias . . . and to what is usually referred to as the utopian practice of capitalism itself: commodities evoking utopian pleasures, the libidinal economy that relies on the dynamic of continuously generating new transgressive desires and practices, right up to necrophilia . . . And one of the strategies of utopia today resides in the aesthetic dimension . . . Does not the curious phenomenon of "flash mobs" represent aesthetico-political protest at its purest, reduced to its minimal frame . . . the act of marking a minimal difference? (IBK 123–4)

How should we understand this strange yoking of interior subjective experiences ("urge of the moment"; "innermost urgency") with formal functions ("changes the co-ordinates"; "marking a minimal difference") in the definition of utopian politics? Strange as it seems, Žižek is making the case that aestheticization is the key to revolutionary political action insofar as it generates minimal self-difference. In order to understand his reasoning, we need to take a closer look at the roles of Möbius subjectivity and extimate causality in the Žižekian revolutionary act.

Headless Revolutionaries

How can Žižek's conflicting accounts of the political Act be reconciled? To do him justice, we must consider the implications for political activity that he draws from two different Lacanian accounts of subjectification. In the more familiar story of the birth of the subject, desire seems to be produced by the symbolic Law's prohibition on *jouissance*. In previous chapters, I have shown how this version corresponds to a neurotic interpretation of subjectification. In the neurotic fantasy, the lack installed in the subject can be removed by getting rid of the obstacle that prohibits access to the fulfilling *objet a*. The neurotic fails to understand that there is no such prohibition, that the lack cannot be remediated by transgressing a prohibition: because the lack constitutes the subject, its elimination would dissolve the subject. In effect, the desiring subject is a fantasy that obscures the truth about the subject in relation to the drive, the truth that the prohibition on reaching the object merely disguises its absence. That is, when we understand the Law in terms of the formal negation, prohibition emerges as a secondary phenomenon, a way that the subject fantasmatically makes sense of its alienation.

Even if there were an object that could completely fulfill the subject's desire and so eliminate the lack at its heart, the subject still would have to "miss" the object in order to remain a subject. This perpetual "missing" is due neither to desire's inanition nor to the strength of the prohibition. It is due to the drive. The drive is what keeps desire alive by producing the illusion that there is an object to aim at as it "circles" the place where the object should be, like a strange attractor. In this way, the drive ensures no encounter with an object while maintaining the illusion of its existence. In this account, the subject is a subject of the drive, not a subject of desire.

Žižek proposes as the properly political subject an "acephalous subject who assumes the position of the object" (OWB 176). In this move from desire to drive, he fundamentally alters the picture of a political subject as one who calculates an intervention to bring about the future it desires. The "acephalous subject" does not function in this intentionalized mode of traditional political discourse: "the subject who acts is no longer a person but, precisely, an object." That is, in his view, we must give up, once and for all, our sense of the political – the political act, the political domain, and the political collectivity – as based on promise or calculation.

To clarify his point that, in the political Act, the subject assumes the position of the object, Žižek rehearses the relationship of subject to object in Lacanian theory. Psychoanalysis, as we have seen, posits that something must be renounced (or formally negated) in order for a subject to emerge.[17] The *objet a* comes to stand in for this lost part: "drive is fundamentally the insistence of an undead 'organ without a body,' standing, like Lacan's lamella, for that which the subject had to lose in order to subjectivize itself in the symbolic space of the sexual difference" (OWB 174). It is in this way that it makes sense to think of *objet a* as the "correlate" of the subject, even if the object is impossible, i.e., an absence that nonetheless functions as a strange attractor for the drive. In his most straightforward statement about the acephalous subject, Žižek draws explicitly on the metaphor of the Möbius band to elucidate how the subject and the object should be thought together:

> [P]ersons and things are part of the same reality, whereas the object is the impossible equivalent of the subject itself. We arrive at the object when we pursue the side of the subject (of its signifying representation) on the Moebius track to the end and find ourselves on the other side of the same place from where we started. One should thus reject the topic of the personality, a soul-body unity, as the organic Whole dismembered in the process of reification-alienation: the subject emerges out of the person as the product of the violent reduction of the person's body to a partial object. (OWB 175)

The acephalous subject, or subject of the drives, has a Möbius topology. In Žižek's thinking, the excessive dimension of the Möbius subject comes into play during the political act as the means by which the subject itself encounters the objective dimension. The *objet a*, the excessive part of the subject, is "the subject's stand-in within the order of objectivity" (OWB 175). When the subject identifies directly with this excess, it becomes genuinely revolutionary because it gains access to the register of the Real, the object. How? According to Žižek, the identification with the object de-personalizes the subject, instituting a gap between its subjectivated individuation (all the little preferences and properties that make up our social identities) and its subject-ness, the "pure" subject that emerges as a function of the drive. This shift in perspective, whereby the subject becomes the object (that it always was) and vice versa, is what Žižek calls *the parallax view.*

It may be helpful to return to our original formulation of the Möbius subject to understand why Žižek places such importance on this de-personalization. If we think of the subject after subjectification as a set, $A = \{x, y, z, \emptyset\}$, we could draw the analogy that the elements of the set (x, y, z as the things-turned-objects by the formal negation) are the subject's "properties" in its symbolic identity: piano-player, husband, chocolate-lover. The excessive dimension of this set derives from the fact that the external brackets marking the set correspond precisely to the internal element of the empty set. Let us recall that set-ness (the externality of the brackets) correlates to the place of the subject's inscription in the Symbolic, prior to any specific content, and the empty set ($\emptyset$) correlates to the impossible *objet a*, which counts as an element of the set but does not have any specific properties. The "pure" subject of Žižek's remarks is reduced to these formal elements, what we have called the **subject*** considered by way of the operation of "subtraction" of the ontic properties from the presentation of the subject.

As long as we are fixated – as happens in multiculturalism and identity politics – on the symbolic identifiers of our personal identities, we obscure the link between the subject and the drive as the true engine of the subject's existence. For when we focus on the symbolic dimension of identity, we are conceiving of the subject as a subject of desire, perpetually seeking to overcome its lack by finding its object of desire. Any political action founded on this premise dooms the actors to a futile search for a utopia which, of necessity, must always be deferred.[18]

In highlighting the difference between the subject of desire and the subject of the drive, Žižek sets the stage for a theory of collective action that does not depend upon the symbolic properties of the individuals involved, including their "common humanity":

> The collective that emerges at the level of such a fighting subjectivity is to be thoroughly opposed to the intersubjective topic of "how to reach the other," how to maintain the openness and respect toward Otherness. There are, grosso modo, three ways to reach out to the other that fit

the triad of ISR: imaginary ("human touch"), symbolic ("politeness," "good manners"), real (shared obscenity). Each of the three has its own dangers. . . It is easy to discern the falsity of such a gesture of empathy [like that of an Israeli soldier towards a Palestinian he is evicting]: the notion [is false] that, in spite of political differences, we are all human beings with the same loves and worries, neutralizes the impact of what the soldier is effectively doing at that moment. (OWB 177)

Other modes, such as shared obscenity, "can function as a fake solidarity masking underlying power relations" (OWB 178). What then does the acephalous subject offer to counter these deficient approaches to solidarity?

In Žižek's view, the political meaning of one's acts has nothing to do with one's "sincerity or hypocrisy" – that is, one's "subjective self-experience" is irrelevant to the objective truth of one's actions. Rather, the subject of the drive institutes a gap between itself and its symbolic-subjective dimension. The subject's identification with *objet a* re-casts it, not as a set of symbolic properties, but as connected directly to the order of objectivity. Introducing a distance towards one's own symbolic identity puts one in a position to act in an "objective-ethical" way (OWB 182). Presumably, it is this link to the objective that makes solidarity possible. The manifold differences or symbolic properties of individuals move to the background, while each subject, as identified with the object of the drive, finds its way to the objective order, the only terrain on which meaningful change can occur. Solidarity, then, emerges not from inter-subjective relations but rather from the relations of subjects purified of their symbolic identities, subjects who meet on the ground of objectivity, as objects.

There is a tentative feel about this argument, as Žižek shifts from considerations of solidarity to ethics to a more general discussion of whether it is possible to distinguish fascism as a form of group solidarity from other political forms that are ranged against it in contemporary theory, and finally to his judgment that the multitude in Hardt and Negri involves the ultimate type of depoliticization. So, the underlying difficulty of articulating the grounds on which subjects – subjects that are avowedly *excessive* – can come together as solidary political groups in a way that avoids fascism is never directly addressed.

Instead, the conclusion to *Organs Without Bodies* returns to the proposition that revolution (somehow already solidary) occurs only through "the suspension of all strategic considerations based on hope for a better future, the stance of *on attaque, et puis, on le verra*," and the ratification of the idea that "in a truly radical political act, the opposition between a 'crazy' destructive gesture and a strategic political decision momentarily breaks down" (OWB 203–4). Whether these are individual or group acts is left open. In any case, Žižek reiterates his earlier definition of a revolutionary Act as a violent one risking both futility and terror. Still, he does open up a new line of argument in *Organs Without Bodies*, one he eventually takes up in *The Parallax View*, which clarifies the link between revolutionary Acts, de-personalization, and the self-aestheticizing function of the extimate cause.

Formal Negation, Constellation, and *Sinthome*

We can glean one clue to Žižek's thinking at this point from the juxtaposition of his statement that truly revolutionary activity depends upon the renunciation of all strategic considerations with his (immediately subsequent) description of the "staged performance" of "Storming the Winter Palace" in Petrograd, November 1920, in which "thousands of workers, soldiers, students and artists" prepared a re-enactment of the October Revolution that had taken place three years before (OWB 203). How does a staged performance qualify as a non-strategic revolutionary act? Žižek describes this performance as a "sacred pageant," a "magic act of founding a new community" (OWB 204). In other words, he claims that the act of the people playing themselves produces solidarity:

> This aestheticization, in which the people quite literally "plays itself," certainly does not fall under Benjamin's indictment of the Fascist "aestheticization of the political." Instead of abandoning this aestheticization to the political Right, instead of a blanket dismissal of every mass political spectacle as "proto-Fascist," one should perceive, in this minimal, purely formal, difference of the people from itself, the unique case of "real life" differentiated from art by nothing more than an invisible, formal gap . . . an indication of this deeper identity of the people playing themselves. (OWB 204)

But let us note that Benjamin's work actually makes it possible to distinguish between the fascist mode of aestheticization and the mode Žižek considers necessary to challenge the status quo, what Benjamin (crucially revised by Adorno) refers to as the *constellation*. The constellation is not the "aestheticization of the political," but rather an aestheticizing *for* the political. In constellative activity, the subject aestheticizes itself by means of a formal gesture, creating a self-distance that brings it into contact with the "objective" and setting aside the given content (socio-historical *données*) of the social universe in order to make a space for the new.

So, surprising as it may be, a dominant tradition in critical Marxist thought explicitly *relies* on formalism and aestheticism to address the problem of external determinants for a materialist-historicist practice, through a reflection on the relationship between aesthetics and politics. The *donnée* of contemporary historicist theorizing – that the presumed neutral or disinterested space of aesthetics serves only as a mask for the ideological de-formation of material reality – does not apply to some foundational writings presumed to belong to the anti-formalist camp: Marx's *German Ideology*, Engels's *The Condition of the Working Class in England*, Adorno's *Aesthetic Theory* (written after *Negative Dialectics*), and even Jameson's own work on Adorno (*Late Marxism: Adorno, or The Persistence of the Dialectic*) all share this emphasis on the political value of aestheticization.[19] The fundamental difficulty engaged by these texts concerns the problem of how newness can possibly enter the world: if everything, including subjectivity, is determined mechanistically by the processes of historical materialism, if all thought is pre-determined and ideologically saturated, from whence will the new, the revolutionary, the emancipatory emerge?

If we want to know how to enable critical thought to stretch beyond existing concepts in a politically relevant way, Adorno (among others) answers that we need the "determinate indeterminacy" of the formal, aesthetic experience. Only this formal reflection can bring us to a mode of construction that is not fully determined by (and therefore in thrall to) the merely given of the socio-historical world. Although the artwork is *made*, it enacts a determinate negation of "what is and has been" – nullifying the given – in order to make a space for some, as yet undetermined, possibility.[20] Negating the "un-truth" of the given opens a door for new-ness to enter the world, something not extant in the given regime.

> That by virtue of which truth-content is more than is posited by works of art, is their participation [*Methexis*] in history and the determinate critique which they execute on history through their form. What history is in the works, is not made, and history first frees the work of art from mere positing or production: truth-content is not outside history, but is history's crystallization in the works.[21]

Adorno here advances a characteristic dialectic. The historical materials deployed by the artwork resist determination by the work (as Jarvis puts it: "these materials are not entirely in the service of artistic production"[22]) and, in so doing, undermine the idea of the artwork as mere "production for its own sake." That is, it undermines precisely the stance entailing the fetishization of labor that characterizes the main obstacle to utopia in our time. At the same time, the artwork's reconfiguration of these historical materials nullifies the sense of their inevitability without however negating the fact of their historicity. Thanks to its materials, the artwork is able to access history, but thanks to its reconfiguration of those materials, it renders a "judgmentless judgment" on what is and has been. Thus, the artwork's determinate negation of untruth results in an indeterminacy, an excess, that does not assure us of a utopia-to-come through some positive assertion. Nor does it offer an explicit historical critique. Rather, the dimension of critique and the opening to the new occur because the artwork must make use of historically given materials which, through the formal reconfiguration of those materials, exposes the possibility that something could be otherwise.

For Adorno, art has a critical function that derives from its formal character as semblance.[23] The audience knows the difference between the artwork and the real world but promotes the artwork to the "dignity of the real," an engagement that enables the audience to experience its own evaluative agency. At the same time, the illusory character of the artwork suspends any application of that agency to the real world while permitting the audience to play with the elements presented in the artwork. Like the people "playing themselves" in the storming of the Winter Palace, the ontic qualities of the world are set off, creating a formal space for the new to emerge. Following Robert Kaufman, we can consider this activity as *constellative*: as he puts it in his discussion of the constellation in Adorno, the artwork "burst[s] the formal contours of extant conceptuality allow[ing] for a renewed sense of capacity or agency vis-à-vis *materials* that can eventually be grasped as reconceived or newly conceived sociopolitical, historical, or ethical *content* in the newly stretched form or formal capacity."[24] This experience requires the formal if provisional negation of the given, the real, or the predetermined – a negation precisely analogous to the formal negation that establishes a set.

Using the example of the empty set to describe extimate causality is a bit risky, given the general agreement among contemporary theorists that formalism is ideologically suspect. Doesn't formalization mean that we are positing a space free from ideological conditioning? Hasn't it been demonstrated that the production of this supposedly neutral space by means of aestheticization is the primary mode of ideological mystification? Isn't the animating fiction of ideology that there is a formal space of disinterested, objective, transcendent judgment – the same problematic assumption for which we have faulted Althusser? With such familiar complaints in mind, it is difficult to see how the kinds of criticisms brought against the ideological valence of Kantian aesthetics and representationalism would not apply to the extimate or formal cause. If we plump for formalism, how will we ever approach considerations of materiality and agency? How is it possible to argue that formalization is a means to forwarding a materialist political interventionism? The critique of formalism mounted by many

Marxists has made it almost impossible to see the value that extimate causality could have for historicist and materialist thinkers.

Yet Žižek's passage encourages us to see that the constellation shares crucial features with the late Lacanian concept of the *sinthome*, in which the subject divests itself of (the fantasy of the significance of) its symbolic properties in order to identify with *objet a* at the end of the analysis. The similarities between constellative activity and sinthomic activity derive from a shared causal problem: both the methodologies of psychoanalysis and socio-political analysis presuppose and present causal patterns in the chaotic flux of given particularities; at the same time, they must locate and mobilize the singularly indeterminate in order to intervene – therapeutically or politically – in the order of determinants. They seek to bring the new into being from a system of apparently total determination.

So, for example, even when interpretation of the meaning of the symptom has reached its fullest extent, that is, even when the symbolic meaning of the symptom has been articulated and the fantasy traversed, the subject is still subject to the drive that organizes her *jouissance*. The problem of intervening in this determinate system – the drive's determination of the subject – can be solved only by creating a new subject, a *neosubject*, who identifies with the symptom in a distanced way, establishing an innovative entity, the *sinthome*:

> . . . normally, that is, neurotically, the signifier of the Name-of-the-Father is expected to take the place of the lack in the Other and to knot the registers of the Real, the Symbolic, and the Imaginary in such a way that the jouissance is forbidden. . . . it is possible for a *sinthome* to take the role of the signifier of the Name-of-the-Father. Lacan invites everyone to follow Joyce's example and to create their own *sinthome* at the place of the lack of the Other; the aim of this *creative* act [my emphasis] is to be able to function without the signifier of the Name-of-the-Father, that is, the Other.[25]

Through analysis, the subject not only learns the meaning of its symptom but also experiences the singularity of the organization of its *jouissance*. This singularity produces the subject (as subject of the drive) in surprising ways: although the drive is always organizing the subject within a finite shape, so to speak, its action is unpredictable both in terms of the materials it seizes and the connections it creates. By dissipating the significatory dimension of the symptom – that is, by identifying, "while assuring oneself of a kind of distance toward one's symptom," with the stochastic dynamics of its wellspring – the neosubject acts *creatively*, in precisely the way that Adorno describes, to nullify the significance of its "given" ontic properties and reveal the possibility of newness.[26] In both Lacanian psychoanalytic and Frankfurt School theories, then, the function of the formal negation in extimate causality is a way of theorizing how the not-yet-conceived might come into being through an aesthetic act, a creative act, of self-distancing. Consequently, it is a way of accounting for the production of a certain form of freedom, or, to put it in a more politically charged idiom, emancipation from the given.

Subjective Destitution and Beginning the New

The question of the provenance of the new is not itself new. We have already seen that Adorno invents the constellation as a way of addressing this question. In Adorno's view, to arrive at new thought, truly new thought, we would have to go beyond thought itself to think the "non-identity" of thought. Adorno arrives at this conclusion by way of a meditation on the double negation in Hegel. He criticizes Hegel for his allegiance to the mathematical proposition that the negation of a negation is an affirmation. This standard logical proposition expresses a principle of identity, according to Adorno, and hence it is necessarily anti-dialectical:

> To equate the negation of negation with positivity is the quintessence of identification; it is the formal principle in its purest form. What thus wins out in the inmost core of [Hegelian] dialectics is the anti-dialectical principle: that traditional logic which, *more arithmetico*, takes minus times minus for a plus. It was borrowed from the same mathematics to which Hegel reacts so idiosyncratically elsewhere.[27]

Only by avoiding "identitary sovereignty," which he considers to be the decisive function in Enlightenment rationality, can we arrive at truly dialectical thought.[28] This (by now commonplace) idea that Enlightenment universality does violence to difference and seeks to abolish otherness sets the agenda for *Negative Dialectics*. Not content with the positing of difference as its aim, because such positing assumes that one knows difference and therefore has subsumed it already to identity, Adorno seeks a way of thinking non-identity, a way that has not yet been found: "what would be different has not yet begun" (quoted in OC 99). His solution is the constellation, which gives up the unification that form imposes: as Badiou puts it, the constellation is "a dispersive explosion such that at no point does the identitary sovereignty of the form govern its construction and its perception" (OC 103).

How can one think non-identity if thought functions by the principle of identity? At this point, Badiou makes what is for us an extremely useful observation: "What is the experience which makes possible the thinking of that which is non-identical to thought? What is the appearance of non-identity to thought? Non-identity is not given to thought as thought; it is given inevitably as *affect*" (OC 103, my emphasis). This observation takes us directly to the point of tangency between Žižek and Adorno, the place at which they touch most closely and from which they utterly diverge.

Žižek's efforts to make a way for the new, as we have seen, lead him to the theoretical conclusion that the Real must erupt in reality: violence is the means for such an eruption. Whether he is speaking about the violence of the political Act or the violence of subjective destitution, he proposes the deliberate facilitation of this eruption of the Real. Lacanians argue that this eruption of the Real, other to the Symbolic and the Imaginary, emerges as affect. The new enters thought by way of the Real, by way of affect.

Adorno treats the necessity of this eruption quite differently than Žižek. Badiou explains the functioning of affect in Adorno in this way:

> Ultimately the sole radical attestation of what thought is, confronted with what does not belong to it, comes in the appearance of suffering. For Adorno, the immediate experience of the essential and the inessential finds measure in what the subject feels objectively as suffering. . . The unique witnessing of difference is, as such, through the position of the victim. The attestation is non-configurable, it is nothing but the constellation of experience, and in this position of the victim stands only what is heteronymous [sic] to thinking. It's here that something like a positive counterpart of *Negative Dialectics* emerges: "the *telos* of such an organization of society would be to negate the physical suffering of even the least of its members." (OC 103–4)

In Adorno, the link between ethics and politics is forged by raising particularity to a universal principle: no wonder that Badiou emphasizes this point in Adorno. Every victim's experience is *sui generis*, yet all such suffering – "objective . . . immediate [and] unconditioned" – has an equal status, such that its elimination serves as a guide to ethico-political action (OC 104). Only this guidance from affective experience can bring us to the threshold of new thought; only this experience of non-identity, of "the thought of what is originally different from thought itself" takes us to the recognition of affect and its ethico-political form of suffering (OC 103). Badiou makes the point that Adorno has left behind logical philosophizing here and turned to ethical prescription: "One can then say that Adorno's system is an ethical historicity, an agenda of beginning which can only begin on the order of a prescription and not on the order of a deduction" (OC 100).

By contrast, Žižek sets aside the question of suffering. Even when he concerns himself with affective states, he focuses on happiness. But more importantly, he simply does not address politics and ethics from the standpoint of the victim reduced to the dimension of the body. In this, he seems to agree with Agamben, that the political gesture to be avoided at all costs is the separation of "bare life" from forms of life, as we discussed in chapter 2. That is, the suffering victim may appear to be subjectively destitute, but in fact, the designation as suffering victim, as one reduced to bare life, simply elevates one ontic property above all others. Žižek is aiming at something different in his turn to the role of affect in the *sinthome*.

Setting Off the Revolution

When the people play themselves in the staged version of the storming of the Winter Palace, it is as though they put in quotation marks or "set off" their real-life substantive properties and, in this way, foster the revelation of their minimal self-difference as Möbius subjects – neosubjects or **subjects***. It is important to remember that this minimal self-difference is what is excessive about the subject, the short circuit or covert identity between the formal cause of the subject (the set-ness that establishes the hollow place for its inscription into the Symbolic, by which it actually becomes a subject) and the *objet a* (empty set) that "merely gives body" to the formal negation (PV 382). This setting-off of ontic properties makes visible the excessive dimension of the subject: once the "fullness" of the subject in terms of Symbolic properties is subtracted, so to speak, what comes into view is this (usually invisible) formal constitution of the subject as Möbius.

In the concluding pages of *The Parallax View*, Žižek appears to be availing himself of these similarities between the constellation and the *sinthome*, where he gives his fullest explanation to date of this form of aestheticization and its revolutionary potential, likening it to the characteristic refusal of Melville's Bartleby:

> [Bartleby's] "I would prefer not to" is to be taken literally: it says "I would prefer not to," not "I don't prefer (or care) to" – so we are back at Kant's distinction between negative and infinite judgment. In his refusal of the Master's order, Bartleby does not negate the predicate; rather, he affirms a non-predicate [adds a negation]. . . This is how we pass from the politics of "resistance" or "protestation," which parasitizes upon what it negates, to a politics which opens up a new space outside the hegemonic position and its negation. . . "I would prefer not to." This is the gesture of subtraction at its purest, the reduction of all qualitative differences to a purely formal minimal difference. . . His refusal is not so much the refusal of a determinate content as, rather, the formal gesture of refusal as such. It is therefore

strictly analogous to Sygne's *No!*: it is an act of *Versagung*, not a symbolic act. There is a clear holophrastic quality to "I would prefer not to": it is a signifier-turned-object, a signifier reduced to an inert stain that stands for the collapse of the symbolic order. (PV 381–5)

Leaving aside for the moment the question of the suitability of Bartleby as an example of this pure negation, we can recognize that, for Žižek, self-aestheticization provides the means for revealing the extimate cause of the subject, its Möbius condition.

In this account, Žižek deploys the Lacanian *sinthome* without naming it explicitly. The refusal (*Versagung*) of all determinate differences – the gesture of formal difference – refers to the extimate cause, the founding gesture of the subject as subject*. We should remember here that the excess attending the Möbius subject arises from the formal addition of a negation (extimate cause) that creates an equation between the place of the inscription in the Symbolic (set-ness) and the little piece of the Real, *objet a*, that must be added as a void (empty set) to form the subject. The refusal of all Symbolic differences puts this equation front and center: the extimate cause not only sets off the subject, producing the hollow that cradles the subject within the Symbolic, it also produces the empty set, which, in a parallax shift, appears to be embodied or substantialized as the obstacle to the Symbolic itself. The same formal gesture that inscribes the subject in the Symbolic also generates the subject's excess over (and therefore apparently athwart) the Symbolic. Setting off the ontic properties of the subject demonstrates their contingency. By creating an aesthetic distance from what seemed to be the given and inevitable characteristics of the situation, the neosubject sets the stage for other coordinates to come into view and into play.

Žižek describes the effect of the elevation to visibility of this formal constitution of the subject as the "signifier-turned-object" – an "immobile, inert, insistent, impassive being" (PV 385). In this way, the neosubject itself becomes the obstacle to the Symbolic, the little piece of the Real that resists symbolization, as he says: "the signifier-turned-object [is] reduced to an inert stain that stands for the collapse of the symbolic order" (PV 385). Or, to put it in our terms, he is arguing that, by finding a way to reduce itself to its formal Möbius conditions, the subject becomes an obstacle to the Symbolic. It is not clear here whether he means that the subject "stands for" the possibility of a different relation to the Symbolic (and so brings the hope of political transformation to the rest of us) or actually, somehow, causes the Symbolic to collapse, or just jams the social machinery. But he appears to be arguing that the kind of violence he has in mind is the "pure violence" of *Versagung* – of the subject against itself, so to speak – which in itself is an act necessary for revolution to occur.

So, here is one way to read his argument. Bartleby's kind of absolute impassivity against the Symbolic links the revolutionary potential of the political Act to the inertness of the acephalous subject through the gesture of self-aestheticization. By deliberately identifying with the extimate cause, the subject changes its relationship to its own drive determinants *athwart* any Symbolic constraints. This neosubject does not seek to act *on* the social field but rather to reveal its true relation *to* the social field – the relation of nonrelation – by explicitly appearing as the excessive dimension in itself and making visible what cannot be accommodated within the encyclopedia of the situation. In Badiou's terms, we might say that the subject makes of itself the *Event* of the revelation of the hidden dimension of the situation and, at the same time, transforms itself into the subject of the process of fidelity by sticking to its self-aestheticization.

If this is Žižek's argument, it is a nifty piece of theorizing that eliminates in one stroke many of the contradictions attending his efforts to distinguish among types of violence while adhering closely to the theoretical requirements of extimate causality and Möbius subjectivity. Because the violence (self-destitution) is *intrasubjective*, it is *nonstrategic* with respect to larger social aims. To the extent that Žižek's earlier proposals for violent acts as mechanisms of change depended upon the (unlikely) serendipity of retroversive politicization, this version appears to have a more secure causal foundation, based on an understanding of the cause of the subject. By situating the locus of transformation at the level of the difference between the Symbolic and what is unsymbolizable (the Real) – by divesting the subject of its ontic properties – Žižek appears to be trying to avoid any reliance on intentional re-signification, the problem bedeviling so many accounts of political agency. And he remains within the framework of the Event and the hidden dimension that he has worked so hard to articulate.

Yet this ingenious conclusion – and to my knowledge, wholly unique deployment of Möbius subjectivity and extimate causality in the service of political theory – unfortunately remains unexplored in any satisfying way. Žižek never offers any examples of events that depended upon the "pure violence" of self-aestheticization for their political value. Perhaps such descriptions are impossible, given that the phenomenon is largely internal to the individual subject. But we need to examine his proposal more closely.

The Political Potential of Self-Aestheticization

Unlike Adorno, who seems to regard aestheticization as a way of finding new, non-ideologically determined but nonetheless Symbolic content,

Žižek situates the revolutionary potential of the subject in its objecthood, its non-Symbolic dimension. We could say that Adorno's inattention to the excess produced by the double negation, i.e. his insistence that it can lead only to affirmation, leaves him with no choice but to emphasize the ontic property of suffering rather than the subject's withdrawal from or subtraction of the ontic – the *given*. In Žižek's view, however, this withdrawal promotes the subject to the register of the Real which *in itself* "stands for the collapse of the symbolic" (PV 385). Revolution does not come about through a replacement of *what is* with something else, not even through a focus on the elimination on suffering, but rather in the stubborn stance of refusal of the entire social universe.

The possibility of refusing the Symbolic *per se*, in fact, points to the heart of Žižek's quarrel with Hardt and Negri's reading of "Bartleby," which they employ as a means of elucidating the grounds for a new community. Where they see Bartleby's refusal as the first step to "acquiring a distance toward the existing social universe" prior to the "painstaking work of constructing a new community," Žižek argues that "the very frantic and engaged activity of constructing a new order is sustained by an underlying 'I would prefer not to' which forever reverberates in it . . . the underlying principle that sustains the entire movement" (PV 383). In our terms we would say that setting off the ontic level (set-ness) of the social universe correlates to the formal negation that brought the symbolic universe into being in the first place and that, like the empty set, persists as a constitutively necessary component of it.

In rejecting Hardt and Negri's program for the intentional building of a new community, Žižek implicitly points up their reliance on the fantasmatic version of communal social life that Nancy debunks. These fantasies seize on the excessive dimension of the **subject*** *both* as the signifier that completes the untotalized chain of signifiers (e.g., Aristotle's *azux* as extra-human) *and* as the signifier that stands in the way of that completion (e.g., the *azux* as *phaulos*, or abjected). In the political fantasies of community, the subject appears either as the obstacle to social harmony or as the savior who resolves social discord once and for all. In either case, ontic properties are made to serve illusory functions: some contingent feature of the subject is imagined to bestow the special quality of obstacle or savior, when the indeterminacy at the heart of the **subject*** itself sets this oscillation in motion. Or, to use the terms we have developed, the formal gesture of the extimate cause produces Möbius subjects who generate the social field through their efforts to rid themselves of their excess: the resulting social relations are relations of *nonrelation*, completely different from those unifying and completing relations fantasized in the discourse of community.

Žižek seems to be formulating an argument for the inherently political nature of aestheticization that depends for its consistency upon the characteristics of the Möbius subjects and the extimate cause. In discussing the difficulties of theorizing social change, we have articulated some crucial properties that any theory proposing political efficacy needs to have and some pitfalls it needs to avoid. Which of these can we find in the subject-turned-object as Žižek describes it? For one thing, Möbius-ness applies to *all* subjects in the social field. Subjectification by way of extimate causality serves as the universalizing function within the theory. More importantly, this universal function is "partisan," because it doesn't appear in the same way for each subject. Even though the extimate cause has a purely formal character, nonetheless "the creative effect of identifying with the symptom . . . [requires a] return to the specific character of this identification [that] belongs to a specific context."[29] That is, Žižek can avoid the disavowal haunting Laclau's equivalential theory, because each subject has its own *unique* relationship to the extimate cause. Insofar as I have to renounce my *particular* symbolic properties in order to highlight the extimate cause of my subjectification, my *Versagung* will look different from everyone else's, although it will bring to light retroversively the same *formal* condition that founds other subjects.

At the same time, Žižek himself seems to disavow some of his own central precepts. His account suggests that the long journey of individual psychoanalysis would be a prerequisite for effective political action. But, as we know, Žižek is no fan of gradual processes. So, he proposes a more direct route that could work to create political groups in a "radical conclusion concerning the figure of the leader":

> . . . as a rule, democracy cannot reach beyond pragmatic utilitarian inertia, it cannot suspend the logic of "servicing goods"; consequently, just as there is no self-analysis, since the analytic change can occur only through the transferential relationship to the external figure of the analyst, a leader is necessary to trigger enthusiasm for a Cause, to bring about radical change in the subjective position of his followers, to "transubstantiate" their identity. (PV 380)

To propose that the leader causes the form of transference his followers experience is both to rely on a discredited intentionalism (which attributes to the leader special powers to will the outcome he desires) and to promote the perverse solution, in which the subject serves as instrument of the Master or the Cause. This perverse instrumentalization is far from Bartleby's *Versagung* and returns us to the politics of *Schadenfreude*. In proposing this role for the leader, Žižek leaves out of account the partisan nature of such transferences, as did Laclau, while at the same time reproducing the dominant fantasy of all political discourse – that someone can repair social discord. This is why this particular solution mirrors the problem in Laclau, repeating the same conceptual dynamic that makes it impossible to distinguish between democracy and repression.

We can notice here as well that Žižek treats the two fantasmatic roles of the subject as stand-ins for the signifier S1 as if each is distinct from the other and on its own could solve the vexing problem of social discord. So, on the one hand, he argues that the de-personalized subject "stands for the collapse of the symbolic" and in this way serves as an *obstacle* to the smooth functioning of the status quo. In this version, political valence derives from a covert equivalence between "Symbolic" and social structure. In fact, of course, if the Symbolic were to collapse, we would have no social universe at all. But by implying that "Symbolic" refers to the set of conventions, institutions, and beliefs that keep things as they are, Žižek can retail the fantasy of a subject-as-obstacle who, by disrupting the status quo, can bring about a new social structure. It is the reversal of the usual political value of "obstacle to the Symbolic" in this fantasy, I think, that makes this sleight-of-hand seem plausible: in this case, when the "obstacle" disrupts the social structure, it is a good thing (brings about revolution), but in other cases, such as Aristotle's representation of the *azux* as obstacle, the disruption is dangerous and undesirable.

On the other hand, in the transferential relation to the leader, we see the fantasy that someone can serve as the *remediator* of social discord. Žižek keeps the fantasmatic status of this version under wraps by arguing that there is an actual (if psychic) transformation ("transubstantiation") of the *subjects* who idealize the leader. He purports to be talking about subjective transformation, in the vein of Bartleby's de-personalization. But whereas in the case of de-personalization the subject reveals its *own* Möbius status and so *exposes* the fantasies of the subject as obstacle to or remediation of social discord, in this example, the subject *immerses* itself in the transferential fantasy that an *other* (the leader) solves the problem. So, even if Žižek were to reply that the leader is not serving the totalizing function of S1 in Phallic mode, he is either arguing that the leader appears to be different from everyone else in having no excess, or that the encounter with the leader as excessive (both obstacle and savior) somehow transforms other people. We'll come back to this latter point in a moment.

Even though Žižek wields the Möbius subject in the most sophisticated way of any of the theorists we've considered, when it comes to arguing for the political charge in the theory, in these passages, he still manages to reproduce the same theoretical difficulties as Bourdieu, de Certeau, Butler, and Laclau. Under the name of the Symbolic, which is in fact a psychic register that is inflected differently by each subject, he often substitutes a social structure that is invariant and so dominantly determinative that only its utter collapse can change it, a version of the error that Bourdieu and de Certeau make. Even as he is arguing for the extimate cause of the subject, he makes Butler's mistake of substituting exclusion for foreclosure when he tries to obtain a political charge for his argument by proposing that the subject can stand in a relation of complete exteriority to the Symbolic, at the level of the Real, leaving aside the fact that ontic properties continue to subsist as part of the **subject***. And, as we have just seen, he reproduces Laclau's disavowal of the partisan relationship to the universal and the function of fantasy in the political field.

And once again we seem to encounter the unnecessary and impossible requirements of an intentionalist dream of political agency. For, under ordinary conditions (that is, prior to any sinthomic effort on the part of a subject), every Möbius subject has precisely the properties that permit other Möbius subjects to regard it as nothing more than an obstacle to the proper functioning of the Symbolic order. Because the property of set-ness (Symbolic inscription) is formally the same as the empty set (object of the Real), the conditions for the parallax shift by which any Möbius subject can appear to be the obstacle to the Symbolic never go away. As we have seen, any citizen of the polis can be regarded as having the double nature of the *azux* (extra-human and *phaulos*/abjected); at any moment, the wolf-pack can turn on one of its members. No subject fully belongs to the social field: although every subject is part of that field, each subject is excessive to it. From some angle, any subject can appear as the obstacle to the smooth running of the social machine or as the savior who resolves social antagonism. So, what gives the "leader" special powers to transform others? Why nominate the sinthomic process as potentially liberatory when a subject can look like an obstacle to another subject without it? Why emphasize the subject's *choice* to de-personalize when whether or not the subject seems to be an obstacle depends entirely on the *other's* fantasies, not the subject's efforts to appear so?

Here we encounter a real sticking point. For even if the subject somehow avoids the perverse position; even if it succeeds in emphasizing its own constitutive gap between its thing-ness and its set-ness (the minimal self-difference that makes it an excessive, Möbius subject); and even if we grant that the subject so aestheticized becomes an obstacle to the Symbolic within its own psychic economy, how does the subject-turned-object become an obstacle to the Symbolic for others? How does an internal transformation affect the social field? How does the "pure violence" of the *Versagung* enable political action or organization? It is difficult to see how Žižek will get the political traction he desires by the route of de-personalization. In the next chapter, we will find a different reason to appreciate the Žižekian account of sinthomic activity.

7

Sinthomic Ethics and Revolutionary Groups

Bartleby and the Non-Orientable Social Field

The Möbius quality of the social field produces a parallax view. The subject's role oscillates between being the *cause* of social discord and its *solution*. This oscillation is another way to describe the "non-orientability" of the social field. That is, there is no point from within the social field that makes it possible to distinguish *on the basis of the subject's ontic qualities* whether it completes the social field or thwarts its completion – because every subject's ability to appear in the social field depends upon being excessive to it. The fact that every subject can appear as *either* the missing piece that will unite the social field *or* as the obstacle to its coherence means that the social field itself "opens and closes" at every point, as fantasies about the other's desirability or danger mobilize defenses to ward off the effects of excess. Even though the parallax oscillation of the subject derives from the fantasy that certain ontic traits embody the qualities of harmonizer or disrupter of the social field, the subject's *actual* Möbius condition has nothing to do with such traits, arising as it does solely from the generation of excess by the extimate cause. The social field's status as both *finite* and *unbounded* (the two conditions of non-orientability) is a function of its *internal* incompleteness due to the extimate cause, not to any particular ontic qualities of the subjects within it.

Bartleby himself instantiates this source of non-orientability when he answers each of the lawyer's proposals for a livelihood with his standard refusal, followed by the statement "but I am not particular." His response seems paradoxical: how can he refuse every option if, as he seems to be saying, he doesn't care which option is presented? But he *is* "not particular" because his grounds for refusing a *specific* option have nothing to do with its substantive, ontic properties. "I am not particular" negates the significance of those properties, their ability to *count* as themselves, as particular elements deriving their identities from the Symbolic. Because Bartleby himself has identified with the meta-level of the formal constitution of the subject-as-excess, the level of substantive particular differences really is of no concern to him, insofar as it deals in ontic properties. The lawyer has no way to separate out the Bartleby who is "particular," in the sense of being just one more substantive difference among others in the social field, from the Bartleby who is "not particular," in the sense of being excessive to that field in his identification with the formal constitution of the field itself as a space of universality. Not until Bartleby pursues this strategy unto death does the lawyer understand the universal form that Bartleby instances: only after he hears the rumor that Bartleby worked in the dead letter office, where every *personal* marker of the letters is removed before burning, can the lawyer say "Ah Bartleby! Ah humanity!"

Now, if *any* subject may appear to any other as "the collapse of the symbolic order," as Žižek says, on account of this non-orientability, what difference could a given subject's decision to identify with its drive determinants make? How does this decision change the Möbius nature of the subject to make it especially *likely* to threaten the Symbolic for others? It is no secret that subjects who are perceived by others as obstacles to the Symbolic order frequently become targets of violence. Even if we replace "Symbolic" with "social field," which would be a more coherent way of talking about potential system-wide effects of individual actions, we would have to say that no subject could *in fact* threaten the social field with collapse by means of symbolic divestiture, because the social field is generated by the circulation of subjective responses to excess. And if Žižek is arguing that individual symbolic divestiture constitutes an attack on the hegemonic structuration of social relations, it is evident that Bartleby himself, Žižek's prime example of symbolic divestiture, does not make that structure collapse: he merely gives the lie to the pretense that it functions by consent rather than force. In the end, the law is not overthrown – it is simply compelled to reveal that its power derives from coercion.

In other words, as I have argued, when the parallax shift takes place and a subject turns object under the gaze of its fellows, the social field *re-generates* itself precisely through these operations. So, while Žižek wants to make use of the subject's Möbius qualities that lead to the parallax shift, he ends up arguing (in a manner reminiscent of Butler) for an exceptional subject with special powers – powers that from our perspective already inhere in each subject. All subjects have the qualities necessary for the parallax shift, and no subject has the power to transform the social field *tout court*.

Given that all subjects are already Möbius subjects, what additional value for social change might the sinthomic activity of a neosubject hold? For example, it might seem that, in refusing the status quo (based as it is on covert and overt violence), the neosubject could become a model for others and just possibly a piece of grit in the social machinery. Of course, by definition, if enough individuals refuse their own social definitions and symbolic identities, the social field will change. However, if Bartleby is to be our model of the neosubject, then he is baffling as the *mechanism* for galvanizing such change in others. For one thing, in the story, he starves himself to death, an act that seems unlikely to hold much promise for either imitation or sabotage. Of course, his act of self-destitution could have social effects through its re-signification, but Žižek specifically refuses to make his case on those grounds – only the "pure" act of violent reduction by the subject itself counts. And even if it were re-signified, as we know, it is not in the subject's power to govern that meaning, so any symbolic divestiture is as likely as not to be interpreted differently from the way the subject wished.[1] Finally, although Bartleby's self-sacrifice in the name of *nothing* certainly avoids the Žižekian bugbears of anti-revolutionary politics (such as intentional strategic action, superego complicity, and what Žižek calls the politics of protestation and resistance), the use of Bartleby as exemplum of the promise of social change raises the question as to how Bartleby's apparently masochistic acts truly escape the perverse position, and if they don't, how perversion enables a revolutionary politics.[2]

When Žižek claims that the "difficulty of imagining the New is the difficulty of imagining Bartleby in power" (PV 383), I plead guilty, because I cannot see how Bartleby, or any subject who purposefully divests itself of symbolic properties, *could* come to power. For one thing, Bartleby kills himself. For another, Žižek describes a confusing temporality. If Bartleby's only "act" is *Versagung*, so that his object-hood stands athwart the Symbolic order, then one of two situations must obtain. *Either* this act in itself brings about the revolutionary new, in which case it is not clear how Bartleby would be "in power" at the end of that revolution. *Or else*, somehow, Bartleby eventually comes to power as a result of his symbolic divestiture, which then causes the revolution to take place.

In any case, in order to contribute to our understanding of the genesis of social change, two important elements must be theorized, elements currently missing from Žižek's discussion. These elements are really two sides of the same coin. First, we need to know how others can be affected and *enabled politically* by an *individual*'s sinthomic activity. Second, we need to know how power can be potentiated, dismantled, or transmitted by an individual's self-aestheticization, that is, by an act of symbolic divestiture. Addressing these issues, as it turns out, also will enable us to articulate the value of extimate causality and Möbius subjectivity for ethics – and ultimately, group transformation.

The Ethics of Infinite Responsibility and the Stockholm Syndrome

As we have seen, Žižek's impatient dismissal of any gradual process of political activity depends for its own claims to political efficacy on the mere chance that some violence will bring about politicization retroversively. He admits that such politicization cannot be guaranteed but must always be a matter of chance. Violence is necessary, not sufficient, for revolution. Had he remained committed to this proposition, we would have no choice, I think, but to believe that he is advocating continued and constant acts of violence as the only possible engine of social change. But once he turns his attention to the potential represented by subjective transformation, making the subject's relation to *itself* the locus and origin of change, Žižek inevitably moves away from political prescription, fantasmatic agency, and the chanciness of violent rupture to an investigation of the role that a transformed *ethical* stance can have on the social field.

In arguing that the subject's relationship to itself changes as a consequence of symbolic divestiture, Žižek promotes a conception of ethics that psychoanalytic theorists will recognize as Lacanian insofar as it depends upon an intrasubjective relationship. Lacan's statement that the only ethics proper to psychoanalysis involves the subject's relationship to its desire ("do not give way on your desire") explicitly contrasts both with the ethics of responsibility to the other extolled in Levinas and Derrida and with the "service of goods" that underwrites utilitarian versions of ethics.[3] While remaining committed to an intrasubjective version of ethics, Žižek derives a somewhat different ethical stance from the later Lacanian theory of the *sinthome*. Decidedly, this is not the ethics of the "service of goods," the traumatic encounter with the impossible demand of the Other, some officious busy-ness in the lives of our neighbors, or adherence to the Golden Rule. Instead, the ethical stance requires taking responsibility for one's own excessive dimension and *jouissance*.[4]

To better understand what is at stake in Žižek's argument for an intrasubjective ethics, I want to take a closer look at a writer who tries to develop an ethical theory that, as it turns out, gives a significant role to a subject with recognizable Möbius characteristics. Simon Critchley's recent work, *Infinitely Demanding: Ethics of Commitment, Politics of*

Resistance, seeks to bring together four philosophical reflections on ethics from Badiou, Løgstrup, Lacan, and Levinas in a new understanding of subjectivity, what he calls the "dividual subject," precisely at the intersection of ethics and politics. Contrasting his version of the subject with the Möbius subject will clarify the logic of the potential for social change that comes with the ethical stance of de-personalization.

Critchley sums up the relationship between ethics and politics near the end of his book:

> the final claim I would like to make is that democratization is action based on an ethical demand. That is to say, political action does not flow from the cunning of reason, from some materialist or idealist philosophy of history, or indeed from some more or less secularized eschatology. Rather, it feeds from what I will now describe as a *meta-political* moment. In my view, at the heart of a radical politics there has to be a meta-political ethical moment . . . the ethical experience of infinite responsibility at the heart of subjectivity, a moment of what I called *hetero-affectivity* prior to any auto-affection and disturbing any simple claim to autonomy. I also described this ethical experience in terms of conscience understood as a splitting at the heart of the self, a constitutive undoing and dispossessing of the self. (ID 119–20, original emphasis)

Wherever he looks, Critchley finds massive political disappointment and disengagement – even al-Qaeda diagnoses liberal democracy as disabling of true citizenry. What Critchley wishes to produce is "a motivating, empowering conception of ethics . . . that is able to respond to and resist the political situation in which we find ourselves" (ID 8). In other words, while his ultimate goal is the re-motivation of the political realm, he finds that he must forge a path through ethics to get there. For Critchley, thinking through the political subject of social change and democratic interaction requires re-conceptualizing the ethical dimension of the subject.

As Critchley, paraphrasing Levinas, puts it: "[t]he subject shapes itself in relation to a demand that it can never meet, which divides and sunders the subject" (ID 40). Still following Levinas, he argues that the autonomous subject – or "self-positing autarchy" – of traditional philosophy is profoundly unethical (ID 121). The autonomous subject grasps all others and the world for itself, using the faculties of perception, reason, and knowledge. Through this grasping, the autonomous self, inevitably solitary and solipsistic, effectively negates the separate existence of the other. Like a Leibnizian monad, the subject cannot recognize anything exterior or other to itself, for it encounters everything in a mode of ego-centric perception, rationality, and knowing. The subject regards itself as the center of its universe: in Levinas, every subject is conceived phenomenologically, as the sole point of reference. In a knowing encounter, the subject will subsume the object, leaving the subject in its solitary, hence unethical, condition. But neither would it be ethical for the subject to lose itself in an other: such "ecstatic" fusion destroys the duality necessary for ethics. For Levinas, the properly ethical act sustains tension between heteronomy and autonomy.[5] In his model, this tension depends upon the maintaining of an absolute distinction between self and other. Naming this relation "hetero-affectivity" to contrast it with the philosophical tradition of the autonomous self, Critchley expands on this affective, processual, and divided notion of the ethical self as the remedy for the "motivational deficit" of secular liberal democracy in the contemporary age.

When Critchley sets out to build an ethical subject that will support a bridge to his political theory, he takes as axiomatic the centrality of a compromised autonomy, starting from a suggestive sentence in Kant's *Grundlegung*: "While we do not comprehend the practical unconditioned necessity of the moral imperative, we do comprehend its *incomprehensibility*" (ID 37). Critchley explains his interest in "this moment of incomprehensibility in ethics," this challenge to the subject's autonomy: "in this situation, I am not the equal of the demand that is placed on me . . . ethics is obliged to acknowledge a moment of rebellious heteronomy that troubles the sovereignty of autonomy" (ID 37). This internalized heteronomy splits the subject so that it becomes an extimate subject, an inside which is also an outside. In a paraphrase, Critchley explicitly draws on Lacan's portrait of the key feature of subjectivity, the "something alien to me but which is located at the core of my subjectivity" (ID 65). Here Critchley illuminates what remains tacit in Rancière's exposition, that is, the need to conceive of the ethico-political subject first and foremost as non-self-coincident.

This non-self-coincidence, in his view, gives the dividual subject a particularly ethical character.[6] In its ethical dimension, "[t]he subject shapes itself in relation to a demand that it can never meet, which divides and sunders the subject" (ID 40). Yet in this definition, the source of the properties of the dividual subject are confusing. Does the autonomous (unethical) subject feel its inability to meet the infinite demand of the other, and in so doing, become divided (ethical)? If that is the case, then why rely on the dividual (ethical) subject to exercise autonomy (unethical) to "shape itself" or commit itself in fidelity, as Critchley proposes? Does the experience of the demand sunder the subject, or does the subject's self-shaping lead to its sundering? Is the subject's ability to commit itself – its autonomous functioning – the means by which it becomes dividual? Or is the origin of the subject's commitment its susceptibility to feeling the other's presence as a demand?

The steps of Critchley's argument seem to be as follows. Autonomous people are self-centered. Because ethics requires us to take another into account, self-centered people are inherently unethical. Something has to happen to make a person responsive to others. People become responsive to others – and hence ethical – when they experience the other as demanding something they cannot give. This experience is traumatic for the subject; the trauma forces the subject to give up (part) of its self-centeredness. As a consequence, the person splits itself between its own interests and those of the other. This internalized heteronomy confers ethicality on the subject.

Not only does Critchley nominate trauma as the agent of change that splits the autonomous subject to make it *ethical*, he also sees this process as the route to *political* action:

> This self-undoing is close to what Judith Butler has recently written about affect undoing us, in particular the affect of grief. In *Precarious Life*, Butler writes with great candour, "Let's face it. We're undone by each other. And if we're not, we're missing something." Such an experience of grief is not depoliticizing, but on the contrary shows our essential interconnectedness and vulnerability to the other's demand. . . . In grief and mourning we undergo an experience of affective self-dispossession or self-undoing that can provide the motivational force to enter into a political sequence. (ID 120)[7]

Let us notice that, in his haste to obtain a *political* valence from Butler, Critchley, apparently unknowingly, equates a motivation to enter politics with a motivation to become ethical. But in his argument for ethical transformation, the subject *begins as incapable* of being able to be affected by the other; that is, the subject only becomes "hetero-affective" when it experiences trauma. Only then does the subject acquire the motivation to become an ethical subject. But in the political transformation described in the passage just quoted, the subject is *already* capable of feeling for the other (already ethical, by his lights), and then *wills* its own entry into a political sequence. So, in the turn to Butler, Critchley unwittingly demonstrates the logical misstep of his argument: subjects must already *be* ethical (sundered, heteronomous) in order to *become* ethical (and political).

In this account, the change-agent is the trauma of the experience of the other's infinite demand: this trauma is required to *produce* the ethical subject. Now the obvious question is, if the initial state of the subject is unethical because it is self-absorbed, grasping, and autonomous, what motivates this self-centered subject to experience the demand of the other as *traumatic*? In fact, what motivates the unethical subject to recognize or respond to the other at all? What will pierce the self-satisfied autonomy of this possessive selfhood so that it will feel the other's presence as infinitely demanding? And what will guarantee that the experience of an infinite demand will call forth a sense of insufficiency, a traumatic sense of insufficiency, on the part of the subject? Or, put another way, why doesn't the subject who encounters the other simply walk away, or try to annihilate the other, or help the other in some limited way and go home to an untroubled sleep?

That is, the Levinasian story as Critchley tells it seems to require that the subject *already* be ethical in order to respond in the way that would *lead* it to ethicality. In this account, the dividual subject is nothing other than an ethical subject from the start, a person who for some *unexplained* reason, responds to the presence of others as requiring more of the subject than the subject can give. Nothing in the story accounts for the transformation of the unethical subject, because the change-agent (trauma) can only be generated if the subject is already responsive to the other. And once we start with an ethical subject, the whole circuitous route to ethicality through trauma is superfluous.

A path through this thicket opens, however, thanks to a small aporia in Critchley's exposition of Levinas's unethical autonomous subject. Levinas regards any subject who takes itself to be the center of the universe (and whose every act of perception, reason, and knowing simply grasps the other as if it were the subject itself) as committed to a subsumption of the other: in its failure to maintain a distinction between itself and the other, such a subject is fundamentally unethical. Levinas's solution to this unethical situation takes two different forms, although Levinas himself does not distinguish them. (This duality is reproduced in Critchley's ambiguous term "hetero-affectivity": does this mean that the subject experiences an affect for the other, or does it mean that the affects the subject experiences are those of an other?) First, the subject can incorporate some dimension of otherness into its own relationship to itself through an act of thought. The ethical subject is produced by the encounter with the "face" of the other, defined as "the way in which the other presents himself, exceeding *the idea of the other in me*."[8] Like the attempt to think the idea of the infinity of God, the subject's attempt to think the idea of the other forces it to think more than it thinks. As the subject encounters the limits of its thought, it is enabled to preserve the alterity and exteriority of the other *inside* itself. Critchley paraphrases Lacan here: "the inside of my inside is somehow outside, the core of my subjectivity is exposed to otherness" (ID 61). The subject, as it might seem to us, has become a **subject***. For convenience sake, I'll refer to this as the *extimate* solution.

In the second solution, in response to the traumatic encounter with the other, the subject tries to transform itself *into* the other or transforms

the other into itself. Levinas proposes that this relation without relation is formed when the subject *tries* to form a relation with something
that exceeds its capacity to relate. In effect, the subject is relating to an
incomprehensible unknown: the subject finds itself in the modality of the
sublime, in which its sense, reason, and ego are overwhelmed. In this definition the social relationship depends upon the idea of infinity and, for
this reason, is considered to be a "relation without relation," because one
cannot have a relation to the infinite. The result is that the subject loses
itself in the other. I'll refer to this as the *subsumptive* solution.

Critchley relies on this second subsumptive possibility for his paradigm of ethicality:

> Levinas makes the extreme claim that my relation to the other is not
> some benign benevolence, compassionate care or respect for the other's
> autonomy, but is the obsessive experience of a responsibility that perse-
> cutes me with its sheer weight. I am the other's hostage, taken by them and
> prepared to substitute myself for any suffering and humiliation that they
> may undergo. I am responsible for the persecution I undergo and even for
> my persecutor. . . (ID 60–1)

We may justifiably ask, what causes the transformation of the other from
radical other (one who persecutes and seeks to annihilate the subject)
into a likeness of the subject? Whatever its mechanism may be, its result,
strikingly, is the series of psychological defenses we know as "Stockholm
syndrome."[9] In other words, the paradigmatic ethical model for Levinas,
at least as Critchley appropriates it, is the identification of the victim with
its persecutor.[10] This solution seems to contradict Levinas's dictum that
ethics demands the maintenance of a radical distinction between self and
other, or a tension between heteronomy and autonomy. If the victim identifies with the persecutor, and even takes upon himself the responsibility
for his own persecution, in effect, the victim is seeking (autonomously)
to destroy itself in order to take the place of the persecutor. How does
this model, which subsumes one pole into the other sustain the requisite
ethical distinction and tension?

Levinas's unethical subject may be a narcissist, but his ethical subject,
at least in terms of the second solution, is a pervert of the masochistic
variety. That is, according to the psychoanalytic definition of the pervert,
the Levinasian "ethical" subject gives up its own subjecthood to become
the object that will rectify (in fantasy) the other's lack. We might even go
so far as to regard this side of Levinas as sadistic: for him, self-interest
is unethical, and the punishment for self-interest is the traumatization of
a subject willing its own traumatic experience of and subjection to the
other.

I submit that there is nothing in this model, other than fantasy, that would lead to the result Levinas proposes. Not only is there no need to traumatize the subject in order to make it feel for and with the other (because only a subject who *already* has the capacity for such feeling will be capable of being so traumatized), but also the subject who responds to traumatic subjection by turning passive into active and identifying with its persecutor is going to be either aggressive or perverse.[11] We are left to imagine what might drive Levinas to nominate this version of a tortured and torturing subject as ethical.

Clearly, the extimate and the subsumptive formulations are at odds with one another. But it is strange to see the subsumptive dominate, especially because it destroys the tension between heteronomy and autonomy (so crucial to ethics in Levinas's view) that the first sustains – urging as it does the subjection of the subject entirely to the impossible demands of the other. Nonetheless, it is this more dramatic and radical solution for which Levinas is famous – and the one Critchley avowedly prefers. Critchley neglects to point out that the subsumption of the subject contravenes his and Levinas's desideratum of heteronomous autonomy.

A larger problem arises here: Critchley never explains what would *motivate* the subject to attempt to relate to a radical other with whom there *can be no relation*. It just seems to him to be obvious that any subject would react to such an encounter with a sense of responsibility, so he never inquires into the *means* by which that responsiveness is achieved. Still, *something* has to make the subject desire a relation with the other, rather than, for example, a rejection or obliteration. Critchley has no way of accounting for this relationality: he simply stipulates it. As a result, his model doesn't explicate the production of the ethical subject, a lack which forces him to build in the ethics that he claims to produce. So, while he provides an excellent *description* of the extimate nature of the ethical subject, Critchley can't explain the motivation to the ethical itself, which after all is his expressed purpose in developing this model.

Möbius Ethical Motivation

It is unfortunate that Critchley casts his lot with Levinas, who not only has no metapsychology but who also is "extremely hostile to psychoanalysis and largely ignorant of it," as Critchley acknowledges (ID 61). Critchley could have found all of the qualities of the ethical subject that he stipulates for his own project, and none of the attendant problems, if he had recognized that he was searching for the Möbius subject rather than the unnecessarily traumatized, perverse subject. I repeat: his story does not provide any motivation for the transformation of a self-centered, autonomous subject into a hetero-affective one. And in the case of the political transformation, the story is evidently either banally tautological (the claim is that empathetic people enter politics where they demonstrate empathy) or spectacularly counter to empirical evidence (the claim is that people engage in political activity solely for "hetero-affective" reasons, as though no self-centered person ever chose politics as a career).

So, let's return to the first, *extimate* solution. Critchley imputes this solution to Levinas, but he acknowledges that it derives from the Lacanian conception of an outside that is at the core of the subject. In our model, rather than producing an excessive subject from a self-coincident one, the process of subjectification produces the **subject***, as non-self-coincident or excessive. One might be forgiven for missing the difference between the Lacanian and Levinasian versions, because in both cases the subject is "produced" by an encounter with an Other.[12] But the two conceptions of the subject are quite different. For Levinas, the sundered subject is the product of a highly unusual process that begins with a narcissistic subject. This process doesn't happen to everyone: many people remain subjects only in the mode of unethical autonomy. For Lacan, by contrast, *every* individual becomes a subject in an encounter with the Other (an Other that is far from *radically other*). This encounter functions as the extimate cause of the **subject***: every subject is non-self-coincident; every subject incorporates the other at its core; every subject's inside is an outside. Every subject is, from the get-go, a Möbius subject. What is more, in Lacan's view, the simple fact of the subject's extimacy is not sufficient to render the subject ethical. It seems, then, that the arduous process Levinas describes as producing an extimate subject is unnecessary. If every subject is a Möbius subject, then every subject fulfills the requirements of ethicality, at least in the terms stipulated by Critchley's Levinas.

Now let's take a look at the problem from the perspective of the Möbius subject to see if we can find some motivation for the ethical stance. We can recall first that the Möbius subject's excess or non-self-coincidence derives from its inability to know its own meaning for others. If the subject experiences another subject *as if* the other holds the secret key to its meaning, this would qualify, I believe, as an encounter with the "face" of the other (in Levinasian, not Agambenian, terms), as an entity (fantasized to be) other than the self insofar as it enjoys what the subject does not, i.e. perfect self-consistency and access to its own meaning. The subject will not take *every* other to have these properties, but when it encounters what Lacan calls the "subject-supposed-to-know," the subject will become aware of its own excess. Of course, the subject itself invests the other with these fantasmatic qualities: the fantasy ties the subject to the other, who seems to hold the key to the subject's meaning (but who, as Möbius subject itself, can never actually provide what the subject believes it needs). The subject's experience of its own excess provides the motive for entering into the social relation, criss-crossed by fantasy though it is. This relation with a fantasmatic other – this relation of nonrelation – in fact produces the social subject as such.

Unlike the subject implied in the Levinasian account, the Möbius subject need not have any prior ethical orientation or properties to experience the other as unsettling. Nor does this model of the subject require any extraordinary motivation simply to establish a relationship between subject and other, for the subject is produced as an instantiation of that relationship. By contrast to the Levinasian model, in which only some subjects (those traumatized by an encounter with an other) become heteronomously autonomous, in the psychoanalytic version, all subjects are Möbius subjects, fissured in the way that the Levinasian believes to be the hallmark of ethicality. Every Möbius subject begins its social life as an extimate subject – its fundament is already a function of otherness.

What is more, the Möbius subject has two driving motivations, that is, motivations at the level of the drive. The first is to maintain the extimacy that is the ground of its existence: as we know, the drive circulates around *objet a*, the missing object, established by way of the encounter with the formal negation, the *Non/Nom-du-Père*. The second is to defend itself against the anxiety generated by its excessive status. This anxiety, understood in Lacanian terms, is simply affect itself, a function of the Möbius condition of subjectivity. These motivations may be at odds, but they derive necessarily from *the subject's* founding. Taken together, they provide the means by which the social space itself is propagated and sustained. Because, at the level of the drive, the subject comes into existence only if it seems as though *objet a* is possible, *prohibited* rather than *impossible*, the subject has a stake in the very condition that produces anxiety – its status as a signifier depends upon the impossibility of *objet a* and its status as a signifier makes its ultimate stability, its final meaning or self-consistency, unreachable. In this dynamic, seen from the level of Symbolic relations, it can seem that the other's failure to stabilize the subject's meaning is willfully aggressive (or negligent) rather than a function of impossibility. As a result, the Möbius subject relates to the other both as the solution and the obstacle to its own inconsistency – a relation of *non*relation. That is, thanks to the excess that sticks to each subject, and thanks to the fantasy that the other is consistent in a way that the subject is not, the social relation necessarily emerges as a relation of nonrelation.

This relation is not Levinas's "relation without relation," in which the subject fails to establish a relationship to something with which it can have no relationship because it is *radically other* – an infinitely demanding and completely inaccessible other. Rather, in the case of a subject who fantasizes a fully determinate meaning blocked by an obstructive other, the subject is driven to perpetually seek out a response from the other. In this model, the subject projects a greater or lesser degree of alterity onto the others in the social field than they actually have, while in the Levinasian version the subject seeks to overcome the radical alterity that, in this view, properly belongs to the other. In the extimate version, the subject must perpetually seek a response from the others because, in fact, the subject will never be sure of the meaning of the response it gets, yet the subject has nowhere else to go to get it. The other is not radically other – it is close enough to the subject in kind to warrant the desire for relationship while distant enough in its ability to fulfill the subject's deepest desire to maintain its otherness. At the same time, the "other" to whom the subject relates does not truly exist in the way the subject believes: this other is a fantasmatic projection of a wish. So the subject has a relation of nonrelation to the actual others in the social space. It is in this relation of nonrelation that we find the sustaining of the duality of subject and other that Levinas requires for ethics but fails to provide.

The hatred and envy that can arise from the subject's frustration at the other's inability to repair the subject's self-inconsistency could easily galvanize the destruction of the very space of the social, as we have seen in the case of the pack in Rancière's discussion of the *azux*, the Aristotelian limit-figure explored in chapter 2. The destruction of that space, however, would spell the demise of the subject *qua* subject. Subjects mobilize a number of (necessarily inadequate) defenses – including perversion and hysteria – to avoid that result. These efforts to avoid the collapse of the social field and to manage non-self-coincidence set up a relay for the circulation of the excess, along with the affects that energize our defenses, something like a game of hot potato in which the potato always returns to scorch the subject's fingers. We don't want to feel that "we're all in this together," if that means everyone is subject to excess. We want to feel that someone can solve this problem or be targeted as its source. But because these wishes do not actually resolve the excess, the best we can do is to try to send it on its rounds, even though it inevitably "returns" to us – since, of course, in reality it never left. We are stuck with and to excess. From this point of view, it appears that the motivation for the social relation is not the preservation of the other's distinct existence, as Levinas and Critchley would have it, but rather the need to preserve the *social field* itself – the field without which the subject (all subjects) as such cannot exist – from a threat of dissolution. That is, the subject fantasizes that the continual dissolution and reassemblage of the social field made possible and necessary by excess is a threat to the field rather than the very condition of its perpetuation.

Although every subject in the field is a Möbius subject, all subjects are marked by their own history and mobilize different defenses against the experience of excess. The individuals within the social space are diverse, even though they share the common characteristic of excess. Put another way, the fact that they are subjects of excess makes it possible for them to be individuated differently and still seek out and maintain connections to one another, even as some of those connections are heavily imbued with aggression and hatred.

But here is the key point. The desire to stabilize meaning (which, I would argue, is desire plain and simple) implies that the space in which meaning emerges is under threat: when we note a need to protect the social space, we are actually acknowledging that it is (always) in the process of being both dissolved and re-generated. The fundamental fact of social relations – the relation of nonrelation due to the excess sticking to each subject – is the engine of the fantasies that assign excess elsewhere, the circulation that produces the social space. What is more, an affective storm swirls through it, a hurricane of hatred, envy, fear, panic, hostility, sadness, loneliness as well as delight, love, joy. In order to take all of these properties of the social space into account, we will need an ethics that is different from the normative morality of "recognizing otherness" or "taking responsibility for others," as we will see in a moment.

One advantage of regarding ethical motivation from the standpoint of the relations of nonrelation structuring the social field is that we need not start out with a subject who embodies specific qualities or who has extraordinary experiences or capacities. More importantly, we are in a position to universalize the ethical, because we begin with a model of the subject that applies to everyone, not just special cases. But another advantage is that, by placing the relation of nonrelation front and center, the *formal* properties of the subject clearly emerge as the route to its universalization and the link to its political potential. In order for social change to come about, something new has to enter the situation, something that is not simply a function of that situation's determinates.

This discussion of the advent of the new as a function of the formal properties of the subject, under the rubric of sinthomic activity or subjective divestiture, has an echo in Critchley's argument: in his account of the dividual solution, he describes the subject's attempts to think the other as the means by which the subject encounters the limits of its own thought. Although he doesn't theorize this formal function as the founding gesture of the subject itself, he does explore its effects on the subject who (in some unspecified way) achieves sufficient self-distance and neutralization of the superego (for here Critchley returns explicitly to psychoanalysis) to be able to mock himself.[13] His privileged example, taken from Freud, is that of a man remarking on his way to the gallows, "Well, the week's beginning nicely," a gallows tale which can also serve us as a reminder of Bartleby's extreme subjective destitution (ID 79). Even though Critchley does not see why this emphasis on de-personalization is at odds with the Levinasian ethics of responsiveness to the Other that he continues to promote, we can see that the ethics of extimacy which respects the relation of nonrelation does not build upon hierarchies of consideration or require recognition for the other over the self.

In fact, Critchley also approaches this self-destitution as an ethical act, and in a way that offers an alternative to individual psychoanalysis as the route to de-personalization. Humor, especially self-mocking humor, provides an excellent example of the subject's self-distanced relationship in a positive affective key, an antidote to the "tragic-heroic paradigm" of ethical action: "The picture of human finitude that I would like to propose is better approached as *comic acknowledgement* than tragic affirmation" (ID 78). In conceiving of humor as stemming from the ego's ability to neutralize the sadistic superego and to observe itself, Critchley adopts a position consonant with the ethical stance arising from the *sinthome*. We might say that self-deprecating humor serves the ethical function of de-personalization by *setting off* ontic qualities, exposing them as contingencies rather than as bedrock properties. It would be reasonable, I think, to propose that the exercise of self-deprecating humor and other strategies of de-personalization have a greater chance of emerging in an environment which decreases the need for defensiveness just as they themselves contribute to such an environment.

What factors conduce to self-observation, self-deprecation, and self-aestheticization? What enables the subject to embrace the ethics of extimacy? And what are the political stakes of this ethics?

The Ethics of Extimacy

The entire trajectory of Žižek's work has been guided by an effort to unearth the political potential of Lacanian thought. From his breakthrough book *The Sublime Object of Ideology*, he has forged innovative links between the materialist and the psychoanalytic traditions, as, for example, when he implicitly draws a connection between the Adornian constellation and the Lacanian *sinthome* in order to argue for the political value of self-aestheticization. As a result of his grasp of the possibilities that psychoanalysis provides for political analysis, he has forever changed the way we think about democracy and capitalism. So, one conclusion that we might draw from this gifted theorist's repeated if frequently unsatisfactory attempts to explain the political Act is that, despite our best efforts, we never leave the terrain of the Imaginary where politics are concerned. The dream of bringing about social change through willed activity – whether violent rebellion, utopian advent, or self-aestheticization – always runs up against the temporality of fulfillment and the problem of intentionalism.

Does this mean that social change is impossible? Obviously not, since social change takes place whether or not we know its causes. What it does mean, however, is that the *politics* of social change is irremediably fantasmatic.

Then what is left for those committed to social change? The conclusion to *The Parallax View* makes social change a matter of a subject's internal relationship to its own minimal self-difference, which is why it forces the question of how an *intrasubjective* change can have broader social effects. In my exploration of this account, I have made an equation between self-difference and the excess sticking to the Möbius subject. But there is a bit more to be said. The minimal self-difference is the difference between the subject prior to subjectification (a notional entity) and the formal function of marking out that subject for inscription in the Symbolic – cutting it away from all other indeterminate "things" and hollowing out the place which will cradle it. The "outline" drawn around this subject in this way *both* encapsulates the subject, so that it can be grasped as a determinate something with its own firm boundaries *and* links it to the social field comprised of other **subjects***. The excess (*) attending the subject, to repeat, is therefore both the medium of its connection to other subjects and the obstacle to that connection. This dual function comprises the "relation of nonrelation" that undergirds the social field, a relation predicated on an obstacle to relationality.

Unfortunately Žižek's emphasis on the obstruction to the Symbolic created by the subject-turned-object neglects the ways in which this excess drives the establishment and maintenance of the social field with all of the connections within it. In his work, the subject is presented as always other to the Symbolic rather than constitutive of it. Even though he acknowledges repeatedly that the Symbolic is sustained by its own obstacle, he doesn't articulate the actual means by which this fact produces the social field, that is, by circulating the hot potato of excess in multiple defensive attempts to ward off being stuck with one's own excess. As a result, Žižek fails to recognize an important social effect of the subject's de-personalization that follows from the focus on extimate causality. In other words, because the Möbius subject encompasses both its symbolic properties (elements of the set) and its formal properties (set-ness, empty set), de-personalization doesn't *rid* the subject of its ontic properties but it sets them off, revealing them as contingent (rather than necessary) bearers of meaning. By making visible the relation of nonrelation through symbolic divestiture the subject situates *itself* as the source of the non-orientability of the social field, without however being able to account for its own effects within that field in any predictive or comprehensive sense. In this way, the subject takes ethical responsibility for its parallax oscillation, exposing the excess that sticks to itself (as if it were being seen from the perspective of others) and establishing distance from it, which is a prerequisite to tolerating it nondefensively.

Following these insights, we could use the analogy of psychoanalysis to show how the ethical potential of de-personalization arises: when the analysand finally traverses the fantasy that her Symbolic identity is sustained by the big Other and embarks on the production of herself as *sinthome* by setting off her ontic properties, she also gives herself the option of ceasing to deploy her characteristic defenses against the excess that sticks to her and makes her who she is. For example, an analysand who has experienced her excess as a lack might imagine that others could supply what she does not have. Such a relation to others is fundamentally hysterical, so, in giving up this defense, the analysand would re-coordinate the situation for herself, locating the excess in herself instead of accusing others of disappointing her and justifying her aggression against them as failed big Others.

To be sure, this ethics does not look much like the ethics of intersubjectivity and recognition of the Other proposed by Levinas and rehearsed in Critchley's subsumptive model of ethics. As far as I can see, the suspension of the defense against excess – or the neutralization of the more destructive defenses – is the only way that the subject's transformation of its relation to its own *jouissance* can affect others. This suspension means that the subject accepts the relation of nonrelation, giving up its fruitless but often destructive efforts to locate the excess outside itself or to eradicate it. By refusing to defend itself (or by refusing to deploy destructive defenses such as narcissism, aggression, projection, and scapegoating), the subject decreases its contribution to the affective storm in a social field that circulates excess like a hot potato. The potentiation of affect decreases, however temporarily, when the subject absorbs some of the affective energy without releasing it back in a destructive form.

Of course, becoming an affective sponge does not guarantee that violent affects will diminish: sometimes violence flares up precisely in reaction to a display of neutrality. Because subjects have individual psychodynamics, we cannot posit one invariant mechanism, one type of effect that the encounter with the neosubject will have. So, people who experience their inability to govern their own social meanings as a wound may respond to the affective neutrality of the neosubject as if it were a display of weakness: such people often become bullies, projecting weakness onto others and then attacking them to reassure themselves of their own strength. Or, to take another case, people who experience their self-difference as if they are missing some crucial part of themselves may respond to the neosubject as a fellow sufferer or as a healer: such people may identify with the neosubject or seek to make the neosubject love them to salve their wounds. Psychoanalytic practitioners know the unpredictable consequences of diminishing defensive activity within a system of individuals: the dynamics of a dysfunctional family or group can change in a way that is intolerable to some of the members. Not every person responds positively to this reduction of tempestuous affects in their vicinity – some people manage their anxiety, for example, by trying to make others anxious. But in general the absorption of affect by one member of the group provides an opening for others to change their own affective posture. Žižek often refers to outbursts of racist violence against others who, as he puts it, are presumed to have stolen *jouissance*; in this example, he highlights one of the most vicious means for locating excess in others. But other, less dramatic defenses also contribute considerably to the generation and circulation of anxiety, anger, and angst. The moderation of these defenses can play a large role in tempering the affective weather in the social field.

In any case, no matter what the specific defense aroused, the encounter with the neosubject will make apparent the dominant identifications and defenses of others. This display of the dominant tendencies in a particular social universe permits reflection on what works and what doesn't, helping to aggregate and focus social energies. These may be actions that put the brakes on violence, stymie bullies, alleviate suffering, secure privacy, promote stability, and so on. That is, the encounter with the neosubject forces into the open the rationalizations for the status quo, and in so doing can foster the conditions under which people will have a choice to make at the level of practices – individual, familial, institutional.

The setting-off of the subject's substantive traits – through, for example, self-deprecating humor – both *exposes* the contingent meaning of those traits and *reflects back* to others the way those traits get used as explanations for social discord. In this way, the subject brings something *new* into the social field – not only a de-emphasis on ontic properties and a revelation of a dimension of universality independent of such properties, but also a new way of being in the social field that nondefensively accepts the relation of nonrelation. What is more, unlike the immanent cause or the exceptional cause, the *effects* of the deployment of the extimate cause, as it generates new behavior and new relations, can be tracked, studied, and analyzed.

This stance corresponds to the analyst's, which has different effects on different analysands and also depends upon the stages of the analysis. In the beginning, the analysand believes that the specific contingent properties of the analyst hold the key to the analysand's meaning. That is, the analysand does not realize that the transference identifications are based on a contingent unary trait, but instead believes that the analyst in fact embodies S1, or the Phallus. The analyst's de-personalization *both* permits the analysand to reveal the specific qualities in the analyst to which she has attributed Phallic power *and* helps the analysand discover the contingency of her identifications. In effect, the analyst's refusal to respond to the analysand as a specific person sets off the analyst's ontic qualities, highlighting the way in which the analysand puts them to use fantasmatically. This double action of the analyst's de-personalization accounts for the way the Lacanian matheme for perversion ($a <> \$$) looks so much like the top half of the matheme in Seminar 17 for the ana-lyst's discourse ($a \rightarrow \$$). In the perverse scenario, *objet a* is imagined to remedy the lack in the other ($\$$). The subject positions itself in the place of *objet a*, in order to create the illusion that excess does not exist: in effect, the subject fantasizes that he and the other form a unity without surplus. Insofar as each transferential fantasy aims to relieve subject–other relations of the excessive dimension through fantasy (the matheme for fantasy being $\$ <> a$), it can swing around into a perverse relation. What keeps the transference from perpetually oscillating between the fantasy that the other can remedy the subject's excess and the perverse belief that the subject can remedy the other's excess is the revelation of the absolute irremediability of the excess itself, through the exposure of the contingency of the apparent meaning-full-ness of all symbolic properties.

To capture the possibility of the terminus of this oscillation, Lacan writes the four social relations in this way:

$$
\begin{array}{ccc}
 & \text{(relation of impossibility)} & \\
\text{agent} & \Rightarrow & \text{other} \\
\hline
\text{truth} & \text{(relation of incapacity)} & \text{production} \\
 & \Leftarrow\!/ &
\end{array}
$$

S1 = master signifier
S2 = knowledge
$\$$ = subject
a = surplus *jouissance*

$$
\begin{array}{cc}
\text{Master's Discourse} & \text{University Discourse} \\
S1 \Rightarrow S2 & S2 \Rightarrow a \\
\$ \;\Leftarrow\!/\; a & S1 \;\Leftarrow\!/\; \$
\end{array}
$$

Hysteric's Discourse

$$\frac{\$ \quad \Rightarrow \quad S1}{a \quad \Leftarrow\!/ \quad S2}$$

Analyst's Discourse

$$\frac{a \quad \Rightarrow \quad \$}{S2 \quad \Leftarrow\!/ \quad S1}$$

In each of the four discourses, the elements are kept apart, either by the bar which occults an element or by relations of impossibility and incapability which prevent their collapsing into one another. This separation of "self-difference" ($) from "excess" (*a*) is a way of diagrammatically pointing out the fundamental engine producing the social realm through the relation of nonrelation, that is, the oscillation between the sense of the social field as incomplete because something is missing ($) and as incomplete because something excessive, something that doesn't belong there, is obstructing its totalization (*a*).

All but the analyst's discourse promote the fantasy of a relation of unity. In the case of the Master's discourse, as we have seen, the actual status of S1 as a signifier which is criss-crossed by its relation to all the other signifiers of S2 (just like any other signifier) is occulted: its self-difference is hidden from view, while it is treated as if it were the agent of remediation of the incompleteness of the social field. For its part, S2 occults its own excessive dimension (*a*): that is, the signifying chain seems to produce a phantom power that is supposed to "stabilize" the meaning of each signifier in the chain and is not subject to the conditions of the chain. The more that S1 is called upon as the remedy for the incompleteness and instability of meaning in S2, the more *objet a* is produced as what needs to be ejected from the system (although in fact it cannot be). This production only serves to galvanize the discourse. The "truth" of the discourse, hidden from view, is the irremediable excess of the subject as signifier, and the incapacity of *objet a* to "reach" and remediate the self-difference of the subject ($) is one of the ways that the discourse presents itself as necessary.

By contrast, the Analyst's discourse correctly exposes the "agent" of the social field as the irremediable excess (*a*) of the subject-as-signifier ($) and highlights their impossible relation. The subject-as-signifier is the other to this agent: that is, the excessive dimension is the cause of the subject in its Möbius condition. The fantasmatic status of S1-as-Phallus is a product of this impossible relation between the subject and its excess, and the truth of the discourse inheres in the chain of signifiers (S2) that supports the subject ($), not as the remedy to its excess but as the mode of its ex-sistence in the social field, the endless circulation of excess among all the subjects-as-signifiers in the field. The reason that the Analyst's discourse does not devolve into the perverse scenario is because the role of S1 is clarified during the analysis. No longer functioning as the exception to the chain of signifiers S2 that would complete them (the S1/S2 connection is "incapable"), and removed from its place as the agent of the subject's constitution, S1 emerges as the production of the subject in its Möbius condition. This discourse, too, has its engine – the excess attending the Möbius subject never goes away – but the work of self-analysis is precisely to keep in view the impossibility of ridding the subject or the social field of excess and to note the constant pressure to produce S1 as the solution. The Analyst's discourse is the means by which the transferential fantasy comes to light and the true nature of S1, as just one contingent signification among all others, is exposed. Once the transferential fantasy has been traversed, through interpretation at this Symbolic level, the analysand encounters the formal constitutive conditions of subjectivity.

At that point, the analysand has some choices. She can disavow her encounter with the excess that underlies all subjects, including the analyst's. In a Freudian idiom, this encounter translates into the disavowal of castration, which, as we know, is the defining element of perversion: the perverse subject seeks to deny and undo the castration or excess of the other, fantasmatically positioning herself as the *objet a* that can cross the barrier of impossibility to remedy the other's self-difference. She also can continue to manufacture new meanings for her symptom as a way of defending against the recognition of her own self-difference; that is, she can make the analysis itself a symptom. But she has a third choice: the *sinthome*. In this case, she can enjoy the creative freedom conferred by her knowledge of her own particular ways of defending against self-difference and of the fantasmatic powers of remediation she had attributed to certain ontic properties – hers and others.

This final option gives the analysand the means for transforming her reaction to excess. And she may choose to consciously adopt – as her analyst does – the stance of de-personalization as an ethical matter. Just as her analyst's ethical stance of self-aestheticization gave her the opportunity to encounter the truth of her own subjectification, so her own self-aestheticization can foster that recognition in others. Not only does this ethics of extimacy decrease a given subject's contribution to the affective storm in the social field, it also opens the door for others to transform their own relationship to self-difference.

Tolerating Bartleby: Symbolic Divestiture

Yet when it comes to the consequences of symbolic divestiture or self-aestheticization, Žižek ignores the possibility that the toleration of excess and affects is the means by which one subject can have an impact on another. Perhaps this is why he has nothing to say about the lawyer who hires Bartleby: is he really the avatar of the Master that Žižek leads us to suppose? There is a longstanding critical tradition of mocking the lawyer as uncaring, unethical, insincere, dominative, self-deluded or unreliable. But isn't the lawyer the person in Melville's novel who has the greatest ability to tolerate excess and the circulation of affect? Nippers and Turkey, his long-time employees, have their diurnal variations of emotional outbursts and intolerance, but the lawyer merely observes them, making no additional contribution to the affective environment. He tolerates Bartleby's self-destitution fairly well from the beginning, and even when he flees his offices to get away from Bartleby, he continues to think about him in compassionate terms. When the new tenants of the lawyer's vacated premises, their landlord, and officers of the law argue that the lawyer is the cause of their problems, they are regarding Bartleby as the source of the excess in the social field and attempting to re-position that excess in the lawyer's purview. The lawyer tempers their aggression by agreeing (however reluctantly) to talk to Bartleby.

The point here is that while the lawyer's efforts to take responsibility for *Bartleby* fail, his encounter with Bartleby as formal negation improves his ability to take responsibility for *his own* defenses against excess. Read in this way, this narrative illuminates what happens to the lawyer's capacity for self-distancing after meeting Bartleby. If, as so many critics are at pains to point out, the lawyer doesn't really understand Bartleby or his social function, nonetheless, the lawyer has a unique response to him. So, for example, he refuses to join the attempts to (violently, if necessary) locate the undesirability of excess solely in Bartleby. In fact, the lawyer surprises himself with his own ability to take on that excess himself. Consider this exchange between them just before Bartleby is taken to the Tombs:

"How then would going as a companion to Europe, to entertain some young gentleman with your conversation – how would that suit you?"

"Not at all. It does not strike me that there is any thing definite about that. I like to be stationary. But I am not particular."

"Stationary you shall be then," I cried, now losing all patience, and for the first time in all my exasperating connection with him fairly flying into a passion. "If you do not go away from these premises before night, I shall feel bound – indeed I *am* bound – to – to – to quit the premises myself!" I rather absurdly concluded, knowing not with what possible threat to try to frighten his immobility into compliance.

Despairing of all further efforts, I was precipitately leaving him, when a final thought occurred to me – one which had not been wholly unindulged before.

"Bartleby," said I, in the kindest tone I could assume under such exciting circumstances, "will you go home with me now – not to my office, but my dwelling – and remain there till we can conclude upon some convenient arrangement for you at our leisure? Come, let us start now, right away."

Even when the lawyer is frustrated by Bartleby's refusal of any symbolic identity offered to him, he does not turn against Bartleby. Instead, he threatens "rather absurdly" to do himself what he wants Bartleby to do – "quit the premises." Žižek says that Bartleby is "so intolerable" because "he couldn't even hurt a fly," but as time goes on, the lawyer finds Bartleby *more* tolerable (PV 385). True, the lawyer seems already to have the capacity to tolerate negative affects without projecting them, but his encounter with Bartleby's symbolic divestiture, by his own account, increases for him the value of locating excess within himself while at the same time making him more aware of his own thoughts, feelings, and preferences – his symbolic properties. In this way, the encounter with Bartleby in the mode of de-personalization, that is, as a revelation of the operation of extimacy, makes the lawyer aware of the contingent quality of his own subjective identifications. This is what, in my view, enables him to moderate his affects and view others at the level of their formal rather than ontic constitution.

Of course, Bartleby's suicide by starvation is regrettable: I am not suggesting that suicide is the route to social change. Nor am I focusing on the lawyer's attempts to take responsibility for Bartleby, attempts that Bartleby refuses. It is not a case of our coming to appreciate (or reject) our ethical responsibilities to others by seeing them reduced to what Agamben calls "bare life." Rather, Bartleby's de-personalization ("definite" but "not particular") forces the lawyer to recognize Bartleby as something *in addition to* a symbolic identity, to treat him as well at the level of the foundation of subjectivity, not as something subhuman.[14] And, in fact, Bartleby seems to express the desire to be seen at the level of the purely formal. In one of the oddest phrasings in the story, he tells the lawyer "I want nothing to say to you." In this comment, Bartleby not only rejects the lawyer ("I have nothing to say to you") but also expresses the wish that "nothing" will have its say, i.e., will speak directly to the lawyer. We might put it this way: if Bartleby wants anything, it is to add a negation. In fact, while he is alive, Bartleby exists as both his particular self and as an identification with Möbius conditions: as a specific entity, he looks like an exception to the social field, but as a Möbius subject, he reveals the field to be non-orientable, for its founding conditions reside in the relation of nonrelation.

The story spotlights the relation of nonrelation between the lawyer and Bartleby as the only *ethical* relation, the only relation that acknowledges the formal dimension of the subject as part of its humanness, rather than something to be eradicated. Only this ethical stance positions the subject within the social field in a way that lets the hot potato of excess cool down.[15] The social field does not disappear as a result, because the excess attending Möbius subjectivity never goes away and the need to obtain a sense of our own meaning from others remains. Yet each individual is responsible for his or her own response to this excess, for the quality and degree of affect that attends the circulation of excess. Seen from this vantage, we have the beginnings of an answer to the question of how an individual's internal transformation of his relationship to his own *jouissance* can affect others in a way that could bring about social change.

I wonder, however, if the story of Bartleby's impact on the narrator is the best example we have of the ethical effect of de-personalization. Another, perhaps better, candidate might be Diogenes of Sinope, who based an entire philosophy on the ethics of refusing the Symbolic and subtracting ontic properties, or at least that is how his legacy has come down to us from Laertius's compilation of anecdotes. The Cynic philosopher tried to live a life as free of social convention as possible – even performing natural acts like defecation and masturbation in public. He considered his simple lifestyle of mendicancy, few possessions, and homelessness to be a "shortcut to virtue." Conceiving of his ethical duty as confronting others with this way of life, he demonstrated his *askesis* in order to force them to see the lineaments of conventionality ruling their lives and to renew public discourse on a more honest basis. Diogenes apparently had the idea that others would transform themselves if they encountered his revelation of the arbitrariness and contingency of the values they took for granted when he himself embodied the de-valuation of all ontic properties.[16] But Diogenes did not expect this transformation to occur immediately or automatically. He took advantage of opportunities and even forced openings, famously barging in on Plato in the act of defining man as a featherless biped, and confronting Plato's students with the counterexample of a plucked chicken. Throughout his life, Diogenes suffered the consequences of his in-your-face actions, most dramatically by being exiled from his home town Sinope: in a gesture Žižek might appreciate as a grasping of the situation by new coordinates, he re-described his sentence as condemning the residents of Sinope to stay put.

I doubt that Žižek, Diogenical as he too can be, finds this turn to individual transformation as appealing as the *coup-de-foudre* of revolutionary violence, even though he himself gestures towards it. The modulation of affect isn't as exciting as the call to arms of violent revolution. But that may be precisely why it is so valuable. We can apply what Žižek has said about revolutionary acts to the adoption of this ethical stance: the insistence on the Möbius subject is "a goal in itself, an act which changes the very concept of what a 'good life' is, and a different (higher, eventually) standard of living is a by-product of a revolutionary process" (PV 380). Who knows what revolutionary social changes the self-willed exposure of the excessive subject could bring about?

Towards Group Transformation

No doubt political activists will scorn the proposition that social change depends upon the subject's self-transformation into a neosubject. Surely, they might retort, we can make some hard decisions, embark on some committed course of action, and make substantial improvements in the status quo without – or at least in addition to – changing ourselves. Let's change the social universe first, and worry about personal transformation later. Isn't self-transformation at best a distraction from the necessary and pressing work of changing the world for the better and at worst a recipe for quietism? The planet is dying and people are suffering: we should act instead of gazing into our navels! And doesn't this idea of "self-transformation" smack of Stalinist and Maoist inquests? Finally, if we turn ourselves into affective sponges, aren't we more likely to tolerate injustice and make revolution less likely?

But before we dismiss the potential for social change that derives from de-personalization, we might recall that the very claim that political action should come first depends upon assumptions about subject formation that in themselves preclude the possibility of political action. The idea that transformations in the political or the economic sphere will change the subjects in a society presumes that those subjects are mere social products. From whence will the "new" arise to make possible political action if subjects are nothing other than the products of the status quo?

That is, activist theory has crucial stakes in understanding the limits of heteronomous conditioning, the roots of social discord, the dynamics of group formation, and the operation of universality. Without the theoretical foundation provided by the Möbius subject, the attempts to answer the most basic questions about how to bring about social change prove unsatisfactory, even self-contradictory, as we have seen. They tend to foster demagoguery or, worse, callous disregard for others who are persuaded to believe that, somehow, consequences can be calculated and governed.

Let's briefly review some of those issues. First, remember that for many theorists it is an open question whether the subject could be anything other than the mere product of social forces that always out-strip individual efforts to cognize or interfere with them. Bourdieu, de Certeau, and Butler all acknowledge the desirability of finding some way to theorize even a small margin of unconditioned freedom for the individual, even though none of their theories does so satisfactorily. Thanks to the tool of extimate causality, we can ground the argument that subjects do have a measure of autonomy, not because of the multiplicity of discourses and subject positions, nor because of the slippage inherent in signification, but because of the constitutive self-difference of the subject and the contingency of its identifications with the unary trait.

Second, the theory of extimate causality not only explains the advent of the subject but also provides a way of thinking causally about the social field. The social field comes into being through the relation of nonrelation, which requires a constant interaction among subjects who seek to get out from under the burdens of the excess that makes that relation inevitable. When subjects regard each other as the solution to social disharmony or the cause of it, they fantasmatically project their own excess onto others defensively, circulating destructive affects throughout the social field. Understanding the reasons for and structures of these dynamics helps any would-be social analyst figure out where to look for the motivating engine of social phenomena in a given situation. Affects, defenses, and fantasies are possible objects of analysis in ways that "over-determined superstructures" and "fluctuating power relations" are not. What is more, they have historically specifiable links to the social field. Anyone trying to understand the power of a political advertisement had best pay attention to this dimension: George Lakoff's admonishments about "re-framing" political discussions will not take us very far unless we add to our thinking the kind of psychological insight into affects and fantasies Drew Westen brings to the mix.[17]

Third, democratic theorists struggle to give due weight to both particularity and universality, both of which are critical for democratic politics as well as for historicity. As we have seen, the Möbius subject meets both conditions, with its partisan bond to a signifier serving the universalizing phallic function for the group (like the S1 as unary trait), a signifier inflected in turn by particular (historicizable) relationships. Failing to appreciate the Möbius condition of the subject promotes the error of imagining individuals as mere congeries of independent variables (ontic properties), even though, as we have seen, no positive (ontic) property can provide the kind of universal required for democratic interaction, because a regime based on an embodied universal is indistinguishable from one based on repressive authoritarianism. Only the formal negation can fulfill the requirements of a universal that is both part of the field and not a positive entity of the field.

Fourth, predominant models of political theory repeatedly propose the elimination of excess as the way to produce groups with strong social bonds. Relying on consensus, shared interests, and common properties to bind groups together means relying upon fantasies that individuals can be tied to one another in a bond of communion, a proposition belied by the fact of contingent and various identifications, with any signifier serving as S1 for the group. And given that subjects are *self-different*, no ties to another person can eradicate fundamental difference – the relation of nonrelation cannot be remediated. Even if it were possible to do so, the resulting Imaginary world of harmonious community would be populated by narcissistic individuals locked in fatal rivalries. The desire to eliminate excess both gives rise to pathological group processes, such as scapegoating, and ill prepares groups to handle the instability that always lurks beneath the surface of even the most tightly knit group.

Fifth, considering the social universe as a non-orientable, regenerating, re-assembling field, changes the way that we view problems in different sectors of the social field, such as economic or legal institutions. Of course, each of these sectors operates according to its own conventions and generates its own forms of knowledge. Each embeds history in its own way. At the same time, each depends upon its own set of assumptions about human nature, social interaction, and causal relations. So, some problems arise within the sector that can be addressed by the terms given within the situation: we may need better regulation of accounting practices, for example. But some problems arise because the sector has inadequately conceptualized the foundations of subjectivity and social relations. For example, economic theories that assume rational (self-interested) behavior on the part of consumers and investors run afoul of the actual importance of fantasy and affect in human behavior. Analyzing the fantasies at work in those assumptions and emphasizing the ethical stance of de-personalization, especially when it promotes the tempering of affects, can foster the recognition of realities and new alternatives to status quo practices. True, it is not obvious how such changes would transform the capitalist system or political institutions. But such modulations make group formation on the basis of something other than hatred (Rancière) or consensus (Habermas) a more viable possibility. If we are right about the social as perpetual re-assemblage, it may well be that alterations in the social field will bring about economic and political change. One thing is certain: any economic or political changes that reinforce the fantasy of social communion or the view that particular ontic traits are the source of social discord will be likely to galvanize aggressive affects in a spiral that all too easily gets out of control.

Finally, the continual re-assemblage of the social field has consequences for thinking the temporality of social change. When Žižek describes the parallax shift that permits a previously hidden dimension of a situation to come to the fore and then change the coordinates by which that situation is grasped, he has no explanation as to why such a shift might come about. While it may seem that an Event takes place in a flash, this does not mean that there were no preconditions for its emergence. These conditions may not have been planned or strategically deployed, and of course, in some sense, *all* of preceding history is the precondition for any given change. It is only possible to distinguish even some of the most significant contributions to the Event after the fact. However, while none of these conditions are predictive or guarantee a given result, some function as indicators that an opening to an Event *may be* possible: that is, in precisely those places in the social universe where the activity of re-assemblage is visibly heightened and where fantasmatic defenses are most prominent, we can find the signals of potential for a shift. As Badiou suggests, the perception of the hidden dimension of a situation might happen innumerable times before the political process of subjectification takes place (if it ever does). Like Diogenes, the sinthomic neosubject can repeatedly offer itself as the exposure of excess in the hope of sparking transformation that has been prepared by myriad other actions. It is reasonable to think that an individual who has adopted the ethical stance of de-personalization could register the intensification of defensive energies and, at the same time, be less likely to be buffeted by them. Such a person therefore might be better able to commit to the process of remaining faithful to the Event. I want to stress, however, that I am not advocating that we all become targets of others' aggression simply on the off chance that violence will spark social transformation. Bartlebyan masochism guarantees nothing.

Symbolic Divestiture and the Transformation of Groups

The examples of Bartleby and Diogenes, however, still do not get at the mechanism of group transformation in a way that could illuminate more clearly the specifically political valence of subjective destitution. We still need to ask whether this focus on individual subjects engaged in the ethical activity of symbolic divestiture can help us understand group processes in a way that is relevant for social change. I want to conclude, then, with one thinker who makes a significant contribution to our understanding of how symbolic divestiture in groups might be put into practice for transformative ends. At the same time, I wish to emphasize what must be clear by now – I am not pulling rabbits out of hats in these accounts: extimate causality, formal negation, Möbius subjectivity, the non-orientability of the social field, and symbolic divestiture are not stepping stones on a royal road to utopia. In my view, however, they are vital and innovative tools that address serious inadequacies in most contemporary conceptions of social relatedness and social change. The utility of these tools ultimately must be addressed through reflection, critique, and praxis.

Once again we have before us a theorist who has been so closely linked with "anti-psychoanalysis" that it may be surprising to find how crucial psychoanalysis is to both his therapeutic and his political theorizing. I will be arguing that Félix Guattari's concept of "transversality" – developed before his collaboration with Deleuze – configures social space as a non-orientable object and that he derives his political charge from the implications of this topology in precisely the ways that we have been outlining. What is more, his argument for transforming social processes by means of a specific type of group therapy involves (what we have been calling) sinthomic activity or symbolic divestiture. Guattari has a story to tell about the potential for social change that starts from what is recognizably a model of Möbius subjectivity, based on an understanding of the significative excess circulating in the social field, and then proceeds by articulating the space of social interaction in terms of group fantasies that recast members in roles of obstacle and resolution to social disharmony. He emphasizes that the variable individual affective responses to significative excess can be analyzed in order to foster the development of groups in which processes involving symbolic divestiture (although he does not use that term) help individuals encounter the fact of the contingency of their meaning for others, which then can be the means for re-channeling unconscious desire and transforming superego introjects for both therapeutic and politically creative ends (MR 21).[18] In short, Guattari provides a way to move from individual psychodynamics to group transformation via a praxis which, in his view, derives its potential for revolutionary politics from the same features of social subjectivity and the social field with which this book has been concerned.

We might do well to start with a warning Guattari delivered just before the events of May 1968:

Either the revolutionary workers' movement and the masses will recover their speech via *collective agents of utterance* that will guarantee that they are not caught up again in anti-production relations (as far as a work of analysis can be a guarantee), or matters will go from bad to worse. It is obvious that the bourgeoisie of present-day neo-capitalism are not a neo-bourgeoisie and are not going to become one: they are undoubtedly the stupidest that history has ever produced. They will not find an effective way out. They will keep trying to cobble things together, but always too late and irrelevantly, as with all their great projects to help what their experts coyly describe as the "developing countries."

It is quite simple, then. Unless there is some drastic change, things are undoubtedly going to go very badly indeed, and in proportion as the cracks are a thousand times deeper than those that riddled the structure before 1939, we shall have to undergo fascisms a thousand times more frightful. (MR 43–4)

"Fascisms a thousand times more frightful": yes, and with no end in sight. We are living in the world against which Guattari warned. So what does he prescribe as a counter to this dystopian future, which seems to be our present state of affairs?

Drawing on his experiences at the Clinique de la Borde, Guattari develops a psychoanalytic and political approach to solving the problem of the institutionalization of anti-therapeutic attitudes and practices in the clinic setting. He comes to see that individual pathology and institutional pathology cannot be treated separately – that they are mutually reinforcing – and this insight leads him to believe that therapeutic aims cannot be isolated from the economics and politics which support institutions and their methods. Because he regards individual psychopathologies as manifestations of morbidity in the politico-economic sphere, he can make a direct connection between certain therapeutic techniques and political praxis:

> I think it is sensible to set out a kind of grid of correspondence between the meandering of meanings and ideas among psychotics, especially schizophrenics, and the mechanisms of growing discordance being set up at all levels of industrial society in its neo-capitalist and bureaucratic socialist phase whereby the individual tends to have to identify with an ideal of consuming-machines-consuming-producing-machines. The silence of the catatonic is perhaps a pioneering interpretation of that ideal. If the group is going to structure itself in terms of a rejection of the spoken word, what response is there apart from silence? (MR 14)

Arguing that "[t]he real subjectivity in modern States, the real powers of decision . . . cannot be identified with any individual or with the existence of any small group of enlightened leaders [but rather is] unconscious and blind," Guattari suggests that we need an "institutional therapeutics" which must take place at the level of the group (MR 13).

What Guattari has in mind, however, is not the kind of group therapy one typically finds in institutions, which simply mirrors the hierarchies structuring institutions (including, by the way, classrooms and training groups). Rather, by "group" he means the involvement of persons from all parts of the institution: in the case of the clinic, staff and patients participate in a nonhierarchical structure. Using the clinic setting as the site of experiments in group therapy, then, has political implications not only because such experiments cut across the structures of authority embedded in the institution – and therefore aim at effects beyond the clinic walls into the state apparatus of such institutions – but also because political groups exhibit the same pathologies – from psychosis to narcissism to hysteria and phobia – seen within the clinic. Political and social groups produce their own centripetal force into regression, which means that psychopathology is more likely to be the product of group interactions than any kind of progressive social change. Without a praxis of group therapy, the political sphere and the clinic will continue to circulate the same characteristic illnesses, which will manifest themselves at every scale.

The "object" of institutional therapeutics is "to try to change the data accepted by the super-ego into a new kind of acceptance of 'initiative'" (MR 13–14). "Initiative" is a key value for Guattari, because he is thinking of groups (and individuals) that can think for themselves, express themselves, act for themselves – groups that have the capacity to invent and encounter the new. Labeling such a group "independent," Guattari lists its three key properties: it has "a perspective, a viewpoint on the world, a job to do . . . a 'vocation'"; it "endeavours to control its own behavior and elucidate its object": and it produces "its own tools of elucidation." These properties enable the group to become "open to a world beyond its own immediate interests," which of course is part of the political valence of the group (MR 14). The independent group "hears and is heard," which is to say that not only can it express, hear, and interpret its own internal processes but also link up with other structures beyond itself without losing its creativity and initiative (MR 14–15). The distinction between an independent group and a dependent group (that is, groups that are "determined passively from outside, and with the help of mechanisms of self-preservation, magically protect themselves from a non-sense experienced as external") is not absolute, however (MR 22). Even independent groups "oscillate" between "two positions: that of a subjectivity whose work is to speak, and a subjectivity which is lost to view in the otherness of society" (MR 14). This oscillation is not the parallax shift but it is related to it, as we will see in a moment.

What techniques might bring an independent group into being from an otherwise dependent group? Guattari emphasizes that the unconscious desire of a group as "expression of the death instinct" in a dependent group cannot be stated directly and therefore will emerge symptomatically. So, rather than trying to cure the group, the task at the outset is to clear a space, "keeping room for a first plan of reference for this group desire to be identified" (MR 15). In this proposal, Guattari is at pains to clarify that he is not speaking of "setting up a community with a more or less psycho-sociological orientation, or group engineering" (MR 15). Nor is he advocating merely interpreting the defenses or group fantasies that develop from the morbid conditions of modern political-economic forces as a pathological response to their powerlessness. Such interpretations can do nothing more than reveal the underlying fact that the real expression of desire of human beings is being blocked at every turn.

By contrast, Guattari is looking for a method that will allow the release of creativity in the expression of desire, which is not the same as interpreting the symptoms that arise from desire's blockage. The *meaning* of symptoms, which is the hoped-for product of standard psychoanalytic practice, can be nothing but a "static truth" (MR 17). In other words, discovering that desire is blocked by the structures and processes of modern life (which is the underlying meaning of the symptoms, each of which develops in order to manage the blockage of desire) does not reveal how to unblock it: "Group analysis will not make it its aim to elucidate a static truth underlying this symptomatology, but rather to create the conditions favourable to a particular mode of *interpretation*" that dispenses with the usual transferential hierarchy of analyst to analysand (MR 17). Such a "fixed transference, a rigid mechanism,"

> like the relationship of nurses and patients with the doctor, an obligatory, predetermined, "territorialized" transference onto a particular role or stereotype . . . is a way of interiorizing bourgeois repression by the repetitive, archaic and artificial re-emergence of the phenomena of caste, with all the spellbinding and reactionary group phantasies they bring in their train. (MR 17)

De-territorializing that structure is the therapeutic and political work of the type of group analysis Guattari invokes. He gives the name "transversality" to this de-territorialized form of transference, an experimental process which not only addresses both the therapeutic needs of the group but also provides an ongoing praxis for the development of a *modus vivendi* for individuals in their group relations (MR 17).

The reactionary and morbid forces generated by group interactions have to be countered by a certain kind of analytic framework and praxis which Guattari describes in spatial terms, as a dimension that is both "*opposite and complementary* to the structures that generate pyramidal hierarchization and sterile ways of transmitting messages" (MR 22, my emphasis).[19] Initially it seems that he is merely looking for a way to describe an alternative to, on the one hand, vertical hierarchies of authority and, on the other, "a state of affairs in which . . . people fit in as best they can with the situation in which they find themselves" – that is, as though they were monads abandoned to groping in the dark through a world that makes no sense to them (MR 17). The term "transversality" captures this alternative. But then Guattari provides a metaphor that makes it clear that transversality addresses a certain kind of *experience* of social relations, an experience we will recognize as a function of the circulation of excess in the social field:

> Think of a field with a fence around it in which there are horses with adjustable blinkers: the adjustment of their blinkers is the "coefficient of transversality". If they are so adjusted as to make the horses totally blind, then presumably a certain form of traumatic encounter will take place. Gradually, as the flaps are opened, one can envisage them moving about more easily. Let us try to imagine how people relate to one another in terms of affectivity. (MR 17–18)

In our terms, the fully blinkered horses do not function as social subjects, because they do not have even a rudimentary sense of being included within signification by way of a Möbius topology. (It may seem unfortunate that Guattari chooses animals for his example, but I think he is right to do so because he is describing an entity that has not entered signification, one that has not been subjectified.) They have no meaning for themselves, and there is no question for them of their meaning for others, precisely because there are no "others" for whom they might have meaning. The other horses are just obstacles. The fully blinkered horses are in the horizontal "serial" relation of monadic disconnectedness: their lives are a series of bumping into obstacles they cannot recognize because these obstacles are both too foreign (completely unknowable) and too close (intrusive).[20]

One solution to this state of affairs is to assign "stable" relations among the entities to give them a permanent place and a fixed meaning. Every horse could be in a stall with its name lettered on the gate, a name assigned by the owner, as though the owner were the (in fact, fantasmatic) big Other guaranteeing the consistency and identity of symbolic relations. The horses exist only at the level of their assigned place: they would not be regarded by the owner as entities like herself, *parlêtres* who are caught in the defiles of the signifier. The price of being relieved of the terrifying existence of blinkered horsedom would be imprisonment. Oh, certainly the horse can move about, it can get exercise, it can whinny with its neighbor; it may even be petted or have sex. But the "stabled" horse has no social being across the entire structure of the world in which it lives and which assigns it its place: it has no way to exercise its subjectivity in social relations because it has no *excess*, no self-difference. The world of the blinkered horse is a world of nonrelation; the world of the stabled horse is a world of fixed relations. In neither case, do we find the essential "relation of nonrelation" that derives from the excessive dimension of subjectivity, the self-difference that makes it impossible for the subject to take account of itself in the social field. The stable (not Guattari's metaphor but my extension) is the typical structure of the mental hospital, a structure based on a retrograde fantasy of mastery and caste. To live a life of real social relations, the subject must give up something to gain something, to be sure. But the cost of the stable is unnecessarily high from Guattari's perspective.

To consider the formation of truly social groups in terms of "affectivity," as Guattari urges, involves some elements familiar to us from our framework of the extimate cause, the Möbius subject, the social field as non-orientable object, and symbolic divestiture. For example, Guattari notes the requirement of a formal negation, effected by the signifier (the same function as the *Non/Nom-du-Père* in individual subjectification), that sets up the group as a site of belonging without subsuming the members completely – an operation that produces each member as excessive. He emphasizes that the only hope for a transformative praxis ("a creative intervention") is that the group members, especially those who would otherwise occupy roles of authority, "accept a form of castration" that derives from being "imprinted by the signifier of the group" (MR 19). Guattari refers to this as a special kind of castration: "[t]he effect of the group's signifier on the subject is felt, on the part of the latter, at the level of a 'threshold' of castration, for at each phase of its symbolic history, the group has its own demand on the individual subjects, involving a relative abandonment of their instinctual urgings to 'be part of a group'" (MR 22). I understand him to mean that the group's demand on each individual requires that the individual give up his or her fantasmatic relationship to "belonging" – a relationship that transpires in the Imaginary – in order to enter into a social relation of nonrelation with the others in the group – an acceptance, so to speak, of the relation of nonrelation. However, even within an independent group, as Guattari admits, forces conducing to fantasies and delusions of group immanence and harmony are considerable.

The instability of the position of "belonging to a group" cannot be avoided, for every person who belongs does so at a fantasmatic level unique to himself or herself, as I noted in the discussion of Laclau's neglect of the unary trait. Only when transversal relations are made to emerge can the individual "manifest both the group and himself. If the group he joins acts as a signifying chain, he will be revealed to himself as he is beyond his imaginary and neurotic dilemmas" (MR 20). Guattari is not arguing here that some fundamental "essence" of the individual comes to light but rather that the individual in his or her social, excessive dimension – not a fantasmatic "stable" identity" – can be recognized. Under these conditions speech is restored to its creative function, rather than its ritual function, because the "delusions and all the other unconscious manifestations which have hitherto kept the patient in a kind of solitary confinement can achieve a collective mode of expression" (MR 20). While every subject will continue to stick to his or her own excess, and excess will continue to circulate, the various modes of defense against excess – such as hysteria, catatonia, paranoia, or other fantasies and delusions – can become available for expression and transformation. So even though at any moment, a given subject can be "nominated" to the position of super-human solution to excess or to the position of scapegoated obstacle to group cohesion, such efforts can be recognized and transmuted through the mechanism of symbolic destitution. This mechanism is what I wish to highlight now in Guattari's account.

In proposing a group psychodynamic process for bringing about real transformation, Guattari is mindful of the differences in response and defense employed in reaction to the relations of nonrelation. Each individual, affected by "the group's signifier," may experience this "castration" in different ways, "from a sense of rejection or even of mutilation, to creative acceptance that could lead to a permanent change in the personality" (MR 22). Once a group embarks on this process, and instinctual demands begin to be expressed in ways that foreground finitude,

> the group becomes ambiguous. At one level, it is reassuring and protective, screening all access to transcendence, generating obsessional defences and a mode of alienation one cannot help finding comforting. . . . But at the other, there appears behind this artificial reassurance the most detailed picture of human finitude, in which every undertaking of mine is taken from me in the name of a demand more implacable than my own death – that of being caught up in the existence of that other, who alone guarantees what reaches me via human speech. (MR 21-2)

The action of the group's signifier cuts two ways: it can dissolve hierarchies, granting "some rights, some authority" to its members, but it also changes the "level of tolerance towards individual divergences" (MR 22-3). This dual action derives from the excess installed by way of the signifier. This is why I believe that when Guattari relies explicitly on the Lacanian advent of the excessive subject as an effect of the signifier, he opens his theorizing to our framework: the consequences of putting such subjects into a group force each subject to function according to the parallax shift. Transversality has a Möbius topology.

Guattari places front and center the role of affects in the social field. "Affectivity" corresponds to the point of excess that permits the crossing of the boundary between inside and outside, injecting a fluidity into the "meaning" of the subjects within the group which permits the circulation of excess to be recognized and interpreted along with the defenses and strategies that such excess generates. Instead of denying the excess – as the stable does – the group uses it as its point of departure for interpretation. The object is to uncover the real lines of power in the group: "real power" has to be distinguished from "manifest power"; real power is unconscious (MR 19). As we noted, the best defense against the regressive pull of "togetherness" is the elucidation of the dimension of excess with its concomitant production of affect and desire within the group.

So, even though Guattari himself doesn't resort to the metaphor of Möbius subjectivity, his description of transversality lends itself easily to representing the social field as a non-orientable object. But what is even more striking is the precise mechanism of transformation Guattari describes, because the therapeutic praxis he has in mind, the praxis that brings transversality into the open, captures the activity of symbolic divestiture very well. Guattari proposes that transversality can work as a hedge against the danger of the regressive pull to a fantasy of "belonging" on the basis of some sort of symbolic role because it brings "to the surface the group's instinctual demands [which] force everyone, whether patient or doctor, to consider the problem of their being and destiny . . . [and to accept] the risk – which accompanies the emergence of any phenomenon of real meaning – of having to confront irrationality, death, and the otherness of the other" (MR 21, 23). Encounters with finitude and alterity are defining characteristics of Möbius subjectivity – the source of the affective engine that drives defensive fantasies galvanized to obscure the constitutive excess that produces us as social subjects. Recast in our terms, we could say that transversality makes appear the fundamental condition of excess, generated through the defiles of the signifier, which assembles and disassembles the social field as a relation of nonrelation. In this way, it can bring to the awareness of the members of the group the fantasies that are generated in order to defend against that excess.

Here is one example of what we would call symbolic divestiture in Guattari's therapeutic praxis:

> The doctor who abandons his phantasy status in order to place his role on a symbolic plane [that is, as opposed to the Imaginary] is . . . well placed to effect the necessary splitting-up of the medical function into a number of different responsibilities involving various kinds of groups and individuals. The object of that function moves away from "totemization". . . . The very fact that the doctor could adopt such a splitting-up would thus represent the first phase of setting up a structure of transversality. His role, now "articulated like a language", would be involved with the sum of the group's phantasies and signifiers. Rather than each individual acting out the comedy of life for his and other people's benefit in line with the

reification of the group, transversality appears inevitably to demand the imprinting of *each* role. (MR 21, my emphasis)

Again, Guattari is not talking about group therapy as "role-playing." In these groups, the doctor, nurses and patients do not act "as if" they were adopting another role and then return to their usual authoritative staff positions. Instead, the group undertakes a project (it has a "vocation") that places each individual in new roles *for real*. More importantly, it questions and "re-defines" roles as part of that project. This overt questioning of roles in relation to the group's project (which is ultimately the production of an independent group), coupled with the undermining of typical hierarchical structures within the institution, requires each individual, "whether patient or doctor, to consider the problem of their being or destiny" (MR 21).

Guattari is cautious about the possibilities of this therapy. Such a practice can modify superego introjects, and it can re-distribute some rights and some authority. But it can also "produce alterations in the group's level of tolerance toward individual divergences" (MR 22). As I noted in my discussion of Bartleby, symbolic divestiture may increase tolerance in the group, but it may decrease it as well: aggression can be potentiated by tolerance. Still, *if* each individual takes turns adopting various roles within the group as different activities are organized, *if* the group has a "significant share of legal *and* real power," *if* the dangers of "togetherness" are addressed – *then* it may be possible for the members of the group to modify ego ideals and with them superegoic introjects that conduce to paranoia, aggression, narcissism, and sadism (MR 21). The means for this modification rests on a voluntary kind of "castration" that Guattari describes in terms strikingly similar to those we used in discussing self-aestheticization, de-personalization, subjective destitution, or symbolic divestiture. Guattari argues that it is

possible to set in motion a type of castration complex related to different social demands from those patients previously experienced in their familial, professional and other relationships. To accept being "put on trial", being verbally laid bare by others, a certain type of reciprocal challenge, and humour, the abolition of hierarchical privilege and so on – all this will tend to create a new group law whose "initiating" effects will bring to light, or at least into the half-light, a number of signs that actualize transcendental aspects of madness hitherto repressed. Phantasies of death, or of bodily destruction, so important in psychoses, can be re-experienced in the warm atmosphere of a group, even though one might have thought their fate was essentially to remain in the control of a neo-society whose mission was to exorcise them. (MR 21)

The blind, unconscious, and ossified structures that regulate social relations (the pathological response to the excess circulating in the social field)
in typical familial and institutional settings can be addressed through
the adoption of a group "vocation" that grants to every person in the
group the same privilege and power of interpreting the group to itself:
"The interpretation may be given by the idiot of the ward if he is able to
make his voice heard at the right time, the time when a particular signifier becomes active at the level of the structure as a whole, for instance in
organizing a game of hop-scotch" (MR 17). This emphasis on symbolic
divestiture – the setting-off of ontic properties to reveal the formal constitution of the subject – counters the regressive pull to a mutual fantasy of
immanent community. Without this counterbalance, Guattari points out,
there will be crises that "endanger the group's future" (MR 23).

Within a political context, he observes that political movements tend
to splinter, not along ideological lines, but along organizational ones,
thanks to these pathological subjective processes within the group (MR
30). In 1968, he argued that our understanding of these processes is
"very inadequate," and it is not clear that we see much improvement
today (MR 35). To locate the seeds of revolution in a new approach to
group organization, rather than in deconstructing ideology or exhorting
"political action," reinforces the insight that conceiving social change
along the lines of traditional politics consigns us to the terrain of the
Imaginary. At the same time, however, we don't (yet?) have a group
praxis or a protocol for recognizing "the series of phantasies which actually make up the real fabric of the whole organization and solidity of the
masses," even though it is at the level of these phenomena that the only
real work of social transformation can be accomplished (MR 35). We
have some help from Guattari, who tries to inaugurate a taxonomy and a
mode of analysis of the provenance and function of the different types of
fantasy involved in group operation as a step on the road to unleashing
the group's potential for social change. But the way is uncertain:

> identification with the prevailing images of the group is by no means
> always static, for the badge of membership often has links with narcissistic
> and death instincts that it is hard to define. Do individual phantasies take
> shape and change in the group, or is it the other way round? . . . group
> phantasizing has no "safety rail" to compare with those that protect the
> libidinal instinctual system, and has to depend on temporary and unstable
> homeostatic equilibria. . . . the tendency is to return to phenomena of
> imaginary explosion or phallicization rather than to coherent discourse.
> (MR 38–9)

Guattari does not postulate any sure-fire consequences of the symbolic
divestiture and the encounter with the formal conditions constituting

subjectivity. It may be that the best we can hope for is that the group will avoid the disavowal or displacement of the relation of nonrelation by means of a process that might "lead the group as a whole to be less ready to evade the lessons" taught by the crises produced within the group when these individual responses to the exposure of excess occur (MR 23).

Guattari's analysis presents a vision of a commitment to a process as a hedge against pathological outcomes. He offers to the excessive subject a mode of belonging that minimizes regressive fantasies and maximizes tolerance without providing any guarantees. The group commits to "short-circuit its [death-dealing] action with a problematic that is open to revolution, even if that group assures me that revolution will certainly not save my life, or provide any solution to certain sorts of problem, but that its role is, in a sense, precisely to prevent my being in too much of a hurry to run away from that problematic" (MR 43). Buffeted by our own and others' discomfort with being excessive subjects, we rush to find any shelter from this affective storm swirling through the social field, even if that shelter turns out to be a prison or the darkness of delusion. Guattari holds out the hope of tempering that storm. Engaging in this praxis means that we have to slow down, express our desire, and accept being "laid bare" in groups where the condition of belonging is simply being there. We have to take the risk of recognizing that our excessive dimension, by virtue of its Möbius topology, not only seals us to finitude but also opens us to change. The revolution starts at the point of excess.

Notes

Introduction

1 Calvino, *Numbers in the Dark*, p. 131.
2 Foucault, *The History of Sexuality*, Vol. I, pp. 92–3.
3 Ibid., p. 92.
4 Copjec, *Read My Desire*, pp. 5–6.
5 Ibid., p. 18.
6 Ibid.
7 The status of the "social" in Lacan has been interpreted in different ways, even by these particularly adept thinkers, in part because Lacan developed the three registers over a long period of time. So, for example, some critics regard the Symbolic register as a repository of social forces that shape individuals ideologically (this is certainly Althusser's and Butler's understanding, for example), while others regard the Symbolic as produced by a content-free operation (the formal negation or *Non/Nom-du-Père*) which makes it possible for the individual to have his or her own idiosyncratic regulatory psychic contents. In this book, I will be pressing the latter version of the Symbolic against the former.

Chapter 1

1 William Sewell has an extensive discussion of this point in his *Logics of History: Social Theory and Social Transformation*, pp. 321–8.
2 Latour, *Reassembling the Social*, p. 3.
3 Ibid., pp. 3–4.
4 Ibid., p. 7.
5 Latour, *Science in Action*, p. 21.
6 Ibid., pp. 25–7.
7 Ibid., p. 28, original emphasis.
8 Sewell, *Logics of History*, p. 328. Pointing out the continuities between

appeals to a divine ontology and appeals to "the social" in the social sciences, Sewell says that "'the social' came to signify the complex and ultimately unknowable reality of human existence, a reality previously represented by such religious concepts as Divine Will or Providence" (ibid., p. 326). Keith Baker argues that "the social (as anyone who presumes to question its priority is reminded) is our name for the 'really real.' It secures the existential ground beneath our feet, presenting a bedrock of reality beneath the shifting sands of discourse" (Baker, "Enlightenment," p. 114; quoted in Sewell, *Logics of History*, p. 326).

9 Ibid., p. 329.
10 In making a related point, Sewell argues for the importance of quantitative methods to register the presence of consequences that occur at a variety of scales and temporalities. See his discussion in *Logics of History*, pp. 351–6.
11 In chapter 4, we will have occasion to discuss the use to which Butler puts a similar insight, although to different ends and with unfortunate internal contradictions.
12 Nancy, *Inoperative Community*, pp. 12–13.
13 Ibid., p. 11.
14 Ibid.
15 Mill, *On Liberty*, p. 60.
16 Althusser, *Lenin and Philosophy*, p. 130.
17 Ibid., p. 128, original emphasis.
18 Ibid., p. 123.
19 Ibid., p. 142, original emphasis.
20 For an overview of Althusser's limitations and the problematic academic appropriations of his work – as well as a review of attempts to use Lacanian psychoanalysis for political purposes – see Ian Parker's succinct and insightful essay "Lacanian Psychoanalysis and Revolutionary Marxism."
21 Amanda Anderson makes this point in her essay, "The Temptations of Aggrandized Agency: Feminist Histories and the Horizon of Modernity."
22 Žižek, *The Sublime Object of Ideology*, pp. 28–9.
23 Ibid., pp. 31–3.
24 Ibid., p. 43.

Chapter 2

1 The most elaborated discussion of extimacy in Lacan's work occurs in *Le Séminaire, Livre XVI: D'un Autre à l'autre*, especially pp. 249 ff. See also Jacques-Alain Miller's excursus on this concept in his essay "Extimity."
2 Badiou, "Towards a New Concept of Existence," p. 65. I should point out that Badiou goes on to define "thing" somewhat differently than I do here in set theoretic terms. But the starting point is the same, and the use to which I am putting this quotation accords with this later development. See Brian Anthony Smith's "The Limits of the Subject in Alain Badiou's *Being and Event*" for a more critical approach to Badiou's use of set theory.

3 This is the significance of the Nietzschean *Mittag* explored by Alenka Zupančič in *The Shortest Shadow*.

4 In another context (a meditation on Number), Badiou describes exactly the same operation and effects: "On the one hand, you have a stable, homogeneous mark: the ordinal. On the other, a mark that, in a certain sense, has been torn from the former; an indeterminate part that, on the whole, does not conserve any immanent stability and can be discontinous, dismembered, and devoid of any concept . . . that which, by extracting a sample of unforeseeable, almost lightning-like discontinuity from matter, allows an unalterable material density to be glimpsed as though through the gaps left by that extraction. . . . What is remarkable is that this simple starting point [the formal extraction] allows one to establish the properties of order and calculation required" (Badiou, *Theoretical Writings*, p. 62).

5 As Cantorian set theory demonstrates, a *power set*, defined as the set of all the subsets of a set, always includes the empty set as one of its subsets. Even a set composed of only one element "p" has three subsets: {p}, {ø}, and {p, ø}. Because the empty set is the equivalent of the outer brackets constituting setness itself, one can draw attention to the persistence of the empty set in any set A by "nesting" A within an additional pair of outer brackets: {A} = {A, ø} = {{A}}. This result is one of the ways in which the formal addition of a negation, e.g. the empty set, produces a "spontaneous" generation of excess.

6 We are speaking here of a formal object only – a minimally determined object, not necessarily the kind of object that we would recognize as an apple, Rome, or a gray-haired person.

7 Zupančič, *The Shortest Shadow*, p. 136.

8 Kojin Karatani's *Transcritique* details the production of this same kind of spontaneous generation in Marx's analysis of capital, where money, routed through the commodity, gives the result of money plus a surplus. A. Kiarina Kordela's *Surplus: Spinoza, Lacan* makes the case for Spinoza as the source of the description of the surplus-generating function that appears in Kant, Marx, and Lacan (as surplus-jouissance).

9 I am indebted to Christine Wertheim for making me aware of this Peircean logical notation. As I read Peirce's works on logic, I am struck by how frequently he seems to be seeking a structure like the Möbius band not only to investigate the properties of double negation or truth-glut formulations, but also to handle the problem of truth-values in situations of indetermination (see Peirce, *Collected Papers* IV, especially pp. 444 ff.).

10 For a helpful discussion of paraconsistent logic, see *An Introduction to Non-Classical Logic*, by Graham Priest, one of the founders of the field, especially chapter 8, "First Degree Entailment" (pp. 140–61). The basic concept here is that it is possible for a formula to be both true and false or neither true nor false, positions inarticulable in classical logic. First degree entailment (FDE) and other forms of nonclassical logic capture this both-and/neither-nor possibility. Paralogic provides for a difference unrecognized in classical logic, that is, the difference between "being false in an interpretation and not being true in it" (p. 140). For non-logicians, it might be helpful here to think of the

Greimasian square where the four positions can be described as true, not-true, false, and not-false: in the square, false and not-true are not the same thing. First degree entailment involves a formal notation that I will not use. For those familiar with FDE, it may be sufficient to note that, in essence, I am explaining a case in which there is a "truth-value glut" as defined in many-valued logic. I should also point out that my use of an asterisk (*) to mark excess should not be taken as indicating the Routley star condition.

11 The Greimasian semiotic square is derived from Aristotle's square of opposition (see Greimas' *Sémantique structurale*). It is used to construct relations of opposition, contradiction, and complementarity. Life is opposed to death; but the negation of life, or not-life, is not the same as death. Neither is the negation of death, or not-death, the same as life.

12 As we will see, Adorno's theory of art as the "determinate negation of untruth" emphasizes the singularity of each work's historical mode of pointing towards "the possibility of a nature which 'is not yet'" without specifying in any way the positive properties of that nature (quoted in Jarvis, *Adorno*, p. 104). Works of art provide no assurances of utopia but merely hold open the possibility of the new by "implying determinate criticisms of what is and has been" (p. 105).

13 Zupančič, following Lacan, considers this figure to constitute an "immanent Twoness." In my terms, the internal doubling of the object, its minimal difference from itself, generates an excess, so that it is indeed more than one. If all we have to reckon with are the cardinal numbers, then by definition more than one is two. But I am resisting the argument that the object so formed is a "two." Rather, by articulating how this figure is "more than one, not quite two," it is possible to bring excess into play as something specific to itself, as we will see.

14 Lacan's interest in and use of the formal negation as a means of understanding the production of subjectivity dates at least from his first seminar, *Freud's Papers on Technique* (1953–54), wherein Lacan asks Jean Hyppolite to produce a reading of Freud's essay "On Negation" (in *The Seminar of Jacques Lacan, Book I*, pp. 289–97). Hyppolite stresses the importance of the French term for denial – *dénégation* – as a form of double negation. Although Lacan points to this moment in Hyppolite's exposition as particularly important for understanding the production of subjectivity and the relation of the subject to the other, he himself doesn't clarify his thinking on the double negation explicitly at this time (ibid., pp. 58 ff.). Still, at the end of the seminar meeting of February 10, 1954, Lacan refers to the "tool" developed by Hyppolite as essential for "the rest of our discussion" (ibid., p. 61). It is clear from his later work that the production of an excessive dimension through a double negation continues to affect his conceptions of *objet a* and the Real.

15 Žižek, *Organs Without Bodies*, p. 92.

16 Zupančič, commenting on these dual levels, puts it this way: "to say 'I am lying' is to say '(it is true that) I am lying' but if we try to eliminate this surplus to formulate it as a statement at a meta-level, we get 'It is true that I am lying' which is in effect the same as '(it is true that) it is true that I am

lying.' This leads to an endless series of levels – trying to eliminate the level of enunciation from the statement by formulating it as part of the statement only multiplies the original problem" (Zupančič, *Shortest Shadow*, p. 141).

17 In the Seminar in Experimental Critical Theory held at the University of California Humanities Research Center in 2004, Joan Copjec referred to this condition as "the subject riveted to being."

18 In chapter 4, I will take up the question as to the difference between a linguistic subject and an embodied subject.

19 This is the point of Lacan's exemplification of the forced choice of the *vel*: Your money or your life! If you choose your money, you will lose both your money and your life. Colette Soler has a concise and clear explanation in "The Subject and the Other (II)"; see especially pp. 46–8.

20 In a lecture given at the Seminar in Experimental Critical Theory held at the University of California Humanities Research Center in 2003.

21 For an extended explanation of the relation of nonrelation, see Badiou's "Scene of Two." Gabriela Riera's collection of essays, *Alain Badiou: Philosophy and Its Conditions*, contains two especially fine essays by Joan Copjec and Juliet Flower MacCannell on this text by Badiou.

22 Rancière himself does not make clear whether, for him, "at odds with themselves" means that they are at odds with one another or at odds internally, but the description of subjects "living rent by passion" indicates that he has in mind *riven* subjects.

Chapter 3

1 See Mark Poster's "The Question of Agency: Michel De Certeau and the History of Consumerism" for a brief discussion of de Certeau and Bourdieu as belonging to the field of poststructuralism along with Foucault, Derrida, Lacan, and Althusser, among others.

2 Bourdieu says that "Sartre's ultra-subjectivist imagination has been outdone by the voluntarism of the anthropological fictions to which the 'rational actor' theorists have to resort . . . in order to make rational decision-making the sole basis of the rational conduct of the 'rational actor', and more especially of the constancy and coherence of his preferences over time" (LP 46–7).

3 Merleau-Ponty, *Phenomenology of Perception*, pp. 143, 144.

4 For a different but related account of de Certeau's criticisms of Bourdieu, see Schirato and Webb, "The Ethics and Economies of Inquiry: De Certeau, Theory, and the Art of Practice."

5 I will revisit the issue of the politics of formalism and aestheticization in the context of Adorno's constellation in chapters 6 and 7.

6 In his "Michel de Certeau: The Logic of Everyday Practices," Michael Sheringham explains de Certeau's emphasis on the "occasion" as coming into being only at the moment it is grasped by "the faculty which identifies or creates" it; his account implicitly invokes the kind of retroversivity which, as I argue below, de Certeau neglects when arguing for the political valence of everyday practices. Ben Highmore's "Opaque, Stubborn Life: Everyday

Life and Resistance in the Work of Michel de Certeau" calls into question the potential for resistance in de Certeau's theory of tactics on grounds different from but compatible with my own.

7 For example, Sheringham, "Michel de Certeau: The Logic of Everyday Practices," p. 29.

8 Tony Schirato and Jenn Webb read de Certeau's discussion of the cut-out and the inversion in his essays on Foucault and Bourdieu and on the arts of theory as though de Certeau approved this procedure of theory. I think they have misread de Certeau here when they say that "this operation allows Foucault and Bourdieu to have, in de Certeau's words, 'access to everything.'" However much de Certeau learned from Foucault and Bourdieu, he regards the operations of cutting out and inversion to be typical gestures of a theory that does not accord the same status to the everyday as he does, and in this essay he is overtly critical of both authors. See Schirato and Webb, "The Ethics and Economies of Inquiry," pp. 98–9, and de Certeau, especially PEL 62–3.

9 Poster, "The Question of Agency," p. 125.

10 Highmore, "Opaque, Stubborn Life," pp. 90, 89, 97.

11 In the section entitled "Method" in *History of Sexuality, Part I*, Foucault attempted to sustain a margin of individual freedom by positing plural systems which situate the individual in conflicting ways, but as his hypothesis about the co-implication of resistance and power demonstrates, any such freedom has unpredictable political value; in any case, pace Highmore, de Certeau explicitly rejects this solution (Foucault, *History of Sexuality*, pp. 92–102).

12 In "The Algebra of Literature," Michel Serres analyzes La Rochefoucauld's story about the tactics of the lion, the strongest animal, succeeding by playing the game of the weak. That is, the "weak" in both the parable and in de Certeau are *a fortiori* the strong: the "tactics" of the weak don't change them from weak to strong because as winners, they are by definition the strong, merely mistaken for (or masquerading as) the weak. The point is drawn from Nietzsche's argument in *The Genealogy of Morals*.

13 Jean-François Fourny makes this point in his "Bourdieu's Uneasy Psychoanalysis," a useful overview of Bourdieu's deployment of psychoanalysis.

14 We see the disavowal of psychoanalysis at work in this passage: as Fourny remarks, just where we would expect to find a reference to Freud, Bourdieu turns to Durkheim for a discussion of the unconscious but continuing presence of "past selves" that "predominate in us" (Durkheim quoted in LP 56; Fourny, "Bourdieu's Uneasy Psychoanalysis," p. 104). As I discuss below, this disavowal preserves the *habitus* as something different from the unconscious, but at the same time, forces Bourdieu to give up precisely what he most needs, the mechanism of the *après-coup* (*Nachträglichkeit*).

15 Bourdieu, *La Domination masculine*, p. 89.

16 For a discussion of psychoanalysis as practical knowledge, the term that both de Certeau and Bourdieu use, with its allusion to Aristotle's concept

of *phronesis*, see Rothenberg, "Articulating Social Agency in *Our Mutual Friend.*"

17 For detailed discussions of these mechanisms as they operate in the vicissitudes of subjectification, see Fink's *A Clinical Introduction to Lacanian Psychoanalysis*, especially chapters 7 and 9 ("Psychosis"; "Perversion"). Philippe Van Haute has an excellent discussion of subjectification that explains Lacan's graphs and mathemes: see *Against Adaptation: Lacan's "Subversion" of the Subject*, pp. 186 ff., for a brief discussion of the child's Imaginary relation to the caregiver and the need for the *Non/Nom-du-Père*.

18 Of course, it also installs the motivation to move from one to the other, but that is a longer story that we will take up elsewhere.

19 I mention the three Lacanian registers here for readers versed in that lexicon, but I will discuss this point more fully later.

20 As we will see in the next chapter, the choice between a highly particularized version of the unconscious and a thoroughly collectivized one is a false choice. We will consider how the nonindividual status of the subject, sought by Bourdieu, de Certeau, and others, should be conceived in terms of transindividuality rather than some supraindividual or collective status. This solution will have implications for the type of political action that can be theorized, but it has the virtue of sustaining a historical dimension to formulations of the individual's relationship to social structures.

Chapter 4

1 In this literature, Butler is by turns congratulated for her "brilliantly nuanced analysis of language as action" and criticized for offering both a faulty version of speech-act theory and an oversimplified version of political agency. Among others, McNay, arguably one of Butler's most sympathetic expositors, finds "the concept of agency that underlies Butler's notion of a politics of the performative . . . abstract and lacking social specificity" (McNay, "Subject, Psyche and Agency: The Work of Judith Butler," p. 176). Martha Nussbaum (in "The Professor of Parody") faults Butler's account of agency and resistance. Kory Schaff notes that "Butler's account of weak agency cannot provide a strategic location for promoting concrete effects of social change" (Schaff, "Hate Speech and the Problems of Agency: A Critique of Butler," p. 190).

2 McNay finds in *Excitable Speech* "a more precise formulation of her [Butler's] conception of the political efficacy of the performative" but she does not discuss Butler's use of psychoanalysis to propose embodiment as a supplement to her account of linguistic performativity, referring only to criticisms of psychoanalysis as ahistorical (McNay, "Subject, Psyche and Agency," p. 178). Butler's later dialogue with Žižek and Laclau touches in part on her theory of the embodied performative and the psychoanalytic conception of subject formation (Butler et al., *Contingency, Hegemony, Universality*). Margaret McLaren has recently discussed Foucault's conception of embodiment in

terms that are relevant to my discussion (see her *Feminism, Foucault and Embodied Subjectivity*).

3 Categorizing Butler as a Foucaultian who "bridges the overpolemicized gap between the psychoanalytic and constructivist perspectives," McNay praises her for "reconfiguring the psyche as an effect of the interiorization of social norms . . . [and avoiding] the tendency towards ahistoricism that hampers psychoanalysis in order to maintain a sense of the social specificity of modalities of desire and gender" (McNay, "Subject, Psyche and Agency,", pp. 175–6). As the discussion to follow will demonstrate, I have a different sense of Butler's use of both Foucault and psychoanalysis.

4 As noted above, critics have faulted Butler's appropriation of speech-act theory for political purposes. I have made detailed criticisms of Butler's efforts to put Austin into such service elsewhere (Rothenberg, "Articulating Social Agency").

5 See Schwartzman's critique of Butler on this point, in "Hate Speech, Illocution, and Social Context."

6 In fact, in her distinction between illocutionary and perlocutionary speech acts, Butler has instanced temporal deferral as the source of perlocutionary iterability (ES 17). This formulation is not Austin's, but it neatly describes Butler's own practice in parsing the iterable nature of acts of signification into those that correspond to the consolidation of meaning through convention and those that correspond to the disruption of traditional meaning through resignification. For a fuller account of Butler's misguided description of Austinian speech acts as referencing two different temporal modalities, see Rothenberg ("Articulating Social Agency"), Schwartzman ("Hate Speech"), and Rothenberg and Valente ("Performative Chic").

7 Butler does talk at some length about how "circumstances alone do not make the words wound . . . and that the deployment of words is not reducible to the circumstances of their utterance," but she applies this caveat only to the first speech act (injurious or hate speech), not to the resignifying speech that responds to it. When she discusses oppressive or injurious speech, she reserves for the victim of this speech the ability to carry out her intentions to subvert the original speech act.

8 See Melissa Clark's discussion of Butler's misrepresentation of the authorizing conventions of Rosa Parks' actions (Clark, "Rosa Parks' Performativity, Habitus, and Ability to Play the Game.")

9 In her last footnote, Butler even references Žižek's discussion of the "phantasmatic promise of the performative" in *The Sublime Object of Ideology*, a discussion she clearly does not take to heart (ES 182 n. 31).

10 Bourdieu explains that "ignorance of the conditions of production and circulation of commentary allows and encourages people to search solely in the discourse in question for the 'conditions of felicity' which, though theoretically and practically inseparable from the institutional conditions of the functioning of the discourse, have been assigned to the domain of external linguistics. . ." (LP 32).

11 This virtually canonical criticism of Bourdieu finds succinct expression in Michel de Certeau's *The Practice of Everyday Life*.

12 The original quotation is in Derrida, "Signature Event Context," p. 15.

13 Butler takes back her initially rigorous account of the universality of iterability, saying that it is "simply not the case" that "the speech act, by virtue of its internal powers, breaks with every context from which it emerges . . . contexts inhere in certain speech acts," which is in fact the position of the pro-censorship opponents against whom she argues in her introduction (ES 161).

14 Here Butler is not innovating on psychoanalysis: this version of continual subjectification is a standard psychoanalytic principle. See, for example, Hans Loewald's "The Waning of the Oedipus Complex," which argues that the psyche continues to negotiate Oedipal conflicts in a continual process of transformation throughout its life.

15 Felman, *The Literary Speech Act*, p. 96.

16 Furthermore, in this attempt to separate speech from performance, Butler undermines a key tenet of Austinian speech-act theory.

17 We can easily see how Butler elides the active role of the audience in a footnote to Felman's work:

> Felman provides a marvelous reading of Austin's humor and irony, showing how the reiterated problem of performative "misfire" reveals how the performative is always beset by a failure it cannot explain. The performative performs in ways that no convention fully governs, and which no conscious intention can fully determine. This unconscious dimension of every act surfaces in Austin's text as the tragic-comedy of performative misfire. (ES 166 n. 8)

In this passage, Butler acknowledges the failure of intentionality but misattributes it to the activity of the speaker's unconscious, rather than to the addressee's (perhaps unconsciously motivated) interpretation. Tellingly, Butler uses the term "misfire" which highlights the role of the speaker rather than the Austinian usage of a failure of "uptake" which highlights the role of the receiver.

18 As noted above, Butler has a syncopated version of iterability; we can see now that this is how she disavows the social dimension of language. For example, in a clever move, she proposes that the performative *opens up* the possibility of "unknown contexts" (ES 161). By focusing on these anti-closural possibilities, she appears to be following the principle of iterability, but rather than bringing to light why these anti-closural effects are merely *possibilities* (because they are not at the disposal of the speaker, not a function of her intentions), she instead states that performatives can be deployed to *open up* contexts closed by other people. Because she has already discussed iterability, which describes the opening of new contexts even as old ones are referenced, she does not bother to explain how a context could come to be "closed," but she speaks as though such closing results from the intentions of certain political forces: "The desire not to have an open future can be strong. In political calculations, it is important not to underestimate the force of the desire to foreclose futurity" (ES 162).

19 As it turns out, Derrida's iterability (rather than the "unknowingness of the body") could ground the social dimension missing from Butler's theory, but only at considerable cost to her political claims. Because, as Derrida demonstrates, performatives are not a special class but the general class of speech acts, the alleged "specific social meaning" of iterability turns out to be a *general* social meaning. Derrida shows that the limits to intentionality derive from two simultaneous operations of signification (repetition and difference) – each equally crucial to the emergence of meaning and *neither dependent on the intentions of the speaker* – that, taken together, guarantee the social dimension of signification. Iterability is a function both of the potential but uncoordinated application of the same conventions by speaker and audience and the potential but uncoordinated application of different conventions used by speaker and audience. Every utterance is split – that is, is self-different – on account of these operations, fissured by constrained conventional usage and unconstrained individual construals. Derrida makes this point when he refers to the "problematic rubric of 'the arbitrary nature of the sign'" ("Signature Event Context," p. 15); in his view, the rubric is problematic because arbitrariness is not a property of the sign itself but a function of the social dimension of signification.

20 In trying to assess Butler on her own terms, I do not address the criticism that she has no theory of collective political action. Obviously, a full discussion of the potential of Butler's work for progressive political thought would have to take up that issue.

21 Laplanche and Pontalis, *Language of Psycho-Analysis*, p. 166.

22 See Van Haute (*Against Adaptation*, pp. 15–18) for a discussion of the particular meaning the paternal metaphor has in Lacanian thought, on which I am relying here. See also Fink's *A Clinical Introduction to Lacanian Psychoanalysis* for detailed elaborations of the paternal metaphor relevant to psychosis, neurosis, and perversion.

23 While this may sound tragic, dooming us to uncertainty about where we stand and what we mean, in fact, for the child, it represents the only way to escape outside determination, the only way to retain a bit of contingency. Thanks to the addition of this negation, the child is enabled to abandon "the belief that there is an adequate object that corresponds to the desire of the mother . . . on the basis of the paternal metaphor the child surrenders itself to the movement of signifiers" (Van Haute, *Against Adaptation*, p. 200). The *Non/Nom-du-Père* supplies the motivation, so to speak, for the child to seek the satisfaction of its desire elsewhere than the mother. The mobilization of desire within the child, derived from the sense that the Other is also desiring/lacking in ways that the child cannot remedy, is what subjectifies the child. The paternal metaphor produces the conditions of signification as irremediable excess: the unrecoverability of the intentions of the mother by the child is the motive force behind the child's subjectification.

24 Van Haute, *Against Adaptation*, pp. 153–4.

25 In an earlier article I discuss another way in which Butler relies on a psychotic form of the subject (Rothenberg and Valente, "Identification Trouble in Butler's Queer Theory").

26 Van Haute, *Against Adaptation*, pp. 232, 230.
27 It is worth noting that in psychoanalytic theory, the person one desires is never desired on the basis of positive characteristics. If that were the case, then all other people who shared those characteristics would be equally desirable. Rather, desire arises from outside the field of positivities.
28 Lacan explains that "[a]nalysis presumes that desire is inscribed on the basis of a corporal contingency. Let me remind you what I base this term 'contingency' on. The phallus – as analysis takes it up as the pivotal or extreme point of what is enunciated as the cause of desire – analytic experience stops not writing it. It is in this 'stops not being written' (*cesse de ne pas s'écrire*) that resides the apex of what I have called contingency. Analytic experience encounters its terminus (*terme*) here, for the only thing it can produce, according to my writing (*gramme*), is S$_1$," (Lacan, *Book XX: Encore*, pp. 93–4). S$_1$ is the master-signifier, the extimate cause or the Law produced in relation to contingency.

Chapter 5

1 See the Introduction to this book for a discussion and critique of the "multiple subject position" solution to this problem offered by Foucaultians.
2 Jacob Torfing has laid out the relationships among structure, agency, power, authority, universality, and particularity admirably in his discussion of Laclau and Mouffe's discourse theory in *New Theories of Discourse: Laclau, Mouffe and Žižek*, especially pp. 135–86.
3 Laclau in Butler et al., *Contingency, Hegemony, Universality*, p. 65, original emphasis.
4 In work subsequent to *Emancipations*, most notably *New Reflections on the Revolution of Our Times*, Laclau focuses on "dislocation" rather than on social antagonism as the crucial property of social systems, as was the case in *Hegemony and Socialist Strategy*. Laclau's preference for a shift to dislocation, and his claim that one "constructs" an antagonism, reveals his disavowal of the psychoanalytic conception of the extimate cause in favor of a theory of subject positions and willed identifications, while continuing to maintain that he is still relying on the entire theoretical edifice he constructed on a psychoanalytic foundation. That is why I have chosen to focus on *Emancipations* as the most sophisticated of Laclau's writings in their reliance on psychoanalysis: this choice allows me to explicate the wrong turn that Laclau makes when he gives up on his insight into social antagonism as constitutive of the social system.
5 Laclau in Butler et al., *Contingency, Hegemony, Universality*, p. 66.
6 In his interview with Lynn Worsham and Gary A. Olson, Laclau emphasizes the crucial function of identification for his theory:

> If one could have identity without requiring acts of identification, one would be entirely at the symbolic level, in Lacanian terms, and the dimension of the real, which is absolutely central and which requires constant acts of reidentification, would not be possible . . . acts of identification

– when they take place – are not acts in which people choose to be this or that because of some set of reasons. The process is much less automatic than that. What I have is an original lack. This original lack requires acts of identification. These acts of identification depend on many things – among other things, availability. (Worsham and Olson, *Race, Rhetoric, and the Postcolonial*, p. 158)

I leave aside here the question as to whether Laclau has gotten Lacan right, simply to point out that, as he presents it, the category of identification functions by way of unconscious processes and in this sense, accords with psychoanalytic precepts.

7 Laclau in Butler et al., *Contingency, Hegemony, Universality*, p. 66.

8 Lacan, *Écrits: A Selection*, p. 316.

9 Laclau in Butler et al., *Contingency, Hegemony, Universality*, p. 66.

10 Badiou refers to this level of being as "generic multiplicity" – the elements exist, they are multiple, but they have no identities or relations to one another: they are generic entities. See, for example, his discussion in "On Subtraction," in *Theoretical Writings*, pp. 107 ff.

11 One can do no better than Zupančič's *The Shortest Shadow: Nietzsche's Philosophy of the Two* for an elaboration of the philosophical implications of the formal negation. Her introduction includes a discussion that provides the crucial connections between this operation, the status of truth, and the possibility of a politics of the new (see especially pp. 13–27).

12 Lacan, *Écrits: A Selection*, p. 285, my emphasis.

13 Freud, *Group Psychology and the Analysis of the Ego*, p. 107.

14 Harari, *Lacan's Seminar on "Anxiety": An Introduction*, p. 47.

15 Lacan, *Book VII: The Four Fundamental Concepts*, p. 103.

16 Let me note in passing that this reinstatement and retention of particular group identities conforms both to Laclau's stated preference for a "liberal-democratic-socialist society" (despite his critique of liberalism) and to his unambivalent endorsement of "multiculturalism [as] one absolutely progressive phenomenon" (despite his caveats about the role of particularist identity politics) (see Worsham and Olson, *Race, Rhetoric, and the Postcolonial*, pp. 143, 161).

17 Lacan stresses that the phallus belongs to the realm of contingency: "the apparent necessity of the phallic function turns out to be mere contingency" (*Book XX: Encore*, p. 94).

18 Lacan takes these discourses as his topic in Seminar 17, and I elaborate on them below in chapter 7. A number of theorists have explicated the discourses very well, including Mark Bracher, Joan Copjec, Bruce Fink, Paul Verhaege, Slavoj Žižek, and Alenka Zupančič.

19 See Schneiderman, *Jacques Lacan: The Death of an Intellectual Hero*, p. 39.

Chapter 6

1 I admire Sarah Kay's discussion of Žižek's political ideas in her *Žižek: A Critical Introduction*. My discussion takes up where hers leaves off – with

texts written after 2002, in which Žižek appropriates elements of Badiou's thought he had not discussed in previous texts. However, I concur with her concerns that Žižek's conception of the political Act has more in common with the psychotic *passage à l'acte* or hysterical acting out than with what for Lacan is its distinct contrast, the true *acte* which "treats the real by way of the symbolic" (Lacan, *Book XI: The Four Fundamental Concepts*, p. 15). I address these issues at the beginning of this chapter because I am trying to show how Žižek's apparent inconsistencies and difficulties turn out to be productive. In the discussion that follows, I will be showing how Žižek's idea of the political Act can be traced not only to the sources Kay references in Badiou and Lacan, but also to more recent Badiouan concepts concerning political action and to the idea of the *sinthome* taken from Lacan's last work.

2 I am drawing on William Sewell's analysis, *Logics of History*, pp. 232–5.

3 *Réimpression de L'Ancien Moniteur*, p. 158, quoted in Sewell, *Logics of History*, p. 238.

4 Sewell, *Logics of History*, p. 265.

5 Ibid., p. 236.

6 Benjamin, *Illuminations*, p. 254.

7 Ibid., p. 255.

8 Ibid., p. 254.

9 I am not discussing here the philosophical issue opened up by Williams' distinction between must and ought, in which considerations of feasibility get entangled with those of permissibility. Neither does Žižek, who deploys Williams in this passage in order to arrive at the conclusion – which is not one Williams suggests – that we are simultaneously responsible for our character and subject to the drive.

10 This non-transcendental and retroversive version of what counts as the truth has roots in Deleuze, Lacan, and other philosophers Badiou considers to be "subtractive ontologists" – those who refuse ontology but nonetheless affirm the possibility of truth. See Peter Hallward, *Out of This World: Deleuze and the Philosophy of Creation*.

11 Badiou makes this point in different ways in his works. For example, he writes that "for philosophy, 'democracy' designates, through its conjunction with the political prescription as such, the seizure of a politics whose prescription is universal, but which is also capable of being conjoined to the particular in a form wherein situations are transformed in such a way as to rule out the possibility of any non-egalitarian statement" (Badiou, *Metapolitics*, p. 92). Or again, from the same work, he remarks that "political sequences take no account of any particular interests. They bring about a representation of the collective capacity on the basis of a rigorous equality between each of their agents" where "'equality' signifies nothing objective here. It is not a question of the equality of social status, income, function and still less of the supposedly egalitarian dynamics of contracts or reforms. Equality is subjective . . . it is a prescription . . . something we declare to be, here and now . . . and not something that should be" (pp. 98–9).

12 Badiou explicitly rejects as unpolitical any act that supports or props up a

statist solution (even a democratic one) to political problems. Žižek seems to share this emphasis in his rejection of democratic legitimation, as we have just seen. Badiou's clearest articulation of his position against statist solutions appears in *Metapolitics*, chapter 5: "A Speculative Disquisition on the Concept of Democracy."

13 Criticizing Badiou on the grounds of his commitment to egalitarianism, Žižek asks: "Did Marx not claim again and again that the whole topic of equality is a bourgeois ideological topic par excellence? The opposition between formal equality and factual inequality, the way the very form of equality sustains the inequality of exploitation, is at the very core of the market logic, and the way toward its overcoming does not lead through 'true equality' but through suspending the underlying conditions of the tension between equality and inequality, namely, the market economy" (OWB 104).

14 See, for example, Badiou's argument against Arendt's claim that truth refuses debate: on the contrary, Badiou rejoins, "a singular truth is always the result of a complex process in which debate is decisive" (Badiou, *Metapolitics*, p. 14). In *Ethics*, Badiou describes the process of becoming a subject of truth: "When all is said and done, consistency is the engagement of one's singularity (the animal 'some-one') in the continuation of a subject of truth. Or again: it is to submit the perseverance of what is known to a duration [*durée*] peculiar to the not-known . . . he can manage to [be faithful to this fidelity] only by adhering to his own principle of continuity, the perseverance in being of what he is" (Badiou, *Ethics*, p. 47). The four truth procedures Badiou outlines, including the political, all require processes of maintaining fidelity as the generator of the subject of truth.

15 I am grateful to one of my anonymous readers who suggests "that there is an easy way to distinguish an 'authentic political Act' from a *passage à l'acte* if the latter is understood to be a mere lashing out against a fantasmatic framework, a desperate and inarticulate attempt to break free (I think of the passage in Lacan in which it is compared to an actor jumping offstage, or Freud's case of the young woman who jumped off a bridge). A proper act is always already doing more to articulate its own framework, its own alternative, if you will. This is not the case for a *passage*." The point that Žižek is making, with which I concur, is that the act's articulation of its framework cannot be foretold in advance and, because in a political context the emergence of the articulation depends upon others' recognizing that this is what has happened, this potential may never in fact come to light.

16 For an illuminating discussion of Žižek's use and abuse of Badiou, see Bosteels' "Badiou Without Žižek."

17 Tracing the temporality of subjectification, Žižek marks out two moments: the moment of renunciation which leads to subjectification, and a prior moment in which a "pure" subject exists. I find this terminology to be unnecessarily confusing, since before subjectification, no subject exists, pure or otherwise. However, the essential point in Žižek's account is that subjectification requires the giving up of something, for which the *objet a* stands in.

18 One might think that Žižek is making a point against capitalism, a political

economy characterized by an interminable search for something that is never "it." By contrast, founding a politics on the subject of the drive, which continues to function only because the object around which it circulates is inaccessible, could have the potential to counter the type of "add-on" infinity belonging to capitalism. A different economy, one that has the power to endlessly circulate within unpredictable limits, that is, not in the open-ended series of capitalist accumulation, might hold out more promise. But he is not reaching for this conclusion: after all, circulation coupled with accumulation describes capitalism very well.

19 Robert Kaufman, "Red Kant, or The Persistence of the Third *Critique* in Adorno and Jameson." Kaufman has elaborated these ideas in a series of recent essays.

20 Jarvis, *Adorno: A Critical Introduction*, p. 105. My discussion in the subsequent paragraph is indebted to Jarvis's explication.

21 Adorno, *Aesthetic Theory*, p. 133. Quoted in Jarvis, *Adorno*, p. 105.

22 Jarvis, *Adorno*, p. 105.

23 In this paragraph, I am relying on Kaufman's essays, especially "Lyric Commodity Critique," but the translation of his ideas into the parallel with the *sinthome* and formal negation/extimate causality, and any errors that follow from that parallel, are mine.

24 Kaufman, "Lyric Commodity Critique," p. 211.

25 Verhaege and DeClerc, quoted in Thurston, ed., *Re-Inventing the Symptom*, p. 75.

26 Lacan, *Livre XXIV: L'insu. . .*, p. 15. Even though the subject cannot identify directly with the object, which retains its heterogeneity to the subject, as Lacan says, one can "identify [with the symptom] while assuring oneself of a kind of distance towards one's symptom" (ibid., pp. 6–7). *L'insu* is one of the three texts in which Lacan elaborates the *sinthome: Seminar XXIII: Le sinthome* and *Joyce-le-sinthome* are the two others.

27 Adorno, *Negative Dialectics*, quoted in Badiou, "On the Connection between Adorno's *Negative Dialectics* and a Particular Assessment of Wagner," p. 101. I am following Badiou's reading of Adorno's views on the negation of the negation here.

28 See Badiou, "On the Connection." The phrase "identitary sovereignty" is Badiou's.

29 Verhaege, quoted in Thurston, ed., *Re-Inventing the Symptom*, p. 75.

Chapter 7

1 In this refusal Žižek may have taken a theoretical false turn, for it is hard to see why any object cannot be taken up as a signifier. Recall that the materiality of the signifier is precisely what makes it available for signification – and it is precisely what inaugurates the subject. It makes sense, then, to conceive of the materiality of the signifier as a mechanism for transforming subjectivity since it is what initiates subjectification in the first place.

2 In addition to Hardt and Negri, and Žižek, two other major philosophers

– Deleuze and Agamben – have commented on Bartleby's value for thinking the problem of social relations. Without taking on board their conclusions, we can nonetheless find some common ground, since they confirm for us the value of regarding Bartleby as a Möbius subject. Both Deleuze and Agamben emphasize the ways that Bartleby escapes from the logic of either/or: Deleuze points out that Bartleby is neither within nor without the law (we would say that he embodies extimacy), while Agamben says that Bartleby's utterance neither affirms nor negates activity. For more on Deleuze's and Agamben's interpretations of Bartleby, see Alexander Cooke's "Resistance, Potentiality, and the Law: Deleuze and Agamben on 'Bartleby.'" I think it is important to note that in the reading of Bartleby as willing his own de-personalization, neither Žižek nor I view him as being reduced to the status of Agamben's "bare life" or the *Mussulman*. Bartleby persists as both his particular self and as an identification with Möbius conditions: as a specific entity, he looks like an exception to the social field, but as a Möbius subject, he reveals the founding conditions of that field to reside in the relation of nonrelation.

3 Lacan, *Book VII: The Ethics of Psychoanalysis*, pp. 321, 319.

4 This is the point at which Žižek comes closest to Badiou in his Lacanian raiments. As we have seen, Lacan's mathemes in the four discourses allow us to track the vicissitudes of affect as it affects the social relation in a variety of defensive structures – hysteria, obsession, narcissism, perversion. Although Badiou doesn't talk very much about affect, he nonetheless relies on the four discourses in his articulation of the ways in which fidelity to an event can go wrong. If, as I would argue, the subject's ability to remain faithful to the (political) event requires the capacity to forego the usual defenses against excess, then Badiou's emphasis on egalitarianism reminds us that the properly ethical stance starts by accepting that excess sticks to us all, that we are each responsible for our reactions to it. One way to discharge this responsibility is to work patiently to deflect and absorb the affective storm in the social field.

5 See, for example, Levinas, *Time and the Other*, p. 41: "through knowledge, whether one wants it or not, the object is absorbed by the subject and duality disappears."

6 Critchley identifies three key components of the ethical subject:

> From Alain Badiou, I am going to take the idea of the subject committing itself in fidelity to the universality of a demand that opens in a singular situation but which exceeds that situation. From Knud Ejler Løgstrup, I take the idea of what he calls "the ethical demand" and his emphasis on the radical, unfulfillable and one-sided character of that demand and the asymmetry of the ethical relation that it establishes. From Emmanuel Levinas, I will try to show how this moment of asymmetry that arises in the experience of the infinite demand of the other's face defines the ethical subject in terms of a split between itself and a [*sic*] exorbitant demand that it can never meet, the demand to be infinitely responsible. (ID 40)

Let us note as well that Badiou doesn't in fact talk about the universality of a demand – this is Critchley's way of linking Badiou to Levinas, a link Badiou explicitly abjures. He does, however, focus on the hidden universal dimension of the situation.

7 It is not incidental that Critchley turns to Judith Butler for support at this crucial juncture in his argument. The term "self-undoing" is another ambiguous term, one that leaves open the question of who is doing what to whom, in the same way that "hetero-affectivity" does. This ambiguity allows Critchley to also have his cake and eat it when it comes to the issue of autonomy versus heteronomy. In other writings, Critchley has proposed that there is a fundamental gap between the ethical and the political, but here he treats the two motivations as the same (see Critchley, "Five Problems in Levinas's View of Politics and the Sketch of a Solution to Them").

8 Levinas, *Totality and Infinity*, p. 50.

9 These defenses include reversal of passivity into activity to counter helplessness, narcissistic overvaluation to counter narcissistic injury, and identification with the one in the active, aggressive position.

10 The defensive purpose of this identification of victim with persecutor is to sustain the subject's integrity in the face of a potentially annihilating assault. So, one distinction between the Levinasian and Möbius subjects is that the Möbius subject's "integrity" is already fissured: it is only because the subject is *already* a function of otherness – a subject of extimacy – that an identification with an other can help sustain the conditions of existence for the subject. The subject seeks to maintain the interior exteriority that is the ground of its existence in the first place.

11 We can see here that one problem for deriving the motive for ethics in this way arises when the source of this sublimity is some other, rather than the Infinite per se. Put simply, we do not feel that the idea of infinity makes a demand upon us to become responsible for it: demands issue from beings that have some *similarity* to ourselves, but the infinite has no such claim insofar as it is *radically other* to ourselves. The ethical relation requires some recognition of the other as being like the subject, for only this similarity allows the subject to experience a connection to the other sufficient to call for a response. Yet, at the same time, in the Levinasian account, the other must embody radical alterity for the subject; only this radical otherness causes the subject to be overwhelmed, subjected to the other.

12 For an extended discussion of the differences between Lacan and Levinas, particularly with respect to the status of the Other, see Donna Brody's "Levinas and Lacan: Facing the Real." In a footnote to this essay, she directly addresses the point at issue here: "It is necessary that the face not have the power of a 'force,' as that would oblige an irresistible (and a counterfactual) response. Rather, the face is an 'authority' that cannot compel. However, this distinction pertains only at the level of the same. It is difficult to make sense of the distinction when applied to the summons of the face, as the response is generated at a 'pre-' or 'a-conscious' level of absolute passivity that cannot be declined or refused. The important issue here, I would suggest, concerns the transition or translation of the ethical command into the sphere of praxis and thought" (p. 78 n. 21).

13 Critchley uses the term "sublimation" from Freud to describe the qualities of a subject capable of self-distance: "humour recalls us to the modesty and limitedness of the human condition, a limitedness that calls not for tragic-heroic affirmation but comic *acknowledgement*" (ID 82). For Critchley, this means that the subject installs a more benign superego that refuses the lure of narcissistic grandiosity. In order to accomplish this task, Critchley rightly tells us, we must work upon ourselves (ID 87).

14 This may be the place to bring up a criticism of Badiou's reliance on set theory for the specification of a situation that, in Peter Hallward's words, leaves us "with 'generic human stuff' that is ontologically indistinguishable from mathematical multiplicity and effectively endowed, in its praxis, with a kind of 'indeterminate' fundamental freedom" (Badiou, *Ethics*, p. xxxii). Badiou is trying to describe a logical situation that is never encountered in reality, corresponding to the state of sheer being. So, pace Hallward, it is an error to conclude that at this level the elements have any kind of freedom, indeterminate or otherwise.

15 In her reading of the title of Seminar XXIV, *L'insu que sait de l'une bévue, s'aile à mourre*, Véronique Voruz notes a pun: one homophonic reading is "The failure (l'insuccès) of the unconscious (de l'Unbewußt) is love (c'est l'amour)" (Voruz, "Acephalic Litter as a Phallic Letter," pp. 133–4). There is a crucial ambiguity here: does the unconscious, bound as it is to Imaginary and Symbolic identifications, fail to love? Or does Real love (of absolute dif-ference) overcome those identifications and in that way make the unconscious fail? This ambiguity binds together the strands of Möbius subjectivity, ontic and formal properties, on display in the sinthome. The love of absolute dif-ference, we might say, corresponds to the ethical stance of the exposure of Möbius subjectivity in its affective dimension.

16 Mazella, *The Making of Modern Cynicism*, pp. 24–7.

17 See Lakoff et al., *Don't Think of an Elephant: Know Your Values and Frame the Debate*, and Westen, *The Political Brain: The Role of Emotion in Deciding the Fate of the Nation*.

18 See in particular two essays, "Transversality" and "The Group and the Person" collected in *Molecular Revolution: Psychiatry and Politics*.

19 "Opposite and complementary" define the dual relations of the elements in the Greimasian square, which I discussed briefly in chapter 2 as an example of a neither/nor structure permitted in paralogical approaches to the double negation. I discuss the formal negation in Guattari's work a bit further on.

20 Here Guattari refers to Schopenhauer's well-known parable of the porcu-pines seeking warmth from each other but having to adjust their distance to avoid the sharp quills of their neighbors. Finding that optimal distance requires constant modulation within the group.

Bibliography

Adorno, Theodor. *Aesthetic Theory*. Tr. Robert Hullot-Kentor. Minneapolis: University of Minnesota Press, 1989.

—— *Negative Dialectics*. Tr. E. B. Ashton. New York: Continuum, 1987.

Agamben, Giorgio. *Homo Sacer: Sovereign Power and Bare Life*. Tr. Daniel Heller-Roazen. Stanford: Stanford University Press, 1998.

—— *Means Without End: Notes on Politics*. Tr. Vencenzo Binetti and Cesare Casarino. Minneapolis and London: University of Minnesota Press, 2000.

—— *The Open: Man and Animal*. Tr. Kevin Attell. Stanford: Stanford University Press, 2004.

Althusser, Louis. "Ideology and Ideological State Apparatuses." In *Lenin and Philosophy and Other Essays*. London: New Left Books, 1971.

Anderson, Amanda. "The Temptations of Aggrandized Agency: Feminist Histories and the Horizon of Modernity." *Victorian Studies* 43.1 (2000): 43–65.

Austin, J. L. *How To Do Things With Words*. Cambridge, MA: Harvard University Press, 1962.

Badiou, Alain. "Being by Numbers." Interview with Lauren Sedofsky. *Artforum* 33.2 (1994): 84–7.

—— *Ethics: An Essay on the Understanding of Evil*. Tr. Peter Hallward. London and New York: Verso, 2001.

—— *Infinite Thought: Truth and the Return of Philosophy*. Tr. and ed. Oliver Feltham and Justin Clemens. London and New York: Continuum, 2004.

—— *Logics of Worlds*. Tr. Alberto Toscano. London and New York: Continuum, 2009.

—— *Manifesto for Philosophy*. Tr. and ed. Norman Madarasz. Albany: State University of New York Press, 1999.

—— *Metapolitics*. Tr. and intro. by Jason Barker. London and New York: Verso, 2005.

—— "On the Connection Between *Negative Dialectics* and a Particular Assessment of Wagner." *lacanian ink* 33 (2009): 72–113.

—— "Scene of Two." Tr. Barbara Fulks. *lacanian ink* 21 (2003): 42–55.

—— *Theoretical Writings*. Tr. and ed. Ray Brassier and Alberto Toscano. London and New York: Continuum, 2004.

—— "Towards a New Concept of Existence." *lacanian ink* 29 (2007): 63–72.

Baker, Keith M. "Enlightenment and the Institution of Society: Notes for a Conceptual History." In *Main Trends in Cultural History: Ten Essays*, ed. Willem Melching and Wyger Velema. Amsterdam and Atlanta: Rodopi, 1994: 95–120.

Balibar, Etienne. "'The History of Truth': Alain Badiou in French Philosophy." *Radical Philosophy* 115 (2002): 16–28.

Balibar, Etienne, and Immanuel Wallerstein. *Race, Nation, Class: Ambiguous Identities*. Tr. Chris Turner. London and New York: Verso, 1988.

Benjamin, Walter. *Illuminations*. Tr. Harry Zohn. New York: Schocken Books, 1969.

Bosteels, Bruno. "Badiou Without Žižek." *Polygraph* (2005): 221–44.

Bourdieu, Pierre. *La Domination masculine*. Paris: Seuil, 1998.

—— *Questions de sociologie*. Paris: Éditions de Minuit, 1980.

—— *The Logic of Practice*. Cambridge: Polity Press, 1990.

Bourdieu, Pierre, and Loïc J. D. Wacquant. *An Invitation to Reflexive Sociology*. Chicago: University of Chicago Press, 1992.

Bracher, Mark. *Lacan, Discourse, and Social Change: A Psychoanalytic Cultural Criticism*. Ithaca and London: Cornell University Press, 1993.

Brody, Donna. "Levinas and Lacan: Facing the Real." In *Levinas and Lacan: The Missed Encounter*. Ed. Sarah Harasym. Albany: SUNY Press, 1998.

Butler, Judith. *Bodies That Matter: On the Discursive Limits of "Sex."* New York and London: Routledge, 1993.

—— *Excitable Speech: A Politics of the Performative*. New York and London: Routledge, 1997.

—— *Gender Trouble: Feminism and the Subversion of Identity*. New York and London: Routledge, 1990.

Butler, Judith, Ernesto Laclau, and Slavoj Žižek. *Contingency, Hegemony, Universality: Contemporary Dialogues on the Left*. London and New York: Verso, 2000.

Calvino, Italo. *Numbers in the Dark and Other Stories*. Tr. Tim Parks. London: Random House/Vintage, 1996.

Clark, Melissa. "Rosa Parks' Performativity, Habitus, and Ability to Play the Game." *Philosophy Today* 44 (2000): 160–8.

Clemens, Justin, and Russell Grigg, eds. *Jacques Lacan and the Other Side of Psychoanalysis: Reflections on Seminar XVII*. Durham and London: Duke University Press, 2006.

Cooke, Alexander. "Resistance, Potentiality, and the Law: Deleuze and Agamben on 'Bartleby.'" *Angelaki* 10.3 (2005): 79–89.

Copjec, Joan. *Read My Desire*. Cambridge, MA and London: MIT Press, 1994.

Critchley, Simon. "Demanding Approval: On the Ethics of Alain Badiou." *Radical Philosophy* 100 (2000): 16–27.

—— *Ethics, Politics, Subjectivity*. London and New York: Verso, 1999.

—— "Five Problems in Levinas's View of Politics and the Sketch of a Solution to Them," *Political Theory* 32.2 (2004): 172–85.

—— *Infinitely Demanding: Ethics of Commitment, Politics of Resistance.* London and New York: Verso, 2007.

Critchley, Simon, and Oliver Marchart, eds. *Laclau: A Critical Reader.* London and New York: Routledge, 2004.

de Certeau, Michel. *The Practice of Everyday Life.* Los Angeles and Berkeley: University of California Press, 1984.

Dean, Tim. *Beyond Sexuality.* Chicago: University of Chicago Press, 2000.

Deleuze, Gilles. *Foucault.* Tr. Seán Hand. Minneapolis and London: University of Minnesota Press, 1988.

Derrida, Jacques. *Archive Fever: A Freudian Impression.* Tr. Eric Prenowitz. Chicago and London: University of Chicago Press, 1996.

—— "Signature Event Context." *Limited Inc.* Evanston: Northwestern University Press, 1988.

Dews, Peter. "Uncategorical Imperatives: Adorno, Badiou, and the Ethical Turn." *Radical Philosophy* 111 (2002): 33–7.

Dor, Joël. *Introduction to the Reading of Lacan: The Unconscious Structured Like a Language.* Ed. Judith Feher-Gurewich with Susan Fairfield. New York: The Other Press, 1998.

Eisele, Carolyn. *Studies in the Scientific and Mathematical Philosophy of Charles S. Peirce: Essays by Carolyn Eisele.* Ed. Richard M. Martin. The Hague, Paris, and New York: Mouton Publishers, 1979.

Feldstein, Richard, Bruce Fink, and Maire Jaanus, eds. *Reading Seminars I and II: Lacan's Return to Freud.* Albany: State University of New York Press, 1996.

—— *Reading Seminar XI: Lacan's Four Fundamental Concepts of Psychoanalysis.* Albany: SUNY Press, 1995.

Felman, Shoshana. *The Literary Speech Act: Don Juan with J. L. Austin, or Seduction in Two Languages.* Tr. Catherine Porter. Ithaca: Cornell University Press, 1983.

Fink, Bruce. *A Clinical Introduction to Lacanian Psychoanalysis: Theory and Technique.* Cambridge, MA, and London: Harvard University Press, 1997.

—— *Lacan to the Letter: Reading* Écrits *Closely.* Minneapolis and London: University of Minnesota Press, 2004.

Foucault, Michel. *The History of Sexuality*, Volume I: An Introduction. New York: Vintage Books, 1980.

Fourny, Jean-François. "Bourdieu's Uneasy Psychoanalysis." *SubStance* 29.3 (2000): 103–11.

Freud, Sigmund. *Group Psychology and the Analysis of the Ego. The Standard Edition of the Psychological Works Vol. 18.* Tr. James Strachey. London: Hogarth Press, 1953.

Giddens, Anthony. *The Constitution of Society.* Cambridge: Cambridge University Press, 1984.

Greimas, Algirdas Julien. *Sémantique structurale.* Paris: Larousse, 1966.

Guattari, Félix. *Molecular Revolution: Psychiatry and Politics*. Tr. Rosemary Sheed. London: Penguin Books, 1984.

Haber, Honi Fern. *Beyond Postmodern Politics: Lyotard, Rorty, Foucault*. New York and London: Routledge, 1994.

Hallward, Peter. *Badiou: A Subject to Truth*. Minneapolis: Minnesota University Press, 2003.

—— "Ethics Without Others: A Reply to Critchley on Badiou's *Ethics*." *Radical Philosophy* 102 (2000): 27–30.

—— *Out of This World: Deleuze and the Philosophy of Creation*. London and New York: Verso, 2006.

Hampshire, Stuart. *Justice Is Conflict*. Princeton, NJ: Princeton University Press, 2000.

Harari, Roberto. *Lacan's Seminar on "Anxiety": An Introduction*. Tr. Jane C. Lamb- Ruiz. New York: The Other Press, 2001.

Harasym, Sarah, ed. *Levinas and Lacan: The Missed Encounter*. Albany: State University of New York Press, 1998.

Hardt, Michael, and Antonio Negri. *Empire*. Cambridge, MA: Harvard University Press, 2000.

Highmore, Ben. "Opaque, Stubborn Life: Everyday Life and Resistance in the Work of Michel de Certeau." *Xcp: Cross-Cultural Studies* 7 (2000): 89–100.

Horkheimer, Max, and Theodor W. Adorno. *Dialectic of Enlightenment*. Tr. John Cumming. New York: Continuum, 1988.

Hyppolite, Jean. "A Spoken Commentary on Freud's *Verneinung*." In *The Seminar of Jacques Lacan, Book I: Freud's Papers on Technique (1953–54)*. Ed. Jacques-Alain Miller. Tr. J. Forrester. New York and London: W.W. Norton and Co., New York, 1988.

Jameson, Fredric. *Marxism and Form*. Princeton, NJ: Princeton University Press, 1971.

—— *The Political Unconscious*. Ithaca, NY: Cornell University Press, 1981.

Jarvis, Simon. *Adorno: A Critical Introduction*. New York: Routledge, 1998.

Jay, Martin. *Adorno*. Cambridge, MA: Harvard University Press, 1984.

Karatani, Kojin. *Transcritique: On Kant and Marx*. Tr. Sabu Kohso. Cambridge, MA and London: The MIT Press, 2003.

Kaufman, Robert. "Aura Still." *October* 99 (Winter 2002): 45–80.

—— "Lyric Commodity Critique, Benjamin Adorno Marx, Baudelaire Baudelaire Baudelaire," *PMLA* 123.1 (January 2008): 207–15

—— "Red Kant, or The Persistence of the Third *Critique* in Adorno and Jameson." *Critical Inquiry* 16 (Summer 2000): 682–724.

Kay, Sarah. *Žižek: A Critical Introduction*. Cambridge: Polity Press, 2003.

Kordela, A. Kiarina. *Surplus: Spinoza, Lacan*. Albany: State University of New York Press, 2007.

Lacan, Jacques. *Écrits: The First Complete Edition in English*. Tr. Bruce Fink with Héloïse Fink and Russell Grigg. New York and London: W. W. Norton and Company, 2006.

—— "On a Question Preliminary to Any Possible Treatment of Psychosis."

In *Écrits: A Selection*. Tr. Alan Sheridan. New York: W. W. Norton and Company, 1997.

—— *The Seminar of Jacques Lacan*, ed. Jacques-Alain Miller:

Book I: *Freud's Papers on Technique (1953–1954)*. Tr. John Forrester. New York and London: W.W. Norton and Co., 1988.

Book VII: *The Ethics of Psychoanalysis (1959–1960)*. Ed. Jacques-Alain Miller. Tr. Dennis Porter. New York and London: W. W. Norton and Company, 1992.

Book XI: *The Four Fundamental Concepts of Psychoanalysis*. Tr. Alan Sheridan. New York and London: W. W. Norton and Company, 1998.

Livre XVI: D'un Autre à l'autre. Paris: Seuil, 2006.

Book XVII: *The Other Side of Psychoanalysis*. Tr. Russell Grigg. New York and London: W. W. Norton and Company, 2007.

Book XX: *Encore. On Feminine Sexuality, the Limits of Love and Knowledge*. Tr. Bruce Fink. London and New York: W. W. Norton, 1998.

Livre XXIII: Le sinthome (1975–76), Paris: Seuil, 2005.

Livre XXIV: L'insu que sait de l'une bévue, s'aile à mourre (1976–77), Paris: Seuil, 2007.

Laclau, Ernesto. *Emancipation(s)*. London and New York: Verso, 1996.

—— *New Reflections on the Revolution of Our Time*. London and New York: Verso, 1990.

Laclau, Ernesto, and Chantal Mouffe. *Hegemony and Socialist Strategy*. London and New York: Verso, 2001.

Lakoff, Gregory, Howard Dean, and Don Hazen. *Don't Think of an Elephant: Know Your Values and Frame the Debate*. White River Junction, Vermont: Chelsea Green Publishing, 2004.

Laplanche, Jean, and J.-B. Pontalis. *The Language of Psycho-Analysis*. Tr. Donald Nicholson-Smith. New York and London: W. W. Norton and Company, 1973.

Latour, Bruno. *Reassembling the Social: An Introduction to Actor-Network Theory*. Oxford: Oxford University Press, 2005.

—— *Science in Action*. Cambridge, MA: Harvard University Press, 1987.

—— "Why Has Critique Run Out of Steam? From Matters of Fact to Matters of Concern." *Critical Inquiry* 30 (2004): 25–48.

Lecercle, Jean Jacques. "Cantor, Lacan, Mao, Beckett, 'même combat': The Philosophy of Alain Badiou." *Radical Philosophy* 93 (1999): 6–13.

Levinas, Emmanuel. *Emmanuel Levinas: Basic Philosophical Writings*. Eds. A. Peperzak, S. Critchley and R. Bernasconi. Bloomington: Indiana University Press, 1996.

—— *Time and the Other*. Tr. Richard A. Cohen. Pittsburgh: Duquesne University Press, 1987.

—— *Totality and Infinity*, Tr. A. Lingis. Pittsburgh: Duquesne University Press, 1990.

Loewald, Hans. "The Waning of the Oedipus Complex." *Journal of the American Psychoanalytic Association* 27 (1979): 751–76.

McLaren, Margaret A. *Feminism, Foucault and Embodied Subjectivity*. Albany: State University of New York Press, 2002.

McNay, Lois. "Subject, Psyche and Agency: The Work of Judith Butler." *Theory, Culture and Society* 16.2: (1999) 175–93.

Mazella, David. *The Making of Modern Cynicism*. Charlottesville and London: University of Virginia Press, 2007.

Merleau-Ponty, Maurice. *The Phenomenology of Perception*. London: Routledge and Kegan Paul, 1976.

Mill, John Stuart. *On Liberty*. London: Harlan Davidson, 1947.

Miller, Jacques-Alain. "A Reading of the Seminar *From an Other to the other*." Tr. Barbara Fulks. *lacanian ink* 29 (2007): 8–61.

—— "Extimity." *Symptom* 9 (2008). http://www.lacan.com/symptom/?p=36. (Accessed May 17, 2009.)

Nancy, Jean-Luc. *Being Singular Plural*. Stanford, CA: Stanford University Press, 2000.

—— *The Inoperative Community*. Ed. Peter Connor. Tr. Peter Connor, Lisa Garbus, Michael Holland, and Simona Sawhney. Minneapolis and London: University of Minnesota Press, 1991.

Nietzsche, Friedrich. *The Genealogy of Morals*. Oxford: Oxford University Press, 2009.

Noys, Benjamin. "The Provocations of Alain Badiou." *Theory, Culture and Society* 20.1 (2003): 123–32.

Nussbaum, Martha. "The Professor of Parody." *The New Republic* 37 (1999): 37–45.

Parker, Ian. "Lacanian Psychoanalysis and Revolutionary Marxism." *lacanian ink* 29, (Spring 2007): 121–39.

Peirce, Charles Sanders. *Collected Papers IV: The Simplest Mathematics*. Cambridge: Harvard University Press, 1933.

Poster, Mark. "The Question of Agency: Michel De Certeau and the History of Consumerism," *Diacritics* 22 (1992): 94–107.

Priest, Graham. *An Introduction to Non-Classical Logic*. Cambridge: Cambridge University Press, 2001.

—— *Beyond the Limits of Thought*. Oxford: Oxford University Press, 2002.

—— *Logic: A Very Short Introduction*. Oxford: Oxford University Press, 2000.

Rabaté, Jean-Michel, ed. *The Cambridge Companion to Lacan*. Cambridge: Cambridge University Press, 2003.

Ragland, Ellie, and Dragan Milovanovic. *Lacan: Topologically Speaking*. New York: The Other Press, 2004.

Rancière, Jacques. *On the Shores of Politics*. Tr. Liz Heron. London and New York: Verso, 1995.

Raskin, Marcus G. and Herbert J. Bernstein. *New Ways of Knowing: The Sciences, Society, and Reconstructive Knowledge*. Totowa, NJ: Rowan and Littlefield Publishers, 1987.

Reekie, Gail. "Michel de Certeau and the Poststructuralist Critique of History." *Social Semiotics* 6.1 (1996): 45–59.

Riera, Gabriela, ed. *Alain Badiou: Philosophy and Its Conditions*. Albany: State University of New York Press, 2005.

Rimmon-Kenan, Shlomith, ed. *Discourse in Psychoanalysis and Literature*. London and New York: Methuen, 1987.

Rothenberg, Molly Anne. "Articulating Social Agency in *Our Mutual Friend*: Problems with Performances, Practices, and Political Efficacy." *ELH* 71 (2004): 719–49.

—— "Down to Cases: The Ethical Value of 'Non-Scientificity' in Dyadic Psychoanalysis," *Journal of the American Psychoanalytic Association* 52.1 (2004): 125–50.

Rothenberg, Molly Anne, and Joseph Valente. "Identification Trouble in Butler's Queer Theory." *Gender and Psychoanalysis* 6.2 (2001): 183–208.

—— "Performative Chic: The Fantasy of a Performative Politics." *College Literature* (1997): 295–304.

Schaff, Kory. "Hate Speech and the Problems of Agency: A Critique of Butler." *Social Philosophy Today* 16 (2002): 185–201.

Schirato, Tony. "Between Practice and Structure: Cultural Literacy and Bourdieu's Notion of Habitus." *Southern Review: Literary and Interdisciplinary Essays* 30.3 (1997): 259–67.

Schirato, Tony, and Jenn Webb. "The Ethics and Economies of Inquiry: Certeau, Theory, and the Art of Practice." *Diacritics: A Review of Contemporary Criticism* 29.2 (Summer 1999): 86–99.

Schneiderman, Stuart. *Jacques Lacan: The Death of an Intellectual Hero*. Cambridge and London: Harvard University Press, 1983.

Schwartzman, Lisa H. "Hate Speech, Illocution, and Social Context: A Critique of Judith Butler." *Journal of Social Philosophy* 33.3 (2002): 421–41.

Serres, Michel. "The Algebra of Literature." In *Textual Strategies: Perspectives in Post-Structuralist Criticism*. Ed. Josué V. Harari. Ithaca: Cornell University Press, 1979.

Sewell, William H., Jr. *The Logics of History: Social Theory and Social Transformation*. Chicago and London: University of Chicago Press, 2005.

Sheringham, Michael. "Michel de Certeau: The Logic of Everyday Practices." *Xcp: Cross-cultural Studies* 7 (2000): 28–43.

Smith, Brian Anthony. "The Limits of the Subject in Badiou's *Being and Event*." In *The Praxis of Alain Badiou*. Eds. Paul Ashton, A. J. Bartlett, and Justin Clemens. Melbourne: re.press, 2006, 71–101.

Soler, Colette. "The Subject and the Other (II)." In *Reading Seminar XI: Lacan's Four Fundamental Concepts of Psychoanalysis*. Eds. Richard Feldstein, Bruce Fink, and Maire Jaanus. Albany: SUNY Press, 1995.

Thurston, Luke, ed. *Re-Inventing the Symptom*. New York: The Other Press, 2002.

Torfing, Jacob. *New Theories of Discourse: Laclau, Mouffe and Žižek*. Oxford: Blackwell, 1999.

Van Haute, Philippe. *Against Adaptation: Lacan's "Subversion" of the Subject*. Tr. Paul Crowe and Miranda Vankerk. New York: The Other Press, 2002.

Vanier, Alain. *Lacan*. Tr. Susan Fairfield. New York: The Other Press, 2000.

Vasterling, Veronica. "Body and Language: Butler, Merleau-Ponty and Lyotard on the Speaking Embodied Subject." *International Journal of Philosophical Studies* 11.2 (2003): 205–23.

Verhaege, Paul. *Beyond Gender: From Subject to Drive*. New York: The Other Press, 2001.

Voruz, Veronique. "Acephalic Litter as a Phallic Letter." In *Re-Inventing the Symptom*. Ed. Luke Thurston. New York: The Other Press, 2002.

Westen, Drew. *The Political Brain: The Role of Emotion in Deciding the Fate of the Nation*. New York: Public Affairs, 2007.

Williams, Bernard. *Truth and Truthfulness: An Essay in Genealogy*. Princeton: Princeton University Press, 2002.

Worsham, Lynn, and Gary A. Olson, eds. *Race, Rhetoric, and the Postcolonial*. Albany: State University of New York Press, 1999.

Žižek, Slavoj. *Iraq: The Broken Kettle*. London and New York: Verso, 2004.

—— *Organs Without Bodies: On Deleuze and Consequences*. New York and London: Routledge, 2004.

—— *The Parallax View*. Cambridge, MA and London: The MIT Press, 2006.

—— *The Sublime Object of Ideology*. London and New York: Verso, 1989.

—— *The Ticklish Subject: The Absent Centre of Political Ontology*. London and New York: Verso, 1999.

—— *Welcome to the Desert of the Real*. London and New York: Verso, 2002.

Žižek, Slavoj, ed. *Lacan: The Silent Partners*. London and New York: Verso, 2006.

—— ed. *Mapping Ideology*. London and New York: Verso, 1994.

——ed. *Revolution at the Gates: Žižek on Lenin, The 1917 Writings*. London and New York: Verso, 2002.

Zupančič, Alenka. *The Shortest Shadow: Nietzsche's Philosophy of the Two*. Cambridge, MA and London: The MIT Press, 2003.

Index

Note: Items easily found by reference to the table of contents, such as the definition of the social (chapter 1) or a discussion of a particular author's work (e.g. Bourdieu) are indexed only as they appear elsewhere in the text or if subheadings for the item are particularly useful.

euporoi
  in Aristotle, 46, 49
  Rancière on, 46–9
Europe, as Möbius space, 52
event
  contrasted with occurrence, 156
  in Žižek 159, 165, 186
  in Badiou, 157, 165
  temporality of, 155, 159, 218
exceptional cause, *see* causality,
  external.
exceptionalism
  as model of interpellation, 25–6
  Butler's reliance on, 98, 104, 106,
    107, 109
  de Certeau's reliance on, 69
  in Marxism, 26
  problems with, 26
excess, 14, 29, 32, 39, 42, 50, 53, 102,
    218
  and historicism, 154–55
  and nondeterminacy, 38
  and social dimension of language, 106
  and subject formation, 23, 41, 88,
    226
  as impossibility of communion, 19
  as source of social change, 229
  Butler's vs. Felman's treatment of, 105
  contrasted with exclusion, 111
  disavowal of, 45, 56, 155
  disavowed in redemptive model, 159
  dual role of, 44
  elimination of, 10, 28
  Guattari's treatment of, 224
  in social field, 186, 223
  irremediable, 28, 36, 88, 105, 106,
    107, 209, 217
  mobilizes desire, 115
  of signification, 55, 97, 106, 111,
    117, 147, 219
  produced by double negation, 187
  speaking body as, 102
  subject of, 10, 12, 30, 44, 89–90, 204,
    224, 229
  see also extimate causality; formal
    negation; negation
exclusion
  abjured in Foucault, 113
  contrasted with foreclosure, 109–13
  in Butler, 93–4, 108, 113
  in subject formation, 108
exploitation, relations of, 24

expropriation, in Butler, 98
external cause, *see* causality
extimacy
  and subject formation, 14, 180
  and the signifier, 145
  coined by Lacan, 11, 32, 164, 231*n*1
  in Butler, 14, 93
  see also extimate causality; Möbius
    subject
extimate causality, 9, 10, 11, 12, 13, 14,
    28, 29, 58, 90, 117, 218
  and Butler, 92, 93, 95, 96, 111,
    114–15
  and ethics, 194, 198–200, 205
  and formalism, 180–1
  and self-aestheticization, 181–2,
    185–8
  and the signifier, 143–5
  as formal function, 86, 188
  as paternal function, 133
  as source of social field, 216
  compared to immanent and external
    causality, 35
  contrasted with empty signifier, 143
  disavowal of 13, 107
  generates S1/S2, 143
  in Guattari, 224
  in Laclau, 118, 127, 131–6, 145,
    240*n*4
  in revolutionary act, 174, 178
  in Žižek, 155, 164, 178
  paradoxical functions of, 139
  produces social subjects, 45, 187, 187
  psychoanalytic model of, 96, 114–15
  quilting function of, 143
  subject formation by, 11, 23, 41, 87,
    133
  see also causality; de-personalization;
    formal negation; subject formation
Extime, see extimacy

face
  as revelation of language, 54–5
  in Agamben, 50, 54–5, 201
  in Levinas, 198, 201, 246*n*12
fantasy, 45, 60, 61, 45, 87
  as screen for lack, 151
  desire as, 174–5
  disavowed in Laclau, 117
  function of, 151
  Guattari on, 224
  in political discourse, 45, 153

Lacan, Jacques (*cont.*)
  in Butler, 13, 91–3, 108
  in de Certeau, 58
  in Critchley, 195, 196, 198
  in Laclau, 131–2, 135–7
  in Žižek, 205
  jouissance in 148
  master signifier in, 240*n*28
  matheme for perversion, 209
  Non/Nom-du-Père in, 39
  notation for four discourses, 41,
    209–11, 245*n*4
  on relation of nonrelation, 44, 148
  parlêtre in, 41
  Phallus in, 135–6, 240*n*28
  political valence of, 117
  Real in, 106, 159
  sinthome, 181, 185, 244*n*26
  sociality in 230*n*7
  subject formation in, 23, 132,
    236*n*17, 240*n*6
  subject in, 43, 201
  subject-supposed-to-know in, 201
  Symbolic, 230*n*7
  two accounts of subject, 174
  twofold moment of the Symbolic, xvii
  unary trait in, 137–40
  vel in, 38, 234*n*19
  Venn diagram in, 39, 52
lack
  Butler's treatment of, 93
  as historicizable, 108
Laclau, Ernesto, 11, 14, 93, 153
  ahistoricality in, 136, 151
  and Hysteric's discourse, 150
  and Master's discourse, 149
  "bad" infinity in, 150
  collective identification in, 118, 126
  community in, 130
  compared to Butler, 117, 146
  compared to de Certeau, 117
  contingency in, 132
  contrasted with Badiou, 164
  criticism of, 128–36, 150–2
  criticism of Butler, 121
  criticism of Foucault, 121
  democracy in, 116, 121, 149, 150,
    117–19, 129–31, 143
  Derrida in, 117, 121
  disavowal of fantasy in, 117
  dislocation in, 240*n*4
  egalitarianism in, 117, 143

empty place-holder in, 120–1, 125,
  128, 131
empty signifier in, 121, 126, 127, 139,
  143, 145
equivalence in, 117, 122, 124–6,
  129–31, 143, 151
exclusionary limit in, 120, 121, 125,
  130, 122
extimate cause in, 118, 127, 131, 136,
  151
fantasy disavowed, 151
floating signifier in, 127, 139
group competition in, 121
group formation in, 117, 119, 129,
  136, 128, 131, 141, 147, 241*n*16
hegemony in, 123, 125–9, 132, 136,
  140–1, 143, 147, 150
his criteria for democratic interaction,
  123, 124
hybrid identity in, 146
Imaginary register in, 136
incarnation in, 120
intentionality in, 146
in Žižek, 161, 163
Lacan in, 131–2, 135, 136
logic of mediation in, 119
master-signifier in, 164
multiculturalism in, 241*n*16
objet a in, 140
on absent fullness of community, 123,
  124, 126–7, 130, 136, 140, 147,
  149
on agent of change, 120
on system limit, 117, 120–1
partisan truth in, 190
Peronism in, 130
Phallic function in, 136
point du capiton in, 127, 132
psychoanalysis in, 117, 124, 141, 150
psychosis in, 132
repression in, 128, 130, 136, 143, 150
retroversion in, 127, 129, 131–2,
  150–1
rivalry in, 146
S1 and S2 in, 136, 143
self-consistency in, 141
self-difference in, 124, 129, 131
semiotics in, 120, 124
signification, 121, 127, 136, 146
signifier/signified, 129, 132
social antagonism in, 123, 130, 131,
  140, 141, 147, 240*n*4

CPSIA information can be obtained at www.ICGtesting.com
Printed in the USA
BVOW08s1124270515

401949BV00006B/15/P